Unmodern
Observations

For Shozo Sato

with admiration,

and all best wishes,

Hers Golder

April 1990

Unzeitgemässe
Betrachtungen

Unmodern
Observations

William
Arrowsmith
General Editor

Friedrich
Nietzsche

YALE UNIVERSITY PRESS

New Haven & London

Designed by Richard Hendel and set in Ehrhardt type
by Brevis Press, Bethany, Connecticut.
Printed in the United States of America by
BookCrafters, Chelsea, Michigan.

Library of Congress Cataloging-in-Publication Data
Nietzsche, Friedrich Wilhelm, 1844–1900.
  [Unzeitgemässe Betrachtungen. English]
  Unmodern observations / Friedrich Nietzsche:
William Arrowsmith, general editor.
    p. cm.
    Translation of: Unzeitgemässe Betrachtungen.
    Includes index.
    ISBN 0–300–04311–2
    1. Strauss, David Friedrich, 1808–1874.
  2. History—Study and teaching.   3. Schopenhauer,
  Arthur, 1788–1860.   4. Wagner, Richard, 1813–
  1883. I. Arrowsmith, William, 1924–   II. Title.
  B3313.U52E5   1990
  193—dc19   89–5658
                                    CIP

The paper in this book meets the guidelines for
permanence and durability of the Committee on
Production Guidelines for Book Longevity of the
Council on Library Resources.

10 9 8 7 6 5 4 3 2 1

for

FRED WIECK

in memoriam

Good friend and best of editors

without whose enthusiastic devotion

to Nietzsche and his translators these

versions would never have been done

Contents

Abbreviations of Nietzsche's Works

Unless otherwise noted, references are to
Nietzsche Werke: Kritische Gesamtausgabe,
edited by Giorgio Colli and Mazzino
Montinari (Berlin, 1969). It is cited in the
notes as *NWKG.*

A	*The Antichrist*
BGE	*Beyond Good and Evil*
BT	*The Birth of Tragedy from the Spirit of Music*
CW	*The Case of Wagner*
D	*Dawn*
DS	*David Strauss: Writer and Confessor*
EH	*Ecce Homo*
GM	*The Genealogy of Morals*
GS	*The Gay Science*
HAH	*Human, All-Too-Human*
HSDL	*History in the Service and Disservice of Life*
NAW	*Nietzsche against Wagner*
NF	*Nachgelassene Fragmente*
PTAG	*Philosophy in the Tragic Age of the Greeks*
RWB	*Richard Wagner in Bayreuth*
SE	*Schopenhauer as Educator*
TI	*Twilight of the Idols*
WC	*We Classicists*
WP	*The Will to Power*
WS	*The Wanderer and His Shadow*
Z	*Thus Spoke Zarathustra*

Foreword

Nietzsche chose his titles with scrupulous care, and these programmatic essays untranslatably entitled *Unzeitgemässe Betrachtungen* are no exception. *Unzeitgemässe* because they contain an explicit disavowal of the *Zeit*, the age, above all the present, *now*. They are not untimely, which means inopportune, nor unseasonable, nor out of season, which means little more than untimely. *Un*fashionable, *un*contemporary, indeed defiantly *un*modern, they are not therefore reactionary or merely antimodern. They aim at transcending the present, at superseding conventional notions of past, present, and future. If Nietzsche repeatedly invokes classical antiquity, he does so not in order to advocate return to an idealized past, but rather to reassess that past, to "judge" it as the first step in surpassing it, and thereby creating a nobler future culture. Understanding the full scope of this very ambitious but finally abortive project is crucial to reading the individual essays. But recidivist culture and the return to an antiquity deformed beyond recognition by contemporary complacency and philistinism are precisely what Nietzsche is here proscribing. The proper task of the present age is emulation, agonistic rivalry with a great past. Properly understood—purged, that is, of its overlay of Christian and bourgeois misprisions—the present can be "overcome" and transformed into a future in which men, no longer self-estranged, may at last become themselves.

Nor are these essays meditations or thoughts, but rather perspectives, observations, views. *Betrachten* in German means to look at, observe, eye, or view; only by extension to consider, meditate, or reflect. What Nietzsche intends by *Betrachtungen* is a persuasively discursive account of what he has *seen* and *considered*, designed to present his reader with the compelling arguments for, and a vision of, that actively aspiring culture so devastatingly absent from contemporary Germany and the life of modern man.

Hence the cultural comprehensiveness of Nietzsche's design. Details of his project varied from year to year, but not Nietzsche's goal of scrutinizing and evaluating the whole of modern culture. Plans that were later scrapped included essays on religion and the school, the press, nature, art, philology, socialism and the state, and one entitled "Man as I." They were to be written at the rate of one page per day, one essay every three months. Ultimately there were to have been thirteen essays in all; the "unlucky" number was obviously chosen to suggest the subversion and "overcoming" of bourgeois Christian culture. In the same competitive spirit, the whole huge enterprise was to have been completed by its author's thirty-third year: *consummatum est!* The concluding essay was to have been titled *The Way of*

Liberation (*Der Weg der Befreiung*), in which Nietzsche would presumably have shown the way to the liberation of his shackled contemporaries, those "helpless barbarians," as he called them, "chained to the present moment, and craving—always craving!"

In this respect *Unmodern Observations* is the culmination of a project more timidly and tentatively advanced in a series of uncompleted lectures, *On the Future of Our Educational Institutions* (*Über die Zukunft unserer Bildungs-Anstalten*), which Nietzsche delivered in Basel in 1872. What those hapless and unhappy contemporaries of his were craving was a manworthy culture, and this required the creation of "true educational institutions." Unlike contemporary schools and universities, these institutions would provide the educational necessities: "goals, masters, methods, models, comrades" (*Our Educational Institutions*, 5). Nietzsche's putative model was of course the old, idealistic, reformist Jena Burschenschaft of 1815, not the jingoistic and anti-Semitic student associations (*Burschenschaften*) of his own day. What he sought, at least in the professorial years at Basel, was the companionship of an elite group of intellectual and spiritual comrades, bonded by a commitment to reforming those cultural institutions, above all the university, on which renewal of German culture depended. "I see a time approaching," Nietzsche wrote (*Our Educational Institutions*, Preface), "when serious men, working together in the service of a completely reinvigorated culture, may once again become the directors of a system of everyday education, designated to promote that culture ... but how remote that day seems!" Five years later, he had resigned his Basel chair in classical philology and abandoned all hope of reinvigorating German culture by reform of secondary and higher education. If culture were ever to be renewed, it could only come about, he believed, through the efforts of individuals to recreate themselves and then, by the contagion of their example, to teach and transform others.

The essential premise of *Unmodern Observations* is that modern educational institutions, although perverted to ends destructive of life, could be radically reshaped. Reform the educational system, eradicate philistinism, and the creation of a manworthy culture became a true possibility. For Nietzsche philosophy, the arts, and the ennobling study of antiquity had all been corrupted by systematic miseducation, the work of so-called educators in the gymnasium and university who, as culture-philistines themselves, had disgraced the highest of vocations. Only by exposing these philistines for what they were could education be rescued and reformed. Nietzsche's term for the small, devoted band of reformers who would undertake this task of demolition was *Destroyers* (*WC*, 4.30). And the vehemence of his attack on the liberal theologian David Strauss in the first essay shows how seriously Nietzsche took his role as destroyer-in-chief. Strauss himself is savaged—somewhat unfairly, as Nietzsche later admitted—as the exemplar of all the vices of a Philistia that deserved total and pitiless extermination.

Why? Because philistine culture stunted the development of the individual and thereby impeded the emergence of Nietzsche's "new aristocrat," the man of genius. Lacking true knowledge, the philistine could only opine, and his pretentious ignorance was inflamed by "educators" and a press that were as illiterate, slavish, and complacent as himself. He was "a man of the crowd," fatuously convinced of his superiority to a past which, from motives of *ressentiment*, he had emptied of greatness and meaning in order to sustain his own vainglory. His culture was like him: vulgar, lifeless, hollow. These "new barbarians" comprised not only the recently affluent German middle classes, but their effective shapers—the imperial Reich, the press, the canting sub-Christian liberal theologians, the state-salaried philosophers, the "scientifically objective" historians, and the anemic classicists. What above all characterized this "high" philistine culture was its fragmentation and the utter absence of any animating unity. Neither in individuals nor in society could Nietzsche detect the slightest sign of integrated culture. Nothing but decentered shards, a chaos incapable of cohering: minds detached from bodies, bodies from heart; actions sundered from words; professions unmatched by behavior; morality at odds with reality. In short, culture so neurotically conscious of itself, so unnatural, that it lacked the slightest title to the name.

Against the organized pretence of this pseudo-culture Nietzsche's whole enterprise is pitted. Thus, it is *culture as unity of style*—style as functional, not decorative, form—which these essays collectively promote. Designed to exhibit the unity they propose, they should not be read as they usually are, in isolation from each other. The reader who reads only, say, *History in the Service and Disservice of Life* will fail to see how its thesis is strengthened and enlarged by the essays that precede and follow it. History is essential, but so too are art, philosophy, and philology. Through their combining agency an evolving cultural "truth"—that is, the enabling myth or "illusion" on which, for Nietzsche, culture rests—is defined and valorized. If art and learning fail to advance life by proposing a revalued "truth" consonant with the fulfillment of human nature, if they fail to serve man's future, they are at best merely decorative graces, at worst an impediment to existence. For life to be *well* served, art, philology, philosophy, and history must interpenetrate, and the compartmentalized life that they lead in universities and in the mind of "theoretical man" must give way to a new integration. As early as 1869, in his Basel inaugural lecture, "Homer and Classical Philology," Nietzsche had concluded that "all philological activities should be enclosed by a philosophical view of things, in which everything individual and isolated is evaporated as something detestable, and in which only great homogeneous views remain." So too with philosophy: it required not only the philologist's reverence for the text in the form of meticulously close reading, but also, and perhaps even more importantly, poetic imagination. To fulfill themselves art and philosophy must be fused in a powerfully unified vision. Thus, Nietzsche could speak of the poetry of Heraclitus and Empedocles as philosophy *en acte* and, in the teeth of the common wisdom, praise Pindar and Leopardi as "poets who think."

Nietzsche's model for this reintegration is ultimately archaic Greece. For artists and thinkers of that period, the nine Pierian Muses composed a sorority whose common mother Harmonia indicated their kinship; it was the collaborative efforts of this sorority that had produced, in the tragedian's famous phrase, "every kind of *arete*." No Greek artist or thinker of the early period, no poet, historian, philosopher, or tragedian could be understood without an intuitive grasp of that family concert, that *unisono* of a single style which, despite individual talents and perspectives, animated the collective Muses.

Furthermore, no integrated culture could meaningfully exist unless it was *lived*, incarnated in the work and behavior of creators, teachers, and audience. Pseudo-culture was passive, bookish, detached; active culture was embodied in behavior and transmitted by example. If Nietzsche detested modern liberal Christianity, it was above all because it was passive, its older, nobler values unlived. He could admire French Christianity because in it "the most difficult Christian ideals have been translated into men and not remained merely ideas, beginnings, falterings" (*Dawn*, 192). Schopenhauer had renewed the spirit of the pre-Socratics not so much by the power of his philosophical thought as by exemplifying that thought. In him thought and behavior were as inseparable as style and substance; unlike the academic philosophers, he *was* what he *knew*. Hence his cultural power; he *educated*. Wagner exhibited the same striking integration, or so Nietzsche thought, until disillusioned by the first Bayreuth Festival.

Artist, sage, philosopher, the man of genius—all were, or ought to be, creators of culture. Exemplary, like the heroes of Greek tragedy, they taught what they knew by virtue of having become what they were. Like Schopenhauer, they paid in person—in solitude, suffering, and rejection—for their sacrifices on behalf of the species. Later Nietzsche would acknowledge that his portrait of Schopenhauer as teacher and culture-hero was in fact pure self-projection. It takes no special insight to see that this role of tragic hero and scapegoat is one to which Nietzsche passionately aspired, as his last, mad allusion to himself as Dionysus and his lifelong contest with Socrates and Christ make terribly clear. Which, let it be said, does not detract one jot from his courage and achievement. He had, after all, fought the *agon* with the greatest exemplars, mankind's supreme teachers, a struggle to "overcome" which, as Dionysus redivivus and self-defined, he recommended to individuals and cultures alike. He practiced what he preached.

The task of this heroic teacher is of course not simply to revive old values, but to revalorize them in accordance with man's changing condition and presumably changeable nature. Renewed culture required a transformation of values; this in turn demanded a "new and improved *physis*" capable of being imprinted with new values. Dogged courage and good cheer in the face of certain suffering—these, Nietzsche thought, were the virtues essential to achieving genuine individuality. And genuine culture could be created only by genuine individuals. Therefore, all manworthy culture had to begin with "inward renovation" (*innerlich Erneuerung*) of the individual, an extraordinarily arduous "overcoming" in which the crucial agent is suffering. Thus, Nietzsche everywhere stresses the duty and dynamics of self-creation that are implicit in the archaic Greek sense of the *daimōn*, an indwelling or unfolding destiny which, through the individual's efforts, could gradually be brought to fulfillment. This is why importance is assigned throughout Nietzsche's work to love of one's destiny (*amor fati*) as a determining trait in the make-up of the Overman or any human being bent upon the daunting ordeal of self-transformation. Again and again the note is sounded, always emphatically. Thus, the Pindaric epigraph "Become the thing you are"— that "granite sentence" (*GS*, 270) which Nietzsche appended to his early monograph on Diogenes Laertius—is also the subtitle of the late *Ecce Homo*. And interest in Diogenes' exemplary lives of the pre-Socratics leads directly to *Schopenhauer as Educator*, thence to Zarathustra's vehement "I teach!" and, finally, to the great educational mission assigned to the philosopher in *The Will to Power*: "Suppose one conceives a philosopher as a great educator, mighty enough from his lonely height to draw a long change of generations up to himself: then one must also grant him the unearthly prerogatives of the great educator. An educator never says what he himself thinks, but only what he thinks of a subject in relation to the advantage of the one he is educating" (*WP*, 352). But despite later modification of the educational methods involved—above all, the teacher's adoption of meaningful "lies"— the point is essentially the same. Men can be educated only by educators who have educated themselves. Culture can be created and propagated only by those who have become themselves.

Decadence, therefore, whether of individuals or of culture, involves the reluctance to oppose one's own nature, to resist the daimonic drive toward fulfillment and "overcoming." Its mark is spiritual torpor, the enervation caused by the absence of a single inspiriting style. Decadent men, decadent cultures, are at odds with their own biology. "Having to fight against the instincts," Nietzsche declares, "is the formula for decadence; so long as life is ascending, happiness and instinct are one thing." The truly healthy individual inhabits and possesses a truly healthy culture. He may even be unaware that he has instincts to fight; the possession of culture means being unconscious of what one possesses, even of one's instincts. True culture possesses us; not we, it.

Consider philosophy. If its practice means merely theoretical examination of life, then philosophers from Socrates to the Hegelians are, in contrast with the pre-Socratics (and their modern counterpart, Schopenhauer), decadent, too conscious of culture to be possessed of it. What to Nietzsche makes Socrates so interesting is that he combines theoretical inquiry with total commitment to the values obtained by such inquiry; by dying for those values, paying for them with his life, he had valorized them. In sum, however much deformed by Platonic "caricature" (*WC,* 4.193), and however consciously, Socrates *educates,* forever changing the lives of those who instinctively emulate him. Without such education culture cannot become a nearly unconscious second nature. "The work of all culture," as Nietzsche wrote in 1874, "is to transform conscious actions into more or less unconscious actions; the history of mankind is in this sense its education."

It was of course Nietzsche's metaphysic of daimonic creativity that led him to place such emphasis upon education as the decisive element in culture.[1] In the following essays, which contain his most sustained, passionate, and cogent account of education (and which deserve a place among the very few classics of the genre), he makes the point implicitly, but also explicitly: "Education is everything we hope for. . . . *Education* is *love for the procreated,* an excess of love beyond love of self" (*WC,* 4.22). This is the conviction which is constantly invoked by the four completed essays. If the Strauss essay is an almost unrelieved jeremiad against philistine miseducation, its very vehemence is fueled by the buoyant educational aspiration that fills the essays on Schopenhauer and Wagner. Indeed, Nietzsche later avowed that the essay on Wagner was intended to present "a unique problem in education, a new conception of self-discipline and self-defense carried to the point of hardness, a road leading to greatness and to world-historical tasks" (*EH,* "The Unmoderns," 3). The Schopenhauer essay, on the other hand, he perceived as a "semiotic" device, like Plato's Socrates, for presenting his own views ventriloqually, through a persona; it is Nietzsche as educator, not Schopenhauer as educator, who is actually speaking. And what Nietzsche-Schopenhauer says has cost him untold suffering: "There are words in it that are literally running with blood" (*EH,* "The Unmoderns," 3).

This might of course be dismissed as the posturing of a man nearing madness. More charitably and reasonably, it can be viewed as Nietzsche's proud assertion that he had accepted the pain of solitude and the loss of love and human warmth in order to suffer at last "into himself," to overcome "the inward dwarf" and become the thing he was. By self-conquest he had earned the right as Dionysiac antagonist to compete against the greatest of teachers and culture-makers, Socrates and Christ, pitting his genius against

---

1. For the (strangely neglected) importance of education in Nietzsche's philosophy, see Timothy P. Murphy, *Nietzsche as Educator* (Lanham, Md., 1984).

theirs. To be the master teacher of a brave new manworthy culture—this was the goal of his life's work. It was the first firm recognition of this goal that provoked these extraordinary essays and the whole ambitious project of *Uncontemporary Observations,* in which Nietzsche's daimon as educator and agonist is fully revealed. But the daimon was present in the teacher before the educator appeared. To his students at Basel he had seemed to speak with an authority that derived from knowledge tested against the experience of a vision. "When Nietzsche's students are asked about him," wrote a contemporary, "they seem to be united in the impression that they had sat at the feet not so much of a pedagogue as of a living ephor from ancient Greece, who had leapt across time to come among them and tell them of Homer, Sophocles, Plato, and their gods. As if he spoke from his own knowledge of things quite self-evident and still completely valid—that was the impression he made upon them."[2] *This* is the Nietzsche, the exemplary master teacher who speaks to us so powerfully, a century later, in these still disturbing and most unmodern essays.

Unmodern Observations appeared essay by essay, beginning with *David Strauss* in August 1873 and concluding with *Richard Wagner in Bayreuth* in mid-1876. Of the numerous German editions the best texts are those of Karl Schlecta (Friedrich Nietzsche, *Werke,* second edition [Munich, 1960]), which includes the four completed essays but not *We Classicists*; and the monumental, indeed indispensable, edition of Giorgio Colli and Mazzino Montinari (*Nietzsche Werke: Kritische Gesamtausgabe* [Berlin, 1969]), which also contains the relevant *Nachlass.* There are numerous English versions of the individual essays; the only other English version of *Wir Philologen* is the incomplete one by Oscar Levy in *The Complete Works of Friedrich Nietzsche* (New York, 1909–11).

This translation aims at fidelity to both the style and meaning of the original. The two are of course inextricable, which means that literal fidelity is impossible. Nietzsche is a great master of German prose style, and an English version of these essays must if at all possible match Nietzsche's verve, variety, and periodic eloquence. If tone and texture are neglected, meaning suffers. Obviously, when several hands are involved, differences of tone and rhetorical level are inevitable, though every effort has been made to achieve stylistic continuity. Nietzsche's German, the reader should be aware, is stylistically extremely diverse. The language, charged with startling energy, leaps with electrical swiftness from colloquial to aulic, from indignant polemic to discursive argument, from sudden explosions of derisive irony to lofty hortatory flights. The style, as Nietzsche surely intended, *is* the man. The prose is no less passionate than it is brilliant, exhibiting the

2. Carl Albrecht Bernouilli, *Friedrich Nietzsche und Franz Overbeck* (Jena, 1908), 1:67.

writer's whole mind. It is therefore addressed not to what Nietzsche contemptuously called "theoretical man," but to the reader capable of responding with passion and intelligence. It is above all this elusive but essential quality of Nietzsche's style in the completed essays that we have tried to convey. The various notes that constitute *We Classicists* present a different problem. Made up of very diverse material in no particular order—random insights, memos, citations, and aphorisms, all jostling longer passages of relatively finished formal prose—the notes had to be translated in keeping with their stylistic variety.

Nietzsche's titles, as noted earlier, often pose problems, especially for his translator. To render *Unzeitgemässe Betrachtungen* as *Unmodern Observations* may puzzle or vex those accustomed to *Untimely Meditations* or *Thoughts out of Season.* But Nietzsche's intention was surely to alert his readers to the fact that he was writing not "unseasonably," but against the grain of the age, and the title must be translated with this in mind. Again, *Vom Nutzen und Nachteil der Historie für das Leben,* for instance, is commonly and catchily rendered as *The Use and Abuse of History,* but this arbitrarily excises the main point—Nietzsche's insistence upon the importance of history "for life," *für das Leben.* Our solution is the title *History in the Service and Disservice of Life.* The title *We Classicists* (*Wir Philologen*) translates Nietzsche's designation of his own profession, one composed of scholars whom Germans still call "philologists" and whom Americans call "classicists." To translate *Philologen* as "philologists" would, I believe, have trivialized Nietzsche's gravamen against his profession. In only one respect, the breaking down of some very long German paragraphs, have we knowingly deviated from Nietzsche's format, for obvious reasons. Except by reducing the cumulative force of the argument, modern English prose cannot tolerate the lengthy rhetorical periods characteristic of nineteenth-century German prose. Purists may object, but four-page paragraphs are a convention impossible to sustain in modern American English; we have formatted accordingly. Finally, the footnotes may strike those who prefer their Nietzsche academically unaccommodated as excessive or even patronizing. But it is difficult these days to know where to draw the annotative line, especially with a writer as rich, allusive, and polemically topical as Nietzsche, whose present audience is both scholarly and general. We have tried to keep both readers in mind, not to daunt, impede, or patronize.

The dedication to the late Fred Wieck expresses the deep indebtedness of the translators, myself above all, to the man without whose energetic support, constant encouragement, discriminating comments, and wide learning this translation could never have become a reality. Warmest thanks are due also to John Silber, who perceptively and forcefully (at times with good-natured abusiveness) commented on several drafts of my versions of *Schopenhauer as Educator* and *We Classicists*, as well as the initial drafts of Gary Brown's translation of *History in the Service and Disservice of Life*. The late Walter Kaufmann gave generously of his time, advice, and his knowledge of Nietzsche. Walter Bland commented closely on Gary Brown's version of *Richard Wagner in Bayreuth*, and colleagues at several universities, in classics, philosophy, and German, responded helpfully to innumerable queries on matters lexical, philosophical, and literary. To Carol Hassman, who diligently typed and retyped the entire manuscript, especial thanks are owed. Our editor at Yale University Press, Edward Tripp, with truly stoic fortitude, tact, and good humor, put up with our persistent failure to meet his always generously extended deadlines.

Boston University   *William Arrowsmith*

Introduction
and translation
by Herbert
Golder

David Strauss: Writer and Confessor

Introduction

In the spring of 1873, four months before the publication of his essay on David Strauss, Nietzsche was hard at work on a study of the pre-Socratic philosophers. This book, *Philosophy in the Tragic Age of the Greeks*, never completed, was not a study of philosophical doctrines as such, but a series of intellectual portraits—portraits of men "who lived uniquely in magnificent solitude for knowledge alone" (*PTAG*, 1.301). In terming sixth- and fifth-century Greece "tragic," Nietzsche argued that ancient Greece had possessed a profound and genuine culture—a tragic one, since such a culture, like a tragic vision, sought Truth. Even in such a tragic world the philosopher would be forced to stand on his solitary peak; but his vision would be reflected and refracted by the culture at large. Where there was genuine culture, Nietzsche believed, the philosopher would "shine like a star in the solar system of culture." Where true culture was lacking, the philosopher would necessarily make his appearance as an "unfathomable and terror-inspiring comet" (*PTAG*, 1.303).

Germany, in Nietzsche's eyes, possessed little more than a "motley carnival of culture." And after the Franco-Prussian War, Germany seemed not only content with but eager to celebrate its modern barbarism. Unmistakable proof of this barbarism was provided by the tremendous popularity in Germany of a new book, *The Old and the New Faith: A Confession* (1871), written by David Strauss, a once-distinguished theologian turned popular philosopher. Strauss's book was a "testament," as Nietzsche called it, "of modern ideas," by which he meant bad ideas conceived in bad faith. Its readers were "culture-philistines" and Strauss their "philistine-in-chief." Nietzsche put aside the book on the pre-Socratics—philosophers who were the brilliant stars of a bright age—so that he himself could blaze with cometary terror in his benighted Germany. These *Unmodern Observations* were to be an impetus for creating in Germany that true and profound culture which Nietzsche so admired among the Greeks. Such a culture was indeed the sole justification of philosophy; and in the first section of the book on the pre-Socratics, Nietzsche equated the health of philosophy among a given people with the health of culture at large. It was his hope that the new project would foster a culture in which the pursuit of philosophy would once again become meaningful.

Even in the best of times, Nietzsche believed that great men—"unmodern" men who thought "unmodern thoughts"—were isolated by their very greatness. Like the intellectual sketches of the pre-Socratics, the *Unmodern Observations* were to be portraits of those few giants of culture who dared to be unmodern—men like Wagner and Schopenhauer, whose struggle and

3

sacrifice were *truly* tragic insofar as their life-affirming visions might someday inspire a genuine German culture. Nietzsche intended the essays to
include sketches in unmodern thinking, like the essay on history (*History in
the Service and Disservice of Life*) and the unfinished piece on the classics (*We
Classicists*). Whatever modern Germans valued was to be resolutely rejected
as worthless, since they regarded as "untimely" what Nietzsche considered
"a timely and urgent need—to speak the truth" (*DS*, 12).[1] One important
question, however, remains: Why was David Strauss given pride of place
among such considerations? Or, perhaps more to the point, what did Strauss
mean to Nietzsche?

The answer lies, at least in part, in the sequence of events leading up to
the composition of the first of the *Unmodern Observations*. While still deeply
involved with his book on the pre-Socratics, which he clearly regarded as
his next major work after *The Birth of Tragedy* (1872), Nietzsche received
an invitation to visit Wagner in Bayreuth during the Easter holidays of 1873.
Nietzsche was still very much the devoted disciple and Wagner the master.
Especially anxious at this time to win Wagner's approval and having every
reason to expect an enthusiastic reception (Wagner had been a supportive
collaborator on Nietzsche's first book), Nietzsche left for Bayreuth with his
latest project in hand.[2]

But Wagner was entirely absorbed with his own affairs. The huge enterprise of the Bayreuth Festival, the realization of Wagner's vision of "artistic
totality" (*Gesamtkunstwerk*), was in grave financial difficulty, caused largely
by the scarcity of subscribers. Wagner was therefore annoyed when his
young protégé arrived eager to discuss his esoteric concoction of Thales
and "Thales' children," as Wagner facetiously described Nietzsche's project. The book had, in Wagner's eyes, nothing whatsoever to do with the
crisis in German culture that now spelled disaster for his Bayreuth undertaking. Wagner expected his disciples, above all Nietzsche, to dedicate
themselves to *his* cause. Nietzsche's seeming indifference was, moreover, a
second offense. Unaware of the extent of Wagner's hypersensitivity, Nietzsche
had refused an earlier invitation to stay with Wagner during the Christmas
holidays in order to visit his mother and concentrate on the essay on the
pre-Socratics. As Nietzsche later learned, Wagner had been deeply offended
and had brooded for several months. When Nietzsche realized that he had
yet again unwittingly disappointed Wagner, he was anxious to make amends.

1. The idea of the philosopher as the "unmodern" man can be found throughout
Nietzsche's writings. "What does a philosopher demand of himself from first to last?"
Nietzsche asks in one of his last essays. "To overcome his time in himself, to become
'timeless' . . . a deep estrangement, a coldness, a sobering up against everything that is
of his time, that is contemporary" (Preface to *CW*).
2. See Nietzsche to Carl von Gersdorff, April 5, 1873.

Almost immediately upon returning to Basel, he wrote to Wagner expressing a desire to be of service and announcing a new project that he felt was sure to please him: a polemical attack on David Strauss.[3] Strauss's new book on German culture had been a subject of conversation during the Bayreuth visit, and also during Nietzsche's previous visit with Wagner,[4] who loathed the book as "terribly shallow."[5] Nietzsche must have read the book as soon as he returned home, and he too was amazed by Strauss's "vulgarity and stupidity as both writer and thinker."[6] Everything else was put aside so that Nietzsche could devote himself to the essay on Strauss, which he hoped to complete for Wagner's birthday in May. The perfect opportunity to serve the master and make amends was now at hand. Wagner and Strauss were old and open enemies.[7] Nietzsche would pay off Wagner's old debt and at the same time advance the cause of German culture to which they were both passionately committed.

Ironically, Strauss had been on Nietzsche's mind just prior to the Easter visit with Wagner. Wilamowitz, the classical scholar who had published a polemic on Nietzsche's *Birth of Tragedy*, had, in a renewed attack, decried Nietzsche's "corroded brain." "The precise words," Nietzsche wrote to a friend, "which David Strauss had used against Schopenhauer."[8] It seemed that all those whom Nietzsche most highly regarded, the true champions of German culture, were under siege—including Nietzsche. Meanwhile, the enemies of German culture, the philistines championed by Strauss in his new book, were growing in influence and arrogance. What is more, Strauss himself had at one time or another pointedly attacked the two men Nietzsche most admired, Schopenhauer and Wagner.

But more was at stake than polemics. By assailing Strauss, Nietzsche was going straight for the jugular of that aspect of contemporary Germany which most disgusted him—its "culture-philistines." It was precisely these *Bildungsphilister*—who had demanded six reprintings of Strauss's book in the first year of its publication—who made Wagner's Bayreuth project so difficult. *The Old and the New Faith: A Confession* (hereafter *Confession*) was a gross vulgarization of German culture and thought by a former theologian who now styled himself a freethinker. It was this "new faith" in scientific materialism that had enabled Germany to defeat France in the Franco-Prussian War. The "old faith" was Christianity: the Christian faith in a

3. Nietzsche to Wagner, April 18, 1873.
4. This event took place in November, when the two met in Strassburg. See *WC*, 5.98.
5. See Cosima Wagner's *Diaries*, Feb. 7 and March 20, 1873.
6. Nietzsche to Wagner, April 18, 1873.
7. Strauss had publicly criticized Wagner for his part in persuading Leopold II to dismiss a rival composer (1865), and Wagner had published sonnets lampooning Strauss (1868).
8. Nietzsche to Gersdorff, April 5, 1873.

personal God. The beliefs of Strauss's Germans, however, were based upon a Darwinian cosmology that vindicated history and deified German "success." Strauss's book, which celebrated this success, was in actuality little more than a curious potpourri of the ideas then most in intellectual fashion: Hegelian Idealism, historicism, social Darwinism, but above all a materialism derived from a mechanistic world view based upon a rational and intelligible cosmos. Worst of all, in the fourth section of his book, Strauss had proudly awarded the wreath of true culture to the new German Reich, whose patriotic spokesman he had already proclaimed himself in a famous open letter to the French theologian Ernest Renan. The book now firmly established Strauss as "philistine-in-chief" in the minds of the German middle class.

An appendix treats the reader to Strauss's vapid views of the German classics—Goethe, Beethoven, Hölderlin, Haydn, and others. Strauss transforms these great "seekers" of German culture into "discoverers," cultural mandarins who, as "classics," reinforced the modern German's smug complacency. The philistine is not encouraged to attune himself to that resonant "striving after truth" which Nietzsche finds audible in every word or note composed by such men, but simply to enjoy his few moments of "cultured" leisure among these precious flowers of his race. Throughout Strauss's book runs a confusion between a certain kind of "cultivated refinement" (*Bildung*, from which comes *die Gebildeten*, "the cultivated") and what Nietzsche defined as culture (*Kultur*): "a unity of style manifest in all the vital activities of a people" (*DS*, 1).

In addition to its intellectual coarseness, Strauss's book was abominably written: cliché-ridden, packed with bizarre solecisms, mixed metaphors, malapropisms, and ungrammatical constructions. Its barbarous thought and style, and the universal praise accorded it, German reluctance to support Wagner's cultural efforts, and Nietzsche's feeling that he had failed Wagner—all these conspired to distract Nietzsche from the pre-Socratics in order to tackle the more pressing problem of renewing German culture. The same life-seriousness which animated the pre-Socratic philosophers, which made them tragic heroes at war with their own times and embodiments of their own ideas, now impelled Nietzsche to do battle for the soul of Germany. His attack on Strauss, who epitomized everything amiss in German culture, became the first, and most timely, of these "unmodern observations."

The Strauss essay is, nevertheless, an apparent anomaly among Nietzsche's works. Elsewhere Nietzsche reserves his polemical attacks for figures with whom he could at least partly identify himself,[9] above all his critical daimon,

9. In *EH* ("Why I Am So Wise," 7), written during his last productive year, 1888, Nietzsche described the value such polemics held for him and articulated the principles

Socrates (in *The Birth of Tragedy*).[10] But which of Nietzsche's many masks or personae can be related to so un-Nietzschean a character as David Strauss? In *Ecce Homo* ("The Unmoderns," 2), Nietzsche gives us a clue. There he describes Strauss as the foremost German "free spirit," that is, a thoroughly contemporary man, presumably liberated from all traditional pieties and beliefs by fashionable scientific skepticism. In fact, Strauss's first book, *The Life of Jesus* (1835–36), an application of myth-theory and historical method to Jesus' life, had made a deep impression on Nietzsche. The book's aim was not so much to demystify Christ as to explain his "myth." In lieu of the historical Jesus, Strauss argued for a Hegelian "ideal Christ" corresponding to something innately human, arising from messianic visions in the Old Testament and the religious need of contemporary Jews for such a myth. The validity of Christianity lay, then, not in its claim to supernatural sanction, but in Christ's exemplary morality. Understandably, the book cost Strauss his career as a professor of theology.

Nietzsche had read Strauss's book while a young student of theology himself. Afterwards, he had confided to a friend, "If you give up Christ, you give up God too."[11] Even Nietzsche's most casual reader cannot fail to hear in these words an anticipation of the famous dictum, formulated nearly twenty years later: "God is dead" (*GS*, 3:125, and *Z*, Preface). In 1865, the year following his introduction to Strauss's book, Nietzsche refused to take Communion at Easter, rejected Christianity, and abandoned his study of theology. The book had clearly made a tremendous impact on him. But he was to develop Straussian ideas in ways and directions of which Strauss could not have dreamt. As so often happened, Nietzsche would freely adopt ideas to which only he himself could do justice.

---

that guided these attacks: "The strength of an attacker is measured by the opposition he demands. Every growth is signaled by the search for a mighty opponent—or problem, for a warlike philosopher challenges problems to single combat. The task is not merely to master whatever resists, but what requires us to risk all our strength, suppleness, and fighting skill—opponents that are *equals*. . . . Equality before the enemy—the first prerequisite of an *honest* duel. Where one feels contempt, one cannot wage war; where one commands, where one sees something beneath oneself, one has no right to wage war. My practice in war can be summed up in four propositions. First, I attack only causes that are victorious—I may even wait until they become victorious. . . . Second, I attack only causes against which I will find no allies, so that I stand alone. . . . Third, I never attack individuals, but use them only as a strong magnifying glass that allows one to make visible a general but creeping and elusive calamity. . . . Fourth, I only attack something when every personal difference is excluded and when any background of bad experiences is lacking. Instead, an attack by me is a proof of goodwill, even gratitude. I honor, I distinguish by identifying my name with that of a cause or person—for or against."
10. For an intelligently comprehensive account of Nietzsche's lifelong obsession with Socrates, see Werner J. Dannhauser, *Nietzsche's View of Socrates* (Ithaca, N.Y., 1974).
11. Paul Deussen, *Erinnerungen an Friedrich Nietzsche* (Leipzig, 1901), 20.

Strauss's "freethinking" was, in Nietzsche's estimation, merely an affectation. The epithet *free spirit* or *freethinker*, however, can be found throughout Nietzsche's works and signifies the highest, the most acutely critical quality of thought. But mankind's genuine free spirits—Goethe, Montaigne, Voltaire, Lessing, Schopenhauer—were, for Nietzsche, prodigiously rare. With his celebration of cultural philistinism, Strauss had betrayed himself as merely one more "buffoon of modern ideas," utterly enslaved to the Christian metaphysics that he pretended to deny. A true free spirit would of necessity be a tragic pessimist, like Schopenhauer, not a fatuous optimist like Strauss. Nietzsche scrupulously distinguished imposters. "They would wage an irreconcilable war," he wrote, "if they understood me: all of them still believe in the 'ideal'—I am the first immoralist" (*EH*, "The Unmoderns," 2).

These soi-disant freethinkers posed radical philosophical problems; Strauss's ostensible rejection of Hegelian Idealism along with Christian faith, for instance, implied the obsolescence of all previous metaphysical systems. But these false free spirits, prone to fall back upon attenuated forms of Hegelian Idealism or to gloss their materialism with Christian sentiment, offered only superficial solutions. Strauss, for example, regarded the universe in purely mechanistic terms, as a cosmic "wheelwork" that flowed with a mysterious "soothing oil." But the cosmic wheelwork was in reality a euphemism, a "modern metaphor," for the Christian heavenly host. Having declared religion itself untenable, Strauss nevertheless retreats to familiar ground: he "reacts religiously," as he says when confronted by the harsh necessities of the cosmos. But these self-contradictory religious reactions cause Strauss the materialist no embarrassment. Instead, he unabashedly justifies them in utterly conventional Hegelian terms as something inherent in man's "elevated consciousness."[12]

For Nietzsche, radical problems required radical solutions; and the Laodicean half-measures and clever circumlocutions of the freethinkers were insufferable impediments. Strauss and his confreres were "admirers of *nil admirari*"[13] who paved the way to nihilism. Genuine courage was the effort to break free of nihilism. "Who will have the heart," Nietzsche wrote, "to waken the imprisoned slave who dreams of release?"[14] In his polemic against Strauss, Nietzsche set out to liberate the freethinker from the fetters of the age by destroying his contemporary caricature. The attack on Strauss was

12. Strauss's *Confession* was regarded as a radical break with his former Hegelian principles in favor of a more purely materialistic world view. But as Nietzsche points out: "Strauss, at least, wants to clamber out of that swamp, and has, in part, succeeded, though he is still a long way from solid ground" (*DS*, 12).
13. "to admire nothing," i.e., to be incapable of wonder or excitement.
14. Nietzsche to Deussen, Nov. 10, 1867.

the "wicked laughter of a 'very free spirit' at the expense of an imposter who imagined himself to be free."[15]

Strauss, however, was merely a symptom of a more widespread and dangerous problem. "In reality," Nietzsche wrote, "I considered Strauss too unimportant for me; I didn't want to fight him." To which he added tersely, and doubtless grudgingly: "Several words spoken by Wagner at Strassburg" (*WC*, 4.98). Later he described Strauss's book, which he attacks so virulently in this essay, as little more than the "senile jottings of an extraordinary critic."[16] His real target was clearly not Strauss himself, but, as Nietzsche admitted in an unpublished preface (*NF*, 27.78) to this essay, the scandalous success of Strauss's book and what that success implied for German culture. Despite factional religious and theological differences, opinion in favor of the book, especially of its stylistic merit, was nearly unanimous. Strauss was fast becoming a national arbiter of culture and taste, while Wagner, Nietzsche's true culture-hero, was struggling desperately in Bayreuth. Nietzsche had caught the Germans "red-handed in a compromising act of bad taste."[17] The time was ripe, and Nietzsche was ripe, for polemic; he felt, as he claimed, "profoundly congested with aversion and oppression" and needed to "disgorge" them before doing some "good work."[18] Strauss was merely the "magnifying glass" that enabled Nietzsche to see "a general but creeping and elusive calamity" (*EH*, "Why I Am So Wise," 7).

That the destroyer's work must precede the creator's is a pervasive Nietzschean theme: "Whoever wants to be creative in good and evil," says Zarathustra, "must first be an annihilator and destroy values" (*Z*, 2). The metaphysical swamps left behind as the flood of religion receded; the cultural chauvinism of Germans combined with their growing militarism; the "objective" historicism and scholarly specialization which were destroying any distinctively German style, value, or character; in short, the culture-philistinism of which Strauss's success was certain proof—all this spurred Nietzsche to the ambitious enterprise of reforming German culture. A Greek pessimist at heart, radically tragic in his outlook, Nietzsche despised above all else the mindlessly optimistic complacency of the philistines, firmly convinced that they stood on the top rung of Darwin's ladder, enjoying the privileged and unlimited prospect that only a Hegelian *Aufhebung* could provide.[19]

15. Nietzsche to G. Brandes, Feb. 19, 1888.
16. Ibid.
17. Ibid.
18. Nietzsche to E. Rohde, March 19, 1874.
19. "Sublation," the standard English translation of Hegel's important term *Aufhebung*, which might also be translated "elevation," implies a dialectical movement towards a synthesis, in which apparent oppositions are dissolved or integrated at a higher level. Unfortuntely, Hegel's philosophical Idealism engendered the kind of fatuous and un-philosophical optimism that Nietzsche found so abhorrent in Strauss.

If Nietzsche undertook the project to please Wagner, it nevertheless became something wholly and uniquely Nietzschean. The redemption of German culture was now *his* project. Nietzsche did not so much abandon his
other projects as convert them into this one. Several long passages in the
Strauss essay are taken verbatim from the lectures on education he had
written in 1872; and the definition of culture, a first principle of the Strauss
essay, is the one already formulated in the essay on the pre-Socratics: "a
unity of style manifest in all the vital activities of a people" (*PTAG*, 1). Unity
of style implies a vital, therefore essential, integrity of form and content, the
unity of a man with his ideas. "To improve one's style," Nietzsche wrote
in *The Wanderer and His Shadow*, "is to improve one's ideas" (*HAH*, 2.131).
Strauss's book, so universally admired for its "exemplary" style, yet so full
of vague, Hegelian abstractions, mixed "modern" metaphors, and sloppy,
sentimental prose, fully revealed the absence among contemporary Germans
of an appreciation for style as fundamental to culture.

Style is the crux of Nietzsche's polemic. "A catalogue of Strauss's utterly
appalling stylistic experiments would clinch the case against him," Nietzsche
wrote to Wagner.[20] And Wagner was so pleased with the essay that he wrote
to Nietzsche: "I swear by God that you are the only person who knows what
I am driving at." But Nietzsche must have been perplexed, even disturbed,
by Wagner's lack of sympathy with the main point of the polemic. Wagner
went on: "All the rest belongs in the chapter on 'style' which, as you know,
I am incompetent to judge, since I bristle, to your great vexation, whenever
the word 'style' is mentioned."[21] It was precisely the profound, the *necessary*,
link between style and culture that Nietzsche felt to be his most important
idea. True, Nietzsche attacks Strauss's muddled metaphysics, his flabby
logic, the structural weakness of his book, and its complacent, self-con-
gratulatory tone.[22] But his most virulent contempt is reserved for Strauss's
mutilation of the German language. Nietzsche, after all, was convinced that
culture began with one's mother tongue, which was wholly dependent upon
an artistically vigorous feeling for its use. Schopenhauer had described style
as "the physiognomy of the mind . . . of culture."[23] The absurd exemplary
status generally conferred upon Strauss's literary style was manifest proof
that Germans no longer possessed any stylistic, and therefore cultural, integrity. For this reason Nietzsche must have been troubled by Wagner's
resistance to his central premise—the equation of *stylistic* unity with cultural

20. Nietzsche to Wagner, April 18, 1873.
21. Wagner to Nietzsche, Sept. 21, 1873.
22. Nietzsche concentrates his attack largely on the extremely glib and pompous fourth
section of Strauss's *Confession*, "How We Regulate Our Lives."
23. "On Authorship and Style," in *Parerga and Paralipomena*, trans. E. F. J. Payne (Oxford, 1974), §282.

cohesiveness.[24] Paradoxically because of, but also in spite of, Wagner, Nietzsche the philologist was now on his way to becoming what he himself called "the philosopher of the future, who would be the higher tribunal of artistic culture."[25] Odd as it may seem, the essay, originally composed as a peace offering and birthday present for Wagner, may also mark the beginning of Nietzsche's disenchantment with Wagner, whom he would later decry as a cultural charlatan, the very embodiment of decadence.

For Nietzsche the enemies of the philosopher were the culture-philistines, the *décadents* who had lost the feeling for life and for language, for the very *life* of language. Affectation was their stylistic means of simulating the signs of life. Strauss's solecisms and stylistic oddities, Nietzsche believed, were calculated to arouse the reader by their very oddity; they come, he wrote, as a "painful stimulus" in the "dry and dusty expanse" of Strauss's book.[26] Behind the posturing of Strauss's "new faith," there was neither instinct nor conviction—in sum, no faith. Or, if Strauss's "confession" was one of faith, then it was a faith in the imagined "rationality" of the cosmos. Vexed by a wordy and obscure passage, Nietzsche demanded of Strauss that he "at least speak like a man of the world."[27] But the culture-philistine lives *against*, not *in*, the world; he cultivates the unnatural; he prefers the abstract to the concrete; his whole orientation is toward some redemptive purpose located in another world, whether a Hegelian Aufhebung, an evolutionary, millennial fulfillment, or a Christian heaven. Nietzsche maintained precisely the opposite: man's highest value and dignity lay in his capacity for art and culture; they were man's sole justification in this life— in this world—and the only means by which the world itself could be eternally justified.

24. Nietzsche wrote the fourth of his *Unmodern Observations*, on Wagner, with something less than the passionate commitment he reserved for the essay on Schopenhauer. In fact, the break with Wagner was imminent, as Nietzsche perhaps knew. Less than two and a half years after the Strauss essay, in 1876, Nietzsche left the Bayreuth première of Wagner's *Ring* in disgust, appalled by its lack of real style and depth.

25. *NF* 19.73 (summer 1872–beginning 1873). It is worth noting that after electing himself to that "higher tribunal," Nietzsche never completed any (though he started many) of the philological projects which had hitherto occupied him.

26. *DS*, 11.

27. An echo of Shakespeare's Falstaff (*Henry IV*, part 2, v, 3), and of Schopenhauer, who quotes it in "On Authorship and Style," to which Nietzsche was clearly indebted: "We find [these German authors] trying to wrap up trivial ideas in grand words and to clothe their very common ideas in the most uncommon expressions and in the most far-fetched, affected, and fantastic phrases. Their sentences constantly stalk and strut on stilts. As regards this pleasure in bombast and generally in that high-flown, bloated, affected, hyperbolical, and aerobatic style, their type is Pistol . . . to whom his friend Falstaff calls out impatiently: 'I pray thee, now, deliver them (the news) like a man of this world!' " (*Parerga and Paralipomena*, §283). Compare below, esp. §10 and 11.

"Speak like a man of this world" is in fact Nietzsche's supreme cultural postulate. Culture, that is, must be understood as humanity's vital artistry and must find its highest expression in art which orders and unifies, which transforms rather than evades the Dionysiac turbulence of life. Great erudition is not essential to culture, at least not in Nietzsche's sense of the word. In fact, as he argues throughout, great erudition is often consonant with barbarism, with the chaotic confusion of all styles. The "cultivation" of which Strauss boasts is actually culture-in-disintegration, a mere accumulation of acquired habits, affected manners, wooden movements. In short, culture that is not centered in *life*.

Utterly opposed to the culture-philistine is the man of true culture—Schopenhauerian man. In fact, the main lines of Nietzsche's own stylistic critique are unmistakably drawn from Schopenhauer's "On Authorship and Style," to which he several times alludes.[28] The Schopenhauerian man already looming in this essay (and fully disclosed in the third of the *Unmodern Observations*) does not inhabit the philistine's tidy, bourgeois "pavilion of culture," but lives in the world. The man of true culture speaks then "like a man of the world." Such men, Nietzsche writes, "really speak; they don't stammer or gossip; they really live and move, unlike other human beings who live such a strange mask-like existence." Among such men, he continues, "one feels human and natural, filled with the desire to shout for joy with Goethe on the glory of a truly living thing" (*SE*, 2). And this contagious good cheer is pointedly contrasted with the philistine's mere "cheeriness."

But how can this good cheer be reconciled with Nietzsche's and Schopenhauer's Greek pessimism? It is akin to the solace that Nietzsche claimed all true tragedy must provide. Tragedy unmasks life, revealing it at bottom as indestructibly powerful and joyous, beneath all suffering and change.[29] The Schopenhauerian man comes to life in his work, and because life is the genuine philosopher's work, his words are like "a forest of tall trees—we breathe deeply and suddenly we feel well again" (*SE*, 2). For Nietzsche,

28. Schopenhauer was Nietzsche's model for this type of polemic. Twenty years earlier Schopenhauer had attacked his contemporaries for their mutilation of the German language; see "On Authorship and Style," esp. §281–89. Schopenhauer had even compiled a catalogue of his contemporaries' awkward and ungrammatical expressions (§283), as Nietzsche does in §12, below.

29. *BT*, 7. Nietzsche of course later rejected Schopenhauer's pessimism on the grounds that it led to resignation (cf. *BT*, "Attempt at a Self-Criticism," 6). Nietzsche's truly tragic spirit, as embodied by Zarathustra, possessed the strength to overcome himself. For Nietzsche, the tragic spirit was eventually transformed into the Will to Power. Wagner and Schopenhauer were employed in these "observations" much as Plato used Socrates in his dialogues, as "pointers to a higher concept of culture." Both Wagner and Schopenhauer were, as Nietzsche admitted, "in one word, Nietzsche" (*EH*, "The Unmoderns," 1).

philosophy is a *vital* activity and therefore its style must be a reflection of its vitality or truth-to-Life—that is, its truth. With every word he writes, the pessimistic writer/thinker of genius creates and destroys. To be creative in good and evil, Nietzsche wrote, the tragic philosopher must first be a destroyer of values. As culture-hero, his powers arise from the depth of his vision and experience and are strengthened by his upward struggle. His words have been written with prodigious care and at immense cost; his revelations are earned. The philistine is merely an optimist and euphemist. Nothing he writes really disturbs or profoundly offends; therefore, he does not truly create. A symptom of the death of culture, his style is uniformly impotent, lifeless. Nietzsche compares a vigorous style to a lean and muscular body, a writer of genius to a conqueror—of everything dull, slow, and stupid in the world.[30] Strauss is described as a pachyderm (the metaphor is again Schopenhauer's) and his prose as viscous and ponderous. "To make language run" was Nietzsche's aim, since "happiness lies in swiftness of feeling and thinking" (*WC*, 3.75). With Strauss's success the German tempo—the cultural pulse of Germany—had slowed to a dead halt.

In *Ecce Homo* ("The Unmoderns," 2) Nietzsche pointedly cites Stendhal's dictum that it is best to enter society with a duel. Germans desperately wanted to believe that their victory over France had been a great *cultural* event, and it was Nietzsche's express purpose to prove otherwise. As might be expected, the essay met with anger but also modest applause. Strauss's adherents, the vast majority of "cultivated" Germans, were outraged that their master had been ridiculed. But a number of old-line theologians hailed Nietzsche's polemic, thinking him, somewhat improbably, their ally against Strauss, the apostate "enemy of Christianity." A discerning few, like the essayist Karl Hillebrand, applauded Nietzsche's attack on the decay of the German language and mind, praising its eloquence and power, and the courage with which Nietzsche had assailed the vile stupor of self-content— so totally destructive of German spirit and culture.[31]

30. In other words, a conqueror of what Schopenhauer called the Will.
31. For critically perceptive and sympathetic commentary on Nietzsche's polemic, see Karl Hillebrand, "Einiges über den Verfall der deutschen Sprache und der deutschen Gesinnung," in *Zeiten, Völker und Menschen*, vol. 2 (Strassburg, 1892), 281–99. Writing in 1873, Hillebrand could not have known who this young essayist was destined to become. There is a certain irony in Hillebrand's sensible criticism of Nietzsche's relatively cursory treatment of the first three sections of Strauss's book. According to Hillebrand, Nietzsche wisely concentrated his attack on Strauss's style and avoided analyzing too deeply the philosophical contradictions created by Strauss's confusing marriage of materialism and Idealism. Fear of falling into the same traps was the motive Hillebrand imputed to Nietzsche's avoidance. Nietzsche must have realized, or so Hillebrand reasoned, that he would only be "bringing coals to Newcastle" ("des Einbrechens offener Türen") if he tried to address these contradictions. But thinking his way through them, "breaking free of nihilism," was to preoccupy Nietzsche for most of his life.

David Strauss died the year after Nietzsche's essay was published. Nietzsche, profoundly disturbed, wrote Gersdorff that he dearly hoped that his polemic had not hastened Strauss's death and that Strauss had died without hearing of it (though Strauss had of course read it).[32] The effect of the essay on Nietzsche's own life was inestimable: an uncanny freedom of thought and speech, since, as he claimed, no one any longer dared to engage him in polemics. Nietzsche had found his "paradise 'in the shadow of my sword'" (*EH*, "The Unmoderns," 2). This, after all, had been his purpose: to free the spirit by destroying the "free spirit." "Write with blood," Zarathustra had commanded, "and you will find that blood is spirit" (*Z*, 1).

32. Nietzsche to Gersdorff, Feb. 11, 1874. Of Nietzsche's attack Strauss wrote to his friend Rapp (Dec. 19, 1873): "First they behead you, then they hang you. . . . Surely not undeserved, if he succeeded in hanging a man already beheaded, or so was the impression he gave. . . . What intrigues me about the fellow is only the psychological problem: how one can get into such a rage against a man who has never crossed his path—in short, the real motive behind his passionate hatred" (E. Beller, ed., *Ausgewählte Briefe von David Friedrich Strauss* [Bonn, 1895], 2:598).

David Strauss: Writer
and Confessor

1   Public opinion in Germany seems almost to
forbid any discussion of the grave and evil consequences of the [Franco-
Prussian] war, especially a war that ended in victory. For this reason, the
writers who find readiest acceptance are those most deferential to public
opinion—those who, in fact, zealously compete in praising the war and
celebrate its potent effect on morality, culture, and art. However, let it be
said: a great victory is also a great danger. In fact, human nature endures
victory with more difficulty than defeat, since it appears easier to win the
victory than to keep from turning it, once won, into a serious defeat. But
of all the ill effects of the recent war with France, perhaps the worst is a
widespread, even universal, mistake made by public opinion and those who
publicly opine: that German culture was also victorious in the struggle and
that, in keeping with this triumphant event, German culture could now be
crowned with the victor's laurels. This delusion is pernicious in the extreme,
not simply because it is a delusion—since mistakes can be very useful, even
fortunate—but because it can transform our victory into total defeat: *the
defeat, if not the extirpation, of the German spirit for the sake of the "German
Reich."**

Even supposing the battle were one between two cultures, the measure
of the victor's worth would be quite relative, and in no case could such
jubilant self-glorification be justified. First, we would have to know the value
of the defeated culture. It might be very small. In this case, the victory
cannot warrant the triumphant rapture of the victors, however spectacular
their show of arms. But in our case there can be no question of a victory
for German culture, and for a very simple reason: French culture still survives, and we still depend upon it. German culture played no part in our
military success. Harsh military discipline, natural bravery and endurance,
superior leadership, unity and obedience in the ranks—in short, qualities
having nothing to do with culture—enabled our victory over an opponent
lacking the most essential of these qualities. One can only marvel that what
is today called "culture" in Germany did so little to inhibit the martial virtues
needed for a great victory. Perhaps, for once, this self-styled culture recognized that it had something to gain by proving useful. But if it is now
allowed to flourish and grow rank, battening on this flattering delusion of
victory, it will have the power, as I said, to extirpate the German spirit—

---

*Translator's note: I have followed Nietzsche's use of italics, in only a few cases adding
italics of my own where rhetorical emphases natural to German cannot in any other way
be captured in English.

15

and who knows if what remains of the German body will be good for anything at all?

If that some tough, well-tempered bravery with which the Germans met the pathetic fury of the French could be turned against the enemy within— against that highly suspicious and, in any case, alien "cultivation," termed, due to a dangerous misunderstanding, "culture"—then all hope for a genuine German culture, the opposite of this cultivation, is not lost. Germany has never lacked astute and daring leaders, but she has often lacked Germans to lead. To give German bravery a new direction seems a doubtful prospect that grows daily more improbable since the war. For I see how everyone is confident that such courage and struggle are no longer needed and that most things have been arranged in the best possible way. In short, all that needed doing has long since been discovered and is now done. And the best seeds of culture have been everywhere sown; some are now sprouting fresh green and others, here and there, are already in full flower. This yields more than mere complacency; it brings joy and jubilation. I sense this ecstatic joy in the incredible self-confidence of German journalists and the manufacturers of novels, tragedies, poems, and histories. These men clearly form a tightly knit club conspiring both to control the hours that modern man devotes to leisure and digestion, that is, his "moment of culture," and to stupefy him with printed matter. Since the war, all is joy, dignity, and self-satisfaction for this little club. After such a "triumph of German culture" its members consider themselves not only established and sanctioned, but nearly sanctified, and therefore speak all the more solemnly. They delight in direct appeals to the German people, publish their collected works in the manner of classical authors, even announce in the journals at their disposal the few from their own ranks who will serve as our new classical models. We might expect the more prudent and enlightened among our educated Germans to recognize the dangers of such an *abuse of success*—to have at least some sense of the distressing spectacle enacted before them. What could be more distressing than to watch a deformed creature strutting like a cock before a mirror, exchanging admiring glances with its own reflection?

The scholarly caste, however, too preoccupied with itself to care about the German spirit, gladly leaves well enough alone. The members of this caste are absolutely convinced that their own culture is the ripest and fairest fruit of the age, indeed of all ages, and cannot comprehend the need to worry about popular German culture, since they consider themselves and numerous of their kind far above such cares. And yet it cannot escape the more careful observer, especially the foreigner, that what the German scholar today calls his culture and that triumphant culture of the new German "classics" differ only in the amount of learning that each presupposes. Wherever the issue is ability and art, not learning and information—that is, wherever life ought to show signs of culture—there now appears to be only *one* German culture—and could this culture have conquered France?

This contention is completely preposterous. All impartial judges—and lastly the French themselves—have ascribed the decisive advantage to the greater expertise of German officers, the superior training of German troops, and their more highly sophisticated military science. So, if we subtract German expertise, in what sense can German culture be considered victorious? None. The moral qualities of strict discipline and unquestioning obedience have nothing to do with culture: it was precisely these qualities that distinguished the Macedonian armies from their infinitely more cultivated Greek adversaries. To speak then of a victory for German education and culture betrays real confusion—a confusion arising from the loss of any clear idea of what constitutes culture.

Culture, is, above all, a unity of artistic style manifest in all the vital activities of a people. Vast knowledge and learning are neither the essential means to, nor even a sign of, culture; in fact, these generally accord much better with the opposite of culture, barbarism—the absence of style, or the chaotic confusion of all styles.

The modern German lives in the middle of this chaotic jumble of styles, and it is a wonder how, with all his expertise, he fails to notice it. Instead, he rejoices with all his heart at the present state of "culture," when in reality, everything—every glance at his clothing, furniture, and house, every walk through the streets of his town, or visit to the showrooms of his fashionable art dealers—should inform him otherwise. In his social intercourse he should be aware of the origins of his manners and movements. In our cultural institutions, concert halls, theaters, and museums, he really ought to see the grotesquely juxtaposed jumbling of all conceivable styles. The modern German amasses the shapes, colors, artifacts, and curiosities of all times and places, creating a motley carnival of culture, which scholars then definitively regard as "modern culture." There, in the midst of this total stylistic turmoil, the German stolidly sits. This phlegmatic culture, this total lack of feeling for culture, has defeated no one, least of all the French. They do possess a genuine, productive culture, which we—regardless of its value—have copied in toto, and rather ineptly at that.

Even if we stopped aping the French, we would not thereby defeat them; we would simply free ourselves of them. Had we imposed an original culture on the French, we might then speak of a German cultural triumph. But meanwhile we depend on Paris, just as we depended before, in all matters of form—and depend we must. For there is no original German culture.

We should all have reached this conclusion ourselves; and, what is more, one of the few entitled to reproach us has already made it plain. "We Germans," Goethe once remarked to Eckermann, "belong to the past. For a century now we have been energetically cultivating ourselves; but a few

more centuries may have to pass before enough intellect and high culture
have sunk into the inhabitants of this land to have it said of them: 'It has
been a long time *since they were barbarians.*' "[1]

2   *If* our public and private lives so clearly lack
the stamp of a creative and coherent culture; *if* our great artists, with the
ardent seriousness and candor essential to their greatness, have avowed, and
still continue to avow, these appalling and, for a gifted people, disgraceful
circumstances, then how can supreme complacency still prevail among educated Germans? Since the last war this complacency tends increasingly to
erupt in wild, triumphant jubilation. We live under the illusion of possessing
a genuine culture. Only a rare few notice the appalling incongruity between
this complacent, even gloating attitude and the patent lack it conceals. All
who assent to public opinion have put on blindfolds—this incongruity simply
must not be allowed to exist. How is this possible? What power can dictate
what "should" and "should not" exist? What species of man has risen to
power in Germany, who can forbid strong, simple feelings or inhibit their
expression? Let me call this power, this species of man, by its name: the
culture-philistine.

The word "philistine," as we all know, is drawn from the vernacular of
student life and means in its broadest sense the opposite of a true son of
the Muses, an artist, or man of genuine culture. The culture-philistine—
whose tiresome confessions we are now forced to hear—distinguishes himself from the common philistine by a superstition: he fancies himself a son
of the Muses and man of culture. This extravagant delusion renders him
incapable of distinguishing himself from his opposite; so it is not surprising
when he solemnly denies his philistinism. With this total lack of self-
recognition, he is firmly convinced that his "cultivation" is the consummate
expression of correct German culture. Since he meets his own cultivated
type everywhere, and finds that all public institutions, schools, and cultural
establishments conform to his brand of cultivation and serve his needs, he
struts about triumphantly, the worthiest representative of German culture,
and makes his claims and pretensions accordingly.

True culture always presumes a unity of style. Even an inferior and degenerate culture is unthinkable unless its diverse strains tend to coalesce in
the harmony of a *single* style. Therefore, the philistine's confusion may arise
from the ubiquity of individuals out of the same mold: he assumes that the
uniformity among the "cultivated" results from the cultivation of a uniform
German style—in short, a unified culture. Around him he perceives needs
and opinions identical to his own. Wherever he goes, the bond of tacitly

1. Goethe's *Conversations with Eckermann,* May 3, 1827. Nietzsche admired the *Conversations,* hailing it as the "best German book" (*WS,* 109).

held conventional attitudes—especially toward art and religion—immediately clasps him. This striking sameness, this spontaneous outburst of *tutti unisono*,[2] tempts him to believe that here culture reigns supreme. But this systematized philistinism owes its power to its system. It represents no culture, not even an inferior one, but the opposite of culture: firmly rooted barbarism. The uniformity among "cultivated" Germans today, which meets the eye at every turn, stems from the conscious, or unconscious, exclusive denial of every artistically productive form and requirement of true style. Unfortunately, something must have warped the cultivated philistine's mind: he claims for culture precisely what culture negates. Proceeding systematically, he arrives, finally, at a coherent body of such negations, a system of nonculture, with a certain "unity of style"—if it makes sense even to speak of stylized barbarism. Whenever he has a choice to act with style or without, he will invariably elect the latter course. Since this is the rule, all his acts bear the same negative stamp. In this way, he recognizes the distinctive character of his patented "German culture." Having judged whatever is at odds with his culture to be hostile opposition, the philistine wards it off, holds his tongue, stops his ears, and looks the other way.

Even in his hatred and hostility he is a negative creature. Most of all he hates the man who treats him as a philistine and tells him what he is: an obstacle to the strong and creative, a maze to the lost and confused, a morass to the weary, a shackle on those reaching for high goals, a miasmic mist falling on all fresh buds, and a scorched desert to the German spirit thirsting for new life. But still this spirit *searches*! And *this* is why you hate it—for refusing to believe that you have found the object of its search.

How, in the first place, could the philistine ever arise, let alone preside as the supreme arbiter of German culture? How is it possible, after the long procession of great heroic figures that have preceded him, men whose every movement, every expression, whose questioning voices and blazing eyes revealed one thing: *that they were seekers*? With ardent determination they sought what the philistine imagines he possesses—the genuine, original German culture. They seemed to ask: Is there a soil so pure and untouched, so virginally sacred that the German spirit might build upon it alone? Probing in this way, they struggled through the tangled wilderness of hard times and cramped conditions and, still seeking, vanished from our sight. One of them, at a ripe old age, could speak for all: "For half a century I have endured hardship and have allowed myself no rest. I have striven and sought, and done the best and the most that I could."[3]

But what view does our philistine culture take of these seekers? It takes them for "finders," apparently forgetting that they claimed only to seek.

2. "everybody, all together"
3. Goethe, *Conversations with Eckermann*, March 10, 1830.

Yes, we have our culture, the philistine then says, for we have our "classics." No? Not only have we a foundation there, but even a structure that already stands upon it—why, we ourselves *are* this structure. With that, the philistine claps his forehead.

To falsify and insult our classics betrays a total ignorance of them. And, in general, such ignorance prevails. Otherwise someone would have realized the one and only way of honoring them: to search on with like spirit and courage, never tiring. Merely to yoke that considered word *classical* around their necks and to feel "edified" on occasion by classical works is to yield to the same feeble, self-serving titillations which our theaters and concert halls hold out to anyone for the price of a ticket. The same applies to erecting statues and to christening celebrations and clubs with classical names—all petty-cash payments to close the account, to rid the philistine finally of these authors and their mandate: Keep searching! The philistine's watchword is: Seek no more!

Once this watchword meant something. In the first decade of this century Germany was plunged into such a bewildering chaos of exploring, experimenting, destroying, promising, foreboding, and hoping that the thinking middle class was rightly alarmed. It was right to shrug off such a concoction of fantastic, word-wrenching philosophies and fanatical, wholly tendentious views of history—a veritable romantic carnival of myths and gods conceived in a drunken frenzy of poetic madness. Of course it was right, since the philistine has no right to a debauch. But with characteristically low cunning he seized his chance and promoted the comfort of discovery by discrediting the searching spirit altogether. The joys of philistinism opened before his eyes. He found idyllic asylum from wild experimentation and opposed the artist's restlessly creative drive with a certain complacency, a contentment with his own limits, his own ease, even his own stupidity. With no undue modesty he stretched his long finger, indicating the nooks and crannies of his life where his innocent, budding joys were just beginning to bloom in the empty hollow of his uncultivated, moorish existence—the modest flowers of philistinism.

A gifted few are on hand to paint, with gentle strokes, the joy, warmth, simplicity, and peasant good cheer—all the comforts belonging to playground, study, and farmhouse alike. Content to cling to such picturebooks of reality, they escape the express provocation of the classics to *go on searching.* Instead, they have invented an age of epigones, and therefore breezily dismiss any new work as "epigonic." To guarantee their tranquility, these easygoing philistines transformed history and the other disciplines that threatened to ruffle their calm—especially philosophy and classical philology—into historical methodologies. With this historical method they spared themselves what Goethe believed the study of history should evoke: strong feelings. Instead, trying to comprehend everything in their own historical terms, these unphilosophical admirers of *nil admirari* made dullness their passion.[4] While claiming to hate all forms of fanaticism and intolerance, they really hated domineering genius and the tyranny of demands made by real culture. Thus, they assiduously crippled, stifled, and demolished wherever new and powerful movements were expected to arise. Coyly veiling the philistine creed of its authors in lacy serifs, a philosophy provided the formula for deifying the trivial. It spoke of the reasonableness of everything real, titillating the philistine, who loves verbal arabesques but above all considers himself real and regards his own reality as the standard of reason for the world. He permits the weighing of problems, the framing of questions, even dabbling in aesthetics. Better still, let anyone compose poetry or music, paint, or even conceive an entire philosophical system, provided he keep faith, for the love of God, with the old forms, and on no account upset the philistine's "reasonable reality." From time to time, even the philistine gladly abandons himself to the delightfully rich extravagance of art and skeptical histories; he would be the last to undervalue the charm of such amusing and diverting entertainments. But he strictly separates the "business of living"—he means his calling, his profession together with his wife and children—from mere recreation, which is all that culture affords. Woe to any art that postures as serious and taxes the philistine's livelihood, business, and habits—what he does take *seriously*. From such art he averts his eyes, as if from something obscene, and with the mien of Chastity's keeper, warns every vulnerable virtue to look away.

Seeing himself as adept at dissuasion, the philistine is grateful to the obedient artist who allows himself to be dissuaded. The philistine reassures him that now he too can go along at a lighter and lazier clip and, as the philistine's trusted intellectual ally, he will be asked for no sublime masterpieces. He has two choices now: apish copies of reality, idylls and mildly humorous satires; or loose imitations of the more widely known classics, as a modest indulgence of popular taste. So long as he prizes iconic portraits of the present and epigonic imitations, he celebrates his peace with "reality" and promotes himself as the arbiter of classical taste. And having already made a permanent peace with the classics, this costs him nothing. Finally, he tags all his habits, views, denials, and endorsements with a roundly effective formula, "good health," and routs all irksome intruders with insinuations of sickness and hysteria. The words of David Strauss, a true *satisfait* of our cultural condition, are typical: "Arthur Schopenhauer's wholly intellectual, yet frequently morbid and unprofitable philosophizing." It is a cruel fact that "intellect" has a particular affinity with the "morbid" and "unprofitable." Likewise, the philistine would find, if he would just

---

4. *Nil admirari*: "to wonder at (or admire) nothing," the famous opening words of Horace's *Epistle* 1.6.

once be *honest* with himself, that the philosophy produced and marketed by his kind is mostly empty of intellect, yet thriving and very profitable.

Now and then the philistines, provided they are by themselves, indulge in wine and think aloud with simple candor about the great war effort. At times things which are otherwise anxiously concealed will come out; and, on occasion, someone will divulge the most carefully guarded secrets of their whole clan. Very recently one such occasion caught a well-known esthete of the Hegelian school of thought completely off guard, and a most unusual thing occurred. A circle of philistines was noisily toasting the memory of a tried-and-true non-philistine who, in the strictest sense of the word, perished by philistines—namely, the noble Hölderlin. This well-known esthete therefore felt that the occasion warranted some talk about tragic souls ruined by "reality," understood, of course, in the sense of philistine reason. But "reality" has now changed. Could Hölderlin have found his way in this grand era of ours? "I do not know," remarked Friedrich Vischer, "whether his delicate soul could endure the harshness of war. Perhaps he would have sunk again into despair. He was one of those vulnerable spirits, a Werther of Greece, hopelessly lovelorn. He lived a life of tender yearning, but with a strong, purposive will and a richly animated, grand style, not unlike Aeschylus. Only his spirit lacked hardness and the weapon of wit. *He found it unendurable that one could be a philistine and still not be a barbarian.*"[5] The final confession—and not the mawkish, after-dinner condolence—does move us. One will admit to being a philistine, but a barbarian—never. Poor Hölderlin was unable to make such fine distinctions. Of course, if we mean by "barbarism" the opposite of civilization, that is, piracy or cannibalism,

---

5. Friedrich Theodor Vischer (1807–88) wrote a six-volume Hegelian *Aesthetik* (1846–47), literary criticism, and a very popular whimsical novel, *Auch Einer* (1879). Outspoken, combatively anti-religious, he was altogether typical of, indeed prominent among, Strauss's circle of "culture-philistines." The speech to which Nietzsche here refers was part of an after-dinner speech by Vischer on March 20, 1870, at Lauften, on the occasion of Hölderlin's hundredth birthday. In *CW*, 2, Nietzsche refers to him as "the fortunately late esthetic Swabian" (*Schwabe* also means "cockroach") and expresses his disgust at Vischer's tendentious falsification of German history.

Hölderlin (the young Nietzsche's favorite poet), whose own work went largely unappreciated during his lifetime, had himself used the term *philistine* to execrate the general state of German cultural barbarism. Nietzsche, in fact, first used the term in an early essay on Hölderlin, written while he was still a student at Pforta. Tradition maintains that this usage—*Philister* as a term of abuse for "townspeople" in student vernacular—arose at Jena, after a "town and gown" row that resulted in a number of deaths. The university preacher, Pastor Götze, chose as his text for the funeral of one of the fatally injured students "The Philistines are upon thee, Samson" (Judges 16). Nietzsche claimed credit for coining the term *culture-philistine*, with its suggestion that the philistine had also infiltrated the ranks of so-called culture and academe. See letter to Georg Brandes, Feb. 19, 1888. Matthew Arnold was largely responsible for anglicizing the term.

then such a distinction is justified. However, the esthete would clearly maintain that a man can be a philistine and still be a man of culture—such wit was lacking in poor Hölderlin, and this lack was his undoing.

On this same occasion, he let still another confession slip: "Not always a strong will, *but sometimes weakness*, sets *us* above those tragic souls with their profoundly felt passion for beauty." This is roughly how it sounded—confessed on behalf of the assembled "we," those "set above," that is, by virtue of their "weakness." We should be pleased with such admissions. We have learned two things straight from the initiate's mouth: first, the "we" are beyond, even above, the desire for beauty; second, it is weakness that exalts them. Of course, at more discrete moments, this weakness goes by a more flattering name: the famous "good health" of the philistine. But in view of all this, it might be more appropriate to call them *weaklings*, or, more emphatically, the *weak*. If only the weak were not in power! Why should they care what we call them? They are our rulers and any true ruler can endure a caricature or a nickname. On the road to power a man has to learn how to laugh, especially at himself. It matters not at all if he exposes himself: royal purple can cover anything. In fact, the philistine reveals his strength by admitting his weakness: the stronger his admissions, and the more cynically he makes them, the more clearly he betrays the strength of his self-importance and sense of superiority. Friedrich Vischer made his confession in a word, but David Strauss made his into a book—and cynical they are, word and book.

3   David Strauss makes his confession of philistine culture both in words and by an act—that is, through *the words of his confession and the act of writing*. His book *The Old and the New Faith* is, in its contents and by virtue of its being a book and an author's creation, an uninterrupted confession. In his very willingness to make public confessions of his faith lies a confession. Everyone over forty should be entitled to an autobiography, since even the most insignificant man has experienced something or seen something at such close quarters that a philosopher would reckon it noteworthy and important. But a confession of one's beliefs is incomparably more pretentious, since it presumes that the confessor places a value not only upon what he has experienced, explored, or observed in the course of his life, but also upon what he believes. By now the serious thinker must be dying to know what natures like Strauss's manage to believe in—what they, "half dreaming, have conjured up" (p. 10),[6] about which

6. All citations of Strauss refer to *Der alte und der neue Glaube: Ein Bekenntnis* (Leipzig, 1872), unless otherwise indicated. The English translation by Mathilde Blind (*The Old and the New Faith: A Confession* [New York, 1873]) redresses many of the solecisms and *bêtises* impugned by Nietzsche. The quotations from Strauss have been translated with a view to approximating, as closely as English will allow, the stylistic oddity of the original.

only they, with their firsthand knowledge, may speak. Who would have wanted the confessions of a Ranke or a Mommsen,[7] although they were, as scholar and historian, in an entirely different class from David Strauss? Had they entertained their faith instead of their scholarly judgments, they would have overstepped their bounds intolerably. And this is precisely what Strauss does in the confession of his faith. Nobody has any desire to hear it, except perhaps a few narrow-minded enemies of the Straussian camp who hope to sniff out the underlying satanic creed that, once exposed, will decisively undercut the learned propositions masking it. Now perhaps these coarse characters can at last settle their score with Strauss. The rest of us, with no cause to suspect hidden satanic motives, have in fact found none, though we would have been grateful to find even a dash of the diabolical. For the Strauss who pleads his new faith is hardly an evil spirit. In fact, he has no spirit, and least of all one of genius. These men, Strauss's "we"—though they be "scholars and artists, civil servants and soldiers, merchants and landlords numbering in the thousands, hardly the worst people in the land"—bore us more in the telling of their faith than they would in the telling of their dreams. If they refuse to leave our land in peace, then at least the din of their *unisono* must not be allowed to disguise the poverty and vulgarity of their melody. How can we freely consent to hear the confession of a multitude when we would have real trouble hearing out any one of them and would interrupt him with yawns no matter how well equipped

7. Leopold von Ranke (1795–1886), father of German historicism. He and his followers were committed to precise and objective determinations of sources and facts—a scholarly commitment which, turned compulsive, destroyed the study of history as a humanistic discipline (see *HSDL*, esp. 2 and 7). Nevertheless, Nietzsche held Ranke in high regard, praising him as a "born classical advocate of every stronger cause, the most prudent of all prudent realists" (*GM*, 3.19) and elsewhere as "clever" or "prudent" (klug) (*EH*, "Why I Am So Clever," 9), one of the truly "objective men."

Theodor Mommsen (1817–1903) was the greatest Roman historian of the nineteenth century. He brought a sociological and anthropological perspective to historical studies, and believed passionately that the purpose of history was to promote political consciousness. His *Roman History* won the Nobel Prize for literature in 1902. In the summer of 1880 Mommsen's house burned down, and with it his voluminous notes. Recalling the story of Mommsen rushing into the flames to recover his notes until at last forcibly restrained, Nietzsche wrote that it made "[my] heart twist around in [my] body" (letter to Peter Gast, July 18, 1880). Nietzsche, however, concluded: "Why this sympathy? I don't even like him." Nietzsche nevertheless admired Mommsen's memory, critical intelligence, and talent for organization, even if he opposed Mommsen's advocacy of liberalizing and democratizing trends.

Nietzsche's point in the present passage is, of course, that neither Mommsen nor Ranke, though men of enormous intellectual distinction and strong convictions, ever imposed their "confessions of faith" upon their readers.

he was to explain it to us? If you hold these beliefs, for God's sake, keep them to yourself.

Once, perhaps, a harmless few looked for a thinker in David Strauss; but, disillusioned, they have found him a believer. Had he kept silent, he might have remained a philosopher to those few. Now he fools no one. But he no longer covets the glories of the thinker. He will be a believer, proud of his "new beliefs." Writing his confessions, he supposed he was inscribing a catechism of "modern ideas" and building the broad "universal highway of the future." Our philistines are no longer gloomy and timid, but cocky to the point of cynicism. Once, very long ago, the philistine was simply tolerated, a creature who did not speak and about whom nothing was said. Then came a time when we stroked his wrinkles and found him amusing to discuss. As a result he became increasingly foppish, taking heartfelt delight in his wrinkles and wrongheaded, simpleminded idiosyncrasies. At last he spoke out on his own behalf, somewhat in the manner of Riehl's *House Music*:[8] "But what's this I see? Is it a phantom, or is it real? Look how my poodle grows long and wide."[9] For now that he lumbers down the "universal highway of the future" like a hippopotamus, his snarling and barking have assumed the proud tone of the founder of a religion. Would it perhaps please you, Master, to found the religion of the future? "The time is not yet ripe. The urge to overthrow any church has not even occurred to me" (p. 8). But Master, why not? It's only a question of ability. And after all, if

8. Wilhelm Heinrich von Riehl (1823–97) was a journalist, novelist, folklorist, and cultural historian. He also had a keen interest in popular music. In 1860 he published a two-volume collection of "house music," intended for performance in the home by family and friends. House music differed from "salon music"—classical music composed for, or performed in, the drawing rooms of aristocrats and the cultural elite—in being associated particularly with the middle class and entirely amateur in nature. Riehl's collection boasted "only simple, easy German Hausmusik." For Nietzsche, who had himself attempted to compose "serious" music, and who believed that a genuine feeling for music, "the language of the will" (see *BT,* esp. 16 and 19), was essential to the revival of true German culture, Hausmusik was an utterly vile and vulgar travesty of music itself—a stupefying middle-class Muzak.

9. The line about the "phantom" comes from Goethe's *Faust,* part 1, 1,247–50. Faust, alone in his study with the black poodle, sees the dog suddenly loom up into a vast shadowy shape, "a fiery-eyed hippopotamus," before emerging from the mist as Mephistopheles. Nietzsche's Strauss is the "spirit who denies," only arrested comically in mid-transformation: the "hippo" lumbering down "the universal highway of the future." The Goethe quotation is not, then, intended to exemplify Riehl's Hausmusik or to mimic the philistine's speech, but to describe the spectacle of the philistine's newly found self-confidence, puffed up like the poodle's diabolical shadow. At the root of the joke, however, there may be an allusion to Strauss as the diabolical enemy of Christianity, for his earlier, radical attacks on its historical basis. Nietzsche scoffs below (§3) at the absurdity of a demonic Strauss.

we may speak frankly, you do believe you're able. Why, just look at the final page of your book. You are convinced that your new road is "the only universal highway of the future, needing but a few finishing touches here and there, and some human traffic above all, to become commodious and agreeable." Deny it no more: the founder of a religion has been revealed, and the brand-new, agreeable, commodious roadway to Straussian paradise has been built. Only the carriage in which you would transport us does not entirely satisfy you, modest man that you are. In closing, you tell us: "I will not claim that the carriage in which my worthy readers have put all their trust meets all the specifications—all along one feels badly jolted" (p. 367). Ah, now, coy religion-founder, you would like to hear a compliment. But we prefer to say something sincere. If your reader required himself to read your religious catechism of 368 pages in the smallest possible doses, one page for each day of the year, we believe that by the end he would feel somewhat sore—sorely frustrated, that is, by the absence of any effect whatsoever. Better to down it at one hearty gulp, the prescription for all timely books. Then the tonic can do no harm and its drinker will escape feeling sore and frustrated. Instead, he will be cheered and enormously gratified, as if nothing had happened, no religion overthrown, no highway to the future built, no confession made—now *this* would be an achievement! Doctor, medicine, sickness—all forgotten! And the uproarious laughter! That steady tickle in our ribs! You really are to be envied, sir, founding the most delightful religion—a religion whose founder is steadily honored with laughter.

4   The philistine, founder of the future religion— *this* is the new creed in its most striking manifestation. The philistine turned religious fanatic—*this* is the shocking phenomenon marking today's Germany. For the time being, let us approach this fanaticism cautiously. None other than David Strauss sagely advises such caution in words that actually remind us more of Christianity's founder than David Strauss (p. 80): "We know there have been genuinely inspired visionaries—visionaries who could stimulate, elevate, and have a lasting historical effect. But we would never choose them as our guides through life. They are bound to lead us astray, unless we temper their influence with reason." We can take this still further. There are also uninspired visionaries who neither stimulate nor elevate, but pose as our guides through life, and control the future by producing a lasting historical effect—which *compels* us to temper their visions with reason. Lichtenberg held: "There are visionaries possessing no gifts, and these are truly dangerous people."[10] For the present, to exercise reasoned control we need

10. Nietzsche regarded the physicist Georg Christoph Lichtenberg (1742–99)—one of the foremost satirical writers of the eighteenth century—with Lessing and Schopenhauer, as one of his stylistic mentors (see letter to Gersdorff, April 9, 1867). Nietzsche consid-

honest answers to three questions. First, how does the new believer imagine his heaven? Second, how much courage does his new faith inspire? And third, how does he write his books? Strauss the confessor must answer the first and second questions; Strauss the writer, the third.

The heaven of the new faith must, of course, be a heaven on earth, since the Christian "prospect of eternal life in heaven," along with other such consolations, has already "fallen beyond redemption" for the man with "just one foot" on the Straussian standpoint (p. 364). The way in which a religion depicts its heaven is revealing: If Christianity knows no heavenly occupation other than music-making and singing, then the Straussian philistine cannot be expected to find this a truly consoling prospect.

But the confession book has its paradisal page (294). Unfurl this scroll first, blessed philistine, and behold the whole of heaven descend. "We only wish to indicate how we occupy ourselves," says Strauss, "and how we have occupied ourselves for a long time. Besides our professional callings—for we follow the most diverse callings, not merely scholars and artists, but civil servants, military men, merchants, and landowners, and again, as I have said before, we are not a few, numbering in the thousands, and not the worst sort in the land—besides our callings, as I was saying, we strive to keep our understanding of humanity's higher pursuits as vital as possible. During the last few years we have played an active part in our great national war and in the establishment of the German state. We find ourselves profoundly heartened by the shift in our much-tried nation's fate, as unexpected as it is glorious. Our understanding of these events has been facilitated by a series of handsomely and popularly written historical works, accessible even to the layman. We strive also to broaden our understanding of the natural world, for which there is likewise no lack of generally available study aids. Finally, in the writings of our great poets and the music of our great composers we find a stimulus for the mind and heart, for imagination and wit, leaving nothing to be desired. This is how we live and make our way—in joy."

That's our man, the philistine cheers; and yes, this is exactly how we live our lives, all the live-long day![11] And how admirably he has mastered the art of euphemism! What, for example, can he mean by "historical works that facilitate our understanding of the political situation" except the morning paper? And what can the "active part played in the establishment of the German state" be except our daily visit to the beer hall? Surely by "generally

---

ered Lichtenberg's *Aphorisms* among the four books of German prose worth reading (see *WS*, 109).

11. Nietzsche alludes to a popular German students' song. The German phrase ("so we live, truly, so we live all day") is fairly close, even in tone, to the lyric from a popular American railroad ballad by which I have rendered it.

available study aids for broadening our understanding of the natural world,"
he must mean a stroll through the zoo. And finally, to say that from our
theaters and concert halls we bring home "stimulus for imagination and wit,
leaving nothing to be desired" does indeed take some real wit—to dignify
such a dubiety! That's our man! His heaven and our heaven are one!

So the philistine cheers. But we are not satisfied and crave to know still
more. Scaliger used to say: "Who cares whether Montaigne drank red or
white wine?"[12] But in these far more weighty matters, how we would treasure
such detailed commentary! If only we knew how many pipes the new faith
recommends that the philistine smoke in a day, or whether he finds the
Spener or *National Zeitung* more agreeable with his morning coffee. But our
craving for this knowledge goes unappeased! On one point only are we more
informed, and that, luckily, concerns his Heaven of Heavens—namely, those
small, private art-rooms consecrated to the great poets and musicians in
which the philistine "edifies" himself and, as he avows, "all his blemishes
are purged and wiped away" (p. 363), as if at some sort of lustral spa. "And
yet this lasts but a fugitive moment; it can only happen, and can only have
validity, in the realm of fantasy. As soon as we return to rude reality and
the cramping constraints of living, our old cares devolve on us from every
corner all over again"—so our master sighs.

If this is the case, let us not waste the fugitive moments we may linger
in these little rooms. They will afford us just enough time to inspect the
ideal image of the philistine—that is, *the philistine purged of all blemishes* and
therefore the purest specimen of his type. But in all seriousness, this could
prove extremely enlightening. No one who has fallen prey to the confession
book should put it aside without reading the two appendices, entitled "On
Our Great Poets" and "On Our Great Musicians." Across their pages the
new covenant's rainbow appears; and whoever is not immediately filled with
joy to behold it is "beyond all help" and—as Strauss has said elsewhere,
and would doubtless say again here—"not yet ripe for our point of view."
Now we are in the very Heaven of Heavens.

Our inspired tour guide begins by showing us around and, enraptured
by the splendor of the place, apologizes for getting somewhat carried away.
"If I perhaps seem," he tells us, "more loquacious than the occasion requires, the reader must indulge me. A full heart must overflow in words.
But he can be sure of this: what he is about to read is not old material
conveniently thrown together, but has been freshly composed for the present
purpose and place" (p. 296). We are stunned momentarily. What do we care

12. Joseph Justus Scaliger (1540–1609), the greatest classical scholar of the Renaissance.
As for Montaigne, one of the true "free spirits," Nietzsche described him as a writer
even more honest than Schopenhauer: "The fact that such a man has written truly adds
to the joy of living on this earth" (*SE*, 2).

if his little chapters were freshly composed? As if it were just a matter of composition! Confidentially, I would rather they had been composed a quarter of a century earlier; then at least I would know why the thinking seems so stale and reeks of modishly rotten antiquities. Anything written in 1872 that is already rancid makes me very suspicious.

Suppose someone fell asleep over these putrescent chapters—whatever would he dream of? A friend of mine confided to me that he did just this. He dreamt about a wax museum: all our classical authors, smartly copied in wax and beads, moving their arms and eyes to the squeaking of an inner screw. Then he noticed something utterly uncanny: a grotesque figure draped with ribbons and yellowed paper; a scrap hanging from its mouth read "Lessing." My friend moved closer and closer, until the very worst became clear: Homer's Chimera, sandwiched between Strauss in front and Gervinus in back,[13] *in summa*, Lessing.[14] He woke suddenly with a shriek of horror—and read no further. Why in the world, Master Strauss, did you ever write such rotten little chapters?

However, we do discover a few new insights there. For instance, how and why, according to Gervinus, Goethe could not have been a dramatic genius; that the second part of *Faust* is merely an allegorical shadow play; that Wallenstein[15] is a Macbeth who is likewise a Hamlet; that the Straussian

---

13. The Chimera was a monstrous mythical amalgam of snake, lion, and goat, which was killed by the Greek hero Bellerophon (*Iliad* 6.179–83).

Georg Gottfried Gervinus (1805–71) pioneered the study of German literary history, relating literary developments to intellectual and political movements. His major work was his *History of German Poetry*, though among English readers he is perhaps best known for his critical study of Shakespeare (*Shakespeare*, 1849–50). He was almost the stereotype of the active and prolific nineteenth-century "political professor." His literary criticism was informed by a kind of Hegelian historial determinism which Nietzsche found superficial (that is to say, unphilosophical, psychologically naive, and historically tendentious). He singled out Gervinus in *BT* (21 and 22), as the prime example of the shallow critic, utterly lacking "the feeling for music as the mother tongue."

14. Gotthold Ephraim Lessing (1729–81), one of the literary giants of his century, ranking in importance perhaps only behind Goethe and Schiller. Nietzsche singled out Lessing in *BT* 15, as the highest type of Socratic man ("the most honest theoretical man"). As a dramatist and critic, Lessing almost single-handedly laid the foundation of modern German drama; in his esthetic, literary, and philosophical views, he was wholly undaunted by the reigning theological and intellectual prejudices of his day. The so-called freethinkers of the nineteenth century, like Gervinus and Strauss, were fond of imagining themselves Lessing's intellectual heirs, a presumption that Nietzsche found intolerable. Their complacency was, he thought, quite alien to the embattled intellectual isolation of Lessing's last years.

15. Wallenstein, the hero of Schiller's tragedy of the same name, based on the life of the charismatic sixteenth-century imperial commander Albrecht Wenzel Eusebius von Wallenstein, who tried to unite Germany and was ultimately betrayed by the emperor himself.

reader plucks novellas from the *Wanderjahre*[16] as naughty children pluck almonds and raisins from a sticky cake batter; that without a gripping and thrilling stage spectacle the dramatic effect is incomplete; and that Schiller emerges from Kant as if from a cold-water cure. This is all certainly very new and striking. I am not quite sure what it strikes; but whatever it is, it is not my fancy. And just as surely as this is new, it will never grow old, since it was never really young. It sprang from the womb a great-uncle already.

What unusual thoughts strike these new-style apostles in their esthetic heaven! But why couldn't they have forgotten even a little of what is at once so unesthetic, so mundanely ephemeral, or, for that matter, so distinctly a mark of absurdity as, for instance, the dogma of Gervinus? It would seem as if the modest greatness of Strauss and the immodest triviality of Gervinus were ideally suited. Long live the blessed ones! And long live the rest of us too, the unblessed, if this redoubtable critic continues to teach us, now and always, his studied enthusiasm and what the honest Grillparzer so aptly termed his hired-horse gallop, until finally the whole heaven resounds with the hoofbeats of Strauss's enthusiastic galumph![17] Then at least we would hear something brassy and lively instead of that shuffling, felt-slippered zeal and lukewarm rhetoric, which, after a time, only bores and disgusts us. I should like to hear a Straussian hallelujah. One would have to listen very closely so as not to confuse it with a polite apology or a lisped gallantry.

I know of an example, instructive but disturbing to recall. Strauss took it badly when one of his enemies spoke of his reverence for Lessing—but this pathetic character simply misunderstood. Strauss, of course, maintained that one must be thick-skinned not to sense that the simple words on Lessing in his ninetieth chapter were warm words straight from the heart.

Now I do not doubt for an instant this warmth. In fact, it is Strauss's warmth toward Lessing that has always bothered me. In Gervinus I find the

---

16. *Wilheim Meisters Wanderjahre* ("Travels"), sequel to *Wilhelm Meisters Lehrjahre* ("Apprenticeship"), was Goethe's last novel. The hero, Wilhelm, is required by a secret society into which he has been initiated to take a journey during which he may not stay in one place for more than three days. The novel, episodic in structure, was attacked by critics like Gervinus for its lack of thematic unity. Goethe himself insisted that the novel had an underlying symbolic scheme ("It has its parts, but it's still of a piece"). The book offended genteel taste, hence Nietzsche's "naughty children." Later Nietzsche wrote that it was only too typically and moralistically German that the decadent sentimentality of someone like Wagner should have been preferred to Goethe's healthy sensuality (see *CW*, 3).

17. See Grillparzer, *Sämmtliche Werke* (Stuttgart, 1872), 2:175. Franz Grillparzer (1791–1872) was a prolific poet, novelist, critic, and, most importantly, playwright. Nietzsche admired Grillparzer's intellectual power and acuity, describing him as "a detached and reflective observer" (*HSDL*, 4, also 6).

same suspicious warmth—only raised to a searing heat. In general, no great German writer is more popular among our lesser German writers than Lessing; but they should not be thanked for this. For just what is it that they praise in Lessing? At times, his universality: he was a critic and poet, archaeologist and philosopher, dramatist and theologian. Then: "this unity of writer and man, head and heart." The latter sometimes distinguishes minor writers as well as great ones: after all, a narrow mind accords only too frightfully well with a narrow heart. And the former, this universality, is, in itself, no great distinction, least of all in Lessing's case, since there it was mere necessity. The remarkable quality of these Lessing enthusiasts is their total blindness to the burning compulsion that drove him through life and to this "universality." They have no sense that such a man may, like a flame, burn out too quickly; nor are they indignant that the narrow poverty of spirit, especially that of his learned contemporaries, which overwhelmed him, may have troubled, dimmed, and finally smothered his softly glowing nature. They cannot see that his touted universality ought to be profoundly pitied. Goethe saw it: "Have pity on this extraordinary man, who lived in a time so miserable that he had to engage continuously in polemics."

How, my fine philistine friends, can you even think of Lessing without feeling ashamed, since it was by *your* stupidity, by his struggle with *your* ludicrous fetishes and idols, and by the killing defects of *your* theaters, scholars, and theologians that he was ultimately destroyed?[18] Not once could he ever even attempt that eternal flight for which he had been born. Do you remember Winckelmann who was so sickened by the sight of your grotesque absurdities that he begged for help from the Jesuits?[19] This

18. Lessing spent the last years of his life in a furious theological dispute. In the third and fourth volumes of his *On History and Literature* (1773–81), he published a series of fragments by a writer whose name, Hermann Samuel Reimarus, was not disclosed for nearly forty years. The fragments addressed religious questions in a rationalist light. The last of these fragments (*On the Objectives of Jesus and His Disciples,* 1778) maintained that Jesus' disciples had distorted his practical and ethical aims in the interests of promoting the faith. Lessing openly declared his sympathy for the unnamed author and "freethinker," but found himself opposed by all parties, orthodox theologians and self-styled liberal thinkers alike. In a flurry of activity, he published a number of polemical pieces attacking his opponents on each front. When the orthodox party at last managed to have further "rationalist" publications suppressed, Lessing turned again to the stage. His last play, *Nathan the Wise,* was principally concerned with the question of religious tolerance.
19. Johann Joachim Winckelmann (1717–68), the more or less self-educated scholar who set the tenor of European classicism for decades with his concept of the "elevated simplicity and serenity" of ancient art. It is commonly alleged that Winckelmann converted to Catholicism in order to facilitate his trip to Rome, where he wrote his famous *History of Ancient Art.* Nietzsche himself was highly critical of Winckelmann's "noble simplicity," preferring to look beneath the Apollonian mask of Greek art and into the Dionysiac experience animating it. Nietzsche compared Winckelmann's and Goethe's idealized

shameful conversion is your shame, not his. Can you even mention the name of Schiller without blushing? Just look at his portrait. The gleaming eyes that stare scornfully beyond you, the fatal flush of his cheeks—do *these* say nothing to you? There you had a noble, godlike plaything to shatter. Had you only been able to deprive his truncated, death-bent life of Goethe's friendship, just imagine how much more swiftly you could have extinguished it.[20]

You have done nothing to help in the lifework of your great geniuses. Will you make it your dogma that no one shall be helped ever again? To every one of them you have proven yourself to be that "repellent stupidity of the world" named by Goethe in his *Epilogue to the Bell*.[21] But in spite of your ill-tempered stupidity, your narrow-minded jealousy, or your self-seeking malice, these men have done their work. Against you they turned their attack; thanks to you they died off too early, with their day's work still undone, and they themselves broken or numbed from the struggle. Should you now be permitted, *tamquam re bene gesta*,[22] to praise these men in words that clearly betray who, in fact, you have in mind—such "warm words straight from the heart" that only a fool would fail to see before whom you really bow? "In truth, we need a Lessing," Goethe cried. And woe to all the conceited masters and the whole heavenly host of esthetes when the

---

Greece with Victor Hugo's Orient, Wagner's Edda, and Walter Scott's thirteenth-century England—"historical fictions that one day will be discovered as the comic creations that they are" (*Aus dem Nachlass der Achtzigerjahre*, in *Werke*, ed. Karl Schlecta [Frankfurt am Main, 1979], 3:644).

20. After a long period of cool formality, Goethe and Schiller at last recognized their close personal poetic affinity. A result of this newly found friendship was their jointly edited literary journal *Die Horen*, which, to the anger of both men, failed to win a readership. They blamed contemporary writers for having nurtured the public's lack of taste and jointly published *Xenien*, a collection of distichs reminiscent of Martial, lampooning the widespread intellectual mediocrity. Their critics were temporarily silenced; and in the wake of this minor victory, Schiller wrote what was perhaps his greatest dramatic masterpiece, *Wallenstein*, and Goethe, his *Hermann und Dorothea*. However, Schiller's plays—drawn along classical lines, charged with the romantic enthusiasm of the Sturm und Drang movement, and influenced by the psychological and ethical awakening of German Idealism—met a public that preferred the crude realism and sentimentality of dramatists like Kotzebue. Possessing neither Goethe's composure nor conciliatory skills, Schiller seems to have spent most of his life at war with all but the rarer spirits of his age.

21. A line from the seventh stanza of a poem composed by Goethe as an epilogue to Schiller's *Song of the Bell*. The epilogue was recited at a memorial service for Schiller (Aug. 1805, Lauchstädt), after a dramatic presentation of his *Song of the Bell*. By Schiller's death Goethe felt that he himself had been robbed of "half [his] being." Nietzsche's own description of Schiller just above—"the gleaming eyes . . . the fatal flush"—is taken from this poem.

22. "as though matters turned out well"

young tiger comes out for the kill, restless strength rippling through his muscles and blazing from his eyes!

5   My friend was wise to abandon the book altogether when that chimerical phantom woke him to the real Strauss, and the real Straussian Lessing. But we read on, we even beg entry into the *musical* heaven of the new faith. The master admits and accompanies us, offering explanations, dropping names—finally we stop dead in our tracks and eye him suspiciously. Couldn't it happen to us—what happened in my poor friend's dream? The composers whom Strauss describes seem, even as he describes them, falsely named. We assume he must really be referring to some other composers, if, in fact, he is not talking about some weird apparitions. When, for instance, he speaks with that suspicious warmth that betrayed his Lessing and starts savoring the name Haydn, as if he were a pope or priest in some Haydn mystery-cult, comparing him to an "honest soup" and Beethoven to "confection" (referring of all things to the quartets, p. 362), this much, at least, is certain: *his* sugar-coated Beethoven is not *our* Beethoven, nor *his* Haydn soup *our* Haydn. Furthermore, the Master considers our orchestra too good to play Haydn and insists that only the humblest amateurs can do his music justice—proof again that he must mean some other artist and some other work, perhaps Riehl's *House Music*.

But who can Strauss's sugar-coated Beethoven be? He is said to have composed nine symphonies, of which a certain *Pastoral* is the "least inspired." We learn that whenever he came to the Third, he felt compelled "to kick over the traces and search for adventure," which conjures up the image of some hybrid creature, half horse, half rider. In the case of a certain *Eroica*, this centaur is attacked in earnest for failing to clarify "whether this struggle takes place in an open field or deep in the human heart." In the *Pastoral* we find an "exquisitely raging storm" interrupting a peasant dance that is "almost too trivial." Therefore, because of this "arbitrary connection with a banal and trivial event," as the classical master so cleverly and correctly puts it, this symphony must be "the least inspired." "With all due modesty," as he says, he suppressed the much stronger word that he had in mind. But no, for once our master is wrong: he is being far too modest. Who else can teach us about this sugary Beethoven, when only Strauss seems to know him? Besides, a judgment, far more severe and spoken with all due *immodesty*, immediately follows—a judgment on none other than the Ninth. It is admired only by those who "regard the grotesque as ingenious and the formless as sublime" (p. 359). To be sure, even a harsh critic like Gervinus applauded it, that is, as a confirmation of his own doctrines; but Strauss is far from seeing the merit of *his* Beethoven in such "problematic works." "What a shame," cries our master with a touching sigh, "to spoil the pleasure we take in Beethoven and the admiration gladly owed him, because of reservations like these." Our master is himself, of course, a darling of the Graces; they themselves told him how they traveled with Beethoven only a short distance and then fell out of sight. "This is a short-coming," Strauss admits, "but could it not also be an advantage?" (p. 355). "The man who pushes a musical idea breathlessly forward with tremendous strain will appear that much stronger and his idea that much weightier" (p. 365). This admission applies not only to Beethoven, but to our "classical author" *himself*, this celebrated writer from whose side the Graces never depart. From the play of light humor—namely, Straussian humor—to the heights of solemn seriousness—that is, Straussian seriousness—they stand unflinchingly by. This classical calligrapher glides lightly and playfully along, while Beethoven struggles breathlessly forward. Strauss, beneath the weight of his burdens, appears to be simply dawdling. And this is an advantage; but could it not also be a shortcoming—of course, only to someone who regarded the grotesque as ingenious, and the formless as sublime? Is this not so, darling dawdler of the Graces?

We begrudge no one the edifying moments he may enjoy in the quiet of his study, or even in a freshly made-up kingdom of heaven; but of all possible edifying pastimes, the Straussian still has to be one of the strangest. For Strauss edifies himself at a small sacrificial fire, into which he calmly tosses the highest achievements of Germany, with whose vapors he censes his gods. Let us for a moment imagine that, by some chance, the *Eroica*, the *Pastoral*, and the Ninth fell into the hands of our high priest of the Graces, and that he had it in his power to purge such "problematic pro-ductions," in order to keep the Master's image pure. Who doubts he would have burned them? And this, in fact, is exactly how our modern Strausses act. About an artist they care to know only what serves their domestic needs. They know only the opposed extremes—either censing or incinerating. No matter, let them be. But that public opinion should be so feeble, wobbly, and docile where art is concerned, that it should tolerate such a pathetic philistine show-and-tell without a word of protest—*this* is what truly aston-ishes.

No one even sees the comedy in this inartistic mini-maestro's passing judgment on Beethoven. As for Mozart, let Aristotle's remark about Plato apply: "His *inferiors* should not even be allowed to praise him." But now all sense of shame has been lost—to the public as well as to the master. Not only do they allow Strauss to cross himself openly before the greatest and purest products of German genius, as though he witnessed godless profan-ities, but they also revel in his frank confessions and admissions of sin, especially since they are not *his* sins, but those supposedly committed by great minds. "Ah, if only our master were always absolutely right," think Strauss's adoring readers, still, from time to time, touched by doubts. But he himself stands there, smiling smugly, perorating, cursing and blessing, tipping his hat to himself, capable of saying at any moment what the Duchess Delaforte said to Madame de Staël: "I must confess, my dear, that I know of no one so consistently right as myself."[23]

6   A corpse is bliss to a worm, but even the thought of a worm sends shudders through any living thing. Worms imagine their kingdom of heaven in a fat, dead body; professors of philosophy imagine theirs to be gnawing on Schopenhauer's intestines. So long as there are rodents, there will be a rodent heaven. With that, our first question—How does the new believer picture his heaven?—has been answered. The Straussian philistines live like vermin on the works of our great poets and composers: they live by what they destroy, they gnaw what they admire, their homage is swallowing.

But now we come to our second question: How much courage does the new religion inspire in its believers? If courage and impudence were one and the same, our problem would be solved. For, in this case, Strauss could be said to possess the true and rightful courage of a Mameluke.[24] In any case, the "due modesty" which Strauss reserves for Beethoven in the passage cited above is merely a figure of speech, not a moral expression. Strauss enjoys his share of that audacity to which every conquering hero imagines himself entitled. All flowers bloom only for him, the conqueror, and he praises the sun for shining directly through *his* window, at just the right time of day. Even the venerable old universe is not immune to Strauss's praise, as though it needed to be sanctified before beginning its revolution around Strauss, the pivotal monad of the world. The universe, he instructs us, is a machine, to be sure, equipped with iron-toothed cogwheels and pistons with pounding rods; but "it moves not only bare, relentless cogs— it also gushes with soothing oil" (p. 365). The universe will be less than grateful to this image-mad master, unless he can find a better metaphor for

23. Baronne de Staël (1766–1817), a French novelist (*Delphine*, 1802; *Corinne*, 1807) and critic who wrote on a miscellany of literary, esthetic, and political topics and is perhaps best known as a theorist of romanticism. She was mistress of a chic literary salon in Paris and at her Swiss estate in Coppet; in many respects, she epitomized European culture of her time. Napoleon, against whom she formed a nucleus of liberal resistance, refused to allow her within forty leagues of Paris and eventually banished her from France altogether. Nietzsche seems to have shared the emperor's contempt for Mme de Staël (see *BGE*, 233).

24. The ruthless courage of this warrior class, which ruled Egypt and Syria from the mid-thirteenth to the sixteenth century, is proverbial. Below (*DS*, 6) Nietzsche again compares Strauss's bravery to the Mameluke's, saying that he feared "neither Schopenhauer nor the devil." Perhaps also to Nietzsche's point is the fact that the Mamelukes, though copious chroniclers, contributed almost nothing to the *culture* of Islam, despite their political and military dominance for nearly two and a half centuries.

his panegyric—if the universe would tolerate, even for an instant, praise from Strauss. What are we to call this oil dripping down the rods and pistons of a machine? And how will it help the worker to know that this oil is gushing all over him, while his limbs are caught in the machinery?

Let us admit that the image is hopeless, and scrutinize another method employed by Strauss to convey his peculiar attitude toward the world. He postures with Gretchen's question on the tip of his tongue: "He loves me— he loves me not—he loves me . . . "[25] Now, even Strauss does not pluck petals or count off buttons, though what he does is just as insipid, even if it requires a bit more courage. Needing empirical proof of whether his feeling for the "cosmos" has, or has not, gone numb or become paralyzed, Strauss pricks himself, knowing of course that he can prick a limb, numbed or paralyzed, without inflicting any pain. But in point of fact he doesn't prick himself at all. Instead, he adopts a still more brutal procedure which he describes like this: "We break out our Schopenhauer, and he takes every opportunity to slap our ideas in the face" (p. 143). Now an idea—even the most beautiful Straussian idea of the universe—has no face. Only the man who has the idea can have a face. A breakdown of the whole procedure would run as follows. Strauss breaks out his Schopenhauer; whereupon Schopenhauer, now *broken out*, steals this opportunity to slap Strauss in the face. At this point, Strauss "reacts religiously" and again breaks Schopenhauer, only this time he breaks him apart, not out, charging him with absurdity, blasphemy, profligacy, finally impugning even his sanity. Strauss wins by decision: "We demand for our universe the same piety which the old-school devotee demands for his God"—in short, "He loves me." Our darling of the Graces does make his life difficult, but he is brave as a Mameluke, and fears neither Schopenhauer nor the devil. Imagine how much "soothing oil" he must consume if this is his regular modus operandi!

On the other hand, we understand the debt of gratitude which Strauss owes the tickling, poking, hard-hitting Schopenhauer. So it is really no surprise when he shows a little kindness: "One may merely leaf through the pages of Schopenhauer, though one would do better to study them closely . . ." (p. 141). Now to whom is our philistine-in-chief actually speaking? He himself has never studied Schopenhauer—and he knows it. In fact, Schopenhauer would have to say of Strauss: "This author does not deserve to be leafed through, much less studied." Apparently, Schopenhauer must have gone down the wrong way; so Strauss now clears his throat, hoping to cough him up. But to achieve the full measure of fatuous praise, Strauss permits himself an approbation of old Kant, designating *The General History and Theory of the Heavens of the Year 1755* a "work that has always struck

25. Goethe, *Faust*, part 1, 3,181. Gretchen (a diminutive form of Margarite) is the innocent peasant girl seduced by Faust.

me as no less significant than his later *Critique of Pure Reason.*" He continues,
"We admire the latter for its depth of insight, and the former for its broad
overview. In the one we see an old man at pains to secure even a limited
domain of verifiable knowledge; in the other we meet the mature man with
all the daring of the conqueror and explorer in the realm of thought." The
Straussian judgment of Kant has always struck me as every bit as immodest
as his judgment of Schopenhauer. In the latter we see our little leader at
pains to articulate even the most limited judgment, while in the former we
meet the renowned prose-writer with all the daring of stupidity, oozing his
eau d'éloges even over Kant.

But the absolutely incredible thing is this: Strauss has no use for the
Critique of Pure Reason in his "testament of modern ideas." His wholesale
preference for the coarsest realism agrees strikingly well with the main
features of this new evangelism, which presents itself as the hard-won
achievement of never-ending historical and scientific investigations and the
tacit negation of all philosophical principles. For the philistine-in-chief and
his "we," Kantian philosophy simply does not exist. He does not even
suspect the basic antinomy that underlies idealism, or the highly relative
status of all science and reason; otherwise, his reason would have told him
just how little things-in-themselves are laid open by reason. But actually,
there are people who, at a certain age, absolutely cannot understand Kant,
especially if, in their youth, they have, like Strauss, understood, or think
they have understood, "that intellectual giant" Hegel; and people who also
must have steeped themselves in Schleiermacher, "a man possessing almost
too much acuity." Strauss will be dumbfounded if I tell him that even now
he remains "utterly dependent" upon Hegel and Schleiermacher, and that
his theory of the universe, his view of things *sub specie biennii*,[26] his cringing
before the German status quo, but above all his shameless philistine optimism, can be explained by youthful impressions, early habits, and certain
disorders. Once infected with Hegel and Schleiermacher, one can never be
completely cured.[27]

---

26. "From the perspective of two years," i.e., with the perspective afforded by entirely
modern considerations. The common expression, of which Nietzsche's is an ironic vari-
ant, is *sub specie aeterni*, "from an eternal perspective."
27. Nietzsche's case against Hegel and Schleiermacher is too complex to be but briefly
discussed. Nietzsche built his philosophy in diametric opposition to the Hegelian notion
of a world-spirit becoming progressively conscious of itself through man. Instead,
Nietzsche was attracted by the Schopenhauerian notion of the world as Will, against
which the human spirit defined itself by struggle. Nietzsche regarded Hegel as the philosophical heir of the Christian theological tradition who had, in effect, simply provided it
with a metaphysical basis. Hegel's historical Idealism actually supports the kind of deification of the present, of historical or material success, that Strauss's book celebrated
and epitomized (though Strauss himself regarded his *Confession* as his materialist depar-

In one passage of the confession-book this incurable Straussian optimism rolls out in high holiday spirits: "If the world is something that would have been better off by not having been, then the philosopher's thoughts, a part of this world, would have been better off by not being thought. The pessimistic philosopher fails to see how, in declaring the world to be bad, he ultimately declares his thinking to be bad as well. But if a thought which thinks the world bad is a bad thought, it follows that the world must therefore be good. As a rule optimism may take things too lightly; and therefore Schopenhauer's remarks on the powerful role played by pain and evil in the world have their place; but every true philosophy is necessarily optimistic, otherwise it denies its own right to exist" (pp. 142–43). If this refutation of Schopenhauer is not the same "refutation attended by loud jubilation in higher spheres" that Strauss employed once against another opponent, then I fail to understand this theatrical turn of phrase. Here, for once, optimism makes light of things for a purpose. But the real trick lies in pretending that it is nothing to refute Schopenhauer—in fact, to write him off so playfully that the three Graces will be tickled by the trifling optimist at every turn. By so doing, he hopes to prove one point: pessimists need not be taken too seriously. The most untenable sophistries are quite enough to show that well-founded arguments need not be wasted on a philosophy as "morbid and unprofitable" as Schopenhauer's, especially when a few words in jest will do. Such words only reinforce Schopenhauer's solemn declaration: Optimism is not merely the mindless chatter of men with only words lodged in their thick skulls, nor just an absurd mental attitude; it is a *malignant habit of mind* that bitterly mocks the nameless sufferings of mankind. When a philistine like Strauss construes optimism as a philosophical system, it is reduced to just such a malignant habit of mind, such an idiotic doctrine of comfort for his "I" and "we"—*we* are indignant.[28]

For example, who can read the following psychological explanation, so clearly stemming from that invidious doctrine of comfort, without getting angry? "Beethoven maintained that he never could have composed a text like *Figaro* or *Don Giovanni. Life had not smiled on him, that he could ever look on it so cheerfully and take men's weaknesses so lightly*" (p. 360). There are even

---

ture from Hegelian Idealism).

Schleiermacher (1768–1834) was the leading Protestant theologian of the German romantic movement; his name literally means "veil maker" (see *EH*, "The Case of Wagner," 3). For a further discussion of Strauss's relation to Schleiermacher, see below, n. 50. On Hegel's stylistic obscurity, see below, n. 55.

28. See Schopenhauer, *The World as Will and Representation*, 1.59 (also 2.46); and *Parerga and Parlipomena*, vol. 2, chaps. 11 and 12). Later, of course, Nietzsche rejected Schopenhauer's pessimism in an effort to find a way out of both Idealism and nihilism. Schopenhauer's Will, before which only tragic resignation was possible, was replaced by the dynamic of destruction and affirmation, i.e., "overcoming."

starker examples of Strauss's malicious vulgarity. A hint will suffice. Strauss explains the dreadfully serious impulse toward self-denial and the disciplined life of religious asceticism characterizing the first century of Christianity as nothing more than the aftermath of a prior age's excess of sexual aberrations, brought on by revulsion and disgust:

> The Persians call it *bidamag bugen,*
> We Germans say: hungover.[29]

Strauss quotes these lines himself, and feels no shame. We must turn away for a moment—to overcome our disgust.

7   In fact, our philistine-in-chief is brave, even brazen, whenever he supposes such displays will amuse his noble "we." For this reason, the asceticism and self-denial of the old hermits and saints are regarded as a species of hangover, Jesus as a fanatic who would barely escape the madhouse today, and the story of the Resurrection as "world-historical humbug." For just once we will endure this, so that we may study the singular courage of which Strauss, our "classical philistine," is capable.

Hear his confession first: "It is certainly an unpopular and thankless duty to tell the world what it least wants to hear. The world likes to conduct business on a grand scale, amassing and spending its wealth like a great lord, so long, that is, as it has something to spend. But the moment someone tots up the expenses and presents the balance, he is branded a troublemaker. Nevertheless, as always, my heart and soul impel me to the task." Such a heart and soul might very well be considered courageous; but whether this courage is natural and inborn or learned and artificial, remains in doubt. Perhaps from the outset Strauss simply fell into the habit of acting like a troublemaker, until by degrees he acquired the courage of his calling. Entirely compatible with this development is that instinctive cowardice which is the hallmark of the philistine. It shows itself in the fecklessness of words that cost Strauss the most courage to utter. They rumble like thunder, but always fail to clear the air. He never acts aggressively; instead, he speaks aggressive words as rudely as possible, and, by so doing, exhausts his resources of energy and power through coarse and raucous outbursts. When his words die away, he is more of a coward than the man who says nothing

---

29. Goethe, "Saki Nameh—Das Schenkenbuch," *Der West-Östliche Divan* ("The Book of the Inn," *West-East Divan*), in *Gedenkausgabe der Werke, Briefe und Gespräche,* ed. E. Beutler (Zurich, 1949), 3:375. In Nietzsche's eyes, a despicable bowdlerization: Strauss quotes from Goethe's mystical poem about love, to illustrate his own insipid and commonsensical views of religious experience. The choice of this quotation is particularly inappropriate in the immediate context, since Goethe's poem represents a fusion of sensual and spiritual experience.

at all. Even in his ethics, that shadow-play of deeds, he reveals himself a hero in words alone, shunning any occasion that might require him to proceed from words to grim earnest. With amazing candor he proclaims himself no longer a Christian; but he refuses to destroy another man's solace. He sees it as a contradiction, that the building of a new order should require the demolition of the old. A contradiction? With a certain coarse complacency, he wraps himself in the shaggy mantle of our simian genealogists, hailing Darwin as one of mankind's great benefactors. But the philistine's ethics baffle us; they are construed with absolutely no regard for the question "How do we view the world?" This is the place for real courage; here he should have turned his back on the "we" and boldly deduced an ethical code for living from the *bellum omnium contra omnes*[30] and the right of the strong. But clearly this can only appear in a deeply intrepid spirit, like that of Hobbes, and in a love of truth utterly different from that which explodes as nasty attacks upon priests, miracles, and the "world-historical humbug" of the Resurrection. A true Darwinian ethic, actually carried through, would make an instant enemy of the philistine; but such outbursts make him feel right at home.

"All moral activity," says Strauss, "is the individual's determination to act in accordance with the Idea of the species" (p. 236). Or, in plain and simple language: Live like a man, not an ape or a seal. Unfortunately, this injunction is totally inane and therefore utterly useless, since the concept of man encompasses such a multiplicity of types, from the Patagonian savage to Master Strauss. And who in his right mind would recommend that we live like either of them? But suppose someone were to challenge himself to live like a genius, that is, as the ideal expression of humanity. And suppose he just happened to be a Patagonian or a Master Strauss. Can you imagine what we would be forced to endure? The importunities of those innately idiotic genius-addicts, who even now mushroom, as Lichtenberg has complained, all over Germany—lunatics wildly howling about how we must hear them confess their latest beliefs.[31]

Strauss has still not learned that a concept cannot make men better or more moral, and that preaching morals is as easy as establishing them is hard. His real task should have been to explain in earnest how human kindness, compassion, love, and self-denial—all of which actually do exist even now—could be deduced from his Darwinian premises. But no, not Strauss. He escapes the task of *explanation* by a leap into the imperative mood, bounding, with his light and nimble intellect, right over Darwin's most basic principle.

30. "the war of all against all"
31. See Lichtenberg's *Über die Schwärmerei* (On fanaticism), in *Werke*, ed. Grenzmann (Frankfurt am Main, 1949), 2:327–39.

"Never forget, even for a moment," says Strauss, "that you are a man, and no mere natural substance; no, never forget, even for an instant, that others are also men; that is, for all their individual differences they are, in their desires and demands, the same as you—and *this* is the essence of all morality" (p. 238). But where does this resounding imperative come from? How can this be innate to man when, according to Darwin, man is just a natural substance, one that attained the height of humanity by adherence to an entirely different set of laws, by forgetting at all times that other creatures like him were also similarly entitled? On the contrary, having perceived his superior strength, he gradually brought about the fall of other, more weakly constituted creatures. While Strauss must admit that no two beings are exactly the same, and that man's entire development, from the bestial stage to the height of philistine culture, hinges on the law of individual differences, he has not the slightest trouble preaching the exact opposite: "Act as if there were no individual differences!" Where is the Strauss-Darwin theory of morals now? Where is that courage?

Immediately, we discover another point at which that courage reverts to its opposite. For Strauss continues: "Never forget that you and everything you perceive in and around you are not disjointed fragments, nor a wild chaos of atoms in random interaction; but that everything arises, according to eternal laws, from the single, primal source of all life, and all reason, and all good—and *this* is the essence of religion" (p. 239). But from that primal source also flows all ruin, all irrationality, all evil, all of what Strauss calls the universe. How can this universe, with its contradictory and self-destructive character, be worthy of religious devotion, or be addressed by the name of "God," as even Strauss addresses it: "Our God does not take us into his arms from without" (here we expect, by way of antithesis, the miraculous feat of being taken into his arms "from within"), "but touches our source of solace deep within. He shows us that chance would make a most unreasonable world-ruler, but that necessity, the chain of all causation, is reason itself" (a deception that only the "we" who have been exalted by the Hegelian worship of reality as reason, that is, the *deification of success*, do not recognize). "He leads us to see that to demand an exception in the fulfillment of even a single natural law is to demand the destruction of the entire cosmos" (p. 365). Quite the contrary, Master Strauss. A true natural scientist may believe in the world's absolute adherence to laws, without ascribing the slightest moral or intellectual value to these laws. Such a claim simply exposes the extreme anthropomorphism of one who has overstepped the lawful limits of reason itself. But at precisely that point where the true scientist yields, Strauss "reacts"—to plume ourselves with his own quill[32]—

---

32. Nietzsche puns on Strauss's name, which means "ostrich." The common German expression *sich mit fremden Federn zu schmücken* is equivalent to the English phrase "to

"religiously" and abandons all scientific method and integrity. He simply assumes that all phenomena possess the *highest* intellectual value, that they are aligned with some absolutely reasonable and purposive plan, and therefore embody the revelation of eternal goodness itself.

Strauss needs a complete cosmodicy, and therefore places himself at a disadvantage vis-à-vis one who only needs a theodicy—someone who, for instance, views human existence as a penance or purgation.[33] At this embarrassing juncture, Strauss, for once, actually ventures a metaphysical hypothesis, a most sterile and palsied hypothesis, in fact, simply an unwitting parody of Lessing: "That other saying of Lessing's—if God held Truth in his right hand and in his left hand only the ever-animating though perpetually erring desire for it, and offered him a choice, he would humbly fall before God's left hand and beg for its contents—has always been esteemed one of the most magnificent statements he left us. It brilliantly evokes his restless desire for inquiry and activity, and has always had a very special effect upon me. For behind his subjective meaning, I hear the faint ring of an objective one, boundless in its scope. And is this not the best rebuttal of Schopenhauer's uncouth remarks about the ill-advised God who, for lack of anything better, entered this miserable world? The creator himself would have shared Lessing's opinion, preferring struggle to peaceful possession" (p. 219). By all means, a God who reserves *perpetually erring* for himself, together of course with a striving after Truth, and who may perhaps even take Strauss humbly by the left hand and say: "Here, take it—the whole Truth is yours."

If ever a God and a man were ill advised, it is this Straussian God, with his taste for error and failure, and this Straussian man who must atone for His taste. Listen closely now. Surely you must hear it: "the faint ring of a

---

deck oneself out with borrowed feathers." Nietzsche's phrase literally translates "to deck ourselves out with his feathers." *Feder* means (quill) pen as well as feather. Above, Nietzsche derisively refers to Strauss as a calligrapher and to his baroque expressions as "lacy serifs."

33. "Cosmodicy" (*Kosmodizee*) is formed on the analogy of theodicy (*Theodizee*), a term coined by Leibnitz and the title of his philosophical treatise, *Essais de Théodicée sur la bonté de Dieu, la liberté de l'homme, et l'origine du mal* (1710) Théodicée derives from two Greek words, *theos,* "god," and *dike,* "justice." Theodicy is, literally, God's justice, a universal system in which everything, including evil, is held to emanate from God and justified as a manifestation of his attributes. By analogy, a cosmodicy refers to a system in which God has been replaced by a metaphysical cosmos ("*All*"). The Leibnitzian term implicitly raises the problem which Leibnitz himself never adequately solved: the existence of evil. Strauss worships the cosmos, a *harmoniously* grinding mesh of gears and wheels, but glosses over the question of evil and misery with either sentimentality or subterfuge (a Christian can at least maintain that suffering is the way to salvation). Strauss never really examines the ethical implications of his materialist world view.

meaning, boundless in scope." With this, the soothing oil of Strauss's cosmic machine begins to flow. With this, we have a presentiment of the reasonableness of all Becoming and every natural law. But is this how it really is? Isn't our world, as Lichtenberg once described it, more like the work of some subordinate being, still rather unsure of his task, a trial or an experiment still being worked on?[34] Even Strauss himself would have to admit that the world is more a showplace of *error* than of reason, and that all the laws of nature provide small comfort, if they are laws of a God who errs, and errs with pleasure. In any case, this is an amusing spectacle—Strauss as a metaphysical master builder, at long last building his castle in the air. But for whom has this spectacle been produced? Why, for the smug and noble "we," to keep them in good cheer. Perhaps they begin to grow alarmed amid the implacably pitiless cogwheels of the cosmic machine, and, trembling now, beg their master's help. So Strauss lets his "soothing oil" flow; and parades his passionately erring God about on a leash, and, this once, even plays the utterly uncanny role of metaphysical architect. He does all this because they are afraid, because now even he is afraid—and here his courage stops, when confronted himself with his "we." He does not dare tell them the truth: "I have freed you from a compassionate and merciful God and shown you that the universe is only an implacable wheelwork. Beware lest its wheels crush you." No, he does not dare. He resorts to an enchantress instead—namely, metaphysics. But to the philistine even Straussian metaphysics are better than Christian metaphysics, and the image of an erring God is more congenial than that of a miracle worker. For the philistine himself errs—but he has never worked any miracles.

This is why the philistine hates the man of genius—because he is rightly reputed to be a worker of miracles. We would especially like to know why Strauss, in one particular passage, poses as a staunch defender of genius and the aristocratic nature of the intellect. Why indeed! Out of fear, and fear especially of the Social Democrats.[35] He makes reference to Bismarck,

---

34. Lichtenberg, *Von den letzten Dingen, "Die Erkenntnis Gottes"* (Of last things, "God's knowledge"), *Werke*, 1:457.

35. The German Social Democratic Party did not formally come into existence until 1875, though the first organized German socialist party (the German Workingman's Association) had been politically active for more than a decade. The Social Democrats, whose formation Marx himself violently protested, advocated the proletariat's assumption of power by constitutional electoral means and rejected the enforced dictatorship of the proletariat so essential to Marxist doctrine. As the self-proclaimed champion of the German bourgeoisie and an ardent advocate of constitutional monarchy, Strauss abhorred the Social Democrats, "the Vandals and Huns of modern civilization" (*Confession*, 4.79; in general, see 76–81). Nietzsche himself had little love for socialism, since he did not believe the historical process to be progressive or "the greatest good for the greatest number" to be the highest aim of a nobly aspiring society. Society's only purpose, he

Moltke, "whose greatness is undeniable, since it has entered the realm of tangible, external fact. Now even the most stiff-necked and surly of that clan deign to look up a little, to glimpse at least the knees of these exalted figures" (p. 280). Are you perhaps, good Master, trying to teach these Social Democrats how to get themselves kicked in the face? Well, rest assured that the goodwill to oblige you in this instruction is everywhere to hand. And you can guarantee the initiates that they, for their part, will catch a glimpse of some pretty exalted knees. "Even in the realm of Art and Science," Strauss continues, "there will never be any lack of kings whose monumental plans will keep a multitude of draymen busy." Good—but what if someday the draymen attempt something monumental? It has happened, Master Metaphysician, as you well know—then the kings may have something to laugh at.

The fusion of impudence and weakness, the brash words with the cowardly trimming, the minute calculations about which words will strike and which words will stroke the philistine, the lack of strength and character disguised as strength and character, the lack of wisdom posing as mastery and mature, worldly experience—*all of this* I detest in Strauss's book. If I believed that our young people could esteem, or even suffer through, such a book, I would abandon all my hopes for their future in despair. These confessions of a bankrupt, hopeless, and truly despicable philistinism are supposed to be the words of that multitude Strauss calls his "we"; what is more, it is supposed that this "we" will father the new generation! This is a ghastly prospect to anyone who hopes to help the coming generation find what the present one has lost: a true German culture. To such a person the ground seems strewn with ashes, the stars blacked out. Every withered tree and wasted field cries out: fruitless! deserted! Spring will never come again! He must surely feel the sadness the young Goethe felt as he stared into the gloomy, atheistic twilight of the *Système de la nature.*[36] He found the

---

held, lay in creating conditions whereby the highest type of man could arise: "Whom do I hate most among the rabble of today? The Socialist who undermines the workingman's instincts, who destroys his satisfaction with his insignificant existence, who makes him envious and teaches him revenge." For Nietzsche, socialism was a historical anachronism, "a residue of Christianity and Rousseau in an unchristian world" (*NF,* ed. Schlecta, 3:633).

36. In 1770, an influential German aristocrat, Baron d'Holbach, the center of a prominent intellectual circle in Paris, published this treatise under the name J. B. Mirabeau. It was an all-out attack upon religion and the articulation of an atheistic, materialistic, and deterministic worldview. One critic described d'Holbach as "a man who came to Paris to wage war on God." He commissioned an entire library of books dedicated to the cause of exposing religion as the source of man's degradation, and he himself contributed 367 articles, mostly translations on scientific topics, to Diderot's *Encyclopédie.* D'Holbach, however, was an insignificant thinker, attacked by both Voltaire and Rousseau as an

book so dreary, so Cimmerian, so deathly that he could hardly bear its presence. It made him shudder, like the sight of a ghost.

8   We now know enough about the new believer's heaven and courage to pose our final question: How does he write his books, and what sort of religious documents are they?

Whoever can answer this question rigorously and without prejudice will be extremely puzzled to discover that six editions of the Straussian pocket-oracle of German philistinism are already in print.[37] He will be astonished to find that it has been hailed as a handbook in learned circles, even in the universities. Students are said to welcome it as the new catechism for strong minds, and their professors raise no objections. Some have actually gone so far as to consider it the new *Bible for Scholars*. Strauss insists, however, that his confessional book is not a reference work intended *solely* for the learned and the cultivated. But his book is in fact devoted almost entirely to them, particularly the scholars, and is held up to them as a veritable mirror of the lives they lead. This is the Master's great feat. He pretends to offer a new and ideal world view; his readers return this compliment with universal praise, since everyone supposes that his own world view and way of life have been described. What Strauss had at first demanded of the future he now appears to see already fulfilled in his present readers. This in part explains the book's extraordinary success. Delighted that others are also delighted, the scholar calls back to Strauss: "Yes, this is how we live, lives blessed in just the way your book declares!" If, by chance, he happens to disagree with the Master on certain points—say Darwin or capital punishment—it is immaterial, since he feels certain that this is, on the whole, the air he breathes, and an echo of *his* voice and *his* needs that he hears. This unanimity must distress every true friend of German culture, who must therefore be relentlessly severe in accounting for this state of affairs, and who must not shrink from making his account public.

We are all too familiar with the way scholarly and scientific inquiry typifies our day and age. We know it because we live it. Therefore, almost nobody

---

intellectual charlatan. The mechanistic scheme of his *Système de la nature*, to which Nietzsche compares Strauss's *Confession*, must have mortified Goethe, who regarded the harmony of nature as one of life's great mysteries and, in general, hated lifeless, conceptual "systems" (see Goethe's letter to Charlotte von Stein, June 15, 1786).

37. "Pocket-oracle" is an allusion to the famous *Oracular Handbook* (*El oráculo manual y arte de prudencia,* 1647) of Baltasar Gracián, a collection of *sententiae* on the ethics of worldly life. Schopenhauer once described Gracián's *Critic,* in which life is presented as "daily dying" and the emphasis is on will and struggle, as one of the most important books ever written; Schopenhauer himself translated the aphoristic *Handbook* into German.

even asks himself what such a preoccupation with scientific inquiry bodes
for the culture at large, even granting that there are people everywhere
exceptionally well equipped and sincerely inclined to promote culture. The
nature of the scientific and scholarly type of man (setting aside his contemporary incarnation) is a true paradox: he acts like an arrogant prig, wholly
at ease with fate; his existence is not an uncertain and fatal business, but a
secure possession, eternally guaranteed. Hence, he fells entitled to waste
his life asking questions whose answers could matter only to someone
vouchsafed an eternity. All around this heir of a few brief hours yawn the
most terrifying abysses. At every step a question should confront him: Where
do I come from? Where am I going? Why? But his soul warms to its work—
counting flower petals or cracking stones along a path—and in this he fully
invests all his curiosity, joy, strength, and desire. This paradox, the scientific
scholar, has lately swept through Germany with such speed that one might
think scholarship has become more like factory work, in which every lost
minute carries a fine. The scientific scholar works hard, as if at slave labor,
his study is no longer a calling: it is a necessity. He looks neither to the
right nor to the left, passing through his life's business and all life's serious
preoccupations with only half his attention, or with that urgent need for
recreation that marks the exhausted laborer.

Now he even treats culture in this way, acting as if his life were merely
otium—but *otium sine dignitate.*[38] Even in his sleep, like a liberated slave who
dreams of rushing around and being beaten, he cannot shed the yoke. Our
scholars can hardly distinguish themselves—and this is not to their credit—
from the common farmer who hopes to increase his slim patrimony by
arduous efforts, toiling from morning until night, sowing his field, driving
his plow, prodding his oxen. Now, Pascal was convinced that men conduct
their business and pursue their scholarship so zealously in order to escape
from the genuinely serious questions that solitude and leisure would impose
on them: From where? To where? And why? How strange that the most
obvious questions never occur to our scholars: What is the purpose of all
this work, this killing pace, these back-breaking frenzies? Not daily bread,
nor even glory. No, certainly not this. And yet you struggle like a man who
hungers and thirsts, greedily and indiscriminately snatching food from the
table of knowledge as if to keep from starving. But if you, scientific scholars,

---

38. "Leisure, but leisure without dignity," the negative version of a phrase, *otium cum
dignitate* (leisure with dignity), found frequently in Cicero's writings. The Romans possessed a refined and essentially aristocratic notion of leisure, to which Nietzsche himself
subscribed (see *GS*, 329, and *NF*, passim). For him, leisure meant freedom from the
tedium of toil, a freeing of the mind for thought and for the pursuit of art and culture,
in which man's highest value and dignity lay—the opposite of the philistine's frantic
busyness.

turn to your scholarship as the worker turns to his labor, driven by poverty and need, what will become of our culture, condemned to await its hour of birth and salvation amid this frantic, racing, gasping, convulsive obsession with scholarship?

For culture no one has time—and yet, what, *above all*, should scholarship have time for, if not culture? At least answer this: To what end should all scholarship lead, if not to culture? To barbarism, perhaps! Our educated class has in fact made astonishing progress in this direction, if one considers that a book as superficial as Strauss's satisfies their present standard of culture. For in Strauss we find that urgent need for recreation, that casual, complacent, drowsy deference to philosophy and culture, and, for that matter, to anything of real life-seriousness. His book reminds us of those scholarly gatherings, after the shop-talk is over, when the signs of fatigue set in and the scholar's desire for diversion at any cost, the randomness of his reminiscences, and incoherence of his life begin to show. Whenever Strauss turns to the great issues of the day, such as the problems of marriage, or the war, or capital punishment, his utter lack of real experience and original insight into human nature is shocking. His judgments are all uniformly bookish, in fact, journalistic. Literary reminiscences are substituted for genuinely fresh insight; an affected restraint and avuncular manner are meant to compensate us for his lack of wisdom and mature judgment. How perfectly in keeping with the spirit of those proclaimed the high priests of German scholarship in our great cities! What a sympathetic conversation their spirits must hold, since in these circles culture has really disappeared and its rebirth been made impossible—so noisy are the preparations for the scholarship they pursue, so like a stampede is the devastating assault of the more popular disciplines on the most important ones. Do we have a light by which we could even search for men capable of delving deeply into the nature, and devoting themselves purely to the spirit, of genius—men with courage and strength enough to invoke the daimons who have fled our age? Viewed superficially, the whole pomp of culture can be found in the scholar's world, with all its imposing apparatus, so like an arsenal, replete with monstrous cannons and war machines. They make such preparations, and with such assiduous industry—as if they were about to storm heaven and draw Truth from the deepest well. And yet in war the largest machines are the hardest to handle. This is why true culture, in its struggle, avoids the scholarly world, instinctively aware that it holds out little hope, and much to fear. The only culture with which the bloodshot eyes and stunted brains of the scholarly working class can be bothered is that philistine culture whose gospel Strauss preaches.

If we look briefly at the basis of this sympathy, linking the scholarly working class to philistine culture, we will come to our last major theme—Strauss the *writer*, the classical writer.

In the first place, that culture wears a smug, complacent expression and will hear of no essential changes in the present state of German education. The philistine is, in fact, utterly convinced of the uniqueness of all German educational institutions, especially the university and gymnasium; he never stops recommending them to foreigners; never for an instant does he doubt that they produce the most cultivated and discerning individuals. Philistine culture believes in itself and therefore in the means and methods at its disposal. Second, it looks to the scholarly community as a high court in matters of culture and taste, while seeing itself as the steadily swelling compendium of scholarly opinions on art, literature, and philosophy. Its first duty is entreating scholars to voice their opinions, which are then mixed, diluted, or systematized, to be offered as a quick pick-me-up to the German people. Any idea that surfaces outside learned circles will neither be noticed nor heard; or, if heard, accorded half-hearted skepticism, that is, until at last a voice—no matter whose, so long as it bears the unmistakable stamp of the scholarly breed—is heard coming from that sanctuary where the infallibility of conventional taste is thought to reside. From that moment on, public opinion has one opinion more, and echoes back a hundredfold the voice of a single man. But, in reality, that esthetic infallibility could reside in this sanctum and be voiced by any scholar at all is highly doubtful, so doubtful in fact that the lack of taste, the triviality, and the esthetic crudity of scholars can be taken for granted until proven otherwise. And only a few could prove otherwise. For, after taking part in the gasping, agitated race of modern scholarship, how many could preserve the calm and courageous gaze of the embattled man of culture, if, in fact, they ever possessed it at all—that gaze that condemns the race itself as a barbarizing force? These few must then live a constant contradiction. What can they do against the uniform belief of a multitude that has unanimously chosen public opinion as its patron saint—a belief that this multitude upholds and, in turn, upon which it depends? When so many have already decided in Strauss's favor, and the masses taken in by them have learned to crave the Master's philistine narcotic (six consecutive doses' worth!), what can one man accomplish by opposing him?

If we simply assume that Strauss's confessional book has conquered public opinion and is now welcomed as a conqueror, its author will perhaps point out that the various reviews of his book, now in print, are neither entirely unanimous nor altogether favorable. In fact, he felt the need, in a postscript, to defend himself against the exceedingly hostile tone, the often insolent and defiant manner, of some of these journalistic contenders. "How can there be any 'public opinion' regarding my book," he will shout at us, "when nearly every journalist brands me an outlaw and abuses me to his heart's content?" This contradiction is easily resolved as soon as we distinguish the two aspects of Strauss's book—the theological and the literary.

Only the latter touches German culture. The work's theological coloring places it outside German culture and antagonizes the various theological factions. For that matter, it antagonizes every single German, since he is a theological sectarian by nature and only invents his odd private beliefs in order to dissent from others. But just listen to what these sectarians have to say when the discussion turns to Strauss the *writer*. Suddenly their dissonant, theological din dies down, and they intone in the purest harmony, like a unified congregation: a *classical writer* he remains! Everyone, even the most obstinately orthodox sectarian, flatters him to his face, be it a compliment on his almost Lessing-like dialectic, or a word about the fineness, beauty, and validity of his esthetic views. This Straussian creation is, so it seems, the ideal book. The dissenting theologians, loud though they may be, account for only a very small fraction of the great public. And so, regarding them, Strauss is right to say: "Compared with my thousands of readers, these outspoken fault-finders constitute an insignificant minority and will be hard pressed to prove that they faithfully represent anyone. As we all know, it's in the nature of these things that dissenters will speak up, while confederates sit by in silent approval." And so, apart from the scandal his theological confessions may have caused in some circles, the judgment on Strauss the *writer*—even among those fanatical opponents for whom his voice is that of a beast howling from the abyss—is unanimous. Therefore, the treatment that Strauss has received at the hands of the literary lackeys of the theological sects in no way disproves our claim. With this book philistine culture celebrates a triumph.

We grant that the educated philistine is, on the average, a trifle less frank than Strauss, or at least more restrained about public proclamations. This is why he finds another's frankness so uplifting. At home and among his peers, the philistine loudly applauds his master, but he is careful not to confess on paper that everything said by Strauss is after his own heart. Now, as we already know, our culture-philistine is something of a coward, even in his strongest passions; and, because Strauss is just a little less of a coward, despite the very strict limits of *his* courage, he has become their leader. If he overstepped *these limits*, as, for example, Schopenhauer does in almost every phrase, he would no longer lead the philistine pack. Instead, they would run from him as fast as they now run after him.[39] Those who term this not exactly wise but clever moderation and mediocre courage an Aristotelian virtue are simply mistaken. This courage is not the mean between two faults, but the mean between a virtue and a fault—and in this mean, between a virtue and a fault, lies *every* philistine trait.

39. In his notes (*NF*, 24.47 [spring–autumn 1873]), Nietzsche describes Strauss as "running before his 'we' like a pillar of smoke," portentous to his acolytes, but lacking substance.

9   "But still, a classical writer he remains!" Let
us see.

Perhaps we can now discuss Strauss as a stylist and master of language.
But we should first consider whether Strauss, the literary man, knows how
to build his literary house and really understands the architecture of a book.
Then we can be certain whether or not he is an orderly, sensible, and skillful
maker of books. And if not, he can always take refuge in his reputation as
a "writer of classical prose." But this distinction alone is not enough to raise
him to the rank of a classical author, at most to that of a classical improviser
or stylistic virtuoso who, in every glib expression and the overall structure
of his work, betrays the clumsy hand and blinkered vision of the bungler.
So our question stands: Does Strauss have the artistic power to create an
esthetic whole, *totum ponere*?[40]

Usually the first rough draft will reveal whether an author has conceived
a totality, and whether his conception conforms to an overall design and is
correctly proportioned. Even with these critical steps taken and the edifice
itself erected to the right scale, much work still remains: there are defects
to be corrected, gaps to be filled, provisional partitions and scaffoldings to
be removed, everywhere you turn, sawdust and shavings, the traces of
work—and work that needs doing. As a house it is still gloomy and unin-
habitable: walls are bare and the wind blows through open windows. But
whether Strauss has finished this necessary and painstaking work is, at
present, of little concern until we can ascertain whether the building has an
overall shape, and is of sound proportions.

Of course, the opposite type of work is familiar enough—a book composed of snippets, the sort of book that scholars write. Trusting that such
fragments somehow all cohere, they confuse logical connections and artistic
ones. In any case, the connections between the four main questions forming
the thematic divisions of Strauss's book are not logical: "Are We Still Christians?" "Do We Still Have Religion?" "How Do We Conceive the Universe?" "How Do We Order Our Lives?" Where is the logical connection?
The third question has nothing to do with the second, nor the fourth with
the third, nor have these three anything to do with the first. The natural
scientist who, for example, raises the third question shows his unsullied
devotion to truth by silently passing over the second. The themes of the
fourth section—marriage, the republic, capital punishment—would become
hopelessly obscured and confused if allied to the Darwinian theories of the
third. Strauss himself, in fact, seems to appreciate this, since he never once
refers back to these theories.

The very question—"Are we still Christians?"—instantly destroys the
freedom of philosophical speculation with its disagreeable theological tinge.

40. "to construct a whole"

Moreover, Strauss has altogether forgotten that the majority of men, even today, are Buddhist and not Christian. Why should the words "old faith" refer simply and solely to Christianity? This only makes it clear that Strauss has never stopped being a Christian theologian and has never learned to become a philosopher. We are even more surprised to find that he cannot distinguish between faith and knowledge and that he constantly speaks of his so-called new faith and the new science in the same breath. Or is this "new faith" just an ironic concession to common usage? So it appears from the naive way in which he interchanges faith and science. On p. 11, for example, he asks on which side—the old beliefs or the new science—"can more of the inadequacies and obscurities unavoidable in human affairs be found." He will moreover demonstrate, according to the plan in his introduction, the proofs that support his modern world view. But all his proofs are derived from the science of knowledge; Strauss conducts himself throughout as a "knower," and not as a "believer."

At bottom, this new religion has less to do with a new faith than with modern science; as such, it is no religion. Now, if Strauss insists that he still has religion, its basis must lie outside the realm of modern science. Very little in Strauss's book—a few scattered pages at most—touches on what could rightly be called a faith: that feeling for the cosmos for which Strauss demands the same piety that the old-style devotee demands for his God. At least here his approach is not wholly scientific. If only he had set about it with a little more strength, instinct, energy—with altogether more faith! What really strikes us is the artificiality of the procedures our author adopts—this pricking and slapping—in order to feel that he still has faith and religion at all. It proves a poor and feeble thing, this artificially stimulated faith. And we shudder simply at the sight of it.

Although in his introduction Strauss promised a comparison, to see whether the new and old faith serve the same purpose, even he finally realized he had promised too much. For to the question of the new faith's purpose, whether the same, or better, or worse, Strauss in the end responds offhandedly, dismissing it with a few pages of embarrassed haste (pp. 366ff.), even by playing his trump: "Whoever cannot help himself in this matter is simply beyond help, and not yet ripe for our point of view" (p. 366). Compare the force of conviction with which the ancient Stoics believed in their cosmos and in its rationality.[41] And, viewed in this light, how does Strauss's

---

41. The ancient Stoics maintained that all phenomena occurred in accordance with a universal *ratio*, or principle of reason, which they made the governing principle of their own severely disciplined lives. A stoical life well lived was a manifestation of ratio itself. Strauss's "faith" in an intelligible "cosmos" is therefore hardly "new"; however, his faith in the cosmos does not require him to live a life disciplined by its laws. In other words, Strauss's cosmos is merely an abstraction.

claim to an original faith appear? But whether a faith is old or new, original or derivative, is immaterial if it shows signs of health, strength, and instinct. However, Strauss himself abandons his distilled faith-in-case-of-emergency whenever he must use erudition to keep us, and himself, out of trouble, or whenever he must display, with a clear conscience, his newly acquired scientific wisdom to his "we." Just as he grows demure at the mention of "faith," he swells up whenever he cites that greatest benefactor of modern man, Darwin. Then he demands belief not only in the new Messiah, but also in himself, the new apostle. At one point, addressing a complex scientific problem, he proudly predicts, like one of the ancient prophets himself: "Some will say I speak of things I do not understand. Very well, but there will be others who will understand—and they will have understood me" (p. 207). Apparently Strauss's renowned "we" are supposed to pledge their faith not only in the cosmos, but in Strauss, the natural scientist, as well. In this case, we can only hope that the task of stimulating their faith in Strauss will not be as cruel and painful a procedure as that required to stimulate faith in the cosmos. Or perhaps this once, pinching and prodding the object of faith instead of the faithful followers might be enough to induce that "religious reaction" which is the hallmark of the "new faith." Think what we would stand to gain by their religious fervor in this event!

Otherwise, we might have reason to fear that modern man will progress without any particular concern for the trappings of the apostle's religious faith—just as, in fact, he has progressed until now without the doctrine of cosmic rationality. Modern scientific and historical inquiry have absolutely nothing to do with Strauss's cosmic faith; that the philistine also has no use for it, Strauss himself makes clear in his fourth chapter, his portrait of philistine life. He is right to doubt that the "carriage" in which his "worthy reader had to entrust himself meets all the requirements." It hardly meets them at all, since modern man progresses more swiftly by never entering Strauss's carriage—or rather, he made swifter progress long before this Straussian carriage ever existed. Now, if it is true that this distinguished "minority not to be overlooked," in whose name Strauss speaks, puts "great stock in results," then they must be as dissatisfied with Strauss the carriage maker as we are with Strauss the logician.

But, for all that, let us abandon Strauss the logician. Perhaps from an artistic viewpoint the book really has a well-wrought form that agrees with the laws of Beauty, even though it fails the requirements of a well-constructed argument. Since he does not act like a scholar, tightly organizing and ordering his thoughts, we must ask: Is Strauss a good writer?

Perhaps the task he set for himself was not so much to frighten people away from the "old faith" as to entice them with a cheerful and colorful picture of life at home with the new world view. Of course, if he considered the learned and cultivated as his most likely readers, he surely must have known from experience that you can bombard them with the heavy guns of scientific proof and they won't budge; yet they quickly succumb to the more scantily clad arts of seduction. Even Strauss calls his book "scantily clad," indeed, "by design." And "scantily clad" is how his public eulogists find it and describe it, as, for example, one of them, a true nonentity, does in the following:

> The discourse proceeds with a graceful symmetry and turns the art of argumentation, by a critical twist, almost playfully against the old, while at the same time ushering in the new, decked out to tantalize simple and fastidious tastes alike. The orchestration of such manifold and dissimilar material is extremely subtle: everything is touched on, while nothing is taken too far. Moreover, the transitions, bridging one section with the next, are particularly ingenious, so that one does not know which to admire more—the skill by which unpleasant issues are side-stepped altogether or that by which they are hushed up.

As the quotation reveals, these eulogists have a much subtler sense of what an author *intends* to do than what he actually *can* do. Strauss betrays his intentions unmistakably in his enthusiastic and not altogether ingenuous praise of those Voltairean Graces in whose service he certainly could have learned the "scantily clad" arts—that is, if virtue can be learned and a schoolmaster can become a dancer.

Who does not have suspicions, after reading the following remarks of Strauss on Voltaire? "As a philosopher he was not at all original but adapted English inquiries to his own use. In this, he proved himself an absolute master of his material, which he understood how to present with inimitable skill, from every possible side and in every possible light. And for this reason, even without being strictly methodical, he can satisfy the demands of thoroughness."[42] The negative traits apply to Strauss: no one will claim that he is a highly original philosopher, or a strictly methodical one. But can we esteem him an "absolute master of his material" or grant him "inimitable skill"? Strauss's confession that his book is "scantily clad by design" makes us wonder if Strauss's design wasn't an imitation of the inimitable: in this case, skill.

Our architect dreamed neither of a temple nor of a home, but of a pavilion surrounded by formal gardens. It even seems that Strauss's mysterious feeling for the cosmos was calculated mainly to produce an esthetic effect, as

---

42. *Voltaire*, in *Gesammelte Schriften* (1878), 2:152–53. Strauss's writings on Voltaire were originally presented as a series of lectures and later published in book form as *Voltaire* (1870). Nietzsche considered Voltaire the real "*grandesigneur* of the spirit," and Strauss merely another "buffoon of modern ideas."

though it were a glimpse of some irrational element, like the sea, from the vantage point of his elegantly rational patio. Our route through the theological catacombs of the first section, with its darkness and scrolled baroque ornamentation, was again only an esthetic stratagem, designed to offset the purity, clarity, and rationality of the section entitled "How Do We Conceive the Universe?" For immediately following our walk through the gloom and our glimpse of the irrational void, we enter a room with a skylight. Sober and sparkling, it greets us; on its walls hang celestial charts and mathematical tables; there is an array of scientific instruments and cabinets full of skeletons, stuffed apes, anatomical specimens. From here we amble on, feeling for the first time truly happy in our pavilion-dwellers' sanctum of comfort. We find these pavilion-dwellers, with their wives and children surrounding them, engrossed in the daily papers or commonplace political discussions. For a few moments, we listen to them pronouncing on marriage and universal suffrage, capital punishment and the labor crisis; and we imagine that the whole rosary of public opinion could not possibly be mumbled more speedily.

Finally, we still need to be convinced of the inhabitants' taste for the classics. A brief visit to the library and the music room gives us all the proof required. Only the best books line the shelves, only the most celebrated compositions are propped up on music stands. Someone is even playing a little piece for us; if it happens to be Haydn's music, Haydn must not be blamed if it sounds more like Riehl's *House Music*. Meanwhile, the master of the household has found an occasion to explain his affinity with Lessing, and even with Goethe, however only as far as the second part of *Faust*. At last, our pavilion-dweller lapses into self-praise, contending that those who are not pleased with his pavilion are beyond help, not ripe enough for his point of view. He thereupon invites us into his carriage, but with a discreet reservation: it may not satisfy every demand and, since his road has been freshly paved, we may get badly bounced about. At this point, with that inimitable skill he learned to admire in Voltaire, our Epicurean garden god bids us adieu.

Who can any longer doubt his inimitable skill? The absolute master of his material has arrived; the scantily clad garden artist is born. Over and over we hear that classical voice: "For once I will not be a philistine! No, not as a writer! I simply refuse! But a Voltaire, a German Voltaire! Or better yet, a French Lessing!"

We have betrayed a secret. Our master does not always know who he would rather be—Voltaire or Lessing—but, in any case, not a philistine. Maybe he can be both, Lessing and Voltaire—so that what has been written might be fulfilled: "He had no character, so, whenever he wanted one, he had always first to assume it."[43]

43. See NF, 27.21 [spring–autumn 1873]). Nietzsche quotes Lichtenberg's remarks on

10   If we have understood Strauss the confessor
rightly, then he is, in fact, a true philistine, with the philistine's dry, cramped
soul and sober, scholarly needs. In spite of this, no one is more outraged
by being called a "philistine" than Strauss the writer. He would like to be
called sportive and daring, wanton and mischievous; but his perfect bliss
would be a comparison with Lessing or Voltaire, since they were anything
but philistines. However, in pursuit of that comparison, he often wavers.
Should he assume the bold, dialectical storminess of Lessing, or affect the
old Voltaire's free-spirited, satyr-like style? Every time he sits down to write,
he strikes a pose, as if he were sitting for a portrait—now Lessing's, now
Voltaire's. His praise of Voltaire (*Voltaire*, p. 217) reads like a bitter diatribe
against the conscience of our age: How could it have for so long ignored
what it possessed in the modern Voltaire? "Even his virtues," Strauss writes,
"are consistently uniform: natural simplicity, brilliant clarity, lively versatil-
ity, and winning charm. Ardor and vigor, when suited, were never lacking,
whereas bombast and affectation were things against which his inmost nature rebelled. If, on occasion, some of his more lewd and impassioned
outbursts tend toward vulgarity, the man, not the stylist, is to blame." From
this it appears that Strauss rightly understands the value of *simplicity* in a
writing style—always the mark of the true genius, who alone is privileged
to express himself with plain and natural grace. An author's choice of a
simple style does not, therefore, spell a mean ambition: for, although many
will recognize the image such an author would *like* to project, there will
always be others willing to accept the image being projected. But an author
of genius does not reveal himself through simplicity and precision alone:
his enormous power makes sport of his material, even when risky and difficult. No one marches in lockstep on an unknown path with a thousand
deep ravines yawning; but the true genius speeds nimbly by, clearing chasms
with bold, graceful leaps, scorning the fearful and cautiously measured step.

Strauss realizes that the problems which he glides over are dreadfully
serious, and have for millennia been treated as such by sages. In spite of
this, he calls his book *scantily clad*. All the dreadfully serious thoughts that
ordinarily attend the question of life's value or man's responsibility cease to
plague us when our highly gifted master goes flitting by, "scantily clad by
design"—more scantily clad, he informs us, than his Rousseau, who is
naked only from the waist down, as opposed to Goethe, naked from the
waist up. Pure, natural genius, it seems, does not drape itself; and perhaps

---

character and makes reference to Strauss's posturing. Both Schopenhauer and Lichtenberg, whose writing considerably influenced Nietzsche at this time, wrote on the link
between character and style. Character, in their view, expressed itself as style ("the
physiognomy of the mind," in Schopenhauer's words); stylistic affectation, then, was a
betrayal of self, or disintegration of character.

"scantily clad" is only a euphemism for "naked" after all. Those few who have seen the goddess of Truth insist that she is naked. And perhaps in the eyes of those who have not seen her but believe those who have, nakedness, or being scantily clad, is already proof of truth, or at least a seductive hint. This suspicion works greatly to the ambitious author's advantage. The reader who sees something naked assumes a more solemn mien than usual and asks himself: "What if this were Truth?" With this, the author has already won a great victory, since he has been able to compel his reader to regard him more solemnly than another, less unbuttoned author. This is the shortcut to becoming a "classic." And Strauss himself tells us: "I have been paid the unsolicited honor of being regarded as a writer of a kind of classical prose." He has reached his goal. Strauss the genius now goes running through the streets, costumed like a scantily clad goddess, cutting a truly "classical" figure; Strauss the philistine, to adopt the genius's original phrasing, must at all costs be "decreed out of fashion" or "expelled, never to return."

But the philistine *does* return, again and again, despite all decrees of banishment and expulsions! And his face, twisted into an expression borrowed from Lessing or Voltaire, keeps bouncing back, from time to time, into its old, true, and original form! Yes, all too often the mask of genius falls off; and never is his look more peevish, or his movements more wooden, than when he tries to spring with that leap, to look with that fiery gaze of genius. It is precisely because he goes around as he does, so scantily clad in our cold climate, that he runs a somewhat higher risk than others of catching bad colds. That the rest of us can see all this must badly distress him. But to be cured he must submit to the public diagnosis: there once was a Strauss, a bold, austere, conservatively attired scholar, as sympathetic a man as any of those in Germany who earnestly and energetically serve truth and know to stay within their bounds. Today, however, this man is a celebrity, known as David Strauss. He has changed. Perhaps the theologians are to blame. But enough: his current theatrics with the mask of genius inspire our hatred, or laughter, as his former seriousness compelled our seriousness and sympathy. Just recently he told us: "It would be ingratitude toward *my genius*, if I did not take any pleasure in having been granted, in addition to unsparing and incisive critical abilities, an innocent joy in artistic creation."

Now, Strauss may be shocked to learn that, despite his personal testimony, quite the opposite viewpoint is commonly held. First, he has never had any artistic gifts. Second, his so-called "innocent joy" is anything but innocent, since his basically strong and profoundly critical scholarly mind, *the essential Straussian genius*, was gradually undermined and finally destroyed by this "joy." Caught in a momentary fit of complete honesty, Strauss himself adds that he has always "heard a Merck within himself, exhorting him:

'Stop producing such trash—others can do that too.' "[44] That was the voice of the real Straussian genius: it tells him what his brand-new, innocent, scantily clad testament of modern philistinism is worth. Others can do it too! And many can do it better! Even those who, endowed with minds more gifted and richer than Strauss's, might do it best would still be producing merely trash.

By now it is clear how highly I esteem Strauss the writer: as an actor who plays at being the pure genius and classical author. Even if, as Lichtenberg once remarked, "a simple style is preferable, since no honest man prettifies and complicates his words," it is still far from being proof of a writer's honesty. If only the writer in Strauss were more sincere, he would write better and be less celebrated. Or—if he must play the actor—at least let him be a good one, and certainly much better at imitating the pure genius and classical author. He might try writing like them, purely and classically. But the truth of the matter is this: Strauss is a dreadful actor, and an utterly worthless writer.

I I   Naturally, the shame of being a dreadful writer is mitigated by the simple fact that in Germany it is hard to be even a tolerably mediocre writer, and highly unusual, if not utterly impossible, to be a good one. A natural soil is lacking: the art of speaking is not valued, promoted, or cultivated. Because in all forms of public speaking—as even the terms *salon, conversation, sermon, parliamentary oratory* suggest—there is no distinct national style, nor even the recognition that one is needed; because no statement made in Germany ever advances beyond the most primitive stage of verbal experiment, the modern writer has no uniform standard and therefore has a clear right to take the matter of language into his own hands. The inescapable consequence—the boundless dilapidation of contemporary Germany—has been most forcefully described by Schopenhauer: "If things go on this way, by the year 1900 the German classics will be unintelligible, since the only accessible language will be the shoddy jargon of noble contemporary speech—whose basic characteristic is impotence."[45]

44. Johann Heinrich Merck (1741–91) was an important eighteenth-century critic and mentor to many young poets, including Goethe, whom he introduced to the prominent literary group known as the Darmstadt Circle. Nietzsche is elliptically ironic here: Strauss, even while criticizing himself, manages fatuous self-praise with his delusions of Darmstadt grandeur.

45. Schopenhauer's term *Jetztzeit* ("contemporary") might be rendered by the current slang expression *contempo*. Nietzsche follows Schopenhauer, his model for this kind of stylistic polemic, in using the term to condemn the inelegance of contemporary German prose—*tztz* being a consonant combination that sounds particularly cacophonous. (See Schopenhauer's "On Authorship and Style," *Parerga and Paralipomena*, vol. 2 §272–89a, esp. 283). "Shoddy jargon" (*Lumpen-Jargon*) is a verbal play on Marx's famous term

Even now, German linguists and grammarians claim in the latest journals that, because of the great number of words, turns of phrase, and syntactical arrangements already lost to us, our classics can no longer serve as stylistic models. In this case, it may be time to collect all the verbal artifices currently employed by our celebrated writers and publish them as our new literary models, as Sanders has already done in his handy little dictionary of heavy-handed expressions.[46] He even includes among our "classics" that revolting monster of a literary stylist, Gutzkow.[47] In general, it seems, we must become inured to a startlingly new breed of classical author, among whom the foremost, or at least one of the foremost, is David Strauss himself, whose style can only be described as worthless.

Now, highly revealing of this philistine pseudo-culture is just how it arrived at its notion of a classic stylistic ideal—the writer who only shows his strength as resistance to any properly severe or rigorously artistic style, a resistance whose tenacity results in a certain uniformity of expression, which in turn almost resembles unity of style. But how is it possible, given the unlimited linguistic experimentation permitted everyone, that certain individual authors still manage to find a generally agreeable tone? What, in fact, is so generally appealing? Above all, a negative quality: the lack of anything offensive—*but everything truly creative is offensive.* The bulk of the German's daily reading material can be found, almost without exception, on the pages of the daily papers and the standard magazines. This language, its continual dripping—same words, same phrases—makes an aural impression. For the most part, the hours devoted to his reading are those in which his mind is too weary to resist. By degrees the ear feels at home with this workaday German and aches when, for any reason, it is not heard. But, almost as an occupational hazard, the producers of these newspapers and periodicals are the most thoroughly inured to the slimy journalistic jargon. They have quite

Lumpenproletariat, his designation of the lowest and most abject classes in a capitalist society. Lumpen are, literally, rags and therefore extend the garment metaphor ("scantily clad") by which Nietzsche has characterized Strauss's writing style throughout his essay.
46. Daniel Sanders (1819–97), a lexicographer responsible for a number of German dictionaries, phrase and quotation books, and linguistic studies. His popular three-volume dictionary contained illustrations of "correct" usage, exemplified by quotations "from Luther to present." Nietzsche refers here to the abridged "pocket" edition; literally, *Hand- und Schand-Wörterbuch* means something like "handy profanity dictionary."
47. Karl Ferdinand Gutzkow (1811–78), a prolific and versatile journalist, dramatist, essayist, and novelist, was one of the most celebrated writers of his day, though now almost forgotten. He wrote with great haste; as a result, his prose was carelessly composed and journalistic. In *On the Future of Our Educational Institutions*, 5, Nietzsche cites Gutzkow as a typical example of impoverished contemporary writing: "He wrote like a semi-educated, vaguely literary, completely desperate schoolboy."

literally lost all taste and relish, above all, the absolutely corrupt and capricious. This explains that *tutti unisono* with which every newly coined solecism instantly chimes in spite of the general torpor and malaise. With their impudent corruptions these wage-laborers of language take revenge on our mother-tongue for boring them so incredibly.

I remember reading Berthold Auerbach's "To the German People." Every expression was un-German, untrue, and perverse; overall, it was like some soulless word-mosaic held together by an international syntax.[48] Of the shamelessly sloppy German used by Eduard Devrient to solemnize Mendelssohn, we should not even speak.[49] Grammatical error—this is the remarkable thing—does not offend the philistine; on the contrary, it is an enticing refreshment in the scorched and treeless desert of workaday German. But anything *truly* creative offends him. The completely twisted, overblown, tattered syntax and laughable neologisms of our thoroughly modern model writers are not merely condoned, but esteemed an asset—their real savor. Woe to the writer with character who scrupulously avoids these vulgarisms, as though what Schopenhauer called "monsters hatched overnight from the contemporary scribbler's pen." When the flat, hackneyed, vulgar, and feckless are accepted as the norm, and the corrupt and malapropos as charming exceptions, then the powerful, the uncommon, and the beautiful fall into disrepute. This is why in Germany we so often hear the story of the handsome traveler who visits a land of hunchbacks. Wherever he went, he was mocked and abused for his apparent deformity—his lack of a hump. Finally, a priest took up his cause, saying to the people: "Have pity on this poor stranger and offer thanks to the gods for gracing you with such stately humps of flesh."

If someone were to write the definitive grammar of today's universal German style and trace its rules, which, like unwritten, unspoken, yet compelling imperatives, hold sway over every writing desk, he would meet with some rather odd ideas of style and rhetoric. Some, perhaps, are reminiscences of bygone schooldays, with their compulsory exercises in Latin composition and French readers, at whose incredible crudity any moderately

48. Berthold Auerbach (1812–82) was one of the most popular German novelists of the nineteenth century. His *Schwarzwälder Dorfgeschichten* (Black Forest village stories) inspired a flood of nineteenth-century German folk and peasant literature. He studied philosophy with Strauss and his novels were, despite their rustic settings, vehicles for the philosophical idealism with which all his work was tinged. Even Nietzsche had been charmed by Auerbach in his youth; see Nietzsche's letter to his mother, end of Feb. 1862.

49. Eduard Devrient (1801–77) belonged to an illustrious family and was himself a director, actor, singer, librettist (*Hans Heiling,* 1883) and theater historian (*Geschichte der deutschen Schauspielkunst,* 1848–74). In 1869 he published a eulogy of his friend, the composer Mendelssohn-Bartholdy, to which Nietzsche here refers.

educated Frenchman would rightly scoff. Nonetheless, it seems that not a single serious German has really considered these odd notions that dictate the way nearly every German lives and writes.

Among these notions is the requirement that, from time to time, an image or metaphor appear, and that the metaphor be "new." To the stunted mind of contemporary writers, however, "new" and "modern" are one and the same; and they are at pains to draw their metaphors from the world of the railroad, the telegraph, the steam engine, and stock exchange. These writers take great pride in their images, which, being modern, must be "new." In Strauss's confession-book, tribute is loyally paid to the modern metaphor. He regales us with an image of modern road repairs, a page and a half long; in an earlier passage he compares the world to an engine, replete with cogwheels, hammers, pistons, and "soothing oil." On page 362: "lunch-break begins with champagne." On page 325: "Kant as a cold-water cure." On page 265: "The Swiss constitution is to the English constitution what a water mill is to a steam engine, or what a waltz or a song is to a fugue or a symphony." On page 258: "Every appeal must be taken through all the stages of appellate procedure. The appellate court, mediating between the individual and humanity, is the nation." On page 141: "If we want to learn whether an organism, which appears dead, is still alive, we should administer a strong, perhaps even painful stimulus, like a stab." On page 138: "The religious domain of the human soul is like the domain of the red man in America." On page 137: "Virtuosos of piety in the cloister." On page 90: "Place the sum total in round figures against the account." On page 176: "Darwin's theory is like a railway only just staked out—where banners flutter gaily in the wind." In this way, this highly modern way, Strauss complies with the philistine fiat that every so often a new metaphor be introduced.

A second rhetorical fiat is also rather prevalent: didactic passages should unfold in long sentences and remote abstractions, while in hortatory passages short sentences and rapid-fire contrasts are preferred. An exemplary sentence in the didactic and scholarly mode, full Schleiermacherian bombast, blown out of all proportion and creeping along with truly tortoise-like agility, is found on page 132: "That in the earlier stages of religion there appears to be a plurality rather than a single origin, instead of one god a multiplicity of gods, follows from the origins of religion, since the various natural forces and vital relationships which rouse in man the feeling of absolute dependence at first work their overwhelming diversity upon him, not yet aware that, with regard to his vital dependence, no difference between them exists; therefore, even the origin, or essence, of his dependence—which it comes back to in the final analysis—can only be one and the same."[50] An example of the opposite sort, the short sentences and af-

---

50. Although Strauss appears to quote Schleiermacher approvingly in this passage, he

fected vivacity that have inspired some readers to place Strauss's name alongside that of Lessing's, may be found on page 8: "I am well aware that what I intend to explain in what follows is something countless individuals know as well as I, many even much better. A few have already spoken up. Should I remain silent then? I think not. We complete one another, all of us, mutually. Another may know some things better; I, perhaps other things. And much I know is what I see in an altogether different light. Let us therefore be candid; let us display our colors and see if they are true." In general, Strauss's style falls somewhere between this frisky goose-stepping and the halting half-step of the pallbearer. The mean between two vices, however, is not always a virtue, but often only a weakness, a palsy, an impotence.

In fact, I was very disillusioned when, with the idea of compiling a catalogue, I combed Strauss's book for elegant, witty expressions. Since I had found nothing praiseworthy about Strauss the confessor, I thought I might at least find something to praise in Strauss the writer. I combed and combed, but the catalogue never took shape. Instead, another list grew, under the rubric "Grammatical Errors, Mixed Metaphors, Obscure Abbreviations, Lapses of Taste, Stilted Language."[51] My collected examples became so numerous that I can only hope to offer a very modest selection. I may have even succeeded in collecting under this rubric the very thing that has caused contemporary Germans to believe in this great, seductive stylist—the oddity of his expressions, which, in the dry and dusty expanse of this book, comes more as a painful stimulus than as a pleasant surprise. Discovering them, we find that, to use the Straussian metaphor, so long as we can still respond to a good prickling, we are not quite dead. But the rest of the book lacks anything offensive, that is, anything creative—a lack today reckoned a positive virtue of the classical author. This extreme dullness and dryness, this bone-dry sobriety, has inspired the unnatural belief among the educated masses that these are signs of health. The author of the *Dialogus de oratoribus* spoke to the point: "Illam ipsam quam iactant sanitatem non firmitate sed

---

was, in the main, opposed to Schleiermacher's theology. In fact, Strauss's *Christ of History and Christ of Faith* (1865) was an assault upon Schleiermacher's notion that man's consciousness of God had been realized prototypically and superlatively in the consciousness of Christ. Strauss denied the divinity of the historical Jesus altogether and rejected Schleiermacher's romantic, highly affective theology, propounding instead a Hegelian, dialectical approach to the historical evolution of Christ's myth. In his *Confession*, Strauss dismisses Schleiermacher's attempt to reconcile supernaturalism and rationalism, i.e., to find "God in Christ," as "a mere phrase" (see "Are We Still Christians?" 17–22).

51. On April 18, 1873, expressing shock over Strauss's vulgarity and insipidity, Nietzsche wrote to Wagner that "a handsome collection of Strauss's utterly appalling stylistic experiments ought to make it instantly clear just how things stand with our so-called 'classical author.'"

ieiunio consequuntur."[52] These Germans hate all *firmitas* with an instinctive unanimity, since it bears witness to a kind of health utterly different from theirs.[53] They are suspicious of firmitas, taut compactness, the ardent strength of movement, the fullness and delicacy of muscles in play. They have conspired to twist the nature and names of things completely around and thence to speak of health where we see infirmity, of sickness and febrility where we find vigorous health. So it comes about that even David Strauss is now a "classic."

If only this sobriety were of a strictly logical kind! But it is precisely simplicity and rigorous thinking that are lacking. At the hands of the "weak" our language has been thrown into an illogical tangle. Just try translating Strauss into Latin! Even with Kant this is possible; with Schopenhauer it would be an agreeably stimulating exercise. The reason Strauss's German will not go into Latin is, in all likelihood, not because his German is more German than theirs, but because it is snarled and illogical, whereas theirs is simple and magnificent. Anyone who knows the pains the ancients took to learn to speak and write well, and how very little moderns bother with this, feels what Schopenhauer called a sense of relief when, having been forced to wade through a German book like this, he can return to the ancients, whose old language is still so alive. "Since in these authors," Schopenhauer wrote, "I find a language fixed by certain rules, with a firmly established and conscientiously observed grammar and orthography, I can devote myself solely to their ideas. However, in German works I am constantly distracted by the impudence of writers bent on establishing their own quirky grammar and orthography and following any crude whim. The pompous folly in this disgusts me. It is a truly painful sight to see a very old and beautiful language, which can itself boast of a classical literature, grossly abused by such asses and ignoramuses."[54]

Schopenhauer's holy wrath cries out. And you cannot say that you were not warned. But whoever chooses to ignore the warning, absolutely unwilling to spoil his faith in a classical Strauss, should, as a final word of advice, try to imitate him. You do it, however, at your own risk. You will have to pay

---

52. Tacitus *Dialogue on Oratory* 23.3: "They acquire the fitness of which they boast through leanness rather than firmness." Tacitus also uses a body metaphor to describe the feebleness of writers who confuse archaizing and prettifying with the adoption of a rigorously classical style, disciplined by classical models. The *Dialogus* was a work which Nietzsche admired; he had once characterized Tacitus's style as "immortal" (*WS*, 44). Nietzsche's polemic against stylistic and cultural decadence, in its analysis of the vital continuity of language and culture, may owe something to Tacitus's *Dialogus*.
53. *Firmitas*: "firmness," "taut muscularity," or "strength."
54. *Handschriftlicher Nachlass*, ed. J. Frauenstädt (Leipzig, 1864), 60–61. This viewpoint is elaborated in Schopenhauer's essay "On Authorship and Style."

for it—with your style and finally even with your head. For you too the Indian words of wisdom will come true: "To gnaw on a cow's horn is useless and shortens man's life; he grinds away his teeth but sucks no juice."

1 2   In conclusion, we would like to present our classical prose writer with the promised collection of his stylistic experiments. Schopenhauer would probably have entitled it "New Proof of Today's Shoddy Jargon." David Strauss may be comforted to know—if this can be considered comfort—that the whole world now writes as he does, and part of it even worse. In the country of the blind the one-eyed man is king. We actually concede him a great deal, if we concede even one eye. We do this because Strauss is at least superior to the vilest corrupters of German—the Hegelians, and their crippled progeny.[55] Strauss, at least, wants to clamber out of that swamp, and has, in part, succeeded, though he is still a long way from solid ground. One can still see that once, in his youth, he too stammered the Hegelian idiom. At that time, he threw something out of joint or overstrained some muscle; his ear, like that of a child brought up amid the beating of drums, must have gone deaf, so he could no longer hear the esthetically subtle and powerful laws of tone that govern the life of the writer indentured to good models and strict discipline. So, as a stylist, he has lost all his worldly goods and is condemned to spend the rest of his life squatting on the barren and perilously shifting sands of journalism—that, or sink back into the Hegelian slime. And yet, for a few short hours in our age, he secured fame; and, perhaps, even a few hours hence someone will remember that he was once famous. But then night comes, and with it, oblivion. Even at this moment, as we enter his stylistic sins into the black book, the twilight of his fame commences. The writer who sins against the German language has profaned the mystery of all our Germanity. Through all the mixing and melding of customs and peoples, the German language alone, as if by some metaphysical magic, has been preserved, and with it the German spirit. It alone guarantees this spirit for the future, provided it does not fall at the hands of the profligate present. "But *di meliora!* Away, pachyderms, away! This is the German language in which men have expressed themselves. Great poets have sung it, great thinkers have thought it. Remove your filthy feet!"[56]

---

55. Hegel and his followers wrote an unidiomatic, ponderously periodic German, full of abstruse abstractions and neologistically compounded terms. Nietzsche described Hegel's style as "an utterly vile greyness ... offensive to the eye" (*NF*, 27.29 [spring–autumn 1873]).

56. *Di meliora*, an abbreviation of the Latin expression *di meliora velint*, "may the gods wish better things," i.e., "God forbid." This entire passage is taken verbatim from Schopenhauer's "On Authorship and Style." §283.

Take an example from the very first page of Strauss's book: *"Even in its accession to power . . . Roman Catholicism recognized the need to consolidate dictatorially all its spiritual and worldly power in the hands of a Pope who was to be declared infallible."*[57] Under this billowy garb various mismatched ideas are concealed, ideas not even simultaneously possible. One might, conceivably, recognize a need to consolidate his power, or to put it into a dictator's hands, but he cannot dictatorially consolidate it in another's hands. If we say that Catholicism dictatorially consolidates its power, Catholicism itself is being compared to a dictator. Obviously, the infallible Pope ought to be compared to a dictator. Only unclear thinking and the lack of any feeling for language can explain this misplaced adverb. To get an idea of the absurdity of this sentence, I recommend the following, simplified version: "The Lord gathers the reins and puts them into the hands of his driver."

Page 4: *"Underlying the opposition between the old consistorial government and the attempts to establish a synodal constitution, lying behind the hierarchical tendency of the one and the democratic tendency of the other, is still a religious and dogmatic difference of opinion."* First, we find an opposition between a gov-

---

57. The Straussian quotations present the translator with an almost insuperable problem: he is required to "mistranslate" from one language to another, to write badly well—and with wit. This accounts, in part at least, for the fact that this section has never before been translated into English. The more than seventy examples of mixed metaphors, ungrammatical constructions, absurd images, and malapropisms offer proof positive that Strauss had indeed lost all feeling for the German language. Following Schopenhauer's model ("On Authorship and Style," esp. §283), Nietzsche proves the worthlessness of Strauss the thinker by demonstrating the appalling absence of thought *in* his style. Moreover, as this essay reveals, style for Nietzsche was an essential element in culture itself. And that Strauss's book had been hailed as a cultural event only confirmed Nietzsche's conviction that Germany has lost "any clear idea of what constitutes culture" (§1). So it is odd that the section to which the entire essay builds, and which Nietzsche himself believed to be the most crucial (see above, n. 51), has been largely ignored by critics and translators alike. To the English reader, some of the distinctions made by Nietzsche may seem pedantic quibbling. But it must be remembered that German grammar is very complex and that clarity depends upon precision of usage. Nietzsche is not, in short, merely demonstrating his own well-honed sense of philological precision, but his artistically vigorous feeling for the use of words and his reverence for the beauty and power of his native tongue.

Insofar as possible, I have tried to approximate, as closely as English usage—or misusage—would allow, Nietzsche's fine linguistic distinctions. Liberties, needless to say, were inevitable, especially in those instances where a rougher English approximation more nearly conveyed Nietzsche's point and provided occasion for humor and sarcasm. On the subject of style, Nietzsche could not be more serious; but it is doubtful that he was ever again as playful and humorous as in these pages. The references to Strauss's original text (the edition cited above in n. 6) are provided in my text for the reader who wishes the check the German.

ernment and certain attempts; underlying this opposition is a religious and dogmatic difference of opinion; and this underlying difference is, in turn, to be found behind a hierarchical tendency on the one hand and a democratic one on the other. Riddle: what thing lies behind two things and underlies a third thing?

Page 18: "*And the days, although framed by the narrator unmistakably between evening and morning,*" etc. I entreat you to translate this into Latin, so that you can see just how shamelessly the language has been abused. Days that are framed! By a narrator! Unmistakably! And framed *between* something!

Page 19: "*Of erroneous and contradictory accounts, of false opinions and judgments, there can be no question with the Bible.*" How sloppily expressed! You have confounded the phrases "with the Bible" and "in the Bible." The former should be placed at the beginning of the sentence; the latter, at the end. I think you meant to say: "There can be no question of erroneous and contradictory accounts, of false opinions and judgments in the Bible." And why not? Because it is the Bible—therefore, "*with the Bible*, there can be no question of . . ." But now to avoid using "in the Bible" and "with the Bible" in the same sentence, yet determined to write shoddy jargon, you mix up the prepositions. You commit the same offense on page 20: "*Compilations into which older pieces are worked together.*" You mean either "into which older pieces are worked," or "in which older pieces are worked together."

On the same page you speak with schoolboy eloquence of a "*didactic poem, which has been put in the unpleasant position of often misreading* [try: being misread], *and then being hated and resisted.*" And on page 24, of "*sharpness, by which they sought to mitigate their severity.*" I am in the unpleasant position myself of not knowing how something sharp could ever mitigate something severe. But on page 367, Strauss again speaks of a "*sharpness, mitigated by a jolt*"!

Page 35: "*Thoroughly typical of both nations stands Samuel Hermann Reimarus on this side vis-à-vis Voltaire on the other.*"[58] A man can only be typical of a nation vis-à-vis the nation, but not typical of two nations vis-à-vis another man. Again, Strauss has brutally violated the German language so as to spare, or sketch in, another phrase.

Page 46: "*Now it came to pass so that only a few years after Schleiermacher's*

---

58. Hermann Samuel Reimarus (1694–1768), a rationalist theologian who prudently died with his *Defense of a Rationalist Reverence for God* unpublished. Strauss published it nearly a century later (1862), along with a study of Reimarus's life and work. Fragments of Reimarus's work, however, had already appeared anonymously in Lessing's *Zur Geschischte und Literatur* (On history and literature) of 1774–77 (see above, n. 18).

death . . ." To such lackey scribblers word order is unimportant. Their drum-deafened ears are insensitive both to the fact that "only a few years after Schleiermacher's death" ought to come before the conjunction, and that the conjunction required by the context must be "that," not "so that."

Page 13: "*. . . and of all the various shades in which Christianity glows today, to us it can only be a question of the boldest and the clearest, whether we can still embrace it or not.*" The question "What is it a question of?" can be answered in one of two ways. It can be a question "of this or that." Or it can be a question of "whether we . . ." Throwing these two constructions together is a sign of slovenly workmanship. Strauss meant to say: "For us it can only be a question of whether, with regard to the boldest, we can still embrace them." But nowadays the preposition in Germany only exists, it would seem, to be used idiosyncratically for its maximum shock value. On page 358, e.g., our classical author shocks us by conflating two common expressions: "a book deals with something" and "it is a matter of something." So we are forced to read sentences like this: "*. . . and therefore it remains uncertain, whether it is a matter with outward or inward heroism, with a struggle in the open field or in the depths of the human heart.*"

Page 343: "*. . . for our high-strung and over-stimulated age, which brings its disease into the clear, above all in its musical preferences . . .*" A shameful confusion of "in the clear" and "make clear." Such improvers of our language, no matter who they are, ought to be chastised like schoolchildren.

Page 70: "*Here we see the thought process by which the disciples worked their way up to the production of the idea of the resuscitation of their martyred master.*" What an image! A chimney sweep's dream! One works his way through a process, up to a production!

When, on page 72, our heroic word wielder terms the story of Christ's resurrection "*world-historical humbug,*" we only want to know by whom, grammatically speaking, this "world-historical humbug" has actually been perpetrated? On whose conscience does this swindle of someone else for personal gain lie? Who is this swindler, this cheat? For we cannot assent to a "humbug" without an agent's seeking to profit by it. Since Strauss has no answer—I assume, of course, that he shrinks from prostituting his god, who errs out of noble passion, as the swindler here— we consider the expression as absurd as it is tasteless.

On the very same page: "*His teachings would have been blown away and scattered like so many leaves in the wind, had these leaves not been bound fast by the hard and sturdy binding of deluded belief in his resurrection.*" Whoever speaks of leaves in the wind leads the reader's imagination astray if he subsequently means that these are leaves of paper, which might be bound together by the art of bookbinding. A careful writer avoids nothing so much as an image that might mislead or confuse. An image should always make a point clearer. But if the image itself is unclear and misleading, the point is more obscured with the image than without it. But, make no mistake, our classical author is anything but careful: he brazenly speaks of *"the hand of our sources"* (p. 76), *"the lack of any handhold on our sources"* (p. 77), and *"the hand of a need"* (p. 215).

Page 73: *"The belief in his resurrection credits Jesus' account."* A man who prefers common mercantile terms to express himself abut so uncommon an event must have spent his life reading remarkably bad books. The Straussian style everywhere betrays a history of impoverished readings. Perhaps Strauss spent too much time in reading his theological adversaries. But where did he learn to molest the ancient Judeo-Christian God with such petit-bourgeois images? For example, on page 105 he treats us to *"pulled the chair out from under the body of the old Judeo-Christian God."* Or, on the same page, *"the ancient personal God ran into something like a housing shortage."* Or, on page 155, we find that this very same god has been removed to a *"spare room where he might still be decently housed and employed after all."*

Page 111: *"with the efficacious prayer, an essential attribute of the personal god once again fell away."* Ink blotter, why not think before blotting! I would have thought your ink would blush red at scribbling that a prayer is an "attribute," and an "attribute falling away" at that. But what have we on page 134! *"Many of the attributes of desire, which man in earlier times ascribed to his gods— I will cite only the ability to cover distances with great speed, as an example—he has now, as a consequence of his rational dominion over nature, assumed for himself."* Who will untangle this knot for us? Granted that man in earlier times ascribed attributes to his gods. But "attributes of desire" is already a little dubious. Strauss means, roughly: "Man supposed that the gods actually possessed everything he desired to have, but which he lacked; therefore, the gods had attributes corresponding to human desires, roughly 'attributes of desire.'" But now, Strauss tells us, man has assumed many of these "attributes of desire" for himself—an obscure process. Compare the obscurity of page 135: *"The desire must supervene here, in order to give this dependence, by the shortest path, a turn advantageous to men."* Dependence—a turn—the shortest path—a desire that supervenes—woe to anyone who actually tries to visualize this image! It is a scene from a picture book for the blind—and so we grope.

Page 222, a new example: *"the ascending course of this movement, which in its ascent overtakes even the individual decline."* But page 120 goes farther still: *"This last Kantian turn, as we have discovered, sees itself obliged to reach its goal by making its way a great distance, far over the field of future life."* Only a mule could find his way in this fog. Turns that see themselves as obliged! Courses overtaking declines! Turns advantageous by the shortest path, turns that make their way a great distance, far over a field! Over what field? Why, over the field of future life! The devil take all this topography! Light! Light! Where is the Ariadne-thread in this labyrinth? No, nobody should be permitted to write like this, not even if he were the world's most celebrated prose writer—and still less a man with a *"fully developed religious and moral disposition"* (p. 50).

A mature man, I think, should know that language is a heritage handed down by our forefathers, to be passed on to our descendants and to be revered as something sacred, invaluable, and inviolable. If your ears have gone deaf, you ask questions, you consult a dictionary, you get yourself a good grammar. But you dare not sin so flagrantly! On page 136, for instance, Strauss writes: *"a delusion, from which it must be the desire of every enlightened man to divest himself and mankind."* This is an impossible construction; and if the cultivated ear of the scribbler cannot hear it, I will shout it out. You may either "remove someone from something" or "divest someone of something." Which means that Strauss would have to say either "a delusion, of which he and mankind must be divested" or "a delusion, from which he must remove himself and mankind." But what he has written is shoddy.

Now what should our response be when we see this stylistic pachyderm wallowing around in old expressions that have been revamped or given new twists; when we hear him speak of the *"leveling tendency of Social Democracy"* as if he were Sebastian Frank (p. 380);[59] or when he imitates Hans Sachs, *"the nations are the god-given, that is, the natural forms by which mankind brings himself into existence, which no reasonable man may disregard, and from which no man of courage may withdraw"* (p. 259)?[60] On page 252 we find: *"The human species is differentiated by races in accordance with natural law."* On page 282: *"to navigate resistance"*? Strauss seems not to grasp why such hackneyed

---

59. Sebastian Frank (1499–1542), originally a Catholic priest, later a follower of Luther, whose dogmatism he finally rejected. Frank was an outspoken man of moral courage and conviction in an age when such traits were regarded as heretical. His mystical inclinations and religious tolerance further alienated him from Lutherans and Catholics alike. He wrote theological and historical works and published a collection of German proverbial expressions. The Frankian paraphrase comes from Frank's well known *Chronika, Zeitbuch und Geschichtsbibel* (Chronicles, book of epochs, and historical Bible) of 1531, whose echo the literate German would presumably have heard in the Straussian expression.

60. Hans Sachs (1494–1756), the mastersinger who became legendary through Wagner's *Meistersinger von Nürnberg* (1868), was one of the most prolific writers of the sixteenth century and indeed a shoemaker by profession. He wrote songs, plays, poetry, fables, verse tales (*Schwanke*), and prose dialogues which advanced the allied cause of nationalism and Protestantism.

phrase-patching is so conspicuous in his threadbare modern idiom. Of course, everyone recognizes these phrases and patches as stolen. But now and then our patchwork tailor shows a little creativity and stitches in a new expression: on page 221 he speaks of *"a self-generating life, wringing itself out and upward."* But "wring out" is used of washerwomen, or "wring" of someone's neck—a hero in the death throes of battle has his life "wrung out." But "wring out" in the sense of self-generate is nothing but Straussian German, like *"all the steps and stages of en-veloping and de-veloping"* (p. 223)—pure diaper-Deutsch!

On page 252: *"in junction with"* for "in conjunction with." Or on page 137: *"In the daily life of the medieval Christian the religious element came to be addressed much more frequently and more uninterruptedly."* "Much more un-interruptedly"—this must be the exemplary comparative, if Strauss is our exemplary prose stylist. Elsewhere, to be sure, he employs the impossible *"more perfect"* (pp. 223, 214). But *"come to be addressed"*!—where in the world did this come from, O verbal trickster? This time I really cannot help you out. No analogy comes to mind. The Brothers Grimm, when addressed on this form of "address," remain silent as the grave.[61] Strauss means, of course, merely this: "the religious element expresses itself more frequently." Once again, out of quite hair-raising ignorance, Strauss has confused the prepositional prefixes: to confuse "express" with "address" is the mark of genuine vulgarity—and I must openly express what he refuses to address.

Page 220: *". . . since I still heard, ringing behind his subjective meaning, an objective one of infinite importance."* As I have pointed out, Strauss's hearing is either bad or plain peculiar. He hears "meaning ringing" and even ringing "behind" other meaning; and, of course, these audible meanings must be "of infinite importance." This is either nonsense or the metaphor of a veteran cannoneer. On page 183 we find: *". . . the external outline of the theory has now been given, and some of its springs, which determine its inner movement, have already been inserted."* Again, this is either nonsense or the unintelligible box-spring metaphor of an upholsterer. But what is a mattress composed of outlines and inserted springs worth! And what kind of springs determine the inner movements of a mattress! We are altogether doubtful about Strauss's theory if he presents it to us in this fashion and must conclude, as Strauss himself so eloquently puts it: *"as to its actual viability, it still lacks some essential joints"* (p. 175). Bring on the joints! Outline and springs are standing by, skin and muscle are ready. So long as this is all there is,

---

61. The Brothers Grimm, Jakob (1785–1863) and Wilhelm (1786–1859), best known to English readers as folklorists—that is, the Grimms of *Grimms' Fairy Tales*. The Grimms were also prolific linguists, philologists, and most notably lexicographers. Their *Deutsches Wörterbuch*, the equivalent of the *Oxford English Dictionary*, was the monumental achievement of nineteenth-century German philology.

Strauss's theory will be a long way from viability. Or to speak *"more disin-terestedly,"* in Strauss's own words: *"so long as one throws directly together two images, so utterly different in value, with no regard to gradations and degrees in between."*

Page 5: *"Yet one may be without a firm position and still not be lying on the ground."* Now here we understand you, scantily clad master! For he who neither stands nor lies, must fly, float, flit, or maybe even flutter. But if you intended to express something other than your flightiness, as the context seems to suggest, you—especially you—should have chosen a different met-aphor—one that evokes something different. On the very same page we find: *"the branch of an old tree, notoriously withered and dead"*—and a style notoriously withered and dead!

On page 6: *"He could not withhold his approval in an infallible Pope, as some-thing required by this need."* One may not, for any reason, confuse the dative and accusative cases. For a schoolboy it is a mistake, for a model prose writer, a crime.

On page 8 we find: *"the new formation of the new organization of the ideal elements in the life of nations."* Let us concede that such tautological nonsense may once have actually spilled from the inkwell onto the page. Should it then have been printed? How can something like this elude correction? And the corrections of six editions? Incidentally, if Strauss is going to quote Schiller (as on page 9), he really should be more precise and less casual about it. He owes that much respect! The line should read: "fearing no man's envy."

On page 16: *"Then it at once becomes a crossbar, a restraining wall of defense, against which the whole onslaught of progressive reason, all the battering rams of criticism, direct themselves with passionate aversion."* Here we are meant to imagine something that is first a crossbar and then a wall of defense, against which finally "a battering ram with passionate aversion," or an "onslaught" with passionate aversion, directs itself. Sir, you might at least speak like a man of this world! Battering rams are directed by someone; they do not direct themselves; and only the one who directs them, and not the battering rams themselves, can have a passionate aversion. For all that, it is still a highly unusual matter for someone to have so passionate an aversion to a wall as that which you describe.

On page 266: *"Wherefore phrases such as these have always constituted the popular arena of democratic platitudes."* What desperate lack of clarity! Phrases cannot constitute an arena! They may, however, be tossed back and forth within one. Perhaps Strauss meant to say: "Therefore, such viewpoints have always constituted the popular arena of democratic slogans and platitudes."

Page 320: "*. . . the inner life of a richly and delicately strung poet-soul, for which, even through all its wide-ranging activity in the realms of poetry and natural science, social life and public affairs, an ever-present need remains to return to the gentle hearthfire of a noble affection.*" I am hard pressed to imagine a soul strung like a harp, which also engages in "wide-ranging activity." This is a soul that gallops, like a dark horse, ranging far and wide, until at last returning once again to the quiet hearthfire. Now this galloping, hearthfire-returning soul-harp, which is even involved in politics, is surely an amazingly original *trouvaille*—about as unoriginal, hackneyed, and illicit as the "delicately strung poet-soul" itself. Through such clever reformulations of the vulgar and absurd, we can recognize our "classical author."

Page 74: "*. . . if only we wanted to open our eyes and to be truly open about what our eye-opening finds.*" In this splendid and solemnly vacuous statement, one is struck by nothing more than the juxtaposition of "being open" and "eye-opening." Whoever opens his eyes to something, and then is not open about what his eyes are now open to, is not really open. Strauss, of course, does just the opposite and feels a need to praise and to confess it publicly. "But who has ever blamed him?" a Spartan asked.

Page 43: "*Only on one article of faith did he draw in the threads more vigorously, and that, to be sure, was the central point of Christian dogma.*" The actual action in question is somewhat obscure. Since when does one draw in threads? Should these threads have perhaps been reins, and the person vigorously drawing them in, a coachman? Only with some revision does the metaphor make sense.

Page 226: "*In the fur coat lies a more accurate presentiment.*" No doubt about it! "*Primal man, an offshoot of the primal ape, was still far*" (p. 226)—far, that is, from knowing he would someday lead the way to a Straussian theory. But now we know it: "*Where it will and must go, where the flags flutter gaily in the wind. Yes, gaily, even in the sense of the purest and most exalted spiritual joy*" (p. 176). Strauss takes such childlike delight in his theory that even "flags" become gay, and strangely gay, "in the sense of the purest and most exalted spiritual joy." But now things get even merrier. Suddenly we see "*three masters, each one standing on the shoulders of his predecessor*" (p. 361). Haydn, Mozart, and Beethoven amuse us with a real acrobatic stunt! We see Beethoven "*kicking over his traces*" (p. 356) like a horse; then a "*freshly shod road*" (p. 367) appears (although until now we only knew of freshly shod horses), likewise a "*rank dunghill of robbery and murder*" (p. 287). In spite of such obvious miracles, "*miracles have been decreed out of fashion*" (p. 176). Then, suddenly, comets appear (p. 167). But Strauss reassures us: "*When among the loose tribe of comets, one cannot speak of inhabitants.*" Words of true consolation! Since, as a rule, when among loose tribes, we had better pray there are no inhabitants. Meanwhile, a new spectacle: Strauss himself "*creeps up*" from "*patriotism to humanitarianism*" (p. 258), while another "*slides down under into an ever-cruder democracy*" (p. 264). Down under into! Not merely down into! commands the master of our mother-tongue, who continues with a truly emphatic and falsely construed phrase: "*an able nobility belongs into an organic structure*" (p. 269).

In another sphere, inconceivably high above us, float dubious phenomena. For example, "*the surrendering of the spiritual withdrawal of man from nature*" (p. 201); or "*the confutation of coyness*" (p. 210); or the alarming spectacle of "*the struggle for survival having been sufficiently abandoned in the animal world*" (p. 241). Miraculously, on page 359 "*a human voice springs to instrumental music*"; but a door is opened through which the miracle is "*cast out, never to return*" (p. 177). On page 123: "*the evidence that sees in death the entire man, as he was, meeting his end.*" Not until the advent of Strauss the language-tamer has "evidence" ever "seen"; but now we have witnessed it in his verbal peep show and want to praise him. From him we also first learned what it means when "*our feeling for the cosmos, upon being wounded, reacts religiously,*" and we still remember the whole procedure this entails. We now know the charm of "*coming within view of at least the knees of exalted figures*"; and consider ourselves privileged to have observed this "classical author," however limited our view may have been.

To speak frankly, what we have seen here are feet of clay, and what appears a healthy flesh tone is only cosmetic veneer. Naturally, philistine culture in Germany will be indignant when we call "painted idols" what it regards as a "living god." But whoever dares to overthrow its idols will not fear to tell philistine culture to its face, in the teeth of all its indignation, that it has forgotten how to distinguish between living and dead, between true and false, between original and fake, and finally between a god and an idol. He will tell philistine culture that it has lost the healthy, virile instinct for everything real and just. It has earned its downfall. Already the signs of its dominion are fading. Already its purple robes have fallen. And when the robe falls, the sovereign soon follows.

With this, I have made my confession. It is the confession of one man; and what can one man do against the whole world, even if his voice were heard everywhere? What would his judgment amount to? "*A subjective truth, subjective to the degree that it lacks objective provability,*" if I may adorn you one last time with a rare and genuine Straussian plume. Is this not the truth, my friends? Therefore, have courage, no matter what! And for the time being, at least, be content with your truth, "*to the degree that it lacks.*" For the time being! For as long, that is, as people consider untimely what always has been, and today more than ever remains, a timely and urgent need—to speak the truth.

Introduction
by Werner
Dannhauser

Translation by
Gary Brown

History
in the
Service and
Disservice
of Life

Introduction

The young Nietzsche described the philosopher as a physician of culture, and his own thought can be understood both as a diagnosis of the crisis or sickness of his time, the nineteenth century, and the quest for a cure. In his first published book, *The Birth of Tragedy* (1872), Nietzsche placed his hopes for the rejuvenation of Germany—and ultimately the world—in the music of Richard Wagner. He sustained that enthusiasm through one of the "unmodern observations" or "thoughts out of season," but thereafter disillusion ensued: he repudiated Wagner and abandoned the possibility of a German cultural revival. With this he entered into the second period of his development, a stage characterized by disenchantment and a leaning toward Western positivism. The typical book of this period, *Human, All-Too-Human* (1878), reflected his new mood in its title, the dedication to Voltaire, and its aphoristic style. Nietzsche articulated his final position in *Thus Spoke Zarathustra* (1883–85) and the books that follow it.

Nietzsche's thought, however, manifests a fundamental unity, or at least continuity, even as it progresses. For example, in *Twilight of the Idols* (1889), the last book he was able to see through to completion, he affirms *The Birth of Tragedy* as his first revaluation of all values. So he also never repudiated, but rather deepened, the view of his age as sick and in critical condition, a view he had expressed from the outset; and the problems he raised during the first stage of his development are problems with which he never ceased to wrestle. For this reason the reader in search of illuminating access to Nietzsche's thought will find *History in the Service and Disservice of Life* as instructive as it is exhilarating and eloquent.

Most readers, to be sure, turn to Nietzsche not primarily to gain access to his thought, but to clarify their own thinking; and they seek instruction not about the crisis of Nietzsche's time, but about their own. In this respect, too, the study of Nietzsche as reflections on the perils and promises of history recommends itself. The problems Nietzsche confronted in the nineteenth century remains those of the twentieth century. Indeed, the passage of time has almost conferred on Nietzsche the status of prophet, so keen were his perceptions of the present and the future. Thoughtful men may reject the cures he recommended, but we ignore his diagnosis at our peril.

In his Foreword to *History in the Service and Disservice of Life*, Nietzsche presents himself as a critic of and against his age, who seeks changes for the benefit of a future age. He also takes pride in identifying himself as "the nursling of past ages, above all of the Greek past." He thus appears to criticize modernity from the perspective of antiquity, to assess and judge the present by standards he had discovered in classical philosophy.

To an appreciable degree that appearance is deceptive. The Greek past that Nietzsche admires is for the most part the Greece that precedes the classical "golden age" of Greek philosophy. He takes his bearings not by an antiquity which Winckelmann could describe as characterized by "noble simplicity and serene grandeur," but by a past whose presiding genius is Dionysus and whose doom was announced by the advent of Socratic rationalism. The tone of the present essay is clearly more moderate and less rhapsodic than the prose of *The Birth of Tragedy*, but Nietzsche's *thought* is nonetheless very different from that of Plato and Aristotle. One small example will suffice. In the first section of his essay Nietzsche refers specifically to the happiness of beasts and children; in the first book of his *Ethics*, Aristotle specifically denies that children and animals can be happy. Nietzsche, then, can be said to admire ancient practice more than he admires ancient theory, which may be why the praise of Athens in his work gradually takes second place to the praise of Rome. What is more, he never thought that a return to more ancient ways was fundamentally possible. In other words, Nietzsche basically effects his critique of modernity from a radically modern, even postmodern perspective.

As the title suggests, Nietzsche's essay is a critique of a specific defect of his own age, which he refers to variously as "historical culture," "the historical movement," "the historical trend," and "the historical sense"—what later came to be called *historicism*. He believes that his own age suffers from the ravages of a historical fever. In criticizing historicism, Nietzsche also critically confronts Hegel, his great predecessor and Germany's philosopher of history. In the latter part of the essay he refers to a "certain famous philosophy," and proceeds to declare: "I believe that there has not been a dangerous turn or crisis in German culture in this century which has not become more dangerous because of the enormous, and still spreading, influence of this Hegelian philosophy" (*HSDL*, 8).

According to Nietzsche, Hegel regards contemporary humanity as the perfection of world history; his philosophy enshrines the sovereignty of history over other spiritual powers such as art and religion. For Hegel, "the climax and terminal point of the world process coincide with his own Berlin existence." Philosophers are not famous for fairness to their predecessors, and Nietzsche oversimplifies Hegel's thought; but the caricature he draws is sufficiently recognizable for him to argue for an opposing view. Against Hegel's doctrine that the historical process is a rational one which culminates in Hegel's own age in an "absolute moment" at the zenith, Nietzsche asserts that the historical process is not and cannot be finally completed.

The completion or fulfillment of history, he insists, is not merely impossible but undesirable; the end of history would inevitably lead to a degeneration of man. Moreover, according to Nietzsche, history is anything but rational; rather, it is demonstrably full of blindness, madness, and injustice.

Once again Nietzsche seems to emerge as the advocate of a premodern perspective and to be reverting to a viewpoint from which history becomes a realm of chance rather than a dimension of meaning. At first sight he seems to be harking back to Plato, who does not include history as a field of study for future philosophers, or to Aristotle, who regards history as inferior to poetry. Once again, however, the appearance proves deceptive. Closer analysis of *History in the Service and Disservice of Life* reveals that Nietzsche actually bases his criticism of Hegel on a crucial area of agreement with him.

The essay begins with a description of the life of animals, who forget each moment in time as soon as it passes. To live in bovine contentment, entirely in the present, unburdened by any memory whatever, means living *unhistorically*. By contrast, human beings remember the past and cannot escape from it; they live *historically*. What is more, they suffer from the awareness of the past and the passage of time, if only because the awareness of transience brings with it an awareness that human beings are imperfect and imperfectible. Happiness depends on our ability to forget, to surrender completely to the present. If we interrupt our total involvement in the moment to step back and contemplate our happiness, we have already abandoned some of the happiness subjected to contemplation. The man who lacks the ability to forget must resign himself to unhappiness, since he comes to see only flux and change, losing all fixed reference points by which to take his bearings.

At the same time, without a memory of the past human beings would not be human. Moreover, only by developing a historical sense and turning the past to the uses of the present does man rise above other animals and become truly man. Human beings enjoy indubitable advantages over beasts, as Nietzsche admits when he ascribes the wish to speak to his "contented cows." Humanity's problem therefore lies in finding the right balance between remembering and forgetting, the balance, that is, most conducive to a full human life. The degree and limits of memory must be fixed by the extent to which a human being can incorporate or absorb the past. A healthy organism instinctively assimilates as much—and only as much—of the past as it can digest; the rest it simply fails to see. The dividing line between the historical and the unhistorical is the horizon of the organism. Nietzsche assigns special importance to his teaching about horizons by promulgating in this connection the only "general law" of his essay on history. "No living being" he asserts, "can become healthy, strong, and productive except within a horizon" (*HSDL*, 1).

A human being's horizon is constituted by his fundamental set of assumptions about all things, by what he takes, or mistakes, for the absolute truth which cannot be questioned. His historical knowledge must be surrounded by an unhistorical atmosphere, the darkness that limits the historical sense. The question arises at once as to the possibility of transcending one's horizon. Nietzsche admits this possibility in his account of the "suprahistorical" man, but he makes it clear that the Olympian vision of such men leads to resignation rather than the productive activity that he associates with happiness. To see too much is to be consumed with a sense of life's meaninglessness. Nietzsche links the supra-historical view to traditional philosophy, and traditional philosophy to a life-disparaging despair. Toward the end of the essay, returning to the supra-historical in a more positive way, he mentions only art and religion. Here at the beginning, he takes care to follow his depiction of supra-historical man with the praise of history.

The proper sphere of history lies within and under an unhistorical atmosphere necessary for the conduct of a full and noble human life. As the title of the essay suggests, Nietzsche thinks that history can render a service as well as a disservice to human life. He writes of three kinds of history which can serve life. *Monumental* or exemplary history supplies models of greatness by its depiction of the great men and events of the past. It can be said to specialize in the heroic, singing as it does of giants on earth. *Antiquarian* history addresses itself to the preserving and revering instincts of human beings, imbuing them with a salutary love of tradition. Nietzsche regards antiquarian history as of special benefit to less favored people and races because it protects them from restless and unproductive cosmopolitanism. Finally, Nietzsche has some kind words for *critical* history, which places obsolete aspects of the past before the bar of judgment and condemns them. He praises this kind of history for bringing to light injustices surviving from the past so that they can be abolished in the interest of the present.

Anyone coming to *History in the Service and Disservice of Life* with the expectation of finding in it a judicious balance between the praise and censure of history will be disappointed to discover that Nietzsche is much more concerned with the latter than with the former. This is immediately apparent in a quick glance at the essay's contents, only two of whose ten sections deal with the "service" of history, the rest stressing its "disservice."

Moreover, even when Nietzsche, in the second and third sections of the essay, discusses useful kinds of history, he is quick to point out how easily these can be abused. Thus, the historical models of past greatness provided by monumental or exemplary history can work to obstruct the emergence of present greatness. One can celebrate Lincoln in order to disparage later presidents; one can praise Shakespeare in order to condemn Yeats. The reverence for the past fostered by antiquarian history can act to stultify the present, since what is good comes to be associated too exclusively with what is old, and we may forget that tradition tends to preserve inconsistently or even incoherently. There is always the danger that critical history—which associates the old with the bad—may uproot more of the past than should be uprooted.

Nietzsche's ambivalence about history becomes even more striking when he suggests a link between the efficacy of each variety of useful history and its blindness to the truth, or at least to the whole truth. Monumental or exemplary history pays insufficient attention to the conditions necessary to the emergence of greatness. Implicitly, it argues that greatness is possible now precisely because it was possible in the past, which need not be the case. Moreover, it is hard to discover what monumental history can do which could not be done as well or better by plays and poems celebrating past heroes or events. In cultivating a general reverence for the past, antiquarian history becomes indiscriminate, praising past events that are in fact deserving of censure. Critical history, in turn, fails to realize the extent to which any present generation has been decisively influenced by the very past which it condemns. It constantly neglects to describe the judges of the past as the products of the past. In short, the uses of the past for the present depend upon a violation of the truth about the past. History in the service of life can never be scientific history.

Science, and the demand that history become a science, disrupt the proper relation between history and life. Throughout his essay Nietzsche emphasizes that the main function and primary justification of history is to serve life, which he characterizes as "that dark compulsive power, insatiably avid of itself." Historical science, however, is motivated by the desire to *know* rather than the desire to *serve* life; it thus forces on human attention more historical knowledge than humanity can properly assimilate. By so doing, history disrupts life, or at least favors declining life at the expense of ascending life.

Nietzsche presents his reader with a veritable catalogue of the calamities that result from an excess of history. Such excess proves hostile to life, first of all by creating the exaggerated inwardness from which moderns suffer, an inwardness to which nothing outward corresponds, and which destroys the organic harmony of the modern human being. Poets who write no poetry tend to proliferate, exonerating themselves by their manifest sincerity. The age deludes itself that it is being more just than previous ages when it is only being more complacent. The callow and jejune replace the truly mature. The affirmative stance toward life succumbs to a corroding self-irony that deteriorates into cynicism, which in turn devolves into cunning but low egotism.

The last calamity which Nietzsche discusses in this connection—the belief in the old age of mankind—causes him to engage Hegel's philosophy. Because of a surplus of historical details, modern man finds himself confronted by a spectacle so vast that he is bound to find it meaningless. He comes to think of himself and his fellow creatures as epigones, late arrivals on the scene for whom nothing whatever remains to be done. The best poems have all been written, the best fights all fought, the best thoughts all thought. If Hegel were right, if the end of history had in fact arrived, Nietzsche and his contemporaries would indeed be epigones, latecomers on the scene. Hegel is wrong, Nietzsche asserts, but the belief in Hegelianism makes men behave as though they were in fact epigones. Those who have no further tasks to accomplish, who believe that nothing epochal remains to be done, will inevitably degenerate, since they will lose what is best in them: their aspirations.

With such arguments Nietzsche manages to score some points against Hegel, but he can hardly be said to have refuted historicism. After all, neither the declaration that the historical process is rational nor the declaration that the historical process has been completed constitutes the most fundamental assertion of historicism. At its core, historicism declares the overwhelming importance of history, the essential determination of human life and thought by history, and the impossibility of transcending the historical process. Now, for the most part, Nietzsche accepts this core avowal, and his assertion as well as his acceptance indicate a crucial degree of agreement with Hegel. The calamities which Nietzsche describes so vividly, and which he attributes to excess of historical knowledge, amount to saying that an excess of history destroys the human horizon. But no permanent horizon for mankind exists. Our fundamental assumptions about all things— what we consider fixed points—are unevident, unsupported, historically variable, and historically determined. There are no eternal things and eternal truths; only flux and change exist. Toward the end of the essay, when he deals briefly with "doctrines of sovereign becoming," Nietzsche admits as much (*HSDL*, 9). These doctrines include evolution, which denies that there are any cardinal distinctions between men and beasts. They are true but they are also fatal. History as the science of universal becoming must be understood as both true and deadly.

If human life can thrive only within a certain fixed horizon which is accepted as absolute truth, but which in reality is merely one of many possible horizons, then human life requires illusions. Then, too, the propagation of truth becomes a life-threatening activity, for, by exposing horizons as *mere* horizons, one removes an essential condition for life. A deadly conflict exists between the demands of truth and the demands of life, or between life and wisdom. In such a conflict, Nietzsche counsels that we should choose the side of life, if only because there can be life without wisdom, whereas there can be no wisdom without life.

That advice, however, solves very little. Life may demand illusions but it would seem quite impossible to accept an illusion once it has been perceived as an illusion. Myths retain usefulness only so long as one mistakes them for truth. Now, a horizon is our most comprehensive myth; it nurtures life, but only so long as we regard it as the final truth about all things. To see our horizon *as* a horizon means that we have transcended that particular horizon.

We might argue to the contrary, of course, by pointing to the phenomenon of myths that we still use even when they strike us as myths. For example, parents continue to send their children to Sunday school long after they have ceased to believe in the lessons taught there; in fact, they themselves continue to attend church long after they have lost their faith. Such practices do not necessarily entail hypocrisy; they simply attest to the fact that human beings, notorious for wanting their cake and eating it too, somehow manage to hold contradictory beliefs at the same time.

As a great psychologist, Nietzsche shows perfect awareness of such human frailties, but without approving of them. Continued acceptance of discredited horizons, he believes, involves a continual and degrading self-deception. One violates one's integrity, and Nietzsche, preeminently concerned with human ennoblement, sets an extremely high premium on integrity. This means that he opposes any ready resolution of the tension between life and wisdom by an accommodating preference for life. It also seems to mean that his thought founders on an impasse.

Yet *History in the Service and Disservice of Life* ends not in despair but on a note of triumph. In asserting an ultimate harmony between life and wisdom, it resembles later writings of Nietzsche—including *Thus Spoke Zarathustra*—in which nihilism eventually yields to celebration. After historicism's exposure of the arbitrary character of all human horizons, man finds himself subjected to an "infinity of hopeless skepticism," as Nietzsche puts it in the final section of the essay. But he professes to sight land: man can recover from the malady of history.

Such a recovery becomes possible only on the basis of a refutation of historicism, which must be shown either to be untrue, or at least incompletely true. Tentatively in *History in the Service and Disservice of Life,* and more comprehensively in his later writings, Nietzsche attempts to overcome and transcend the insights of historicism. He thus embarks on the most remarkable of his many remarkable journeys of thought: what begins as the questioning of the objective truth of historicism ends as a questioning of the very possibility of any and all objective truth.

Not every kind of history necessarily culminates in historicism; that fate is reserved for the kind of history that understands itself as, or pretends to be, scientific and objective. As a theoretical assertion, historicism depends on an examination of historical phenomena and assumes that it has comprehended the latter correctly. Nietzsche's attack begins with his doubts as to whether historical phenomena can be adequately understood by objective or scientific history and historians. He questions whether history will yield its secrets to disinterested inquiry. After all, it takes historical actors, also known as great men, to make genuine history. The makers of history all manifest their intense dedication, their steadfast commitment to a cause. The world-historical figures for whom Nietzsche has words of admiration—from Pericles and Alexander the Great to Luther and Napoleon—all acted within a horizon of commitment, unhistorically believing in the absolute validity of the goals they were pursuing. The great figures of history—world-historical men, as Hegel had labeled them—were the great creators, facing the future and devoting themselves to that which was to be. The greatest creators are those who create horizons within which future generations will live and flourish; from this perspective the traditional distinction between statesmen and religious founders simply vanishes. Great historical actors create such horizons unconsciously; they are subject to the nurturing illusion that they are merely discovering truth. This amounts to saying that all previous horizons, no matter how substantively different from each other, embodied a common belief in an absolute truth which can never be created but which may at privileged moments be discovered.

Can objective or scientific history do justice to world-historical actors and the events they shaped? Objective history stands or falls by its fidelity to its object; to use Ranke's terms, it must justify itself by its ability to present the past as it really was. Nietzsche approves of the ancient maxim that like can only be understood by like. Thus, only creative men and committed men confronting the future can understand the creations of the future-directed and committed heroes of the past. The objective historian does not fit this description. At best he criticizes, but he does not create; and he resolutely faces the past instead of the future. He ascertains facts, but does not penetrate to the essence of things. For example, a historian of art may well excel at establishing the dates of Michelangelo's birth and major productions, but only a fellow artist can really understand Michelangelo. Most objective historians, to be sure, would shrug off such criticism. They might say that Nietzsche has simply perpetrated a case of mistaken identity. They do not pretend to interpret the past, let alone evaluate it. Modestly they advance the modest claim that they simply set forth the uncontested or uncontestable facts. To them objectivity means no more, but also no less, than that.

Nietzsche exposes such rejoinders as illusions on the part of objective historians, since ultimately an illusion, amounting to a delusion, lurks in the very word *objectivity*. Any statement about facts is already an interpretation of facts. Indeed, the very selection of data from a potential infinity of data already amounts to an interpretation. Historians evince naiveté by considering even the possibility of objectivity. For example, if they recount the story of a war, they must impose a beginning, a middle, and an end on the flow of facts; but this means that in one way or another they weight the facts on subjective grounds. The only alternative would be to assemble facts in something resembling a statistical abstract or a registry, but here too there would have to be an order, or at least a sequence of facts to be related. In the last analysis, then, one has no choice between objective and subjective history; all history is subjective. One does, however, have a choice between a noble, rich interpretation of the past and a base, impoverished one. So-called objective history stands exposed as arid subjectivity.

We must note that Nietzsche does not deny the validity of the insight that all horizons, far from being "the permanent horizon" of which philosophers have spoken at times, are human creations. He pursues a different strategy, attacking historicism as a particular interpretation of that insight.

Nietzsche attempts to transcend the apparent deadlines of the historicist insight by interpreting, or reinterpreting, it nobly. One does well to admit— or even assert—that the values by which human beings have lived in the past have been their own creations, fictions, or myths. On close inspection, however, this turns out to be an ambiguous fact, admitting of diverse interpretations. Nietzsche moves in the direction of viewing this insight as a revelation of human creativity and hence of human power. Philosophers have hitherto viewed man as the rational animal, but he now stands revealed as the animal—the only animal—who is able to create horizons. In the past, horizons have been created unconsciously, but the possibility now arises of consciously created horizons, horizons of a glory and splendor never before achieved in human history. No wonder, then, that Nietzsche is able to end his essay on history with such bright images of a wondrous human future.

This sketch of Nietzsche's views depends for its plausibility on a consideration of his work as a whole, which is to say that only hints of it can be found in *History in the Service and Disservice of Life*. Moreover, the questions raised by those hints can scarcely be said to be resolved by the essay. If horizons are the subjective creations of human beings, why do we not—why can't we—find, in principle at least, as many horizons as there are human beings? If horizons are free projects, how do we choose nonarbitrarily among different and differing horizons? The reader who wishes to follow Nietzsche's struggles with these questions must turn to the main body of Nietzsche's work; but a study of this early work should enable him to appreciate the importance Nietzsche persistently assigned to the historical process. Two instances from later work suffice to make the point. As previously indicated, Nietzsche's so-called middle period begins with *Human, All-Too-Human.* The very first aphorism of that lengthy work distinguishes between metaphysical and historical philosophy, and clearly places Nietzsche's own thought in the second category. The second aphorism explicitly charges philosophers with a lack of historical sense, a charge from which the author of the aphorism obviously considers himself exempt. The concern with history continues into the final stage of Nietzsche's thought, as we can see in *Beyond Good and Evil.* The seventh part of that work is entitled "Our Virtues," and the 224th aphorism deals with the historical sense, one of the two most prominent virtues of Nietzsche's time (the other is intellectual integrity) and of Nietzsche himself. One might additionally note the numerous references to history in the titles and subtitles of his books.

In short, Nietzsche couches his own philosophy in terms of a vast historical analysis; he deals with human history in order to place it in the service of life. His early essay sets an agenda for his own philosophical labors. And it is difficult to read his depiction of mankind as horizon-creating without seeing here the first stirrings of the doctrine of the Will to Power.

An exposition of Nietzsche's final teachings, the doctrines of the Will to Power and the Eternal Recurrence of the same, lies far beyond the scope of an introduction to this early essay. Suffice it to say that even the most sympathetic reader of Nietzsche may come away from a study of his work with grave doubts as to the way he answered the questions he asked of himself. The doctrine of the Will of Power may yield great insights into human nature; it may even be the best available account of human beings as creative. But what are they to create? According to Nietzsche, they must create the meaning of their lives. But does not meaning *mean* that there are things beyond the power of man to make, so that he can take his bearings by them? Nietzsche's answer to that question remains obscure. Needless to say, the doctrine of the Eternal Recurrence of the same muddies matters rather than clears them up. On the one hand, Nietzsche seems to regard the Will as sovereign, but if everything will happen again as it has happened before, the Will is revealed as impotent.

In the case of most philosophers, one can afford to respond with a benevolent shrug when told that his thought, in its totality, fails to persuade. Philosophy does not, like the sciences, have to progress over previous endeavors; one expects no more of it than that it once more pose basic problems. That toleration may well mask a certain contempt for philosophy as such, but other considerations as well should make one wary of giving Nietzsche every benefit of the doubt. First of all, he constantly asks to be judged as exactingly as possible; indeed, this side of his thought may constitute its most enticing aspect. The very intellectual integrity which Nietzsche praises demands that we acknowledge the historical and intellectual link between him and fascism. The praise of cruelty, the loathing for the common man, the mockery of common decencies, the hallowing of war over peace—these and other excesses caused Nietzsche to become the one philosopher whose shrine was honored by Hitler himself. It would be foolish to deny that by abusing Nietzsche the Nazis, by exaggeration and misinterpretation, did him a great disservice; it would be almost as foolish to deny that Nietzsche's extreme views performed a real service for the extremists of the Right. The Nazis not only *abused* Nietzsche; they *used* him.

What then remains valuable and viable in the thought of Nietzsche? The answer must be that a great deal of Nietzsche remains viable, that he remains one of the greatest of cultural critics of Western civilization. What is still alive in Nietzsche's thought needs no commentary, for Nietzsche wrote with astonishing vigor and clarity. The insights seem almost to leap off the page, but it may be helpful, by way of conclusion, to indicate several of them.

To begin with, Nietzsche's strictures on modern academic life are still remarkably valid. The modern university, especially the modern American university, suffers from listlessness, above all in the humanities, Nietzsche's prime concern. The sciences flourish but the liberal arts decline, offering no grounding for the sciences and no guidance to their students. They are held in contempt and in truth they have become contemptible. Nietzsche saw and foresaw as much. He diagnosed the academy's rampant pedantry and its pitiful attempt to seek refuge in arid historical studies that can be justified before the bars of neither reason nor passion.

Those within the academy who specialize in castigating the society around them will find Nietzsche extremely helpful. His scathing comments on such phenomena as rootlessness, cynicism, and the overly scientific cast of mind anticipate whole battalions of modern Cassandras. He writes of the perils of conformity and other-directedness more beautifully than contemporary social scientists and depicts despair more profoundly than contemporary existentialists.

The radicals in the academy can take comfort in Nietzsche's pitiless dissection of bourgeois society. Those on the Right may find his condemnations refreshing because they so clearly emanate from the Right—and because Nietzsche's great competitor on the Left, Marx, cannot begin to match Nietzsche as prose stylist. Nietzsche condemns bourgeois society for its complacencies, its shameless reliance on the baser motivations of human beings, its petty yearnings, its bald abandonment of the poetic and the heroic. Though bourgeois society is anything but heroic, yet, when it possessed a crude but energetic self-confidence, it too once enjoyed a heroic age. Bourgeois society has lost its certitudes. It no longer knows itself to be right, it no longer knows *what is right*. In other words, it has succumbed to relativism.

On this point, Nietzsche most clearly and very interestingly differs from Marx, who ascribes the crisis of bourgeois society primarily to material conditions and economic factors. Nietzsche, on the contrary, regards the crisis as spiritual. God is dead, mankind has lost its bearings. To those who attempt to find satisfaction in their relativism, understanding it as a sign of superiority over past times—a sign of great openness—he shows its inescapable links to nihilism.

It may, of course, be true that the antidotes to nihilism which Nietzsche, as physician of culture, prescribes are worse than the disease he diagnoses. The consequences of his thought are surely in many respects dangerous, but a thinker is not to be refuted by pointing to the dangerous consequences of his thought. Those readers who take Nietzsche seriously will discover that he holds up a dauntingly accurate mirror to his own time, the nineteenth century, but, no less importantly, to their own time as well.

History in the Service and Disservice of Life

"Furthermore, I hate everything that merely instructs me without increasing or directly conferring life on my activity." With these words of Goethe,[1] as with a boldly expressed *ceterum censeo*,[2] our consideration of the worth and worthlessness of history may begin. Our purpose here is to show why instruction which fails to confer life upon—why knowledge which dampens—activity, why history as an extravagant intellectual excess and luxury, must arouse, in Goethe's words, our intense hatred. For we still lack our greatest necessity, and the superfluous is the enemy of necessity. To be sure, we need history, but not in the way the pampered dilettante in the garden of knowledge, for all his elegant contempt for our coarse and graceless needs and wants, needs it. I mean, we need history for life and action, not for the smug evasion of life and action, or even to gloss a selfish life and a base, cowardly action. Only insofar as history serves life do we wish to serve history. But history can be professionally practiced and valued to a degree that encourages the atrophy and deterioration of life—a phenomenon which, because of certain remarkable symptoms of our age, is as essential for us to diagnose as it may be painful to do so.

I have attempted to describe a feeling that has frequently tormented me; I take my revenge on it by making it public. Perhaps this description will give the reader opportunity to declare that he too is quite familiar with my feeling, but that I have failed to feel it with adequate purity and originality, that I have not expressed it with the confidence and maturity of experience which it requires. A few perhaps will so assert; but most will tell me that my feeling is completely perverted, unnatural, heinous, and positively illicit; and that by feeling it I have shown myself unworthy of the dominant historical orientation of our time—one which, as everyone knows, has been powerfully visible for two generations, especially among the Germans. In any case, by daring to step forward with the natural description of my feeling, I will be promoting, not injuring, the general respectability, insofar as I provide many with an opportunity to pay compliments to that historical orientation I mentioned. As for myself, I gain something of much greater value than respectability—I mean, being publicly instructed and corrected about our own time.

1. See Goethe's letter to Schiller, Dec. 19, 1798.

2. Thematic allusion to the celebrated sentence with which the elder Cato (the Censor) invariably capped his every speech to the Roman Senate: "Ceterum censeo Carthaginem esse delendam" ("I believe that Carthage must be destroyed").

These reflections are unmodern because I attempt to understand something of which our age is justly proud—its historical education—as a defect, an infirmity, a deficiency of the age. And because I also believe that we are all suffering from the ravages of historical fever and we should at least know what we are suffering from. But if Goethe was right in saying that we cultivate our faults along with our virtues; and if, as everybody knows, an excessive virtue—as the historical sense of our age seems to me to be—can destroy a people as easily as an excessive vice, then my reader might this once allow me to have my say. Also, by way of exoneration, I should not conceal the fact that the experiences which provoked these tormenting feelings in me were for the most part my own, and that the experiences of others are cited for comparison's sake. And furthermore that only insofar as I am the nursling of past ages—above all of the Greek past—could I, as a child of my age, have such uncontemporary experiences. But this much must be conceded me by virtue of my profession as a philologist. For I cannot imagine what would be the meaning of classical philology in our own age, if it is not to be unmodern—that is, to act against the age and, by so doing, to have an effect on the age, and let us hope, to the benefit of a future age.

I   Consider the herd grazing before you; aware of no yesterday, no today, it frolics about, feeds, sleeps, digests, and frolics again, from morning till night and from day to day, tethered by its pleasures and aversions, pegged to the moment, and therefore neither sad nor satiated. This spectacle is hard on man since he boasts of his superiority to the animals, but looks with envy on their happiness. His desire is futile because he refuses to be like them. He may ask the animal: "Why do you just look at me instead of telling me about your happiness?" The animal wants to reply, "Because I always immediately forget what I wanted to say"—but then it forgets even this answer and says nothing. Man is left to wonder.

But he wonders about himself, too, wonders that he cannot learn to forget, but always clings to the past; that however far or fast he runs, that chain runs with him. It is a wonder that a moment now here, now gone, a nothing before, a nothing afterward, still returns like a specter to disturb the calm of a later moment. Loose sheets from the scroll of time are forever falling out, fluttering away—and suddenly floating back into man's lap. Then the man says, "I remember," and envies the animal who immediately forgets and sees each moment really die, lapse back into fog and night and disappear forever.

So the animal lives *unhistorically*. Like a number that leaves no remainder, it merges entirely into the present, it knows nothing of dissembling, hides nothing, and always seems exactly what it is, and so cannot help being honest. Man, on the other hand, struggles under the great and ever-growing burden of the past, which weighs him down and distorts him, obstructing his movement like a dark, invisible load, a load he can disown at times for appearances, and is only too glad to disown among his peers—in order to arouse their jealousy. And so the sight of a grazing herd or, closer to him, a child who does not yet have a past to disavow, who plays fenced in between past and future in blessed blindness, shakes him as though he remembered a lost paradise. And yet the child's play must be disturbed; only too soon will it be summoned from obliviousness. Then it learns to understand the phrase *it was*, the password that brings strife, suffering, and satiety upon man to remind him what his existence basically is—an imperfect tense that will never become perfect. And if death finally brings the forgetfulness he longs for, yet at one stroke it robs him of both the present and existence, and seals his realization that human existence is merely an uninterrupted past tense, a thing that lives by denying and consuming itself, by opposing itself.

If happiness, if striving for fresh happiness, is in any sense what binds men to life and urges them on to more life, then perhaps no philosopher is more right than any cynic. For the happiness of an animal, the consummate cynic, is living evidence of the truth of cynicism. The smallest happiness, if only it is uninterruptedly there and makes us content, is incomparably more than the greatest, which comes only episodically, like a mood or a wild inspiration, in the midst of sheer listlessness, yearning, or privation. But in the smallest and in the greatest happiness, there is always one element which makes it happiness: the power to forget or, in learned language, the power to feel *unhistorically* while it lasts. The man who cannot pause upon the threshold of the moment, forgetting the entire past, the man who cannot pivot on a tiny point like a goddess of victory, without dizziness or fear, will never know happiness, and even worse, will never do anything to make others happy. Take the most extreme example—a man who totally lacks the power to forget, who is doomed to see becoming everywhere. Such a man no longer believes in his own being, no longer believes in himself; he sees everything disintegrating into turbulent particles and becomes lost in this flux of becoming. Like a true disciple of Heraclitus,[3] he will end by scarcely daring to lift a finger. Forgetting is necessary to all activity, just as dark, as well as light, is necessary to all organisms. A man who wanted to live an utterly historical existence would be like a man forced to go without sleep, or like ruminant animals compelled to survive solely by chewing and re-

3. I.e., the sophist Cratylus, a young contemporary of Socrates. According to Aristotle (*Met.* 4.1010a.12), Cratylus took Heraclitus's doctrines to their logical extreme by asserting that since the universal Flux prevented the utterance of any truth, one should say nothing, merely wag his finger.

chewing their cud. That is, it is possible to live almost without memory, indeed to live happily, as the animals show us; but without forgetting, it is utterly impossible to *live* at all. Or to make my point still clearer: *There is a degree of insomnia, of rumination, of historical awareness, which injures and finally destroys a living thing, whether a man, a people, or a culture.*

To determine this degree and thereby the boundary beyond which the past must be forgotten if it is not to bury the present, we would have to know precisely how great is the *shaping power* of a man, a people, or a culture. I mean the strength to develop uniquely from within, to transform and assimilate the past and the alien, to recover completely from wounds, to redeem losses, and to refashion broken forms. There are men who possess so little of this strength that a single experience, a single pain, or, often and especially, a single subtle wrong, the tiniest scratch, makes them bleed help-lessly to death. On the other hand, some men are so lightly troubled by life's most savage and terrible misfortunes, and even by their own evil deeds, that while these are taking place or soon afterwards, they achieve reasonably good health and a kind of peaceful conscience. The more strongly rooted a man's inner nature, the better he will assimilate or overcome the past; and if we imagine a man of the strongest and most exceptional nature, we would realize that in his case there would be no boundary beyond which his his-torical sense would overwhelm and injure him. He would summon up and engage the entire past, his own as well as that most alien to him, and transform it into his own blood. What his nature cannot master, he knows how to forget—for him it no longer exists. His horizon is closed and com-plete, and nothing has the power to remind him that beyond this horizon there are still men, passions, theories, and goals. It is a general law that no living being can become healthy, strong, and productive except within a horizon; if it is incapable of describing its own horizon and yet too selfish to enclose its vision within another horizon, then it will fall into feeble decline or perish prematurely. Cheerfulness, good conscience, joyful action, faith in the future—all these depend, in an individual as in a people, upon the existence of a line that separates the bright and lucid from unilluminable darkness, upon knowing how to forget at the right time as well as how to remember at the right time, upon sensing, vigorously and instinctively, when the historical and when the unhistorical sense is needed. This is the thought I ask my reader to consider: *The unhistorical and the historical are equally necessary to the good health of a man, a people, and a culture.*

It is common observation that a man's historical knowledge and percep-tion may be severely limited, that his horizon may be as constricted as that of some inhabitant of an Alpine valley, that he may be unjust in all his judgments, and that he may, mistakenly, think himself the first to have his experiences—and yet, despite all his injustices and mistakes, he may stand there, invincibly healthy and vigorous, rejoicing every eye. By contrast, close beside him stands a man far more just and knowing, who grows sick and collapses because the limits of his horizon are constantly shattered by fresh uncertainties; because he cannot untangle himself from the much finer strands of his rationalizations and truths in order to will and desire strongly. In contrast with the latter man, we saw the animal, totally unhistorical and living within a horizon no larger than a mere point, yet with a certain happiness, living at least without satiety and hypocrisy. We must therefore regard the capacity for a certain degree of unhistorical awareness as the more important and primordial capacity, since it provides the only foundation upon which any just, healthy, great, or truly human enterprise can develop. The unhistorical resembles an enveloping atmosphere; within its confines alone is life engendered, only to disappear again with the annihilation of this atmosphere. It is true that a man diminishes this unhistorical element when he thinks, reflects, compares, analyzes, and synthesizes, that inside this enfolding vaporous cloud a brilliant incandescence flares up. And it is therefore true that a man becomes human only by using the past for the purpose of life and by making history anew from events. But with a surfeit of history he stops again; without that unhistorical envelopment he never would have begun, and would never dare begin. What could a man possibly accomplish without first entering that vaporous region of the unhistorical?

Or, putting images aside in order to illustrate my point with an example, imagine a man seized and carried away by a violent passion for a woman or a powerful idea. What a transformation of his world! He becomes blind to what lies behind him, deaf and insensitive to all that is unfamiliar around him, but what he actually notices was never before so real, so palpably near, so colorful, resonant, or brilliant—as though he now grasped it with all his senses simultaneously. All his evaluations are so changed and debased he can no longer honor them, because he can scarcely feel them anymore. He asks himself why he has so long been the dupe of strange expressions, strange beliefs. He marvels that his memory turns ceaselessly in a single circle, yet he is too weak and tired to attempt even a single leap out of it. His is the most unjust condition in the world, narrow, ungrateful to the past, blind in the presence of dangers, deaf to warnings, a tiny, living whirlpool in a dead sea of night and oblivion. And yet this condition—unhistorical, antihistorical through and through—is the womb not only of an unjust act, but of every just act as well. No artist would ever paint a picture, no general would win a victory, no people would gain its freedom without first having longed for and struggled toward that end in such an unhistorical condition. Just as the man of action, in Goethe's phrase,[4] is always unscrupulous, so he is always ignorant too. He forgets almost everything in order

4. *Dichtung und Wahrheit,* 3:13.

to accomplish just one thing; he is unjust to what lies behind him, and he knows only one truth: what must be done now. Thus, every man of action loves his achievement immensely more than it deserves to be loved, and his superlative exploits happen with such exuberance of love that in every case they must be unworthy of it, even though otherwise invaluable.

If in many cases a man were capable of sensing and savoring the unhistorical atmosphere in which every great historical event begins, then perhaps this man, as a knowing being, might be able to elevate himself to a *supra-historical* vantage point—a vantage point that Niebuhr[5] once described as a possible result of historical reflection. He says: "When history is clearly and fully understood, there is at least one thing it is useful for. Through history we know what the greatest and loftiest human spirits do not know: how fortuitously they received the forms through which they see, and through which they forcibly demand that everyone else sees—forcibly because of the extraordinary intensity of their consciousness. The man who has not fully ascertained and comprehended this is in many cases enslaved by the appearance of a powerful spirit who imbues a given form with the loftiest passion." This vantage point described by Niebuhr would be called supra-historical because those who attained to it would no longer feel tempted to go on living or taking part in history, because they would have recognized that the one condition for all events is the blindness and injustice in the soul of the man of action. Henceforth, they would even be cured of taking history too seriously. Have they not learned to answer the question—for every man, for every event, whether among the Greeks or the Turks, whether from a day in the first or in the nineteenth century: How and why is life lived?

If we ask our friends whether they would want to relive the last ten or twenty years, we will easily recognize which of them are suited for that supra-historical vantage point. Very likely they will all say "No!" but they will give different reasons. Some may console themselves by saying, "But the next twenty years will be better." Of these David Hume says sarcastically,

> And from the dregs of life hope to receive
> What the first sprightly running could not give.[6]

These men we will call historical men. A glance into the past drives them

---

5. Georg Barthold Niebuhr (1776–1831), renowned German historian, author of a magisterial *Römische Geschichte,* who discovered the *Institutes* of Gaius as well as fragments of Cicero and Livy, which he edited. As a pioneer in the *scientific* study of history, he was generally regarded by Nietzsche with sternly critical disapproval.
6. David Hume, *Dialogues Concerning Natural Religion,* 10, a quotation drawn from Dryden's play *Aureng-Zebe,* iv, 1.

on toward the future, inflames their courage to go on living, kindles their hope that justice will someday come, that happiness lies hidden on the other side of the mountain they are approaching. These historical men believe that the meaning of human existence will be increasingly revealed in the *process* of life. Thus, they look backwards only in order to understand the present by reflecting on the processes leading to it, and to learn to desire the future even more acutely. In spite of all their history, they have no idea how unhistorically they think and act, and how their pursuit of history serves not pure knowledge, but life.

But there is still another answer to this question than the one we have just heard. Admittedly, it is another No! but its basis is different. It is the no of the supra-historical man who sees no redemption in process; for whom, instead, the world is complete, fully consummated, at every single moment. What could ten more years teach them that the last ten could not?

Now, supra-historical men have never agreed whether this idea implies happiness or resignation, virtue or repentance. But in contrast to all the historical deliberation of the past, they unanimously believe that past and present are one and the same, that they are archetypically equivalent in all their diversity, and, like omnipresent, imperishable types, are motionless forms of unchanging value and eternally equal meaning. Just as the hundreds of different languages conform to the same typically recurrent necessities of men, so that those who understand these necessities could learn nothing new from any of these languages, so too the supra-historical thinker illuminates the entire historical experience of peoples and of individuals from within himself, clairvoyantly divines the primordial meaning of the different hieroglyphs, and by degrees finally turns in exhaustion from this constantly rising flood of recorded scripts. How could he, in the endless profusion of events, avoid becoming satiated and more than satiated—indeed, nauseated? Finally, perhaps, the most daring of supra-historical men is ready, with Giacomo Leopardi, to say in his heart:

> Nothing is worth your moving.
> Earth is unworthy of your sighs. Life
> is bitterness and boredom, nothing more.
> And the world is foul.
> Now be still.[7]

7. The lines come from Leopardi's bitterly beautiful poem "A se stesso": "Non val cosa nessuna / I moti tuoi, nè di sospiri è degna / La terra. Amaro e noia / La vita, altro mai nulla; e fango è il mondo." For the poetry and prose of Giacomo Leopardi (1798–1837), Nietzsche, like Schopenhauer, felt intense admiration. Schopenhauer had seen in Leopardi the supreme contemporary poet of human unhappiness; and it was to Nietzsche, qua Schopenhauerian and author of *The Birth of Tragedy*, that Cosima Wagner's first husband, Hans von Bülow, dedicated his translation of Leopardi into German, which

Let us abandon these supra-historical men to their nausea and their wisdom. Today for once we want rather to rejoice in our unwisdom, and, like effective and progressive men, like men who venerate process, we want to enjoy ourselves. Our esteem for history may be merely a Western prejudice. If only we could progress at least within these prejudices, and not stand still! If only we could get better at studying history in pursuit of life! Then we would gladly admit to the supre-historical men that they are wiser than we are; that is, if only we could be certain that we have more life than they do. Then, in any case, our unwisdom would have more future than their wisdom. And now, to banish all doubts about the meaning of this opposition of life and wisdom, I will adopt the standing practice and directly advance some themes.

A historical phenomenon which is clearly and thoroughly understood, and which is resolved into a phenomenon of knowledge, is dead to the person who has understood it, because he has understood the madness, the injustice, the blind passion, and, in general, the whole dismal and earthly horizon of that phenomenon, and thence its historical power too. To the extent that he is a knower, this power has now become powerless in his hands, but to the extent that he is still alive, it is perhaps not yet powerless.

History, regarded as a purely scientific discipline and accorded supremacy, would resemble a balancing of the books of life and a liquidation of mankind's accounts. On the other hand, if historical scholarship is to be a beneficent enterprise, holding future promise, it must itself move in the wake of a fresh and powerful torrent of life—for instance, a newly emerging culture. History, therefore, must be guided and controlled by a higher power and must not itself guide and control.

Insofar as it serves life, history serves as an unhistorical power; and because of its subordinate function, it could never, and should never, become a pure science like mathematics. But the question of the degree to which life needs the services of history is one of the supreme questions, of supreme concern because it involves the health of a man, a people, or a culture. For there is a certain excess of history that causes life to degenerate and to be destroyed, and through this degeneration, history itself is finally destroyed.

2   But that life needs the services of history must be as clearly understood as the principle—to be demonstrated later—that too much history harms the living. In three respects history is relevant to the living. It is relevant to the man of action and ambition, to the man who

---

Nietzsche cites here. Of Leopardi Nietzsche remarked (*WC*, 3.23 and note thereon) that he was "the modern ideal of a classicist" and one of "the last great followers of the Italian poet-scholars" (*RWB*, 10), and who, along with Merimée, Emerson, and Landor, could rightly be called "a master of prose" (GS, 92).

preserves and venerates, and to the man who suffers and needs liberation. These three relations correspond to the three kinds of history, insofar as we can distinguish between *exemplary*[8] or *monumental, antiquarian,* and *critical* history.

History is especially relevant to the energetic and powerful man, the man who fights a great battle, who needs exemplars, teachers, and comforters, and is unable to find them among his companions and contemporaries. History of this kind was relevant to Schiller, for, as Goethe observed, our age is so wretched that the poet no longer encounters qualities he can use in the human beings around him. Polybius, for instance, was thinking of the man of action when he called political history the proper preparation for government and the incomparable educator, which, by reminding us of the misfortunes of others, admonishes us to endure the vicissitudes of fortune without flinching.[9]

The man who has mastered history in this sense will be infuriated by the sight of curious tourists or scrupulous students of trivia clambering about on the pyramids of a great past. Here where he finds the inspiration to emulate and surpass this greatness, he has no desire to meet the dilettante in quest of amusement or excitement, who saunters through history as though it were some gallery of priceless paintings. In order to avoid feeling despair and disgust among these weak and impotent tourists, among these apparently active, but actually merely busy and agitated, companions, the active man looks to the past and, in order to catch his breath, interrupts his progress toward his goal for a while. But his goal is some happiness or other—not his own, perhaps, but usually that of a people or of all mankind; he shrinks from resignation and history is his remedy against it. For the most part, the only reward that can tempt him is fame, the hope of an honorable place in the temple of history—a temple where he in turn can become a teacher, comforter, and cautioner of those who come after him. His standard: anything that once had the power to extend and fulfill the idea of "man" more beautifully must also be always available in order to be perpetually capable of doing so again.

That the great moments in the struggle of individuals form a chain; that in them a great mountain ridge of mankind takes shape through the millennia; that the peaks of such long-lost moments might be still alive, still luminous, still great, for *me*—that is the crucial idea in the belief in humanity which the demand for *exemplary* history expresses. But this very demand— that greatness should be immortal—kindles the most frightful battle. Every

8. In German, *monumentalische.* Since English "monumental" fails to convey Nietzsche's particular inflection of the German, the word has here and there, as needed, been rendered as, or supplemented by, "exemplary."
9. Polybius *Histories* 1.1.2.

other living man cries out No! The monumental *shall* not reappear—that is the password. Lifeless custom, triviality, and vulgarity fill every cranny of the world; like a heavy, miasmal fog, they blur everything great, they occupy the path the great must take toward immortality—obstructing, deceiving, smothering, and suffocating them. But this path leads through human brains! Through the brains of frightened and transient animals who rise over and over again to the same needs and who are kept from deteriorating only briefly and with great effort. They want only one thing above all else: to live at any price. Who could imagine that the arduous torch-race of exemplary history is run amidst such men—the race without which greatness cannot survive!

And yet persistently a few men awaken—men who look back at greatness, are encouraged by reflecting on it, and feel themselves blessed, as though human life were a splendid thing, as though the loveliest fruit of this bitter plant were the knowledge that before them one man lived his life with pride and strength, another profoundly, and a third with compassion and benevolence—but all bequeathed the same lesson: the man who is ready to risk his existence lives most beautifully.

If the ordinary man clutches at his mortal span so morbidly and greedily, these great men, on their way to immortality and monumental history, knew how to treat it with Olympian laughter or were proud enough to disdain it. And they often climbed into their graves with an ironic smile—for what was left of them to be buried? Only what they had always regarded as mere ashes, refuse, as something vain and bestial, and which now lapses into oblivion after long exposure to their contempt. But one thing survives, the personal signature of their most inward nature—a work, a deed, a rare perception, a creation; it survives because future generations cannot do without it. In this, its most transfigured form, fame is even more than a supremely delicious sop to our vanity, as Schopenhauer called it.[10] It is the belief in the solidarity and continuity of the great men of all ages; it is a protest against the mere succession of generations and the brevity and transience of human life.

Of what use to the man of the present, then, is exemplary or monumental study of the past, the pursuit of what is classical and rare in the past? From this study he concludes that greatness was at least *possible* once, and therefore may be possible again. He goes his way with greater courage because the doubt that assails him in his weaker moments—that he is perhaps demanding the impossible—is now banished. Imagine a man who believes that you need only a hundred fruitful men, men educated and working in a fresh spirit, to do away with that "cultured" refinement which has now become so fashionable in Germany. How encouraged he must feel to see that the

10. See *Parerga and Paralipomena*, trans. E. F. J. Payne (Oxford, 1974), 1:449ff.

world of the Renaissance was raised aloft on the shoulders of a hundred such men.

And yet—to learn at the same time a lesson from the same example—how loose and tentative, how imprecise such a comparison would be! How many differences have to be overlooked before it can have that invigorating effect! How violently the uniqueness of the past has to be crammed into an abstraction, and all its angularities and edges smoothed away in the name of congruity! In point of fact, what was once possible could be possible again only if the Pythagoreans were right in their conviction that, given the same configurations of heavenly bodies,[11] earthly events must be repeated down to the minutest detail—so that every time the stars resume a certain pattern, a Stoic will conspire with an Epicurean and murder Caesar, and every time they reach another position, Columbus will discover America. Only if the earth always began its drama anew after the fifth act; only if it were certain that the same tangle of motives, the same deus ex machina, the same catastrophe would recur at fixed intervals, would the powerful man want exemplary history to repeat everything with utterly graphic *exactitude*—that is, to describe precisely the peculiarity and uniqueness of every fact—which is improbable unless astronomers become astrologers once more. Until then exemplary history will have no need for absolute accuracy. It will continue to approach dissimilar events, make generalizations about them, and finally declare them identical. It will persist in attenuating the diversity of motives and circumstances in order to present the *effects* as monumental—that is, as exemplary and worthy of emulation—to the detriment of the *causes*. Since monumental history therefore disregards causes as much as possible, there would be less exaggeration in calling it a collection of events that will affect every age. What we celebrate in public festivals, on days of religious or military commemoration, is really such an "effect in itself." It troubles the sleep of the ambitious; it lies like an amulet over the heart of the adventurous. But it is not the true historical *connexus* of causes and effects which, completely known, would only prove that its exact counterpart could never recur in the dice game of future and chance.

So long as the heart of historiography is the great *encouragement* a powerful man receives from it; so long as the past must be shown as worthy of emulation, as imitable and capable of repetition, it is doubtless in danger of being a little distorted, too favorably described, and, therefore, assimilated

11. See G. S. Kirk and J. E. Raven, eds., *The Presocratic Philosophers* (Cambridge, 1960), 223. According to Eudemus, the Pythagoreans held that "the same individual things will recur, then I shall be talking again to you sitting as you are now, with this pointer in my hand, and everything else will be just as it is now, and it is reasonable to suppose that the time then is the same as now." The passage, one hardly needs to add, is plainly germinal to Nietzsche's later development of the idea of the Eternal Recurrence.

into free invention. Indeed, there are times when we simply cannot distinguish between an exemplary past and a mythical fiction, since precisely the same encouragement can be taken from the one world as from the other. So, if exemplary study of the past *prevails* over the other modes of consideration—I mean antiquarian and critical history—then the past itself is *damaged.* Large portions of it are neglected, despised, and washed away on the grey, monotonous tide of oblivion, out of which a few richly embellished facts emerge like islands. The rare man who surfaces at all seems a little unnatural and miraculous, like the golden thigh which disciples of Pythagoras claimed to see on their master.[12] Exemplary history is deceptive in the use it makes of analogies; by means of seductive similarities it provokes courageous men to rash action and enthusiastic men to fanaticism. And imagine the effect of such history on the minds and activities of talented egoists and fiery malcontents; empires would be destroyed and princes murdered; there would be wars and rebellions, and the number of historical "effects in themselves"—that is, effects without sufficient causes—would be constantly multiplied. But this reminder of the damage caused by exemplary history in the hands of powerful and energetic men, whether good or evil, is enough. Think also of its effect when it is usurped and exploited by weak and passive men.

Consider the simplest and most ordinary example. Think of effetely inartistic natures clad and armored with the exemplary history of art. At whom will they now aim their weapons? At their traditional enemies, the strong artistic spirits, hence at those who are unique in being able to really learn—that is, to learn to live—from that history and to translate what they learn into heightened purpose. For these strong artistic spirits the path is blocked and the atmosphere darkened when zealous idolaters dance around the shrine of some half-understood monument of a great past, as though they wanted to say: "See, this is real art, authentic art! What concern of yours is this new art that is now appearing?" This dancing swarm seems even to have a patent on "good taste," since the creative man is always at a disadvantage in comparison to the dilettante who merely looks and creates nothing, just as the beer-hall politician has always been more clever, more just, and more reflective than the statesman in power. But if the practice of referenda and majority rule is transferred to the world of art, and the artist forced to defend himself before a council of dilettantes, as it were, then we could solemnly swear in advance that he will be found guilty—and this not although, but *because*, his judges have solemnly proclaimed the canon of exemplary art (which means, according to our earlier explanation, art which "has had an effect" at all times). But for all art that has not yet become monumental or exemplary simply because it is contemporary art, the judges

12. See Diogenes Laertius *Lives of the Eminent Philosophers* 8.11.

lack, first, need; second, genuine inclination; and third, precisely that authority of history. On the other hand, instinct tells these judges that art can be killed by art; they cannot tolerate a rebirth of the exemplary, and, to ensure that none will take place, they employ precisely that past art which has long been canonized as monumental. This is the method of connoisseurs, because they would like to eliminate art altogether. They pose as physicians while actually scheming to poison art. They hone their tongues and their tastes in order fastidiously to explain why they so persistently refuse all the artistic nourishment which the present might provide them. They do not want a rebirth of great art; their strategy is to say, "Look, we already have a great art!" Actually, this great art of the past is of no more concern to them than the art now being created—a fact to which their own lives bear witness. Exemplary history is the masquerade in which their hatred for the great and powerful artists of their own age appears as a complacent admiration for the great and powerful artists of the past. They use this disguise to transform the true meaning of monumental history into its opposite. Whether they recognize it or not, they nonetheless act as though their motto were "Let the dead bury the living."

Each of the three kinds of history is valid only in its own soil and its own climate; in any other soil it becomes a ravenous weed. If the man who wants to create any great thing has any need of the past, then he will take possession of it by means of exemplary history. Those men, on the other hand, who want to remain firmly within the bounds of hoary and venerable custom, will cherish the past as antiquarians. And only the man who is oppressed by a present need, the man who wants at any cost to rid himself of a burden, needs critical history—that is, history which judges and condemns. If these historical growths are carelessly transplanted, great damage is done. The critic without need, the antiquarian without reverence, and the authority on greatness with no capacity to be great, are such growths—plants that have run wild and, torn from their nurturing soil, have therefore degenerated into weeds.

3   Second, history is relevant to the man who preserves and venerates the past, who looks back with love and loyalty to his origins, where he became what he is. Through his veneration of the past he gives thanks, as it were, for his own existence. By cherishing with loving hands the remnants of the past, he means to preserve the conditions in which he grew up, for those who will grow up after him. And by so doing he serves life. In such a soul the possession of its ancestral patrimony[13] changes its meaning, for it is he, instead, who is possessed by this patrimony. Small, humble, fragile, old-fashioned things are endowed with dignity and

13. An echo of Goethe, *Faust*, part 1, 408.

sanctity when his antiquarian spirit, preserving and venerating, enters into them and makes itself a home and nest. His city's history becomes for him his own biography. He understands its wall, its towered gate, its laws, and its popular festivals as an illustrated diary of his youth, and he rediscovers himself in all of these things—finds in them his strength, his energy, his joy, judgment, follies, and improprieties. "Here men could live," he tells himself, "since men can live here now. And men will be able to live, because we are tough and can't be broken overnight." With this "we" of his, he looks beyond his fleeting, quaint, individual life and feels himself to be the spirit of his house, his kind, his city.

At times he even greets the spirit of his people across the vast distance of dark and confusing centuries as though it were his own. Empathy and a feeling for the future, a nose for almost obliterated traces, an instinctive capacity for reading accurately a past still concealed beneath many later layers, a quick understanding of palimpsests, indeed polypsests—these are his gifts and virtues. It was with such gifts that Goethe stood before Erwin von Steinbach's monument; in the storm of his feelings the historical veil of clouds separating them was torn apart, and he saw the German monument again for the first time, "exerting its effect out of the robust and rugged German soul."[14] It was this kind of feeling and impulse that guided the Italians of the Renaissance, and reawakened the ancient Italian genius in their poets to a "marvelous new resounding of the ancient lyre," as Jacob Burckhardt put it.[15]

But that antiquarian sense of historical reverence is of the greatest value when it fills the modest, coarse, even miserable conditions in which a man or a nation lives, with a simple, poignant feeling of pleasure and contentment. Niebuhr, for example, admits with genuine candor that he lived happily and with no regrets, without missing art, on moor and heath, with free peasants who possess a history. How could history better serve life than by binding less-favored races and populations to their native land and native customs, by settling them in one place, and preventing them from straying beyond their borders in search of better land, and competing for that in war? At times it seems as though stubbornness and unreason are the ties that bind the individual to these companions and environments, these tedious customs, these barren mountain ridges. But this is the healthiest, most generally beneficial sort of unreason—a fact known to everyone who recognizes the terrible aftermath of that adventurous migratory yearning which sometimes possesses a whole population, or who has studied the plight of

14. See Goethe's brief essay "Von deutscher Baukunst," dedicated to the "shades" (*dis manibus*) of Erwin von Steinbach.
15. Jacob Burckhardt, *The Civilization of the Renaissance in Italy*, trans. S. G. C. Middlemore (Oxford, 1945), 153.

a people that has lost its loyalty to its past and succumbed to a restless cosmopolitan craving for the new and always newer. The opposite feeling, the satisfaction of a tree in its own roots, its happiness in knowing that it is not a wholly arbitrary and chance growth, but the inheritor, the blossom, and the fruit of a past, and that its existence is thereby excused and even justified—this feeling is what I now prefer to call the true historical sense.

Now, clearly this is not the condition likeliest to enable a man to reduce the past to pure knowledge. So in this case too we observe what we have already observed in regard to exemplary history, that the past itself suffers so long as history serves life and is governed by the instincts of life. Or, to put it more metaphorically: a tree can feel its roots better than it can see them, but it measures their size by the greatness and strength of its visible branches. If a tree could be wrong about its own roots, how much more wrong it will be about the whole surrounding forest! A forest which it knows and feels only as a hindrance or support—but nothing more. The antiquarian sense of a man, a township, or a whole nation always has an extremely limited visual field; it simply does not notice most things, and the little it does see, it sees in isolation and much too closely. It cannot measure anything, and hence regards everything as equally important, and hence each single detail as excessively important. Furthermore, there is no criterion of value and no sense of proportion for the things of the past which would really do them justice in relation to each other; invariably there are only the measurements and proportions applied to things by the antiquarian individual or nation looking back at them.

There is always an immediate danger in this. In the end every old or venerable thing that is still part of our visual field is simply accepted as equally venerable, while everything that fails to welcome the ancient with reverence—that is, everything new, everything emerging—is rejected and condemned. In the plastic and graphic arts even the Greeks tolerated the old hieratic style alongside a freer and greater style. Indeed, they later not only tolerated the pointed noses and the frozen smiles, they even honored them as refinements of taste. When a people's sensibility hardens in this way; when history serves the life of the past so that it undermines further life and, above all, higher life; when the historical sense no longer preserves life but embalms it—then the tree dies unnaturally, withering from the top slowly downward to the roots—and finally the roots themselves usually die. The moment antiquarian history is no longer inspired and quickened by the vigorous life of the present, it degenerates. Now piety withers, the scholarly habit persists without piety, revolving egoistically and complacently about its own center. Then we witness the revolting drama of a blind mania for collecting things, an incessant, restless accumulation of everything which has ever existed. The man envelops himself in mustiness. By this antiquarian behavior he succeeds in degrading an even more significant talent, a nobler need, into an insatiable craving for the new, or, more accurately, for the old, for everything old. Frequently he sinks to the point where he is satisfied with any fare, and devours dusty bibliographical trivia with gusto.

But even if this degeneration fails to occur, even if antiquarian history does not lose the ground in which it must take root in the service of life, the danger that it may become too powerful and suffocate the other modes of viewing the past always remains. It understands merely how to *preserve* life, not how to create life; hence it always undervalues becoming because it lacks the divining instinct for it—the instinct which exemplary history, for instance, possesses. Hence antiquarian history impedes the powerful resolve for the new; hence it paralyzes men of action who, precisely because they are men of action, always will, and always must, offend against some piety or other. The fact that a thing has acquired age now creates the demand that it should last forever. For if we add up the experience accumulated in such things—an old ancestral custom, a religious belief, an inherited polit-ical right—during the course of their existence; if we add up the cumulative piety and reverence felt by individuals and generations, then it seems rash or even ruthless, to set such a past aside for a new present, and to compare the single, one-time fact of things present and becoming to the cumulative multiplicity of past pieties and old reverence.

By now it is clear how urgently man often needs to supplement the exemplary and antiquarian modes of viewing the past with a *third*, the *critical* mode; and that he needs this too in life's service. In order to live, man must possess the strength, and occasionally employ it, to shatter and disintegrate a past. He does this by haling that past before a tribunal, interrogating it carefully, and in the end condemning it. But every past deserves to be condemned, for this is how it is with human things: human violence and weakness have always been potent in them. It is not justice that sits in judgment here; even less is it mercy that here pronounces the verdict; but life alone, that dark, compulsive power, insatiably avid of itself. Its verdicts are always unmerciful, always unjust, because they never flow from a pure fountain of knowledge. But in most cases justice herself would pronounce the same verdict, "for everything that comes into being *deserves* to perish. It would be better if nothing began."[16]

It takes very great strength to be able to live and to forget to what degree living and the practice of injustice are synonymous. Luther himself once supposed that the world began only through an oversight of God; that is, if God had thought of "heavy artillery," he would not have created the world. But at times the same life that requires this forgetfulness also requires its periodic abolition. Then it becomes extremely clear precisely how unjust it is that certain things—a privilege, a caste, or a dynasty, for instance—exist

16. Goethe, *Faust*, part 1, 1339–41.

at all, and how thoroughly they deserve destruction. It is then that we consider its past critically; then that we attack its roots with a knife; then that we cruelly trample on all the pieties of the past. The process is always dangerous, dangerous even to life itself. Men or ages that serve life in this way, by judging and destroying a past, are always dangerous and always endangered. For since we happen to be the products of earlier generations, we are also the products of their blunders, passions, and misunderstandings, indeed, of their crimes; it is impossible to free ourselves completely from this chain. If we condemn those blunders and exempt ourselves of guilt for them, we cannot ignore the fact that our existence is rooted in them. At best we create a conflict between our inherited, ancestral nature and our knowledge, and perhaps even a revolt of a strict new discipline against what was long ago inbred and inborn. We plant in ourselves a new habit, a new instinct, a second nature, so that the first nature withers. It is an attempt to give ourselves a past a posteriori, as it were, a past from which we prefer to be descended, as opposed to the past from which we did descend—always a risky task since it is so difficult to set limits to this rejection of the past, and because second natures are generally weaker than first natures. Too often we know the good but fail to do it because we also know the better but are incapable of doing it. But now and then a victory does occur, and for those who struggle, for those who use critical history in the service of life, there is significant consolation in knowing that even this first nature was once a second nature, and that every victorious second nature will become a first.

4   Such are the services that history can render to life. Every man, every nation, requires, according to its goals, strengths, and necessities, a certain knowledge of the past, a knowledge now in the form of exemplary history, now of antiquarian history, and now of critical history. What is never needed is a crowd of pure thinkers merely observing life, or individuals hungry for knowledge who are satisfied by knowledge only, whose sole purpose is the increase of knowledge. What is always needed is history whose aim is life and which must therefore be subject to the authority and ultimate control of life. That this relation to history—one created by hunger, governed by the degree of need, and limited by the inward shaping power of an age, culture, or nation—is the natural one; that knowledge of the past in every age is desirable only insofar as it serves the future and the present, and does not weaken the present or eradicate a vital future—all this is as simple as the truth is simple and is immediately convincing to anyone who does not first insist upon historical proof.

And now glance quickly at our own age! We recoil in shock. What became of all the clarity, all the naturalness and purity of the bond between life and history? How confusing, exaggerated, and disturbing is this problem now looming! Are we, the observers, to blame? Or has the old constellation of life and history really been altered by the intervention of some powerfully malignant star? Let others prove our perception false; we will say what we think we see. Actually, just such a star, radiant and magnificent, has intervened; the constellation of life and history has really changed—*because of science*, because of *the demand that history be a science*. Life alone no longer dominates and limits the knowledge of the past. Instead, all the boundary markers have been knocked down, and everything that ever was now plunges down upon man. As far back into the past as becoming reaches, back into infinity, all perspectives have shifted. No past generation has ever seen so boundless a spectacle as that which history, this science of universal becoming, now presents to us; but this spectacle is also presented to us with history's dangerously bold motto: *fiat veritas, pereat vita.*[17]

Now let us imagine the spiritual effect this science has had on the soul of modern man. Historical knowledge constantly overwhelms him from its inexhaustible sources; strange, disconnected facts crowd upon him; memory throws open all its doors but cannot open them wide enough; he does his best to welcome, sort out, and honor these alien guests, but they quarrel with each other, and it seems that man must conquer and subdue them all lest he himself perish in their quarrels. Accustoming himself to this rowdy, boisterous, quarrelsome household gradually becomes second nature, though there can be no doubt that this second nature is much weaker, much more nervous, and in every way less healthy than the first. In the end modern man carries around with him an enormous load of these indigestible stones of knowledge, which then at every opportunity, as the fairy tale has it,[18] rattle loudly inside his stomach. This rattling reveals modern man's most characteristic trait. And that is the strange contrast between an inward nature that has no corresponding exterior, and an exterior nature that lacks a corresponding interior, a contrast unknown to the ancient world. Knowledge consumed to excess, in the absence of hunger, and even against a man's need, is now powerless to transform or make itself manifest, but remains concealed in a certain chaotic inner world which modern man, with curious pride, calls his characteristic "inwardness." He says of course that he possesses content and lacks only the appropriate form; but this is a wholly unnatural disjunction for any living thing. Our modern culture is not a living thing precisely because it cannot be understood without this dissociation; that is, it is not in fact a real culture, but merely a kind of knowledge about culture. It stops at the thoughts and sentiments of culture, but never becomes cultural resolve. What actually motivates modern man instead, and becomes externally visible as action, usually means little more than a trivial

17. "Let truth be done, though life perish."
18. Grimm, "The Wolf and the Seven Little Goats."

convention, a pitiful imitation, or even a coarse caricature. His feelings then doze inside him like the snake that swallowed rabbits whole, stretches out peacefully in the sun, and avoids all unnecessary movements. The inward process: this is the real thing today, this is "genuine" culture. The casual observer can only hope that this kind of culture does not die of indigestion.

Imagine a Greek, for instance, happening on a culture of this kind. He would notice that for modern man the terms *educated* and *historically educated* are apparently so close that they mean the same thing and differ only in the number of words. If this Greek then observed that a man might be well educated and yet historically ignorant, we would shake our heads in disbelief, as though we had not heard him rightly. That famous small people of the not-so-remote past—I mean the Greeks—had, during the period of their greatest vigor, stubbornly preserved an unhistorical sense; if a contemporary were magically transported to the Greek world, he would probably find the Greeks very "uncultured"—which would clearly expose the carefully concealed secret of modern culture to public ridicule. We moderns, in point of fact, possess nothing which is truly ours. Only by stuffing, and overstuffing, ourselves with alien customs, ages, arts, philosophies, religions, and perceptions do we become worthy of notice, that is, as walking encyclopedias, as which we might perhaps be regarded by a Greek of the archaic period marooned in the modern world. But with encyclopedias everything of value lies within, in the contents, not on the outside, on the binding and jacket. And so all of modern culture is essentially inward; on the cover the binder has stamped some title like "Handbook of Inward Culture for Outward Barbarians." Indeed, this contrast between inward and outward makes the exterior even more barbaric than would be the case if a primitive people had developed solely on its own according to its own harsh needs. How else could Nature cope with the excessive richness of the past pouring in upon it? Only by one means, that is, accepting it as superficially as possible, in order to dispose of it rapidly and reject it. Hence the habit of not taking real things seriously; the "weak personality," which prevents reality and existence from making a deep impression. In the end we become outwardly ever more lazy and self-indulgent, and the dangerous gulf between form and content is widened until we become insensitive to our own barbarism; memory is always freshly stimulated, there is a constant flow of new things, things worth knowing, which can be stored away in the drawers of our memory.

The culture of a people as the opposite of that barbarism has been defined, appropriately, I think, as unity of artistic style in all the vital manifestations of a people. This definition should not be taken to imply an opposition between barbarism and beauty of style. A people to whom we attribute a culture must be a vital unity in every aspect of reality; it cannot be wretchedly fragmented into inward and outward, or form and content.

If you want to establish and foster a national culture, then establish and foster this higher unity, and devote your efforts to destroying modern "culture" in the name of true culture. Have the courage to consider how a nation's health, damaged by history, can be restored; how its instincts, which means its integrity, can be recovered.

I want to speak directly only about ourselves, about contemporary Germans. More than the people of any other nation we suffer from this weakness of personality, from this dissonance between form and content. Among Germans form is commonly regarded as a convention, a disguise, and a fiction. If we do not hate it, we certainly do not love it. It would be still more accurate to say that we have an extraordinary fear of the word *convention* and even more of convention itself. In this fear the Germans deserted the school of the French, because they wanted to become more natural and thereby more German. But it now seems that they miscalculated with this "thereby." Having escaped the school of convention, they simply let themselves follow their own inclinations wherever they led, and imitated sloppily, indiscriminately, and almost mindlessly what we once painstakingly and often successfully imitated. So, even today, we still live, as compared with earlier times, by a slovenly and incorrect French convention, as revealed in our mode of walking, standing, speaking, dressing, and dwelling. While we believed we were escaping to naturalness, we merely chose freedom from restraint, our own convenience, and the smallest possible degree of self-mastery. Merely wander through a German city. Every stylistic convention, in comparison with the distinctive national traits of foreign cities, reveals itself in a negative way. Everything is colorless, decrepit, badly copied, slipshod; everyone does as he wishes, not from vigorous and deliberate desire, but according to laws prescribed in part by the universal haste, in part by the prevalent passion for comfort. A piece of clothing requiring no ingenuity to design, whose making costs no time—therefore clothing borrowed from abroad and copied with extreme sloppiness—is immediately viewed by Germans as a contribution to German fashion. The feeling for form is flatly rejected by Germans, and ironically: because they have a *feeling for content*. Aren't they, after all, a nation famous for its "inwardness"?

But a notorious risk also exists in this inwardness. The content itself, which we assume to be completely invisible from the outside, might someday evaporate. And neither its disappearance nor its earlier presence would be outwardly apparent. Yet even supposing that this danger to the German people is extremely remote, there is still truth in the foreigner's reproach that our inner life is too weak and chaotic to act externally and achieve form. Our inner life, however, is quite capable of being sensitive, serious, powerful, intense, good, and perhaps even richer than the inner life of other peoples. But as a whole it remains weak because all those fine individual strands are not interwoven into a single hard knot. Consequently, our visible acts are not the complete action nor manifestation of our inner life but merely a crude, weak effort by one or two strands to represent the whole. This is why we simply cannot judge a German by his behavior; even after he has acted, he remains completely concealed as an individual. He must, as we know, be measured by his thoughts and feelings, and these are now expressed in his books. If only these books of his did not make it more doubtful than ever that his famed inwardness still resided in its inaccessible little temple. It would be frightful to think that this inwardness may someday disappear, leaving only that exterior—now arrogantly clumsy, now meekly indolent—as the distinguishing mark of the German. Almost as frightening to find that inwardness was still there, concealed from view, disguised, rouged and retouched, that it had become an actress, if not something worse! So Grillparzer, for instance, a detached and reflective observer, seems to conclude from his dramatic and theatrical experience. "Our feelings are abstract," he says, "we hardly any longer know how our contemporaries express their feelings. We let our feelings kick up their heels with an extravagance unknown today. Shakespeare has spoiled all us moderns."[19]

This is an individual case, and generalization may be premature. But how monstrous this generalization would be if proven accurate, if the individual cases too often imposed themselves upon the observer! How desperate would be the statement that a German's feelings are abstract, that we have all been spoiled by history—a statement that would utterly destroy every hope of a future national culture. For every hope of this kind grows from a faith in the authenticity and immediacy of German feeling, from a faith in our unimpaired inwardness. What have we to hope for, or believe in, if the spring of our belief and hope is muddied, if our inwardness has learned to kick up its heels, dance, paint its face, express itself abstractly and with calculation, and gradually dissipate? And how can a great, creative spirit exist among a people no longer certain of its inward coherence, and divided into an educated class whose inwardness has been crippled and corrupted, and an uneducated class of inaccessible inwardness? How can he exist if people have lost all solidarity of feeling; if he also knows that the feelings of those who consider themselves educated and claim to provide the nation's artists, are false and corrupt? Even if there are a few individuals here and there whose judgment has become more refined and sophisticated—this does not compensate him. It torments him that he must address himself to a mere sect, as it were, and is no longer deeply necessary to his people. Perhaps he will now prefer to bury his treasure, since he loathes being pretentiously patronized by a sect while his heart feels compassion for all. His people's instinct no longer turns toward him; it is futile for him to

19. Grillparzer, *Sämtliche Werke* (Stuttgart, 1872), 9:187. The quotation has been slightly altered.

stretch longing arms toward them. What can he do now but turn his inspired hatred against that limitation which obstructs him, against those barriers raised by the so-called culture of his people, in order at least to condemn, as judge, what for him, a vital and creative spirit, is destruction and degradation? So, for the godlike joy of creator and benefactor, he exchanges a profound insight into his fate, and ends as a lonely wise man, a disgusted sage. It is the most painful of spectacles; anyone who sees it will recognize in it a sacred urgency. He tells himself that help is needed, that the higher unity in a people's spirit and nature must be renewed, and that this gulf between inward and outward must, under the hammer blows of necessity, once again disappear. But how can he possibly help? All that is now left to him is his profound knowledge. By expressing, by diffusing, by strewing this knowledge from heaping hands, he hopes to plant a need: from strong need strong action will someday emerge. Lest there be the slightest doubt as to what I mean by this necessity, this need, this knowledge, I hereby explicitly declare that it is *German unity* in its highest sense to which we aspire, and we aspire to it more passionately than to political unity—*the unity of German spirit and life, after we have annihilated the gulf between form and content, between inwardness and convention.*

5   In five respects, it seems to me, an excess of history in a given age is hostile and dangerous to life. For it is through such an excess that the gulf between the inward and outward life, already discussed, is created, and personality thereby weakened. Through this excess an age falls victim to the conceit that it possesses, to a higher degree than any other age, that rarest of virtues—justice. Through this same excess, a people's instincts are disturbed, and both the individual and the whole society are prevented from maturing. Through this excess is distilled the belief, always damaging, that mankind has grown old, that we are its epigones and the product of its old age. Through this excess an age falls into a dangerous attitude of self-irony, and from that into an even more dangerous state of cynicism. But in a state of cynicism, an age increasingly ripens toward cunning and egoistical behavior by which the vital forces are paralyzed and finally destroyed.

To return now to our first proposition. Modern man suffers from a weakened personality. Just as a Roman of the Empire ceased to be Roman in regard to the world he had conquered; just as he lost himself in the inrush of the foreign, and degenerated in that cosmopolitan carnival of gods, arts, and customs, so modern man—who makes his historical artists prepare for him the feast of a continual world's fair—must suffer a similar fate. He has become a spectator wandering around and enjoying himself, reduced to the point where even great wars and great revolutions barely succeed in changing his condition for a moment. Even before the war is over, it has already been converted into a hundred thousand pages of printed paper; it has already been served up as the latest appetizer for the jaded palates of these historical gluttons. It seems almost impossible that a richer or stronger tone can be produced even with the most intense plucking of the strings. It promptly fades away, and in the next moment it already has a historical ring, delicately volatilized, impotent.

In moral terms: you can no longer maintain the sublime; your deeds are not rolling thunder now but sudden bursts. Accomplish great and wonderful things, they will still go down to Hades, silent and unsung. For the moment you stretch the canopy of history over your actions, art shuns you. The man who wants immediately to grasp, assess, and understand something in matters where he should, with prolonged emotion, experience the incomprehensible as the sublime, can be called rational, but only in the sense in which Schiller speaks of the reason of rational men. He cannot see things that even a child can see; he cannot hear the things that even a child can hear,[20] and these are surely the most important things. This means: he has destroyed and lost his instinct; he can no longer rely on his "divine animal," giving it free rein when his intellect vacillates and his way leads him through desert regions. So the individual becomes hesitant and uncertain, and can no longer believe in himself. He sinks down into himself, into his inwardness, or in this case into the cumulative wasteland of his knowledge, which has no outward effect, of learning which fails to become life.

Look at modern man's exterior and you will see how the expulsion of his instincts by history has almost transformed him into pure abstractions and shadows. No one any longer dares to risk his own person, but wears the mask of the cultured man, a scholar, a poet, a politician. If we take hold of these masks, in the belief that they are serious and not merely farce—for they all flaunt their seriousness—we suddenly find ourselves holding nothing but patches and tatters.

So we must refuse to be deceived, we must order them to take off their coats, or be what they seem! The authentically serious man must not become a Don Quixote; he has better things to do than tilt with such fictitious realities. He must rather scrutinize each mask closely, cry out "Halt! Who goes there?" and rip off the disguise.

Strange! One would think that history would encourage men to be *honest* above all—even if only to be honest fools. And this has always been its effect, but this is so no longer. Historical learning and the garb of bourgeois uniformity together prevail. Although "free personality" was never more glowingly spoken of, we see no personality at all, much less free personality, but merely mass man in his timid disguise. The individual has retreated inward; outwardly we see nothing more of him. And this makes us wonder

20. See Schiller, *Die Worte des Glaubens.*

whether there can in fact be causes without effects. Or do we require a generation of eunuchs to guard the great historical world-harem? Certainly pure objectivity is superbly suited to eunuchs. But it almost seems as though their task is to watch over history so that nothing comes of it except precisely more histories—surely not events!—and to prevent personalities, by means of history, from becoming "free," that is, sincere with themselves, sincere with others, both in word and deed. Only through this sincerity will the distress and inner misery of modern man be exposed. And then art and religion, like true helpers, will be able to replace that conformity and timid masquerade whose sole purpose is concealment, and jointly plant a culture that answers man's true needs and does not merely teach us, like modern culture generally, to lie about these needs, and thus become walking lies.

In an age that suffers from general education and culture, how unnatural, artificial, and utterly unworthy is the condition in which Philosophy, that goddess of naked sincerity, must find herself! In this world of enforced outward conformity, she remains a learned monologue of the man who walks alone, the chance prey of the individual who hunts her, a secret hidden in the study, or the innocent chatter of academic greybeards and children. No one dares fulfill in himself the law of philosophy, no one lives philosophically with that simple, manly loyalty that compelled an ancient, wherever he was and whatever he did, to act like a Stoic, once he had promised loyalty to the Stoa. All modern philosophizing is political and policed, limited to a learned specter by governments, churches, academies, and the customs and cowardices of men.

It stops with a wistful "if only" or the notion of "once upon a time." Whenever philosophy becomes more than ineffectual, inward knowledge, she is banned from the fold of historical culture. If only modern man were courageous and resolute, if only he were not, even in his hatreds, an inward creature, he would banish her. So he contents himself with prudishly disguising her nakedness. To be sure, he thinks, writes, publishes, speaks, and teaches philosophically—up to that point almost everything is permitted. Only in action, in what is called life, is it different. Here only one thing is permitted and everything else is simply impossible. Historical culture requires this. Are these still men, we ask ourselves, or perhaps only machines for thinking, writing, and speaking?

Goethe once said of Shakespeare: "No one despised the outward garb more than he. He knows the manner of the inner man all too well, and here all men are alike. He is said to have portrayed the Romans superbly. I disagree. They are simply flesh-and-blood Englishmen, but they are certainly men, real men, and the Roman toga fits them well."[21] Now I ask whether there is the slightest possibility of portraying our present literati,

21. See Goethe, "Shakespeare und kein Ende," 1.

popular leaders, functionaries, or politicians as Romans? Absolutely not, because they are not men, but merely incarnate compendia and, as it were, concrete abstractions. If they have a character and style of their own, it is all so deeply concealed within them that it can never emerge into the light of day. If they are men, they are men only to those who "examine their innards." To all others they are something else, not men, not gods, not animals, but products fashioned by history, fashioned through and through, mere image, form without demonstrable content, but unfortunately only bad form, and uniform at that. And so the reader should understand and ponder my thesis: *Only strong personalities can endure history; the weak are completely annihilated by it.*

Why? Because history confuses those feelings and sensibilities that are insufficiently vigorous to measure the past by themselves. The man who is afraid to trust himself, who instead instinctively interrogates history about his feelings—"How should I feel here?"—gradually, out of fear, becomes an actor and plays a role, very often many roles, and therefore performs each one badly and superficially. Gradually all congruence between a man and his historical area disappears. We see saucy little schoolboys treating the Romans as though they were their equals; and they dig and burrow in the remaining fragments of the Greek poets as though even these *corpora* were ready for them to dissect and were mere *vilia*—as their own literary *corpora* well may be.[22] One of them, let us say, is busy with Democritus; but the question always comes to my lips: Why Democritus? Why not Heraclitus? Or Philo, or Bacon? Or Descartes? And so on. And then: Why a philosopher anyway? Why not a poet, an orator? And why a Greek at all? Why not an Englishman or a Turk? Isn't the past great enough to find something in it that doesn't make you appear so ridiculously arbitrary? But, as I said, they are a generation of eunuchs. To a eunuch any woman is as good as another, merely a woman. Woman-in-Herself, the eternally unapproachable. So it does not matter what they study, so long as they—who could never themselves make history—keep history nicely "objective." And since the Eternal Feminine[23] will never draw you heavenward, you drag her down to your own level, and, being neuters yourselves, take history to be a neuter, too. But lest someone suppose I am seriously comparing history with the Eternal Feminine, let me make it clear that I rather regard history as

22. Sarcastic play on the plural of Latin *corpus*—"body" or "body of work," i.e., literary oeuvre. The philologists dissect the corpus of Greek lyric poetry as though it were—like their own writings—"cheap" stuff.

23. Goethe, *Faust*, part 2, 1,210–11. "Das Ewig-Weibliche / Zieht uns hinan" (The Eternal Feminine / Draws us upwards). The Eternal Feminine is the driving inspirational force behind earthly existence, and the impulse to human transcendence. Compare Dante's "Love that moves the sun and the other stars."

the Eternal Masculine; though for those who are in the fullest sense "historically educated," it can be no great matter whether it is masculine or feminine. For they themselves are really neither masculine nor feminine, nor even epicene, but always and only neuters, or, in more cultured terms, simply the Eternal Objective.

Once personalities have been snuffed out, in the manner described, by being reduced to eternal nonsubjectivity, or, in our terms, "objectivity," nothing can any longer affect them. Suppose something good and just happens: an action, poetry, music. Immediately the man who has been hollowed by education passes over the work and inquires about the author's biography. If the author has already done several things, he must immediately submit to an interpretation of his past development and the putative course of his future development; he is immediately compared to other authors, analyzed, dissected in regard to his choice of material and his handling of it, and then cleverly put back together again and generally chastised and reprimanded. No sooner does something remarkable occur than the historical neuters come crowding around, always ready to supervise the author from a great distance. There is an immediate echo, but it is always a "critique," whereas a little earlier the critic did not even dream of the possibility of such an achievement. At no point does the work produce an effect, but always and only another critique; and the critique itself has no effect in turn, but is simply subjected to a new critique. It is moreover agreed that many critiques are the same as a positive effect, and only a few or none a failure. But basically, despite this "effect," nothing has changed. People of course chatter for a while about some novelty, but later about some newer novelty, and in the meantime everyone does what he has always done. The historical education of our critics does not in fact permit a work to achieve a genuine effect; that is, to affect life and action. No matter how bold and black the penmanship, they immediately blot it; the most graceful design is smeared with their thick brushstrokes, which are viewed as corrections, and that again is the end of it. But their critical pens never cease flowing because they have lost control of them, and instead of guiding them are guided by them. Precisely in this excessiveness of critical effort, in this lack of self-mastery, in what the Romans call *impotentia*, the weakness of the modern personality is revealed.

6   But let these weaknesses be. Pose instead an admittedly painful question about modern man's highly acclaimed strength. Does modern man's famous historical "objectivity" give him the right to call himself strong, that is to say, *just*—juster in a higher way than men of other ages? Is it true that the course of his objectivity lies in an increased need and longing for justice? Or does this objectivity, as the effect of utterly different causes, merely give the impression that justice is the cause of its

effect? Does this objectivity, by flattering us too much perhaps, lure us into a pernicious prejudice about the virtues of modern man?—Socrates thought it was a misfortune verging on madness for anyone to imagine himself in possession of a virtue and not possess it. And this illusion is surely more dangerous than its opposite, that of suffering from a flaw, a vice. For thanks to this delusion we still might improve ourselves, whereas the former illusion makes a man or an age become daily worse—which means, in this case, more unjust.

Clearly, no one has a higher claim on our reverence than the man who possesses the instinct and the strength for justice. For in him the highest and rarest virtues are combined and concealed, just as an unfathomed sea absorbs the rivers flowing into it from every source. The hand of the just man with the authority to pass judgment no longer trembles while holding the balance. Stern with himself, he adds weight to weight; there is no flicker in his eyes as the scales rise and fall; and when he proclaims the verdict, there is no harshness or quavering in his voice. If he were a cold demon of knowledge, he would radiate the icy halo of a terrible superhuman majesty, which we would have to fear, not revere. But the fact that he is a man, still trying to rise from indulgent doubt to a stern certitude, from mild tolerance to the imperative "You must," from the rare virtue of generosity to the rarest virtue of all, justice; the fact that he now resembles that demon of knowledge, although from the very beginning he has been only an ordinary human being; and, above all, the fact that in every moment he must constantly expiate his own humanity, the tragic victim of his own impossible virtue—all this lifts him to a solitary height as the *most venerable* exemplar of the human species. For what he wants is truth, not merely as cold, inconsequential knowledge, but as an ordering and punishing judge; truth, not as a private, individual possession, but as the sacred authorization to pull up all boundary stones of egoistic possession—truth, in short, as the Last Judgment, as anything but the captured prey and plaything of the individual hunter. Only insofar as a truthful man possesses the absolute will to be just, is there any greatness in the aspiration for truth that the world so mindlessly glorifies. Whereas in the eyes of less clear-sighted men a whole host of quite different impulses—curiosity, fear of boredom, envy, vanity, frivolity—which have nothing whatever to do with truth—are confused with that aspiration toward truth which has its roots in justice.

Hence, the world indeed seems full of those who "serve the truth." Yet the virtue of justice is very rarely found, even more rarely recognized, and almost always hated with deadly hatred, whereas the regiment of seeming virtues has always been accorded honor and pomp. Few men, in truth, serve the truth, because only a few men possess the pure will to be just; and even among these only a very few possess the strength to be capable of justice. In fact, the will to be just is not enough; and man's worst miseries are the result of justice that lacks discernment. This is why the general welfare demands above all else that the seeds of judgment be sown as widely as possible so as to distinguish between fanatic and judge, and to recognize the difference between the blind desire to be judge and the ability to judge. But how can we possibly develop such discernment?—Hence, when you speak to men about truth and justice, they persistently, timidly, vacillate, doubtful whether a fanatic or a judge is speaking to them. So we should forgive them for always welcoming, with especial kindness, those "servants of truth" who lack both the will and the strength to judge, and who impose upon themselves the task of seeking knowledge which is "pure and without consequences," or more bluntly, a truth which amounts to nothing. There are many indifferent truths; there are problems whose solution costs no effort, let alone sacrifice. In these safe and indifferent areas, a man undeniably succeeds in becoming a cold demon of knowledge. But despite this! Even if, in especially favored times, whole regiments of researchers and scholars are transformed into such demons, it is still unfortunately possible that such an age suffers from the lack of great and strict justice—lacks, in short, the most noble kernel of the so-called passion for truth.

Now look at the historical virtuoso of the present. Is he the justest man of this time? True, he has cultivated in himself a sensibility so subtle and sensitive that nothing human is alien to him. Radically different times and people immediately arouse sympathetic echoes in his lyre. He has become a resonant passivity, whose vibrations in turn influence other passive natures of his kind, until finally the whole atmosphere of an age throbs with these delicately related, crisscrossing resonances. Yet it seems to me that, of every original, basic historical tone, we hear only, as it were, the corresponding overtones. The harsh, powerful quality of the original can no longer be inferred from the shrill, ethereal vibration of the echoing strings. The original tone usually awakened actions, anxiety, and terrors, whereas the echo lulls us to sleep and turns us into flabby sensualists—as though Beethoven's *Eroica* had been adapted for two flutes for the benefit of dreaming opium smokers. From this we may infer what value for these specialists is to be assigned to modern man's loftiest claim, his pretense to a higher and purer justice. This virtue of justice never has anything pleasant about it; it possesses no exciting vibrato; it is hard and terrible. Compared to this justice, how low magnanimity stands in the scale of virtues—that magnanimity which is the property of only a few, rare historians! But far greater is the number of those who only get to tolerance, to recognizing what can no longer be denied, to tidying and prettying up the past, with moderation and benevolence, on the cunning assumption that the novice reader will be led to think that an account of the past which lacks harsh tones and expressions of hatred is the virtue of justice. But only superior strength can judge;

weakness must be tolerant, unless it wants to feign strength and transform regal justice into a comic actor.

Now there still remains another frightful species of historian—good, decent, honest, serious fellows, but narrow-minded. Here we find the same strong desire to be just, the same judicial pathos; but all their verdicts are false for roughly the same reason that the decisions of ordinary juries are erroneous. How improbable, therefore, is any frequency of historical talent, even if we leave aside altogether those disguised egotists and partisans who assume very objective appearances in order to conceal their dirty games. So too we discount the truly mindless crowd of those who write history in the naive belief that all the popular views of their own age are true, and that to write in conformity with the age is quite the same as being just (a belief which sustains all religions and on which, in religions, nothing more will be said). These naive historians say that "objectivity" means judging past opinions and accomplishments by the standard of current public opinions; this is their sole criterion of all truth. Their job is to accommodate the past to the triviality of the present. Conversely, all historiography that refuses to accept these popular opinions as canonical, they call "subjective."

But might there not be an illusion in even the loftiest interpretation of the word *objectivity*? For in this sense the word implies a state of mind in the historian in which he contemplates an event so purely, with all its motives and all its consequences, that it has no effect on his subjectivity. It connotes that esthetic phenomenon, that detachment from personal interest by which a painter, in a stormy landscape threatened by lightning and thunder or on an angry sea, perceives his own inner image; it connotes complete immersion in things. But it is superstitious to suppose that the image which things reveal to a man so attuned reproduces their empirical reality. Or are we to suppose that in these moments things actively sketch, paint, or photograph themselves, so to speak, upon a purely passive mind?

This would be a mythology, and a bad mythology at that. Besides, this would mean forgetting that for the artist these are the most powerful and spontaneous moments of creativity, compositional moments of the highest kind, whose result will be a painting that is clearly artistically but not historically true. To envisage history objectively in this way is the quiet work of the dramatist and consists in imagining everything at once, in weaving isolated particulars into a whole, always on the supposition that a unity of design must be imposed on the material if it does not inhere in it already. This is how man spins his web over the past and masters it, this is how he manifests his artistic instinct—but not his instinct for truth or justice. Objectivity and justice have nothing to do with each other. We can imagine a historical writing utterly devoid of simple empirical truth, but which can still make the highest claim to objectivity. Indeed, Grillparzer boldly asserts:

What else is history but the way in which the spirit of man assimilates *impenetrable events*; in which he combines things whose relationships only God could know, and replaces the unintelligible with the intelligible; in which he introduces into a whole his own concept of an external purposiveness when there is only an internal purposiveness, and, what is more, assumes chance where a thousand little causes are at work? Every man simultaneously has his own particular necessities, so that millions of paths, crooked and straight, run along side by side, intersecting, reinforcing, and impeding one another, striving forwards or backwards, thereby assuming vis-à-vis each other the character of chance, and in so doing (apart from the influence of natural events) making it impossible to demonstrate the effective and comprehensive necessity of what happens.[24]

But it is precisely this necessity which ought now to be revealed as a result of that "objective" view of things! If stated as a historian's article of faith, this assumption can only assume a very odd form; Schiller of course is quite clear about the essentially subjective nature of this assumption when he remarks of the historian, "One phenomenon after another begins to emerge from blind chance and lawless freedom, and to take its place as a proper part of a harmonious whole—*which exists, however, solely in the historian's conceptualization.*"[25]

But what are we to think of the following assertion by a famous historical scholar—an assertion introduced with such conviction and balanced so nicely between tautology and absurdity? "It cannot be denied that all human action and behavior are subject to the course of events, events which are trivial and often undetectable, but powerful and irresistible." In an assertion like this the cryptic wisdom is no more evident than the obvious inanity, as in the maxim of Goethe's court gardener "Nature can be forced, but not compelled," or in the sign on a booth at the fair described by Swift: "Here is the largest elephant on earth, except for itself." What inconsistency is there after all between the activities of man and the course of events? I am particularly struck by the fact that historians like the one cited above cease to instruct as soon as they begin to generalize, betraying in their obscurity the sense of their weakness. In other disciplines generalizations are the crucial factor since they contain laws. But if such assertions as that cited are meant to be valid laws, then we could reply that the historian's work is wasted. For whatever truth is left in such statements, after subtracting that

24. A conflation of two different passages from Grillparzer, *Sämmtliche Werke*, 9:129 and 140.
25. A quotation from Schiller's inaugural lecture (May 26, 1789) as professor of history at Jena.

mysterious and irreducible residue we mentioned earlier, is obvious and even banal since it is self-evident to anyone with the slightest range of experience. But to make whole nations uncomfortable and devote years of tiresome labor to this effort would be like constantly amassing experimental evidence in the natural sciences when existing evidence is sufficient to establish the law in question—a pointless, supererogatory effort which, incidentally, according to Zöllner,[26] plagues modern natural science. If the value of a play lay solely in its final, governing theme, then the play itself would be the most lengthy, roundabout, and tiresome means of attaining its goal. And so I hope that history may discover that its meaning is not general ideas as the final fruit of its effort, but that its value lies precisely in the spirited retelling, enhancing, and heightening of a familiar or even ordinary theme, an everyday tune, into a comprehensive symbol, and thereby intimating in the original theme the presence of a whole world of profound meaning, power, and beauty.

But to achieve this requires above all a great artistic power, a creative buoyancy, a loving immersion in empirical data, a poetic elaboration of given types. Clearly this means objectivity, but objectivity of a positive kind. So often, however, objectivity is merely a verbal expression. In place of that imperturbable calm of the artist's gaze, inwardly flashing but outwardly dark and impassive, we get an affectation of calm, just as an absence of feeling and moral strength habitually disguise themselves as a piercing coolness of observation. In some cases that banality of mind, that vulgar wisdom, which solely by virtue of its own boredom creates the impression of disinterested calm, sallies forth disguised as that artistic state of mind in which the subject becomes silent and disappears from sight altogether. Then there is an effort to suppress everything that might excite, and the driest word is precisely the right word. Indeed, it is even thought that a man to whom a past moment *is of no concern whatever* has a vocation to describe it. This is often the relation that exists between classicists and the Greeks; neither has any relevance to the other—and this, too, is then called "objectivity." But when it is a case of describing precisely the noblest and rarest things, then this deliberate, pretentious indifference, this calculatedly cold and pedestrian exposition, is utterly revolting—when, that is, the historian's *vanity* drives him to this indifference posing as objectivity. Moreover, our judgment of these historians should be based specifically on the principle that a man is vain precisely to the degree that he lacks intelligence. No, at least be honest! Don't affect the appearance of that artistic power which can truly be called "objectivity"; don't pursue the semblance of justice unless you are dedicated to the terrible mission of justice. As though it were the duty of each age to be just to everything in the past! Besides, no age or generation ever has the right to

26. Johann Karl Friedrich Zöllner (1834–82), German astronomer.

pass judgment on all preceding ages and generations. This uncomfortable mission falls only and always to individuals, and only to the rarest among them. Who then compels *you* to judge? And then too—ask yourselves if you could be just, even if you wanted? As judges you must stand above what you are judging, whereas you have merely come later. The last guest to arrive at the table rightly deserves the last place, yet you want the head of the table? But in that case at least do the noblest and greatest deed. Perhaps then, even though you come last, a place will really be found for you.

Only from the highest power of the present can you interpret the past. Only by the most vigorous exertion of your noblest qualities will you sense what in the past is great and worth knowing and preserving. Like for like!

Otherwise you drag the past down to your own level. Do not trust history unless it springs from the most extraordinary mind; the quality of the historian's mind becomes apparent whenever he has to express a general truth or restate a familiar truth. The true historian must have the power of making the familiar sound like something wholly new, and of stating universal laws with such simplicity and profundity that we overlook the simplicity because of the profundity, and the profundity because of the simplicity. No man can be a great historian, an artist, and a simpleton at the same time. But those drudges charged with the task of carting, storing, and winnowing do not deserve our contempt simply because they cannot become great historians. Still less should we confuse them with great historians. Rather, we should recognize them as the journeymen and apprentices required for their master's service, just as the French, for example, with greater innocence than is possible for Germans, used to speak of "les historiens de M. Thiers."[27] These workers should eventually become great scholars, but they can never, by dint of diligence, become masters. The same hat easily fits both a great scholar and a simpleton.

In sum, only men of experience and superiority can write history. The man whose experience is not higher and greater than all other men's cannot understand the greatness and sublimity of the past. The past always speaks with oracular voice. Only as master builders of the future, who understand the present, will you comprehend it. The only conceivable explanation we can now offer for the extraordinarily deep and pervasive influence of the Delphic oracle is that the priests of Delphi were scrupulous students of the past; we must now recognize that only those who build the future have a right to judge the past. By looking ahead, by setting a great goal for yourself, you also master that excessive analytical drive which now devastates your present and makes all calm, all peaceful growth and ripening impossible.

---

27. Louis Adolphe Thiers (1797–1877), French statesman and historian. His reputation as a historian rests mainly upon his ten-volume *Histoire de la révolution française* and his immense (and diffuse) *Historire du Consulat et de l'Empire.*

Enclose yourself in a great barricade of hope, a hopeful striving. Form a mental image to which the future must correspond and forget your false conviction that you are epigones. You have enough to think about and discover as you meditate on that future life; but don't ask history to show you how and by what means. If, instead, you revive in yourselves the biographies of great men, they will teach you the highest commandment of all, to ripen and escape the paralyzing spell of modern education—whose true purpose is *not* to let you ripen, in order to control you and exploit you in your unripeness. And if you want biographies, shun those books with titles like *The Life and Times of*————, and choose instead a biography subtitled *A Fighter against His Time*. Steep your mind in Plutarch and dare to believe in yourself as you believe in his heroes. With a hundred men educated in this unmodern way, that is, with men who have ripened into themselves and are accustomed to the heroic, we could reduce the whole noisy sham of modern culture to eternal silence.

7   When the *uncontrolled* historical sense prevails and reveals all its implications, it uproots the future by destroying illusions and depriving existing things of the only atmosphere in which they can live. Historical justice, even when applied in a true and pure-hearted way, is therefore a frightening virtue because it always undermines and destroys living things. Its judgment is always a destruction. If no constructive urge is at work behind the historical urge; unless demolition and clearing away are carried out in the hope that a future, already alive in hope, may build its home on the cleared ground; if justice alone rules, then the creative instinct is weakened and discouraged. A religion, for instance, which is converted into historical knowledge under the jurisdiction of pure justice, a religion thoroughly and scientifically analyzed, will also finally be destroyed by this process. The reason is that historical research inevitably reveals so much falsehood, coarseness, inhumanity, absurdity, and violence that the compassionate atmosphere of illusion, indispensable to everything that wants to live, necessarily vanishes. But only in love, only in the shadow of the illusion of love, does man create; that is, only when he believes unconditionally in perfection and truth. A man who is unconditionally forced to surrender love is severed from the roots of his own strength; he inevitably withers, that is, becomes dishonest.

In such effects art is opposed to history. And only when history can be transformed into a work of art—that is, become pure artistic creation—can it perhaps preserve or even awaken instincts. But such historiography would be wholly at odds with the analytical and anti-artistic temper of our times; indeed, it would be regarded as a perversion of it. But history which, unless guided by a constructive instinct, only destroys, eventually makes its instruments jaded and unnatural. For such men destroy illusions, and "the man who destroys illusion in himself and others is punished by Nature, the strictest of all tyrants."[28]

For a while, of course, one may take up the study of history quite ingenuously and unconsciously, as though one vocation were as good as any other. Modern theology in particular seems to have devoted itself to the study of history out of pure naiveté, and even now it tries to ignore the fact that by so doing it serves, no doubt quite unwillingly, Voltaire's *Écrasez [l'infâme]*. No need to assume, behind this theological concern with history, the existence of fresh, vigorous, and constructive instincts; otherwise we would have to accept the so-called Protestant League as the matrix of a new religion and perhaps the jurist Holtzendorff[29] (who edited and introduced what has been widely dubbed as the Protestant Bible) as John the Baptist by the River Jordan. This innocence will perhaps for some time be propagated by Hegelian philosophy, still smoldering on in the heads of the older generation through its distinction between the "idea of Christianity" and its many imperfect "phenomenal forms," thereby allowing us to believe that the "passion of the Idea" is to reveal itself in ever purer forms, and finally to attain its purest, most transparent, indeed almost invisible, form in the mind of the contemporary *theologus liberalis vulgaris*.[30] But if one listens impartially to what this supremely purified form of Christianity says about the earlier impure forms of Christianity, he often gets the impression that the subject is not so much Christianity, as—well, what are we to think when we find Christianity described by the "greatest theologian of the century" as the religion which can "empathize with all actual religions and other merely potential religions," and when the "true Church" is necessarily a church which "becomes a fluid mass in which there are no extruding parts, in which every part is found at every point, and everything tranquilly blends together"—again, what are we to think?

What can be learned from Christianity is that it has become apathetic and unnatural through historicizing treatment, and in the end a totally historical—that is, a just—treatment has now reduced it to pure knowledge about Christianity, thereby destroying it. This same process can be observed in connection with any living thing; its life ceases when completely dissected; it becomes painfully sick the moment we begin to dissect it historically. There are men who believe in the healing, revolutionary, and reforming influence of music among Germans. To them it is an outrage and a crime against what is most vital in our culture that composers like Mozart and

---

28. This passage from Goethe is taken word for word, along with alterations, from Eduard von Hartmann, *Die Philosophie des Unbewussten* (Berlin, 1869), 620.
29. Franz von Holtzendorff (1828–89), jurist and professor at Berlin and, later, Munich, an authority on civil and criminal law.
30. "ordinary liberal theologian"

Beethoven should now be swamped by the learned zeal of biographies and tortured by historical criticism to yield the answers to a thousand impertinent questions. Is not a man's living influence destroyed or at least paralyzed long before being exhausted, when curiosity is directed to the countless trivial aspects of his life and work, and intellectual problems are sought precisely where we should learn to live and forget all problems? Imagine transporting a few of these modern biographers to the birthplace of Christianity or the Lutheran Reformation; their cold, pragmatic curiosity would be just enough to render every spiritual *actio in distans*[31] quite impossible— just as the most pitiful animal can, by eating the acorn, prevent the mightiest oak from sprouting. Every living thing needs a surrounding atmosphere, a shrouding aura of mystery. If this shroud is removed, if a religion, an art, a genius is condemned to move like a star without an atmosphere, no wonder they soon harden, dry up, and cease to bear. So it is with all great things "which never without some illusion prosper," as Hans Sachs puts it in *Die Meistersinger.*

But every nation, indeed every man, that wants to reach *maturity* needs such an enveloping illusion, such a protective, concealing cloud. Yet at present we hate the process of becoming mature because we honor history more than life. Indeed, we rejoice in the fact that "scientific methods are beginning to govern life." Conceivably this may happen. But surely a life so governed is nearly worthless, since it is far less *life*, and promises far less life for the future, than the life which was once governed not by knowledge, but by instinct and vigorous illusions. But this age of ours should certainly not be, as observed earlier, one of complete, fully developed and harmonious personalities, but one of shared and, as much as possible, productive labor. In other words: men must be adapted to the goals of the present so they can be put to work as soon as possible. They must labor in the factory of public utility before maturing, indeed in order to keep them from maturing—because maturity would be a luxury that would subtract a quantum of energy from the "labor market." There are birds which are blinded to make them sing better; I am not convinced that modern man sings more beautifully than his grandfather, but I do know that he has been blinded in his youth. And the instrument, the vile instrument, which is used to blind him is knowledge and learning, a *light* which is *too bright, too sudden, too varied.* A young man is literally flogged through the millennia; boys utterly ignorant of war, diplomacy, and the politics of commerce are presumed to be worthy of instruction in political history. But just as the young race through history, so we moderns race through art galleries or listen to concerts. We may well feel that one concert sounds different from another, or that one affects us differently from another, constantly losing our sense of surprise, no longer

31. "action at a remove," i.e., "distanced action"

being awed by anything, and, finally, being pleased with everything—this is now called the historical sense, historical culture.

In plain words, young minds are so overwhelmed by the mass of material imposed upon them, so enormous, astonishing, barbaric, and violent, so "tangled into hideous knots," that they can save themselves only by deliberate apathy. In those of finer and stronger sensibility, another symptom may even appear—nausea. In this way the young person is alienated, he becomes suspicious of all traditions and ideas. Now he knows that every age is different, what you're like changes nothing. In depressed indifference he discards one opinion after another, and he understands what Hölderlin felt when he read Diogenes Laertius on the lives and teachings of the Greek philosophers;: "Here I have once again experienced something I have often noticed before, that the transience and mutability of human ideas and systems affected me almost more tragically than those tragedies which are usually called the only real ones."[32]

No, so overwhelming, stupefying, and violent an exposure to history is surely unnecessary to youth, as the ancients demonstrate; and it is exceedingly dangerous, as the moderns demonstrate. But now consider the student of history, the heir almost from childhood of a precocious apathy. Now, for his own work he has acquired the "method," the right touch and the superior tone, of his master; a totally isolated little chapter of the past has fallen victim to his acumen and the method he has learned. He has already produced, or to put it more arrogantly, he has already "created"; he has now actually become a servant of the truth and a master of the world-domain of history. If he was already "accomplished" as a boy, he is now over-accomplished; we need only shake him and his wisdom falls into our arms with a plop. But the wisdom is rotten, and every apple has its worm.

Believe me: if men must labor in the factories of scientific scholarship before they ripen, then scholarship itself will be ruined as swiftly as these factory slaves whom it employs all too early. I regret having at this point to use the jargon of slave-owners and bosses to designate relationships which should properly be viewed as free of utility and exempt from life's necessities. But the words *factory, labor market, supply, productivity*—notice how these expansions of egoism sound—come spontaneously to the lips when one wants to describe the most recent generation of scholars. Solid mediocrity becomes ever more mediocre; scientific scholarship is becoming, in an economic sense, ever more profitable. Actually the youngest scholars are wise in one respect only, though in this wiser than all the men of the past, but in every other respect they are only immensely different—to put it mildly—from all scholars of the old school. Nonetheless, they demand honor and benefits, as though the state and public opinion were obliged to

32. See Hölderlin's letter to Isaak von Sinclair, Dec. 24, 1798.

accept this new currency contract and decree that genius is superfluous—
by restamping every teamster a genius; but a later age is likely to see that
their structures were only collectively carted, not collectively built. I would
say clearly and plainly to those who tirelessly sound the modern cry to battle
and sacrifice—"Division of labor!" "Join the ranks!"—that if you want to
promote scientific scholarship as swiftly as possible, you will also ruin it as
soon as possible, just as pullets are ruined by being forced to lay too many
eggs unnaturally.

Admittedly, scholarship in recent decades has advanced remarkably fast,
but look at the scholars too, all those exhausted pullets. They cackle more
than ever, not because their natures are more "harmonious," but because
they lay eggs more frequently; yet their eggs have become increasingly small
(but their books have gotten bigger). The natural and final result of this
process is the universally applauded "popularization" (along with "femini-
zation" and "infantization") of scholarship; that is, the infamous fitting of
the garment of scholarship to the body of the "general public"—to make
deliberate use of tailor's German to describe a tailor's task. Goethe saw in
this an abuse and called upon the scholarly disciplines to affect the outside
world only by means of a higher practice. Moreover, older generations of
scholars had good reason to regard this abuse as oppressive and burden-
some. For equally good reasons the younger scholars find it quite easy,
since, aside from their little niche of knowledge, they themselves are a part
of the general public and share its needs. Simply by settling comfortably
into their chairs, they manage to open up their own little field of study to
the compulsive curiosity of the general mixed public. They then term this
act of accommodation "the modest condescension of the scholar to his
public," but in fact that scholar, insofar as he is not learned but vulgar, has
only condescended to himself.

No matter how you conceive of the "people," you can never form a
concept sufficiently noble and lofty. If you regarded the people as capable
of greatness, you would be compassionate with them, and would take care
not to offer them your historical *acquafortis*[33] as a rejuvenating elixir of life.
But in your heart of hearts you think poorly of them, since you cannot,
deeply and sincerely, respect their future. And you act like practical pessimists; that is, like men living with the presentiment of disaster—men who
have grown indifferent and careless about the welfare of others, indeed,
even about their own. "If only the earth will still support *us*! But if it no
longer will, that's all right too." Thus they feel, and live, an *ironic* existence.

8   It may seem very odd, but surely not contradictory, that I should attribute to our age, so accustomed to loud and en-

---

33. Diluted form of nitric acid.

thusiastic outbursts of reckless jubilation over its historical culture, a kind of *ironic self-consciousness*, a haunting suspicion that there may be no reason for rejoicing, a fear that all the enjoyment of historical knowledge may soon be done with. A similar puzzle regarding individual personalities has been provided us by Goethe in his remarkable study of Newton. He discovers at the base (more precisely, at the peak) of Newton's being "an obscure presentiment of his own error, an expression, as it were, observable only in rare moments, of heightened, critical awareness which had attained a certain ironic perspective of its own necessary inner nature." Similarly we find, precisely in the greater and more highly developed historians, an awareness, often reduced to a general skepticism, of the great absurdity and superstition in the belief that a nation's education should be as radically historical as ours now is. Whereas the strongest nations, strong in both deeds and works, have lived differently from us, have educated their youth in a different way.

But this absurdity, this superstition, suits us—or so the skeptical objection runs—because we are the latecomers, the last, anemic descendants of strong and happy generations—the very generation predicted by Hesiod when he said that someday men would suddenly be born with gray hair, and that Zeus, as soon as he saw this visible sign, would destroy them. Historical culture is in fact a kind of congenital grayness, and those who bear the mark of it from childhood are destined to achieve an instinctive belief in the *old age of mankind.* But old age is quite properly devoted to the activities of old men, that is, to looking backwards, making its reckonings, concluding accounts, seeking comfort in the past by means of memory—in short, historical culture. But the human species is tough and tenacious, and it dislikes being observed in its steps—forwards and backwards—after several thousands of years, or hardly even after hundreds of millennia; that is, mankind as a whole does *not want* to be observed from the perspective of that infinitesimally small atomic mite, the individual man. For what do a few millennia (or, alternatively, the span of thirty-four consecutive human lives of sixty years) matter, if at the beginning we can speak of the "youth" of the species, and of its "old age" at the end?

Isn't there rather a tincture in this paralyzing belief that mankind is already decaying, a misunderstanding bequeathed us by the Middle Ages, of the Christian theological concept of the imminent end of the world, of the dread expectation of the Last Judgment? Could it be that this concept has disguised itself as an increased need for historical judgment, as though our age, the last possible, age, were authorized to pronounce, on the whole human past, the Last Judgment—a judgment which Christianity expected not from man, but from the "Son of Man"? In the past, this memento mori,[34] addressed to the species as well as the individual, was a terribly

34. "Remember you are mortal."

painful goad, the summit, as it were, of knowledge and conscience in the Middle Ages. But the reply of the modern age—*memento vivere*[35]—sounds, to speak frankly, quite timid; it lacks resonance; there is a hint of insincerity. For mankind is still fixed on the old memento mori, as its universal historical need makes clear. Knowledge, despite very energetic beating of its wings, is still earthbound and cannot fly; a deep sense of hopelessness persists, and it has taken on that historical coloring which now casts a depressing gloom over all higher education and culture. A religion which regards the last hours of a human life as the most important, which predicts the end of all earthly existence and condemns the living to live in the fifth act of a tragedy, certainly will arouse the profoundest and noblest resources; but it is hostile to all new cultivation, all daring experiment, free desiring. It is opposed to every flight into the unknown, since it feels neither love nor hope for such a flight. Against its wishes, it lets events take their own course in order to choose the right moment for repudiating them, or for sacrificing them as corruptors of life, as a lie about the value of existence. What the Florentines did when, under the influence of Savonarola's call to repentance, they organized those notorious bonfires of paintings, manuscripts, mirrors, and masks, is precisely what Christianity would like to do to every culture that incites men to further striving and adopts *memento vivere* as its motto. And when it proves impossible to do this directly without subterfuge, which is to say, by violence, it achieves its purpose just as effectively by allying itself with historical culture, usually without being detected. And then, speaking in the name of this culture, it shrugs off all new movements, enveloping them in the feeling that they are too late, the work of epigones— in short, that they are congenitally gray. The bitter and profoundly depressing reflection that no event has any value, that the world is ripe for judgment, is dissipated into the skeptical conviction that it is good at least to know everything that has happened because it is too late to do something better. In this way the historical sense makes its servants passive and retrospective; and it is almost solely in a moment of forgetfulness, when the historical sense is absent, that the man who is ill of historical fever is able to act. But no sooner is the action done, then he dissects it, and, by analyzing it thoroughly, prevents it from continuing to have an effect, finally stripping it bare and reducing it to "history." In this sense we are still living in the Middle Ages, and history is still for us a camouflaged theology, just as the reverence with which the layman regards the learned is a reverence passed on from the clergy. What people once gave to the Church, they now give, less generously, to education. But the fact that they give anything at all derives from the Church, not from the modern spirit, which, despite its other good traits, is notoriously stingy and, in the aristocratic virtue of generosity, a bungler.

35. "Remember you are alive."

This observation is perhaps distasteful, as distasteful perhaps as my derivation of the excess of history from the medieval memento mori and Christianity's profound hopelessness in regard to the whole future of our earthly existence. But the reader will provide better explanations than those which I have somewhat hesitantly advanced; for the origin of historical culture—as well as its intrinsic and absolutely radical inconsistency with the spirit of a "new age," a modern consciousness—*must* itself in turn be historically understood. And the problem of history *must* also be solved by history itself; knowledge *must* apply the goad to knowledge. This triple *must* is the spiritual imperative of the "new age," provided that this age genuinely contains something new, powerful, original, something that promises life. Or, leaving aside the Latin notions, is it true that we Germans must always remain mere "descendants" in all the higher areas of culture simply because this is all we are *capable* of being? In a statement worth pondering, Wilhelm Wackernagel[36] once asserted: "We Germans are a nation of descendants; in all our higher knowledge, even in our beliefs, we are mere descendants of the ancient world. Even those who are bitterly opposed to that role, never cease breathing in, with the spirit of Christianity, the immortal spirit of ancient classical culture; and even if they succeeded in separating these two elements from the atmosphere in which they live and breathe, little would be left to sustain us in our spiritual lives." But even if we gladly accepted this fate of being the descendants of antiquity, even if we resolved to accept it energetically, seriously, and with greatness, and to acknowledge this very energy as our unique distinction and privilege, we would still have to ask whether we were forever doomed to be the *disciples of an ancient world in decline.* Someday in the future we might be permitted to set our sights progressively higher and farther; someday we should perhaps be able to praise ourselves for the splendid and creative renewal in ourselves—even by means of our universal history—of the spirit of Hellenistic and Roman civilization—a renewal so splendid that we may, as our supreme reward, set ourselves the still greater task of going back in time far beyond this Alexandrian culture, and with bold gaze seeking our models in that primitive and archaic Greek world of the great, the natural, and the human. *But there we also find the reality of a basically unhistorical culture, a culture which, despite its lack of history or rather precisely because of it, is unbelievably rich and vital.* Even if we Germans were nothing but descendants, we could, by viewing this culture as our inheritance, ours for the taking, find no greater or higher destiny than being "descendants."

I mean to say this and only this: that even the thought, so often painful, that we are epigones can, greatly imagined, guarantee to both the individual

36. Wilhelm Wackernagel (1808–69), distinguished Germanist, editor of Hartmann and Walther von der Vogelweide.

and the nation generous results and a hopeful hunger for the future. It can do so insofar as we regard ourselves as the heirs and descendants of remarkable and classical powers and see in this our honor, our incentive. Then we will not be the pale, emaciated, last descendants of vigorous generations, eking out chilly lives as the antiquaries and gravediggers of those generations. Clearly, such late-born offspring live an ironical existence; annihilation follows their steps as they hobble through life. They shudder when they enjoy the past since they are living memories; but without heirs their memory is meaningless. So they are overwhelmed by the gloomy suspicion that their life is a wrong since no future life can justify it.

But let us imagine that these late offspring, turned antiquarians, suddenly exchanged their sad, ironic resignation for outright impudence. Imagine them loudly, shrilly, proclaiming that the race has reached its peak since it now finally possesses self-knowledge and has become open and honest with itself. The result would be a spectacle that would, as in a simile, explain the puzzling significance for German culture of a certain famous philosophy. I believe that there has not been a dangerous turn or crisis in German culture in this century which has not become more dangerous because of the enormous and still spreading influence of this Hegelian philosophy. Clearly the belief that we are the late offspring of the ages is enervating and depressing; but then brazenly one fine day to turn this belief upside down in order to deify ourselves as the true meaning and purpose of all previous history, defining our own conscious misery as the consummation of world history—this would be monstrous and destructive. Such a way of thinking has accustomed Germans to talking about the "world-process" and justifying their own age as the inevitable result of this world-process; this way of thinking has established history in the place of the other spiritual powers, art and religion, as sole sovereign, insofar as it is the "self-realizing concept," the "dialectic of the spirit of nations," and the "universal judgment."

This Hegelian notion of history has been scornfully dubbed God's sojourn on earth (though this God himself was first created by means of history). But in Hegelian heads this God has become visible and intelligible to himself and has already ascended all the dialectically possible stages of his Becoming up toward this self-revelation. Thus, for Hegel the climax and terminal point of world-process coincide with his own Berlin existence. Indeed, he might have claimed that everything after Hegel should be regarded as a mere musical coda of the world-historical rondo, or, more precisely, as superfluous. He did not claim this; instead he has instilled in the generations nurtured in his philosophy that admiration for the "power of history" which in point of fact is constantly transformed into naked admiration of success and leads to idolatry of the fact—a form of behavior which we now, in a very mythical and also truly German way, tend to call "taking account of the facts." But once a man has learned to bow and scrape before the "power of history," sooner of later, like a Chinese puppet, he nods approval to every power, whether that of government, public opinion, or numerical majority, dancing in perfect time to the tune of any "power" that pulls his strings. If every success contains its own rational necessity; if every event is a victory of the logical or the "Idea," then fall to your knees this minute and kowtow to the whole scale of "successes"! What, are we no longer ruled by mythologies? What, are religions dying out? But look at the religion of historical power! Observe the priests of the mythology of ideas, note their bruised knees! Aren't all the virtues adherents of this new belief? Or isn't it self-denial when the historical man allows himself to be flattened into an objective crystal mirror? Isn't it magnanimous to reject all force in heaven and on earth by adoring in every force only force itself? Isn't it justice always to hold the scales of power in your hand and carefully observe which pan sinks, which is the stronger and heavier power? And what an education in "propriety" is this view of history! To accept everything objectively, never to be angered by anything, to love nothing and understand everything—how soft and submissive this makes a man! And even if someone reared in this school is publicly irritated and exasperated, we find it pleasant because we know very well that everything is being done for artistic effect, that it is *ira* and *studium*, but utterly *sine ira et studio*.[37]

My thoughts about this pastiche of mythology and virtue are very old-fashioned. But, however ludicrous, they must be expressed. So I would say that history always teaches "Once upon a time . . ." and morality always says "Thou shalt not" or "Thou shouldst not have. . . ." Therefore, history is a compendium of effective immorality. How grave an error it would be to view history at the same time as the judge of this effective immorality! It is, for example, a moral outrage that Raphael should die at thirty-six; a man like Raphael should never die. If, as apologists of the actual, you wish to come to the aid of history, you will say that Raphael expressed everything that was in him; longer life would only have enabled him to repeat himself, not to create new beauty, etc., etc. You would thereby become the devil's advocate, precisely because you idolize the event, the fact; but the fact itself is always stupid and has always resembled a calf more than a god. Besides, as apologists of history, your prompter is ignorance, since it is only your ignorance of a *natura naturans*[38] like Raphael that hinders you from being

37. The Roman historian Tacitus avowed (*Annals* 1.1) that he would write "sine ira et studio" (without indignation and partisan involvement). But Nietzsche is here playing upon the German word *Studium*, a formal course of studies grounded in scholarly detachment and "objectivity."

38. Scholastic term meaning "nourishing" or "creative nature," usually opposed to *natura naturata*, i.e., "created" or even "man-made" nature. Compare, for instance, the dialogue

outraged that he lived and will never live again. Somebody recently tried to tell the world that Goethe at eighty-two had exhausted himself. Yet I would happily exchange whole cartloads of fresh, ultramodern lives for a few years of the exhausted Goethe, simply to take part in conversations like those with Eckermann, and, by so doing, spare myself all the modish teachings of the legionnaires of the present moment. How few men there are, in comparison with the great dead, who really deserve to live! That the many live and these few no longer do, is nothing but a brutal truth, an irremediable stupidity, a crude "That's the way things are" as opposed to the moral response, "Things shouldn't be that way." Yes, as opposed to morality! Mention what virtue you will; speak of justice, generosity, bravery; talk of wisdom and human compassion—in every case the man of virtue rebels against the blind power of facts, against the tyranny of the actual, subjecting himself to laws which are not the laws of historical flux. He always swims against the tide of history, whether he is struggling against his passions as the most immediate, stupid "given" fact of his existence, or devoting himself to honesty, while the lie everywhere around him weaves its glistening nets.

If history were nothing more than "the universal system of passion and error," mankind would have to read it in the same way Goethe advises it to read *The Sorrows of Young Werther*: as though it shouted, "Be a man and do not follow me!" But, fortunately, history also preserves for us the memories of the great fighters *against history*, that is, against the blind power of actuality, and indicts itself by exalting as truly historical men precisely those who disregard "the way things are" in their serenely proud quest of "the way things ought to be." What drives them indefatigably lies not in carrying their generation to the grave, but in creating a new generation. And if they themselves were born latecomers—there is a way of living which annuls the memory of that fact—future generations will know them only as the forerunners.

9   Is our age perhaps such a forerunner? In point of fact, our historical sense is so vehement, expressing itself in such sweep-

between Perdita and Polixenes in Shakespeare's *Winter's Tale*, iv, 4, 86ff.:

Perdita: For I have heard it said
        There is an art which in their [gillyvors] piedness shares
        With great creating nature.
Polixenes: Say there be;
        Yet nature is made better by no mean
        But nature makes that mean: so, over that art,
        Which you say adds to nature, is an art
        That nature makes. . . .
                        This is an art
        Which does mend nature—change it rather—but
        The art itself is nature.

ing and absolute language, that in this respect at least our age will be honored as a forerunner by future ages—assuming, of course, that there will actually be *future ages*, that is, cultured ages. But this very assumption remains gravely doubtful. Directly related to modern man's pride are his *irony* about himself, his awareness that he must live in a historicizing and twilight atmosphere, as it were, his fear that in the future he will be quite unable to preserve his youthful hopes and vigor. Here and there some go further, they become *cynical*, quite literally justifying the course of history, indeed the evolution of the world, for modern man's convenience according to the cynical axiom that everything was destined to be precisely what it now is. Men had to become what they now are and not something else, and against this "necessity" there can be no rebellion. The comfort afforded by this kind of cynicism is a refuge for those who cannot bear to live ironical lives. Besides, the last decade has provided them with one of its finest inventions, a rich and sonorous rhetoric for their cynicism; their opportunistic and mindless mode of living is now dubbed "the total surrender of personality to the world-process."

Personality and the world-process! World-process and the personality of the flea! If only we were not endlessly forced to listen to this most hyperbolic of hyperboles—the word *world, world, world,* inasmuch as it is only about *man, man, man* that we can, with honesty, speak. Heirs of the Greeks and Romans? Of Christianity? All this seems insignificant to these cynics. But heirs of the world-process! Apex and goal of the world-process! Ripest fruit on the tree of knowledge, meaning and solution of the whole riddle of Becoming—this is what I call inflated grandeur—the sign by which the first forerunners of all epochs can be recognized, even if they are the latest of latecomers. Never, even in dreams, has the conception of history soared so high. For human history has now become merely the continuation of the development of plants and animals; indeed, in the lowest depths of the ocean, in the living slime, the historical universalist still finds traces of himself. Gazing in amazement at the immense distance already traversed by mankind, he reels before the sight of an even more incredible miracle—modern man himself, whose vision can survey this long ascent to himself. He stands tall and proud atop the pyramid of world-process; at the apex he sets the capstone of his knowledge, and he seems to shout aloud to nature listening all around him, "We have reached the peak; we are at the goal; we *are* the goal; we are the fulfillment of nature!" Overproud European of the nineteenth century, you are raving mad! Your knowledge does not fulfill nature; it merely kills your own nature. Assess your height as a man of knowledge by your depth as a man of action. True, you climb toward heaven on the sunlight of knowledge, but you also sink downwards toward chaos. Your mode of moving, the fact that you climb by what you know, is what dooms you. Earth and soil crumble uncertainly beneath you; your life has nothing to support it, nothing now but spiderwebs, torn by every fresh lunge of your knowledge. —But enough of these grim forebodings, since we can speak of more cheerful matters.

The fact that all foundations are being torn apart and destroyed with mindless rage, their dissolution into a ruinous flux of Becoming, the tireless unraveling and historicizing of everything that *has* become by modern man, the great spider tangled in the universal web—all this may interest and worry the moralist, artist, and religious man, perhaps even the statesman. But we, for our part, should for the moment be delighted to see this spectacle in the shimmering magic mirror of a *philosophical parodist,* a parodist in whose mind our age has achieved an ironical self-consciousness, and has done so with a clarity which, to use Goethe's expression, "approaches villainy." Hegel once taught us that "when the Spirit makes a sudden leap, we philosophers are there too." Our age made a leap toward self-irony, and lo, there was Eduard von Hartmann[39] too, author of the famous philosophy of the Unconscious—or more precisely, the philosophy of the ironic unconscious. Rarely have we read a more humorous fiction or a more philosophical fraud than Hartmann's work. Anyone whom he fails to enlighten, indeed, utterly re-educate, on the subject of *becoming* clearly deserves to be called a "has-been." The beginning and the end of the world-process, from the first startling shock of consciousness to the final plunge back into nothingness, including the exact description of our generation's role in this world-process—all this he derives from the unconscious, the inspirational source which Hartmann so ingeniously invents, and bathes in such apocalyptic light; all this he counterfeits so cunningly, with such candor and sincerity, that it seems like serious, not merely burlesque, philosophy. — An achievement of such magnitude establishes Hartmann as one of the leading philosophical parodists of all times; so let us make sacrifice upon his altar, let us sacrifice a lock of hair to Hartmann, the inventor of a genuine panacea—to borrow Schleiermacher's[40] formula of admiration. For what better cure for the excessively historical bent of our culture could there be than Hartmann's parody of all world history?

---

39. Eduard von Hartmann (1842–1906), metaphysician and author of *Die Philosophie des Unbewussten* (1869), whose liberal and optimistic spirit captured a wide and admiring readership in Nietzsche's Germany. Essentially late romantic in its outlook, it stressed both traditional teleology and irrationalism, based upon a perversion of Schopenhauer— whence, in part, Nietzsche's persistent contempt for Hartmann—fashionably adulterated with doctrines drawn from Fichte, Schelling, and Hegel. In the main, however, Hartmann's philosophy is an effort to combine Schopenhauer's notion of the Will with Hegel's ideas of the unconscious self-realization and revelation of the Idea or Reason in human history.

40. Friedrich Daniel Ernst Schleiermacher (1768–1834), the most eminent German Protestant theologian of the romantic period.

If we were to state succinctly the oracle pronounced by Hartmann from his smoky tripod of unconscious irony, we would say: he proclaims that our age must only remain precisely what it is, if humanity is someday to become truly glutted with existence—a belief with which I heartily concur. That alarming ossification of our age, that restless rattling of bones—which David Strauss has naively described as the most splendid concrete reality—is justified by Hartmann not only from the standpoint of the past, *ex causis efficientibus*,[41] but even on the basis of the future, *ex causa finali*.[42] From the Day of Judgment back to the present, this scoundrel floods his light on our age, and he finds it very good; that is, for those who want to suffer as much as possible from the indigestibility of life, for whom Judgment Day cannot arrive too soon. True, Hartmann refers to the age which humanity is now approaching as its "manhood,"[43] but, according to his description, this manhood will be a blissful state in which there is nothing but "solid mediocrity,"[44] and art will be the equivalent of "a late evening's farce for, say, a Berlin stockbroker";[45] a period in which "we no longer need genius, since that would be throwing pearls before swine, or even because the age has progressed beyond the stage at which genius is relevant, to a more important stage"[46]—that is, to the period of social development in which every worker "has working hours allowing him sufficient leisure for his intellectual improvement, and leads a comfortable life." Scoundrel of scoundrels, you express modern man's yearning; but you also know what sort of specter will appear at the end of this manhood of mankind as a result of that intellectual education toward solid mediocrity. I mean *nausea*. Obviously things are wretchedly bad, but our wretchedness will become much worse—clearly "the Antichrist will gain more and more ground."[47] But we are wretched of *necessity*, and it must *necessarily* happen, for only in this way can we enter on the good road—to the feeling of disgust for every living thing. "So, as laborers in the vineyard of the Lord, let us strive vigorously to advance the world-process, since only process can bring us to our redemption!"[48]

The vineyard of the Lord! The process! The road to redemption! Is there anyone who cannot see that here historical culture, which knows only the word *becoming*, deliberately disguises itself behind this caricature, saying the most petulant things about itself behind its grotesque mask? For what does

---

41. "through efficient causes"
42. "through a final cause"
43. *Philosophie*, 619ff.
44. Ibid., 618.
45. Ibid., 619.
46. Ibid., 619.
47. Ibid., 610.
48. Ibid., 637–38.

this final fraudulent appeal to the laborers in the vineyard really ask of them? What task should they vigorously strive to advance? Or, to put it another way, what tasks remain to be performed by the man of historical culture, the modern fanatic of process, swimming and drowning in the river of becoming, in order someday to harvest this vineyard's most delectable grape—nausea? —All he can do is to go on living as he has lived, loving what he has always loved, hating what he has always hated, and reading the newspapers he has always read. For him there is only one sin—living in a different way. But his way of life is described to us with extraordinary, lapidary clarity on that celebrated page, its propositions printed in bold capitals, that page over which all the cultural scum of the present are so blindly rapturous and ecstatic, believing it to be the vindication of their own lives, one which they read in an apocalyptic light. For every individual the unconscious parodist required "the full surrender of his personality to the world-process, for the sake of its goal, the redemption of the world."[49] Or even more clearly and distinctly: "The affirmation of the will to live is now the only thing whose rightness can be asserted; for only in the full surrender to life and its sorrows, not in cowardly personal resignation and withdrawal, can anything be done for the world-process";[50] and: "The striving toward individual negation of the will is as foolish and useless, indeed even more foolish, than suicide";[51] and: "The thoughtful reader will understand without further explanations what form a practical philosophy based on these principles would take, and will realize that such a philosophy must necessarily embrace a full reconciliation with life, not an estrangement from it."[52]

The thoughtful reader will understand. As though Hartmann could be *mis*understood! And how incredibly funny is the fact that he was misunderstood! Are modern Germans very subtle? An observant Englishman feels that they lack "delicacy of perception"; indeed, he boldly says that "in the German mind there does seem to be something splay, something blunt-edged, unhandy, and infelicitous."[53] Perhaps our great German parodist would care to object? True, according to his explanation, we are approaching "that ideal state in which the human race makes its own history in full consciousness of what it does," but we are clearly rather far from that presumably even more ideal state in which humanity will read Hartmann's book in full consciousness. If we ever reach that state, it will be impossible for anyone to speak of "world-process" without smiling, for the phrase will

49. Ibid., 638.
50. Ibid., 638.
51. Ibid., 635–36.
52. Ibid., 638.
53. A quotation, I believe, from Walter Bagehot, whose *Physics and Politics* (1869) enjoyed very wide and enthusiastic circulation throughout Europe. See *SE*, 3 and n. 12.

recall an age when Hartmann's evangelistic parody was actually heeded, studied, debated, admired, elaborated, and canonized with all the sincerity of the "German mind" our Englishman has described, or rather, in Goethe's phrase, with "the grotesque seriousness of the owl." But the world must progress; we cannot achieve this ideal state of consciousness merely by dreaming on it; we must fight it and conquer it, and only through serenity lies the road to redemption—redemption, that is, from this owlish serious- ness. The time will come when we will wisely avoid all interpretations of the world-process, or even human history; when historians generally will no longer consider the masses, but rather those individuals who form a kind of bridge over the wild torrent of Becoming. These individuals by no means continue a process, but, thanks to history which makes concerted effort possible, they live as timeless contemporaries in that republic of genius described by Schopenhauer.[54] Across the desolate gulfs of time, giant calls to giant and, undisturbed by the noisy, clamoring dwarfs creeping around below them, the high discourse of spirits proceeds. It is the task of history to mediate between them and, by so doing, to provide fresh opportunities and to concert our forces in the creation of greatness. No, the *goal of hu- manity* cannot lie at the end of history, but only in the *highest human ex- emplars*.

   Our droll authority, of course, with that admirable dialectic of his, no less genuine than his admirers are admirable, asserts precisely the opposite:

> It would be quite as incompatible with the concept of evolution to ascribe infinite duration to the world-process in the past—since in that case every conceivable development would already have taken place, which is clearly not the case (O villain!)—as to impute to it an endless duration in the future. For both assumptions would nullify the idea of evolution towards a goal (O damnable villain!) and reduce the world- process to the vain labor of the Danaids. The completed triumph of the logical over the illogical (O damnably villainous villain!) must coin- cide, however, with the temporal end of the world-process, with the Last Judgment.[55]

No, you transparent mocker, so long as the illogical still prevails as it does at present; so long, for instance, as you can still elicit general approval for your doctrine of the "world-process," Judgment Day is still a long way off. It is still too pleasant here on earth, and many illusions still flourish (like your contemporaries' illusion about you), and we are not yet ready to plunge back into your nothingness. We believe that life here on earth will become even more pleasant when people at last begin to understand you (O mis-

---

54. *Parerga and Paralipomena*, §256.
55. Hartmann, *Philosophie*, 637.

understood, unconscious scoundrel!). But if you should, nevertheless, be overcome with nausea as you prophesied to your readers; if your description of your present and future proves to be right—and nobody has ever felt more loathing for the present and the future than you—then I am quite ready to cast my vote with the majority in the way you proposed, to end your world next Saturday evening on the stroke of midnight. And our decree will conclude: "As of tomorrow there will be no more time, and no more newspapers will appear." But if our decree has no effect and we fail to bring about the desired results, well, in any case we will still have time to perform a splendid experiment. Let us take a pair of scales; set Hartmann's unconscious in one pan and his world-process in the other. There are some men who believe that both would weigh the same since both pans hold equally bad words and equally good jokes. —When Hartmann's joke is at last understood, people will only use his phrase *world-process* in jest. But in point of fact it is high time to train every engine of satirical destruction against the excesses of the historical sense; against the immoderate delight in process at the expense of life and being; against the mindless dislocation of all perspectives. And we should always praise the author of *The Philosophy of the Unconscious* for his success in first clearly recognizing the ridiculous element in the idea of "world-process" and, thanks to the extraordinary seriousness of his argument, in making us realize the absurdity of it with even greater clarity. Why the world exists, why mankind exists, should now not trouble us in the least unless we want to joke about it; in fact, the pretension of the tiny human worm is surely the most comical, the funniest scene on the face of the earth. But why do you as an individual exist? Ask yourself this question, and if no one can tell you, then try to justify the meaning of your existence a posteriori, as it were, by determining your own purpose, a goal, a "reason why," a high and noble "reason why." Then go perish in the attempt—I can conceive of no greater aim in life than to die while attempting a great and impossible task, *animae magnae prodigus*.[56]

If, however, the doctrines of sovereign Becoming, the fluidity of all concepts, types, and species, the lack of all cardinal distinctions between man and beast—doctrines which I consider true but deadly—are inflicted on the public for another generation in the modern craze for education, then no one should be surprised if the nation perishes of egoistical triviality and misery, of ossification and selfishness, that is, if it begins to fall apart and ceases to be a nation. Then perhaps in its place organized groups of individual egoisms, brotherhoods whose purpose is the greedy exploitation of nonbrothers, and similar creations of utilitarian vulgarity, will appear. —To make ready for such groups, we have only to go on writing history from the

---

56. Literally, "prodigal of a great soul," i.e., "careless of a great life." The phrase comes from Horace *Odes* 1.12.38.

standpoint of the *masses*, exploring that viewpoint in search of those laws that can be deduced from the needs of these masses, in other words, the laws that govern the movements of society's lower strata, its loam and clay. Only in three respects does it seem to me that the masses are deserving of notice: first, as faint copies of great men, printed with worn-out plates on cheap paper; second, as resistance to the great; and third, as instruments of the great. For anything else, let the devil and the statistician have them. What, can statistics prove that there are laws in history? Laws? Yes, they prove how vulgar and disgustingly uniform the masses are. Are we to apply the term *laws* to the effects of gravity, stupidity, mimicry, love, and hunger? Well, suppose we grant it; but if so, the corollary is also true: insofar as there are laws in history, the laws are worthless and history is worthless. But at present the style of history most admired is precisely that which views the great instincts of the masses as crucial and paramount, and all great men as merely the clearest expression of these drives, quite as though great men were simply bubbles floating on that great mass-tide. Thus, the masses presumably generate greatness, in the same way that chaos of itself gives birth to order; and, in conclusion, of course, these historians chant their hymn to the great life-giving masses. Then the word *great* is applied to everything which for a considerable time has moved the masses, which has been, as they say, "a historical power." But isn't this deliberately confusing quantity and quality? If the clumsy masses have found some idea—a religious idea, for instance—satisfactory, if they have tenaciously defended this idea and clung to it for centuries, then and only then is the originator and founder of the idea said to be great. But why? The highest and noblest ideas have no effect on the masses. The historical success of Christianity, its historical power, tenacity, and endurance, fortunately prove nothing about the greatness of its founder, and indeed would even be evidence against it.

But between him and that historical success lies a very worldly layer, dark with passion, error, hunger for power and honors, the still-active forces of the *imperium Romanum*, from which Christianity inherited that earthy taste and earthy residue which made possible its persistence in this world, and its staying power. Greatness cannot depend upon success, and Demosthenes is great, even though he failed to succeed. The purest and most authentic disciples of Christianity have always doubted and obstructed, rather than promoted, its worldly success, its so-called historical power. In early times they habitually took their stand outside the "world" and gave no thought to the "process of the Christian idea." This is why, for the most part, they remain wholly anonymous and unknown to history. In Christian terms, it is the devil who rules this world, who is the lord of success and progress; he is the real power behind all historical powers, and so he will essentially remain—though this may be painful news to an age accustomed to deify success and historical power. That is, it has acquired the habit of giving new names to things and baptizing even the devil.

This is unmistakably an hour of great peril. Men seem on the verge of discovering that the egoism of individuals, groups, or masses has always been the motivating power of historical movements. But at the same time, they are not in the least alarmed by this discovery: egoism will be our god. Armed with this new faith, they set out, transparently determined to make egoism the foundation of future history, on condition that this egoism should prudently impose a few limits on itself in order to strengthen itself and endure; an egoism, in short, which studies history precisely in order to acquaint itself with imprudent egoism. From this study they have learned that, in the universal system of egoism they want to establish, the state has a very special role; it must act as patron of all prudent egoisms and protect them by its military and political power against the terrible explosions of imprudent egoism. To the same end they have taken pains to indoctrinate the working classes and the dangerous (because imprudent) masses with history, both natural and human, knowing that a light rinse of historical culture will subdue desire and the cruder, dark instincts, or lead them on the road to refined egoism. In sum, modern man, in the words of Hartmann, is concerned with "a practical, comfortable accommodation of his earthly home, an accommodation which prudently has its eye on the future."[57] The same writer calls such an age the "manhood of humanity," thereby making a mockery of what is now called "man," as though it referred only to the disenchanted egoist. In the same way he prophesies an old age corresponding to such a manhood, but obviously only venting his sarcasm on his older contemporaries. For he speaks of the ripe contemplation with which they survey "all the stormy, dissolute sufferings of their former lives, and realize the vanity of what they had once supposed to be the goals of their striving." No, the old age that corresponds to the manhood of this cunning and historically educated egoism is one devoid of dignity, which clings to life with disgusting greediness, and then a final act—

> That ends this strange eventful history,
> Is second childishness and mere oblivion
> Sans teeth, sans eyes, sans taste, sans everything.[58]

Whether the dangers threatening our life and culture come from these dissolute, toothless, and tasteless old men or from Hartmann's so-called men, we will sink our teeth into the rights of the young in defiance of both, and in our youth tirelessly defend the future against those vandals who

57. Hartmann, *Philosophie*, 625.
58. Shakespeare, *As You Like It*, ii, 7, 164–66.

assault the images of the future. But in this struggle we must also make an acutely painful observation: *The excesses of the historical sense, from which the present suffers, are deliberately promoted, encouraged, and—utilized.*

But these excesses are utilized against youth in order to train them to that mature egoism to which the whole world aspires. They are used to overcome youth's natural aversion to egoism by showing the young, by means of scholarship's magic lantern, an enlarged image of this manly yet unmanly egoism. We know, of course, what the study of history is capable of when it holds sway; we know only too well. It is capable of eradicating youth's strongest instincts—ardor, obstinacy, unselfishness, love—and of casting a cold spell on youth's passion for justice; of suppressing or repressing youth's desire to ripen slowly, encouraging instead youth's opposite desire to be immediately ready, immediately useful, immediately productive; of infecting youth's honesty and passion of feeling with doubt. Yes, history is even capable of defrauding youth of its loveliest privilege, its strength for planting inwardly, with invincible confidence, a great idea, and letting an even greater thought grow from this. We have seen that a certain excess of history is capable of all this, precisely because, by continually shifting perspectives and horizons, by eliminating the surrounding atmosphere, it prevents man from feeling and acting *unhistorically*. From the infinity of this horizon, he then retreats into himself, into the smallest parish of his egoism, and is there doomed to arid sterility. He will probably attain cleverness, but never wisdom. He compromises, calculates, and adjusts himself to the facts; he shuns outbursts of anger, he winks, he knows how to pursue his own opportunity or his party's to advantage or disadvantage; he liberates himself from unnecessary modesty and becomes by degrees an "old man," a "Hartmann-man." But this is what he is *fated* to become; this is precisely what is meant by the cynical demand that he should "completely surrender his personality to the world-process"—in order to achieve his goal, which, as the scoundrel Hartmann assures us, is the redemption of the world. Now the goal and purpose of these "men" and Hartmann's "old men" can hardly be the "deliverance of the world." But surely the world's deliverance would be brought much nearer, if only it could be delivered of these "men" and dotards. And the kingdom of youth would be at hand.—

10   Remembering *youth* at this point, I cry out, "Land ho!" Enough and more than enough of this passionate, wandering journey on dark and alien seas! Landfall at last! No matter where it is, we must disembark; even the poorest haven is better than being swept back into the infinity of hopeless skepticism. Our first task is to make land. Later we will find good harbors and help others who come after us to put in to shore.

Our journey was exciting and dangerous. How far we have come from that calm contemplation with which we first saw our ship launched! We went in quest of the dangers of history, and yet it was we ourselves who were especially exposed to these very dangers; we ourselves bear the mark of the sufferings with which an excess of history has afflicted modern man. And I would not deny that this essay itself, in its excessively critical spirit, in its immature humanity, in its veering between irony and cynicism, from pride to skepticism—evinces its modern character, its characteristic weakness of personality. Nonetheless, I have confidence in the inspiring power which, in the absence of a tutelary genius, guides my course, confident that *youth* has guided me well if it now compels me to *protest against the historical education imposed on the young by modern man,* and if in my protest I demand that man must above all learn to live, and use history only in *service of the life he has learned to live.* One must be young to understand this protest, and, given the precocious senility of modern youth, it is almost impossible to be sufficiently young to grasp precisely what I am here protesting.

An example will suffice. In Germany, not much more than a century ago, a few young men were stirred by a natural instinct for what is known as poetry. Are we to suppose that earlier generations or their own contemporaries were wholly silent about the art of poetry, which was intrinsically strange and unnatural? On the contrary, we know that these generations, with all the strength at their command, thought, wrote, and debated about poetry with words about words, words, words. The ensuing rebirth of the word did not also mean the death of these word-smiths; in some sense, they are still alive today. For if, as Gibbon asserts, nothing but time—but a great deal of that—is needed for a world's decline and fall, then nothing but time, but a great deal more time, is required in Germany, the "land of the gradual,"[59] for a false idea to disappear. Nevertheless, there are now perhaps a hundred more men who understand what poetry is then there were a century ago; in another hundred years perhaps there will be a hundred more who have learned what culture is, and that, for all their chatter and preening, Germans still do not possess a culture. In their eyes the prevalent complacency of the Germans about culture will seem as incredible and shallow as the classicism attributed to Gottsched[60] or Ramler's[61] reputation as a German Pindar now seem to us. They will perhaps conclude that this culture of ours is merely some sort of knowledge about culture and, furthermore,

59. Hartmann, *Philosophie,* 638.
60. Johann Christoph Gottsched (1700–66), German literary critic and francophile. His avowed hope was to create a linguistic reform designed to forge a single educated German speech, and at the same time to make French classicism the model of German poetry and drama.
61. Karl Wilhelm Ramler (1728–98), professor of logic at a Berlin military academy, but also an aspiring poet of classicizing bent.

that the knowledge is quite false and superficial. False and superficial, that is, because we tolerate the gulf between life and knowledge; because we never exhibit the characteristics of a culture—a culture which can only grow and flourish from life, whereas, among the Germans, it is like a paper flower, pinned to us, or spread on like icing, and therefore doomed to perpetual falsehood and sterility.

But the education of German youth derives precisely from this false and sterile concept of culture. At its purest and loftiest, its object is certainly not to produce the liberally educated man, but rather the learned man, the scholar, and above all the scholar who can be put to use at the earliest possible age, who removes himself from life in order to observe it as objectively as possible. The result, apparent from the most ordinary empirical observation, is the cultural philistine, stuffed with history and aesthetics, always ready to chat with an air of precocious wisdom about religion, politics, and art—a *sensorium* for thousands of borrowed sentiments; an insatiable stomach, as it were, utterly ignorant of real hunger and real thirst. The fact that such an education, with this purpose and these results, is unnatural is recognized only by those who have not yet been fully formed by it. It is instinctively recognized only by the young, because they still possess natural instincts which have not yet been accurately and violently destroyed by this education. But those who in turn would like to destroy this education must help the young to express themselves, must use the clarity of their ideas to illuminate the unconscious resistance of youth and convert this into outspoken consciousness. But how can such a breathtaking purpose be achieved?

Above all, by destroying a superstition, the conviction that this educational operation is *necessary*. It is still believed that there could be no possible alternative to this terribly painful modern reality of ours. With this belief in mind, one need simply examine what has been written in recent decades on secondary and higher education. To his surprise and indignation, he will discover that, despite all the divergence of opinion and violent controversies, there is no significant disagreement about the general aims of education; he will discover how mindlessly the current product, the "educated man" as now defined, is assumed to be the rational and necessary basis of all future education. The doctrine of our educationists is monotonously the same: the young must start with knowledge of culture, not with knowledge of life, even less with life and experience itself. And of course this knowledge is instilled or inculcated in the youth in the form of historical knowledge, which means that his mind is stuffed with an enormous quantity of ideas drawn not from immediate intuition of life, but from an expertly mediated knowledge of past ages and nations. The youth's yearning to experience things for himself, to feel his own experiences growing inside him, in vivid, integrated coherence—this desire is drugged and intoxicated as it were by the delightful delusion that in a few short years he can assimilate the most sublime and unusual experiences of past ages, above all the greatest ages. It is precisely the same idiotic method that sends our young painters to museums and galleries rather than the workshops of a master, and, above all, the unique workshop of that unique master, Nature. Quite as though, like tourists hurriedly escorted through history, we could pick up the skills and arts of the past! As though life itself were not a craft which had to be thoroughly and constantly mastered, which must be relentlessly practiced, if bunglers and busybodies are not to take over!

Plato thought it necessary for the first generation of his new society (in the ideal state) to be educated by means of a great, *necessary lie.*[62] Children had to learn to believe that for a certain time they had all lived in a dream-state beneath the earth, where they were shaped and formed by the de-miurge of Nature. Impossible to rebel against this past! Impossible to oppose the work of the gods! This must be regarded as an inviolable law of nature: those who were born to be philosophers had bodies of gold, guardians only of silver, and laborers of iron and bronze. Just as these metals, Plato explains, cannot be mixed, so the caste system cannot be overthrown or blurred: faith in the *aeterna veritas*[63] of this order is the basis of the new education, and, therefore, of the new state. The modern German now has the same faith in the aeterna veritas of his education, in his brand of culture; yet this faith would founder, just as Plato's Republic would founder, if the necessary lie were ever confronted with a *necessary truth*—namely, that the German does not possess a culture since, given his educational grounding, he cannot have one. He wants the flower without root and stem; so his wanting it is futile. This is the simple truth, unpleasant and crude, but a necessary truth.

But *our first generation* must be reared in this necessary truth; it clearly suffers most severely from it since this truth is the means by which each member of our generation must educate himself, and this means educating himself against himself, in new habits and a new nature, abandoning his old nature and earlier habits. Hence, he could say to himself, in classical Span-ish, "Defienda me Dios de my"—God protect me from myself, that is, from the nature I have already acquired. He must savor this truth drop by drop, like a strong and bitter medicine; and every individual of this generation must overcome himself in order to pass judgment on himself—a judgment which he might find more endurable as a general judgment on his whole age, namely:

> We have no culture; even worse, we are spoiled with respect to life, to seeing and hearing clearly and simply, to taking joyfully what lies to

62. See Plato *Republic* 3.414b.
63. "eternal truth"

hand, the near and natural things. To this day we still do not have even the basis for a culture because we ourselves are not convinced that an authentic life is ours. Here I am, disintegrated and fragmented, my whole nature almost mechanically split into interior and exterior, sown with concepts like so many dragon's teeth, breeding conceptual dragons, suffering also from the disease of words and lacking faith in any feeling which has not yet been stamped with words. Being what I am, this lifeless but incredibly busy factory of words and concepts, I may perhaps have the right to say of myself, "Cogito, ergo sum,"[64] but not "*Vivo, ergo cogito.*"[65] Empty "being" is granted to me, not full, fresh life; my most personal awareness merely assures me I am a thinking, not a living, being; that I am not an animal, but at best some sort of *cogital.* "First give me life, and from it I will then create a culture for you!"—that is the cry of every individual of this first generation, and we all recognize each other by virtue of that cry.

But who will grant them this life? Neither god nor man, but only their *youth.* Unshackle youth and by so doing you will have liberated life. For in actuality it was merely hidden away, in prison; it is not yet decaying and dying. Ask yourself!

But it is sick, this unshackled life, and must be healed. It is sick with many ills, not only the memory of its chains, but also—and this is of special concern to us—with the *historical sickness.* Excess of history has exhausted the shaping power of life, it can no longer take potent nourishment from the past. This illness is frightful, and yet, unless youth possessed Nature's clairvoyant gift, nobody would recognize that it is an illness and that we have lost a paradise of health. But with the healing instinct of that same Nature, youth also divines how our lost paradise can be regained; it knows the simples and remedies for our historical sickness, for the excess of history.

What are the names of these remedies? Don't be surprised that the names of these remedies are poisons. The antidotes to history are the *unhistorical and the supra-historical.* With these terms we return to the beginning of our discussion and its serenity of spirit.

By the term *unhistorical* I mean man's skill and power to *forget,* his ability to seclude himself within a limited *horizon.* By *supra-historical* I mean those forces which direct our eyes away from Becoming and toward that which gives existence its eternal and unchanging character, toward art and *religion.* *Scientific scholarship*—for it is this that would speak of poisons—sees in these forces and powers forces antagonistic to its own since, according to it, only that view of things is true and genuine, that is, scientific, which everywhere

64. Descartes' famous formula: "I think, therefore I am."
65. "I live, therefore I think."

observes the Becoming, the historical element, always ignoring the Being element of the eternal. Just as it is inherently opposed to the eternalizing forces of art and religion, so too it abhors all forgetting and the death of knowledge, as it struggles to annihilate every limitation of the horizon and plunges man into that eternally infinite sea of shimmering waves, in the sea of known Becoming.

If only men could live in that sea! Just as cities collapse when devastated by earthquakes and men nervously and fearfully build their houses on volcanic ground, so life also collapses, becoming discouraged and feeble, when a conceptual upheaval provoked by science deprives man of the basis of all his security and peace, his faith in the enduring and eternal. But should life prevail over knowledge, over science, or should knowledge govern life? Which of these two powers is higher and decisive? Nobody will doubt that life is the higher and dominant power, since if knowledge destroyed life, it would have destroyed itself, too. Since knowledge presupposes life, it has as much interest in preserving life as has every being in prolonging its own existence. For this reason scientific scholarship needs the supervision and surveillance of a higher power. A *hygiene of life* has its own place at the side of science, and one of the principles of this hygiene would be that the unhistorical and the supra-historical are the natural antidotes to the suffocation of life by history, by the historical sickness. It is probable that we, the historically sick, will have to suffer from these antidotes, too. But the fact that we suffer from the antidotes is no argument against the correctness of the chosen therapy.

And here I recognize the mission of this *youth*, this generation of warriors and dragon-killers who presage a more felicitous, more beautiful culture and humanity, without experiencing anything more than an auspicious presentiment of this future happiness and beauty. This youthful generation will suffer from the evil and the remedy at one and the same time; and yet they believe they can boast greater health and vigor, and, in general, a more natural nature than their predecessors, the cultured "men" and "old men" of the present. But their mission is to upset modern concepts of "health" and "culture" and arouse scorn and hatred against these monstrous conceptual hybrids. And the health and vigor of these young people are guaranteed precisely by their inability to use a single concept, a single party slogan, from the stock of words and concepts now current, to designate their own nature. Rather, their conviction comes solely from their faith in a power which is active in them, a power which struggles, discriminates, analyzes, and, in their best moments, in their own increasingly heightened sense of life. It might be objected that this generation lacks culture, but what young man feels this to be a reproach? They might be accused of being rude and intemperate, but they are not yet old and wise enough to know their place. But above all they have no need to feign or defend a ready-made education, and they enjoy all the privileges and consolations of youth, especially the privilege of bold and courageous honesty and the consolation of an inspiring hope.

I know that in their hearts they understand the abstractions on which these hopes are founded and that through their own experience they will translate them into a doctrine that is personally meaningful. Others in the meantime may see nothing but covered dishes, which might well be empty, until the day when to their astonishment they see with their own eyes that these dishes are full, and that imbedded and compressed in these abstractions are assaults, challenges, vital impulses, and passions that could not long remain concealed. Referring these doubters to time, which reveals everything, I turn in conclusion to that hopeful community and tell its members by means of a parable the course and progress of their cure, their deliverance from the sickness of history, and therefore their own personal story up to the moment when they will once again be well enough to resume the study of history and, under the direction of life, make use of the past in the three historical ways we have described, that is, exemplary, antiquarian, and critical. At that moment they will be less knowledgeable than our contemporary "educated men"; for they will have unlearned much and even lost all desire to give their general attention to what the educated man especially wants to know. The signs by which we will recognize them, from the perspective of our "educated men," are precisely their "lack of culture," their indifference and reserve toward much that is famous, even toward much that is good. But, at the end of their cure, they will once again have become *men* and ceased being human robots. And that is something! There is still hope. Do not, therefore, your hearts rejoice, O ye of good hope?

"But how will we attain our goal?" you will ask. As you begin your hard journey toward your goal, the god of Delphi calls out to you with his famous imperative "Know yourself." It is a hard saying, since the god, in Heraclitus's words, "neither reveals nor conceals, but merely gives a sign."[66] What does his sign mean?

There were centuries in which the Greeks found themselves threatened by a danger similar to that which menaces us, that is, of being submerged by things foreign and past, of perishing by "history." They never lived in proud isolation; on the contrary, their "culture" was for a long time a chaos of foreign ideas and concepts—Semitic, Babylonian, Lydian, and Egyptian; and their religion a genuine conflict among the gods of the whole Orient, just as "German culture" and religion are now an inwardly warring chaos of all foreign countries and all past ages. And yet, thanks to that command of Apollo, Hellenic culture did not become a conglomerate. In accordance with the teaching of Delphi, the Greeks gradually learned to *organize chaos*

66. Kirk and Raven, *The Presocratic Philosophers,* 211.

by concentrating on themselves, that is, on their own needs, and letting their apparent needs die out. By so doing, they regained possession of themselves; not long did they remain the glutted heirs and epigones of the entire Orient. After an arduous struggle with themselves, as a result of their practical interpretation of Apollo's command, it was their supreme good fortune to enrich and increase the treasure they had inherited, and to become the forerunners and exemplars of all civilized peoples who succeeded them.

This parable applies to every one of us. Each of us must organize his own inward chaos by concentrating on his own true needs. At some point his sincerity, native strength, and honesty of character must rebel against constant imitation—against imitated speech, imitated learning, imitated behavior. It is then that he begins to grasp the fact that culture can still be something very different from adornment of life—that is, nothing but a sham and a disguise, since all ornaments conceal the thing they adorn. In this way the Greek concept of culture—in contrast to the Roman—will be revealed to him, the concept of culture as a new and improved physis, unified, without the gulf between interior and exterior, without dissimulation and convention; of culture as a harmony of life, thought, appearance, and will. In this way, from his own experience, he will learn that it was by the superior strength of their *moral* character that the Greeks were victorious over all other cultures and that every increase in truthfulness is a necessary step on the way to *true* culture, even though this truthfulness may sometimes do grievous harm to the "concept of culture" in vogue at the time, and even though it may hasten the collapse of an entire decorative culture.

Introduction
by Richard
Schacht

Translation by
William Arrowsmith

Schopenhauer as Educator

Introduction

Among Nietzsche's writings, there is perhaps no better introduction to his thought than *Schopenhauer as Educator* (1874). Written when he was still a young professor of classical philology at Basel, just beginning to discover his own voice and philosophical calling, it reveals many of the fundamental concerns and convictions that animate later works. It is a remarkable essay. Though flawed by lack of philosophical sophistication and romantic tendencies of thought and expression that Nietzsche had not yet learned to check, it presents an astute, often eloquent discussion of a broad range of intellectual, cultural, and social issues, and calls powerfully for a reorientation of philosophical and human endeavor. It is also one of the most sustained, vigorous, delightful, and radically discomforting works Nietzsche ever wrote. Subjecting many contemporary practices and institutions to searching and powerful criticism, it offers a perceptive critique of the scholar and of scholarship, and concludes with a violent polemic against academic philosophy. And all of this Nietzsche provides in the context (or in the guise) of an appreciation of "Schopenhauer as educator."

As these remarks suggest, the essay is not really "about" Schopenhauer. Nietzsche made the point himself fourteen years later in *Ecce Homo* (1888) in a retrospective comment on his earlier work:: "Now that I am looking back from a certain distance upon the conditions to which these essays bear witness, I do not wish to deny that at bottom they speak only of me. . . . In *Schopenhauer as Educator* my innermost history, my *becoming,* is inscribed. Above all, my promise! . . . At bottom it is admittedly not 'Schopenhauer as Educator' that speaks here, but his opposite, 'Nietzsche as Educator.' "[1]

Schopenhauer is certainly honored in this essay, and is frequently mentioned; but his thought is hardly discussed at all—and when Nietzsche does occasionally purport to present certain aspects of it, more often than not he interprets them in ways that will seem strange indeed to those familiar with Schopenhauer's work. Since the title of the essay presumably indicates its subject, its general neglect of the main content of Schopenhauer's worldview may at first seem surprising, especially in view of Nietzsche's obvious debt to it in *The Birth of Tragedy* (published only two years earlier), and Schopenhauer's continuing influence upon his thought. (While he came to be very critical of Schopenhauer's understanding of the "will" and his interpretation of our fundamental nature and of life and the world as developed

---

1. *Ecce Homo* and *On the Genealogy of Morals,* trans. Walter Kaufmann (New York, 1967), 281.

in terms of the Will, Nietzsche's own interpretation in terms of Will to Power owes a good deal to it.)[2] But the purpose of this essay is to honor Schopenhauer for the *kind* of thinker and philosopher Nietzsche took him to be, rather than for his doctrines; to declare how much it had meant to him to encounter such an *example*; and to argue for the importance of "education" through such teachers and encounters.

The essay is instructive on several counts. It affords considerable insight into Nietzsche's early intellectual development. It also contributes to the understanding of changes in his thinking, as he moved beyond the first major formulation of his views in *The Birth of Tragedy* toward positions elaborated in *The Gay Science* and subsequent writings. But the essay can and should also be read for its interest in its own right. This is perhaps the most rewarding way of reading it, and the one which does greatest justice to its author.

Nietzsche had been appointed associate professor of philology at the University of Basel in 1869 at the astonishingly early age of twenty-four, without even having earned his doctorate, and was promoted to full professor the following year. Great things were expected of him in classical studies; but in his first book (*The Birth of Tragedy*) and in his Basel lectures, he showed himself to be unwilling to conform to the disciplinary norms of classical scholarship, and indeed to be deeply hostile to its limitations and conventional concerns—a critical stance that soon developed into profound discontent with the very character of scholarship and education in the universities of the period. Rather than remaining professionally concerned with classical culture, even in the oblique way of *The Birth of Tragedy*, Nietzsche turned his attention directly to cultural issues of his own day. Over the next three years, he published only the four essays of *Unmodern Observations* (and made notes for a fifth, *We Classicists*, on his own profession), and until 1878 nothing else.

He never returned to classical philology, but instead focused his attention first on cultural, social, and psychological matters, and later on more overtly philosophical issues. Ill-health forced him to resign his Basel post in 1879, but both academic life and philology both had long ceased to be congenial to him. Indeed, five years earlier in *Schopenhauer as Educator* he had effectively repudiated both. And while he came to see his concerns as fundamentally philosophical and to think of himself as a philosopher during the last decade of his productive life, even in this early essay he distanced himself in no uncertain terms from the academic philosophy of his time. Philosophy as he wanted it understood, as he found it exemplified by Schopenhauer, and as he later practiced it himself, is far removed from what

2. See my *Nietzsche* (London, 1983), chaps. 4 and 5.

commonly passed for it among his contemporaries—and passes for it among us still.

Schopenhauer as Educator is thus, at least on one level, Nietzsche's declaration of intellectual independence—from the academic establishment, from the kind of scholarship practiced and honored by his philological peers, and from the sort of philosophy that had become dominant in the universities. It is also an impassioned appeal for a different kind of intellectual activity, more truly deserving of the title of "education" and "philosophy," and also healthier, more productive, and better suited to the cultivation of our humanity as he conceived it. Owing partly perhaps to his hesitation at this early point to speak directly for himself, but also to his grateful recognition of Schopenhauer's example and its importance for him, he chose to cast his appeal in the form of an appreciation. In so doing, he perhaps gives Schopenhauer more credit than is due, imputing to him intentions and convictions that are clearly Nietzsche's own. But in the end, this matters little. What does matter is what Nietzsche had to say about the great cultural issues that concerned him—issues with which we too would do well to concern ourselves.

       Something should be said about Schopenhauer himself, to enable readers unfamiliar with him to appreciate how remarkable it is that Nietzsche could have regarded him so highly. Arthur Schopenhauer was born in 1788, the son of a successful businessman. He studied philosophy at Göttingen and Berlin, received his doctorate from Jena in 1814, and taught for some years at Berlin. He retired to private life in 1831, after contending in vain with Hegel for influence there, and died in 1860. Both before and after his retirement he was extremely productive, but never received the recognition he felt he deserved. Most of his adult life he lived in isolation, resentful of his neglect, and bitterly hostile to his philosophical rivals, above all Hegel. Greatly influenced by Kant, he conceived himself to be Kant's rightful heir. Taking Kant as his point of departure, he developed certain ideas advanced by Kant into a comprehensive philosophy of his own which, as he saw it, at once completed and superseded Kant's philosophical project.

His most important work, in which he systematically developed his basic views, was *The World as Will and Representation.* First published in 1818, it was reissued in greatly expanded form in 1844, the year of Nietzsche's birth. Starting from Kant's distinction between phenomena and things-in-themselves, he argued that it is possible (contrary to Kant's denial) to come to know the fundamental nature of things in themselves and of the world in general, and that their nature is to be conceived in terms of a dynamic principle which he called "will." The phenomenal world is its manifestation in experience. The world is thus "will" (in itself) and "representation" (in its phenomenal manifestation).

But for Schopenhauer the world is also fundamentally irrational and meaningless, characterized throughout by blind striving, ceaseless conflict, and pointless suffering. In the belief that there is neither a God nor any world-historical development in relation to which existence in such a world might be rendered meaningful, and that there is no prospect of transforming the conditions of existence to make possible its justification in terms of the satisfactions it may afford, he considered life and the world to stand condemned before the bar of evaluative judgment. His philosophical pessimism thus verged on nihilism; and his counsel was to withdraw as completely as possible from all worldly activity, either through detached contemplation or—preferably—through complete asceticism, repudiating all forms of active willing. A better world he deemed impossible; and so his ultimate ideal was the utter annihilation of the "world-will" and all of its manifestations: "No will: no idea: no world."[3]

In his assessment of the world's nature and of the meaning and value of human existence, Schopenhauer thus broke radically with the entire Western religious and philosophical tradition. His bleak worldview and deep pessimism clashed fundamentally both with the Judaeo-Christian interpretation of the world and human life and with beliefs in the world's basic rationality, in historical progress, and in the possibility of human well-being and happiness, by his time widely embraced as secular articles of faith. Dismissed by most of his contemporaries as a morbid crank, he impressed and disturbed Nietzsche greatly, since in Nietzsche's opinion both the questions he raised and the challenge of his pessimism needed to be taken very seriously indeed. It might even be said that, despite Nietzsche's eventual radical opposition to Schopenhauer's conclusions and other criticisms of him, Schopenhauer was his primary inspiration. In any case, Nietzsche's recognition of the importance of coming to terms with Schopenhauer and the challenge he posed radically influenced the direction and development of his own thought from *The Birth of Tragedy* to his last works.

But Nietzsche's encounter with Schopenhauer was indirect; he was only sixteen when Schopenhauer died, and so they never met. He knew him only through his published work, and made his first acquaintance through *The World as Will and Representation,* discovered quite by accident one day in the late 1860s in a second-hand bookstore in Leipzig, where he was studying classical philology. No other one discovery had such powerful and immediate impact on him: he could not put the book

3. For fuller discussion of Schopenhauer's thought, see Patrick Gardiner, *Schopenhauer* (Baltimore, 1963) and D. W. Hamlyn, *Schopenhauer* (London, 1980).

down until he had read it through. It was his introduction to philosophy, to the thinker who became his "educator," and to the basic problems that were to occupy him with increasing urgency for the rest of his productive life, the course of which it altered dramatically and to great effect. For this we too are greatly in Schopenhauer's debt.

Our essay bears the title *Schopenhauer as Educator*. But what does Nietzsche mean when he speaks of "educating" and cites Schopenhauer "as educator"? It is of no small importance that the word he employs in his title is *Erzieher*. The kind of educator and education with which he is concerned is not that signified by the words *Lehrer* and *lehren*—the educator as instructor, and education, the imparting of some body of knowledge or doctrine (*Lehre*). Schopenhauer advocated certain doctrines, and sought to persuade others to accept them; but this is not why Nietzsche lauds him as Erzieher. He does so rather in recognition of Schopenhauer's significance for Nietzsche's own intellectual development—by challenging, provoking, stimulating, and inspiring, but above all by serving as an *example*, by what he sought to do and how he sought to do it. It is in this sense that "educator" is here to be understood. Nietzsche offers his own response to his encounter with Schopenhauer as an example of the way in which one thinker may be educated by another without thereby becoming a mere disciple. And his larger purpose is to suggest, in contrast to all more conventional forms of instruction, learning, and scholarly training, the importance of such education for the realization of one's intellectual and human potential.

The kind of educating Nietzsche has in mind is thus linked to what he calls "the task of making human beings human," by developing their intellectual and creative abilities to the full. For him education has the sense of liberation, self-realization, and the transformation of one's spiritual life. And a true "educator" is someone capable of stimulating this development in those who encounter his example, in person or through his work, and who are ripe for such an encounter. In contrast, Nietzsche contends, modern educational practices and institutions fail to provide such educators, and are indeed dangerously stultifying, stunting rather than fostering the development of spiritual life. They enslave rather than liberate, distort rather than cultivate, and restrict rather than stimulate. They also establish norms of intellectual activity that divert those capable of achieving real autonomous and creative spirituality into sterile endeavor, squandering their potential in the pursuit of arid ideals. Thus they not only fail to serve but are actually detrimental to the true end of education, which has to do not with transmission or accumulation of knowledge of various objects of abstruse inquiry, but rather with the enhancement, enrichment, and fulfillment of human life.

Early in the essay, Nietzsche sounds a theme that is at once all too familiar and all too easily misunderstood: "Sei du selbst! Das bist du alles nicht, was du jetzt tust, meinst, begehrst" (Be yourself! You are none of those things you now do, think, desire). This appeal can be properly understood only if notice is taken of what sort of "self" he calls upon one to "be" (or "become"). It is one's *"true* self" he has in mind; and this is something other than one's biological, social, and personal identity. "Finding oneself" is a task Nietzsche regards as both difficult and dangerous. It involves restraining, sacrificing, overcoming, and transforming most of what makes up one's initially acquired identity. One's true self, he suggests, transcends this ordinary plane of all-too-human existence, and the self as commonly understood. Moreover, it is something that "does not lie hidden deep inside you," already formed and waiting to emerge, but is rather "high above you," to be achieved only through great effort. Nietzsche conceives of it in terms of one's potential for creative activity, and self-realization is construed in terms of the realization of that potential.

True selfhood for Nietzsche is thus not a matter of individuality per se. Individuality is to be desired and given scope only insofar as it is either a precondition or a consequence of such self-realization; and it may assume negative significance if its pursuit interferes with the development of one's creative abilities. As one might expect in view of the importance he attached to the artistic transfiguration of human life in *The Birth of Tragedy*,[4] artistic ability and activity are obviously paradigmatic for Nietzsche here. And in this light we may easily understand how he can accord special significance to "genius" and to exceptional individuals possessed of it, since in them the capacity for "productive uniqueness" (which he is prepared to attribute in some degree to everyone) is present in far greater measure—a fact which renders their self-realization of exceptional importance.

If, as Nietzsche supposes, "the task of making human beings human" has above all to do with the actualization of this potential, it is easy to see why he takes the fullest self-realization of these exceptional human beings to represent the attainment of a higher form of humanity. And since "culture" is the sphere in which such self-realization finds its primary expression and the strongest impetus to its further cultivation, it should also be clear why he associates the enhancement of human life and the emergence of a higher humanity with the flourishing of culture (which he sharply distinguishes from the flourishing of social, political, and economic institutions in response to the more mundane imperatives of human existence). Nietzsche is often thought to have advanced a conception of humanity which reduces it to its natural rudiments. But this essay shows that such a view is mistaken, since great significance is attached to the difference between humanity and mere animality, and to culture as its source (with "genius" as its instrument). Nature and merely natural existence are viewed as devoid of meaning and standing in need of "justification" and "redemption"; and this, Nietzsche

4. See my *Nietzsche,* chap. 8.

contends, can be accomplished only by their transformation through the development of culture.[5]

Culture is the sphere in which, for Nietzsche, human animality is sublimated and transmuted into spirituality. "The task of making human beings human" may thus be conceived as the task of spiritualizing human animals through their introduction to and participation in cultural life. And the exhortation to "become yourself" is to be understood not as a call to return to nature or to intensify one's subjectivity, but rather as an appeal to *ascend* to culture, and to contribute what one can to its enrichment. To be sure, this is possible only by drawing upon energies and cultivating abilities rooted in one's human animality, which is fundamentally but a piece of nature. For Nietzsche, however, everything depends upon what one does with those energies and what one makes of those abilities, and so upon transcending the plane of merely natural existence and the commonplace forms of social existence which in his view still belong essentially to it.

Nietzsche distinguishes a number of general images of humanity which differ from each other as well as from the all-too-human type of social-animal humanity he regards as the human rule. He identifies three images of a more genuine humanity competing for attention and allegiance in his own time (and which bear a strong resemblance to the Dionysian, Apollinian, and tragic types he had depicted in *The Birth of Tragedy*). He designates them with the names of three more recent figures whom he regards as champions and exemplars of the apposite ideals: Rousseau, Goethe, and Schopenhauer (here actually Nietzsche himself)—all Nietzschean "educators" par excellence.

Rousseauean man—for Nietzsche the most problematic of the three—represents naturalized humanity, renewed by emancipation from the shackles of society and restoration to its basic instincts. Goethean man—less dangerous for Nietzsche, but lacking in vitality—is the image of contemplative humanity, cultivated and sophisticated and therefore more truly human owing to its attainment of high spirituality, but essentially withdrawn from active involvement in life. Schopenhauerian (or Nietzschean) man, on the other hand, combines elements of both and also supersedes both. This is the image of a "truly active," creative humanity, at once vital and spiritualized, and which has therefore become most truly itself because most fully human.

The significance of these image-types for Nietzsche is that they have the power to liberate, stimulate, inspire—in short, to *educate*. But because of

5. This echoes his contention in *The Birth of Tragedy* that it is only as an *aesthetic phenomenon* that existence and the world are externally justified" (trans. Walter Kaufmann [New York, 1966] §5).

the different forms of human development that each tends to foster and the shortcomings of the Rousseauean and Goethean models, he regards them as differing not only in kind but also in value. Only the Schopenhauerian (the heir to the tragic type and model of art and spirituality in *The Birth of Tragedy*) holds out the promise of an attainable form of humanity healthy and vital enough to have a real future in this world, and sufficiently creative and spiritualized to justify itself—and human life and the world as well. Rousseauean man neglects human spirituality and the importance of engaging the forces of our natural humanity in its service in such a way that, when tapped, these forces are creative rather than merely destructive. Goethean man neglects to give these forces their due and thereby fails to promote the active expression of human spirituality, without which it necessarily becomes sterile. It is therefore the image and ideal Nietzsche associates with Schopenhauerian man which he commends to us here, and which he subsequently elaborated and celebrated.

A second set of types is intended to anchor this ideal in human reality by singling out certain actually attained exceptions to the human rule in whom, in various respects, this ideal is anticipated. These are the types of the *philosopher,* the *artist,* and the *saint.* Nietzsche here sounds themes developed in later works where he invokes the *Übermensch* as the apotheosis of the enhancement of life, in relation to which a variety of types of "higher humanity" are significant, but are only partial and all-too-human approaches and approximations.[6] In this early essay Nietzsche honors these three types because some significant aspect of the human ideal he envisions has been realized in each of them (albeit in limited and merely provisional form), thereby demonstrating that this ideal is no mere fantasy but one which lies within human reach and legitimate human aspiration.

Having more fully identified the "true man," through whom life may be "redeemed" and "justified," Nietzsche can also identify "the goal of culture": "to foster the production of the true man." Moreover, to the question of how one's life may "be given the highest value and deepest significance," he can now answer: by contributing in whatever way one can to this development. In addition, he considers it possible to "derive a new set of duties" founded upon "the fundamental idea of culture" and its advancement. So he contends that both the advancement of culture and the enhancement of life depend upon the "production" of the philosopher, artist, and saint, because of the emergence and development of certain traits he associates with them. These types are importantly linked to his conception of genius, which is not to be equated with them but embraces and draws upon them.

Thus the figure of the saint is meant to evoke the idea of self-overcoming, of transcending the willful, self-centered individual ego, and attaining unity

6. See my *Nietzsche,* chap. 5.

with all of life and existence. The figure of the philosopher conveys the idea of spiritual liberation, enlightenment with respect to the nature and conditions of human existence generally, and knowledge of the world's basic character. The figure of the artist is employed (rather oddly) to represent the achievement of a fuller knowledge of the various forms of life and existence as well as their creative transfiguration. In each case Nietzsche alludes to both a kind of knowledge and a related kind of transformation. And it is of no small interest that in this essay he considers such special forms of knowledge—as well as the kinds of creative activity mentioned— to be attainable; and, further, that he takes their attainment to be crucial, not only to the enhancement of life and consummation of nature, but also as constituent features of life so enhanced and nature so consummated.

Schopenhauer (whom Nietzsche follows in assigning special importance to the philosopher, artist, and saint) was clearly his model for the philosopher in this trinity of higher types. Nietzsche has much more to say, however, about the kind of philosopher he conceives Schopenhauer to have been; and his remarks in this connection are of particular interest for the light they cast on his emerging conception of the genuine philosopher and on his own later philosophical activity. For Nietzsche, Schopenhauer was no ordinary philosopher or scholar of the types he so astutely and severely portrays in the last sections of the essay. His sketches of these types, vividly anticipating his later critiques of their characteristic modes of thought,[7] serve to underscore the contrasting significance he found in Schopenhauer's example. Schopenhauer stands out in bold relief; and the entire discussion plainly demonstrates that Nietzsche considers a different sort of intellectual-philosophical activity to be humanly possible, and that he takes the realization of this possibility to be of immense importance.

Once molded into creatures of their disciplines, the academic philosophers and scholars he describes and criticizes neither are nor can become truly and fully human beings; nor do their labors help others to do so. A philosopher like Nietzsche's Schopenhauer, however, is an exception in both respects. He can hardly be regarded as exemplifying Nietzsche's conception of true humanity completely; but he does represent what Nietzsche means by "genius" in philosophical thinking, and he is viewed by Nietzsche as the kind of philosopher through whom human life might be enhanced.

One of the qualities Nietzsche stresses in his portrait of Schopenhauer as philosopher is *independence*—independence of one's time and of prevailing institutions and interpretations. The philosopher may not be able to escape them entirely—indeed, he cannot and should not ignore them—but a *critical*

7. See my *Nietzsche*, chaps. 1 and 2.

relation to them is both possible and necessary to genuine philosophical thinking. Philosophy, as Nietzsche would have it understood, presupposes a measure of such independence and also makes possible a fuller liberation from the constraints of conventional thinking, from the structures and imperatives of existing institutions (social, political, and also academic), and even from the thinker's own biological and historical conditioning. The idea and ideal of the philosopher as pure knowing subject, spectator of all time and existence, may be a Platonizing myth to which Schopenhauer should not have subscribed and which Nietzsche rejects; but there *is* an attainable form of transcendence, exemplified by Schopenhauer, which Nietzsche regards as a crucial distinguishing mark of a truly philosophical thinker. The quest to know nature and one's own time and the human norm and prevailing modes of thought *in order to transcend them*—and, by so doing, not only do justice to them but also criticize and transform them—is for Nietzsche an aspiration that sets Schopenhauer apart, and an essential aspect of what it means to be a genuine philosopher.

The three specific virtues he attributes to Schopenhauer—honesty, cheerfulness, and constancy—add additional detail. All are required in order to persevere and advance in true philosophical endeavor. But these three virtues must be supplemented by the courage to think and live independently and the intellectual ability to *reinterpret* and *revalue* life and existence. Thus, according to Nietzsche, Schopenhauer was not merely a "profane and secularized" thinker no longer under the sway of religious and metaphysical ideas whose time had come and gone, important though Nietzsche believed that to be. He also had a sharp eye for truly fundamental problems—problems that must be freshly and radically reckoned with, such as "the problem of existence itself" and whether life has, or may come to have, meaning and value. He further had the creative originality to develop a new and comprehensive worldview, to present "a picture of life as a whole" with significant implications for the meaning of one's own life. Nothing less, Nietzsche suggests, is to be expected of a truly philosophical thinker, in contrast with those who occupy themselves with merely investigating, refining, and applying inherited interpretations and conceptual schemes. And nothing less than this is what he himself subsequently sought to do.

Philosophical thinking, so understood, proceeds through and beyond the analysis, comprehension, and criticism of various matters to their more fundamental and comprehensive interpretation. This in turn makes possible a *re*interpretation and *re*valuation of many specific phenomena of human life. In embracing this conception of philosophy, Nietzsche renounces neither the conception of any sort of truth deserving of the name, nor its pursuit (contrary to the claims of some of his recent interpreters). His emphasis here on the importance of truthfulness and honesty, and the attainment of knowledge by the philosopher (and by artist and saint as well), makes this abundantly clear. And he has in mind something more than the kinds of truth and knowledge which are abstracted from life and may be pursued only by restricting oneself to problems and methods that depend for their clarity and rigor upon the artificiality of the reasoning patterns and experience in which they are formulated.

A parallel (by no means merely fortuitous) may be discerned between the aims of philosophy and those of education as Nietzsche construes them here. Education of the sort he envisions is associated very revealingly with the attainment of a kind of "truth"; but it is related only incidentally (if at all) to the learning of facts or the mastery of forms of theoretical inquiry. Its focus is rather upon human-spiritual self-realization through the cultivation and employment of one's full intellectual powers. And the measure of "truth" here is the extent to which our lives come to manifest our highest possibilities, we come to be what we have it in us to be, and true humanity is thereby achieved.

The philosophical endeavor Nietzsche champions is likewise concerned above all with the pursuit of a kind of "truth" that is not merely a matter of fidelity of thought and expression to the way things are, even though it presupposes their clear and candid apprehension. More importantly, it also relates to what may become or be made of human life, and therefore of life and the world more generally, as the merely natural is transfigured and higher forms of existence are attained. "Truth" here requires that justice be done to the possibilities inherent in life and the world generally, as well as to their present character. It is this "truth" of existence, at once sobering and promising, and to be grasped through its unflinchingly honest, unmyopic, and imaginative assessment, which Nietzsche suggests may make possible its affirmation, justification, and redemption. It has nothing to do with the illusory forms of metaphysical and religious "comfort" which he earlier (in *The Birth of Tragedy*) had supposed were needed to make life endurable. It differs from most of what does and should count as true, but it still deserves the name of "truth." Indeed, it constitutes a higher form of truth—a truth of the greatest human significance. For it alone may be able to sustain us, whereas truthfulness and honesty in their merely analytical and critical employment only weaken and destroy such illusions without offering anything better in their place.

There are many ways of doing some justice to our developmental possibilities and to life and the world as well. For this reason it is to be expected and even desired that genuine philosophers will be creative in their interpretations, and that these interpretations will differ. Their differences, moreover, should not be taken to mean either that some are wrong or that all are meaningless. If philosophers do what they should be doing, they will think in creatively original as well as analytical and critical ways. They will elaborate a wealth of perspectives diversely illuminating what we and the world are and have it in us to become, thereby summoning us to lives which will further transform the aspect of existence. To serve and pursue the attainment of this highest kind of truth in this way is, for Nietzsche, their fundamental task.

The endowment of human life with meaning and value through its creative transformation is a central theme of Nietzsche's thought. In the earlier *Birth of Tragedy* he first detected this idea at the heart of the ancient Greek response to the problems of rendering life in a harsh and inhuman world endurable and worth living. Subsequently he came to view it as the key to overcoming that nihilistic crisis in which, he believed, this problem had in his own age returned with a vengeance. In *Schopenhauer as Educator* this problem and this conception of its only viable resolution both loom very large. They define the context in which Nietzsche inveighs against what commonly passes for philosophy and education and in which he honors Schopenhauer as a different kind of philosopher and educator—a kind for whom there is now the greatest need. Without such philosophers and educators, he holds, there is little hope that mankind will be able to meet this grave nihilistic challenge and to redeem itself—and nature with it—from meaninglessness. For him the vindication of life depends upon its qualitative enhancement; and that in turn depends upon the emergence of exceptional human beings through whom the potential as well as the reality of our existence and the world are revealed and more fully realized, and by whose examples others are induced to exert themselves in like manner and to still greater effect. In this way mankind may succeed in educating and transforming itself, drawn toward the higher spirituality of which it is capable by a vanguard through whose genius its possibility is envisioned and its realization is furthered. Its attainment may never be widespread; but enough exceptions to the general human rule may occur to justify all.

There is a celebrated image, certainly familiar to Nietzsche, which may well have influenced his conception of the enhancement of life through an educational process of this sort. This is the great image of the "ladder of love" in Plato's *Symposium*. The image is employed by Plato's Socrates to suggest how the soul may, by its attraction to beauty, be liberated and drawn upward toward the highest state of which it is capable. This attraction serves to render the soul responsive to a succession of exemplifications of beauty of progressive refinement. Responding at first only to cruder beauties, it may gradually be educated and elevated as it is drawn to others of a similar but more refined nature. As the process is repeated, the soul may ascend the "ladder of love" to a spirituality far above the rung on which it began, and so become what it ought to be.

For Nietzsche true education may be conceived as involving a comparable ascent and development through one's attraction to a succession of ideas and of exemplary others. Toward the end of the first section of the essay, he even speaks of "love" and employs the image of a "ladder" in this connection. Through such encounters and responses, we may in fact become what we have it in ourselves to be. And by reflecting upon them, we may achieve a better understanding of our true natures, since our attraction to these objects of interest reveals us to ourselves. Our real educators, our liberators and "educers," are all those special influences which have this significance for us, even if certain individuals stand out, as did Schopenhauer for Nietzsche.

It is fitting that, as Nietzsche turned from philology to philosophy, and looked to philosophy liberated from conventional scholarly and social expectations for the resolution of some of the most fundamental problems of human life, he should echo Socrates here. For Socrates engaged in philosophical inquiry in a similar spirit and with similar concerns. He likewise loathed the sterile and servile substitute for it practiced by the sophistic counterparts in his own day of the academic philosophers castigated by Nietzsche. And though he undoubtedly would have been as critical of Nietzsche's interpretation and assessments of many matters as Nietzsche was of his, he surely would have agreed with Nietzsche about the nature and importance of true education and educators.

Given Nietzsche's preference for the pre-Socratics,[8] and his profound ambivalence toward Socrates in *The Birth of Tragedy* and later writings, it is hardly surprising that Socrates is not included along with the pre-Socratics in Schopenhauer's company here. But he could have been, and perhaps even should have been. For Socrates was unmistakably one of Nietzsche's greatest educators, and furthermore one who arguably satisfies Nietzsche's own account of the true educator and the genuine philosopher at least as well as Schopenhauer. And, of all Nietzsche's writings, this essay not only anticipates the literature of existential philosophy most closely, but also is perhaps the most Socratic in spirit. For many this will mean that, early Nietzsche though it may be, it is also Nietzsche at his best.

---

8. See Nietzsche's early essay (which he did not publish or even finish, but which is of considerable interest in connection with the present essay, *Philosophy in the Tragic Age of the Greeks*, trans. Marianne Cowan (South Bend, Ind., 1962).

Schopenhauer as Educator

1   A traveler who had visited many countries and peoples and several continents, was asked what trait he had discovered to be common to all men, and replied: a tendency to laziness. Some will think that he might have answered more accurately and truthfully: they are all afraid. They hide behind customs and opinions. Basically every man knows quite well that he is on this earth only once, a *unicum*, and that no accident, however unusual, could ever again combine this wonderful diversity into the unity he is. He knows this, but hides it like a bad conscience. Why? From fear of his neighbor who demands convention and wraps himself inside it. But what compels an individual to fear his neighbor, to think and act as part of a herd, rather than joyously being himself? Modesty perhaps, in a few rare cases. But with the vast majority it is convenience and indolence— in short, that inclination to laziness observed by our traveler. He is right; men are more lazy than fearful, and above all they fear the burdens that unconditional honesty and nakedness would impose upon them. Artists alone despise this aimless drifting about in borrowed manners and super- imposed opinions, and they expose the secret, everyone's bad conscience, the principle that every man is a unique miracle. They dare to show us how man, down to each twitch of his muscles, is himself, himself alone, and what is more, that in this rigorous coherence of his uniqueness, he is beau- tiful and worthy of contemplation, as new and incredible as any work of nature, and anything but boring. When the great thinker despises men, it is their laziness he despises; it is laziness that makes them seem mass- produced, indifferent, unworthy of association and instruction. The man who does not want to belong to the mass has only to stop being lazy with himself. Let him follow his conscience, which cries out to him: "Be yourself! You are none of those things you now do, think, desire."

Day and night every young soul hears this cry and trembles at it; for when it thinks of its true liberation, it has an intimation of the happiness destined for it from eternity. But so long as it remains bound in the shackles of opinion and fear, nothing can help it attain this happiness. And without this liberation how bleak and meaningless life can become! There is no drearier and more repulsive creature in nature than the man who has evaded his own personal destiny,[1] his eyes squinting left and right, behind him, every-

---

1. In German, *Genius*. But Nietzsche, here and elsewhere, often uses the word in its Latin sense, i.e., as an indwelling tutelary divinity, as in the phrase *genius loci* or "the genius of a nation." In this sense, *genius* is the equivalent of the Greek word *daimōn*, but the resonance of daimon is far richer than that of the Latin genius. And it is essentially the Greek sense on which Nietzsche constantly draws. Daimon, for instance, connotes

where. In the end a man like this can no longer be touched or grasped because he is all shell and no kernel, a shabby, puffed up, painted garment, a gaudy ghost that can arouse no fear and certainly no compassion. And if it is rightly said that the lazy man kills time, then we must ensure that a time that entrusts its salvation to public opinion—which is to say, to private lazinesses[2]—should itself be killed, and killed for good, by which I mean stricken from the history of the true liberation of life. Imagine the revulsion of later generations in coping with the legacy of a time governed not by living men, but by publicly opining mockeries of men—which is why our own age may for some distant posterity be the darkest and least known, because least human, chapter of history. I walk through the new streets of our towns and I think how a century from now not one of all these frightful

---

an individual *destiny* or fate, a potentiality unfolded and revealed in the individual's life-history. Just as an acorn contains the daimon of the oak-to-be, so a man contains in his *physis* (see n. 19 below) the daimon of his own realized—or realizable—future, his personal potential destiny. It is this principle of organic potentiality that underlies Nietzsche's favorite Pindaric maxim, "Become the thing you are," which also animates Nietzsche's dynamic of transcendence or "overcoming," and his insistence upon the acceptance of one's own nature and the nature of life generally, i.e., *amor fati.* The idea of a daimon *realized,* for instance, is present in the Dionysiac boast in the title of the last section of *Ecce Homo*—"Why I Am a Destiny." Culturally and metaphysically, it is the dynamic expressed in Zarathustra's prologue: "Man is a rope, tied between beast and overman— a rope over an abyss. . . . What is great in man is that he is a bridge and not an end."

A simple but vivid example: I once saw, on the way to Priene high above the Meander valley in Turkey, on a day in late April, a whole hillside covered with what looked like enormous floral candelabra. Everywhere, a base of curling leaves, a three- or four-foot stalk with many arms, each arm bearing a burst of yellow blossom. I looked at the leafy base and recognized the plant: wild *fennel.* And I suddenly understood why Prometheus carried fire to man in a stalk of fennel. Not, as rationalizers would have it, because fennel is fibrous and makes good tinder, but because the stalk of fennel has in it, by nature, the daimon of *fire*—those yellow bursts of blossom, the "force that through the green fuse drives the flower."

To this ancient sense of the word, Nietzsche adds Schopenhauer's idea of genius as intellect which has gradually emancipated itself from the domination of the Will, which is therefore *disinterested,* and capable of devoting itself to the advancement of the species. The Schopenhauerian genius is the instrument by which Man becomes himself, becomes truly Man. See, for instance, *Parerga and Paralipomena,* 1:201ff., but esp. 209–12 and 221–23, where Schopenhauer defines daimon and equates it with a general and immortal aim which transcends the individual but at the same time harmonizes with the individual's will, which is simply the unique individual incarnation of the Will to Live.

2. A glance at the subtitle—"Private Vices, Public Benefits"—of Bernard de Mandeville's (1670–1733) *Fable of the Bees.* Nietzsche was attracted to this work because of Mandeville's thesis—an ironically perverse defense of human vices founded on the argument that, insofar as they are all motivated by self-interest, they are necessarily all vicious, despite the fact that their results are beneficial to civilization.

houses built for themselves by the breed of public opiners will be left standing, and how the opinions of those builders will have collapsed as well. How
hopeful, by contrast, are all those who feel that they are no citizens of this
time. For if they were, they would join in "killing the time" and perishing
with it—whereas they want rather to quicken the age to life, so that they
may go on living in this life.

But even if the future allowed us no hope, our remarkable existence in
this Now—the inexplicable fact that we are living now and yet have had
endless time in which to appear; that we possess nothing but a brief today
in which we are to show how and for what purpose we came to exist at just
this moment—this gives us the strongest encouragement to live according
to our own standards and law. We are accountable to ourselves for this
existence of ours; and this is why we want to be the real helmsmen of our
lives and keep them from resembling the mindless result of chance. One's
life must be lived with a certain danger and boldness since one will always,
at best and at worst, lose it. Why cling to your clod of earth, to your trade,
who heed what the neighbors say? It is so provincial to obligate oneself to
views which a few hundred miles away are no longer obligatory. East and
West are lines chalked by someone before our eyes in order to mock us
with our own timidity. I will make the effort, says the young soul, to attain
freedom. Should that effort be hindered simply because two countries happen to hate each other and go to war, or because an ocean lies between two
continents, or because a religion that did not even exist two thousand years
ago is being everywhere taught? All this is not yourself, the young soul says
to itself. Nobody can build you the bridge over which you must cross the
river of life, nobody but you alone. True, there are countless paths and
bridges and demigods that would like to carry you across the river, but only
at the price of your self; you would pledge your self, and lose it. In this
world there is one unique path which no one but you may walk. Where
does it lead? Do not ask; take it. Who was it who said, "A man never rises
higher than when he does not know where his road may take him"?[3]

But how can we find ourselves again? How can man know himself? He
is a dark and veiled thing; and whereas the hare has seven skins, man could
skin himself seventy-times-seven times and still not say, "This now is you
yourself, this is no longer skin." Besides, it is an agonizing, dangerous

---

3. Cited by R. W. Emerson in "Circles" (*Essays: First Series*), which Nietzsche read in
the German translation of G. Fabricius (Hanover, 1858). Nietzsche had great admiration
for Emerson. On Dec. 22, 1884, he wrote to Overbeck: "I am having translated into
German for me . . . a longish essay by Emerson, which provides some clarity about his
development. . . . I don't know how much I would give if only I could bring it about, ex
post facto, that such a great, glorious nature, rich in soul and spirit, might have gone
through some *strict* discipline. . . . As it is, in Emerson we have lost a *philosopher*."

enterprise to dig down into yourself, to descend forcibly by the shortest route the shaft of your being. A man may easily do himself such damage that no doctor can cure him. And again, why should it be necessary, since everything bears witness to our being—our friendships and hatreds, the way we look, our handshakes, the things we remember and forget, our books, our handwriting? But there is a way by which this absolutely crucial inquiry can be carried out. Let the young soul look back upon its life and ask itself: what until now have you truly loved, what has raised up your soul, what ruled it and at the same time made it happy? Line up these objects of reverence before you, and perhaps by what they are and by their sequence, they will yield you a law, the fundamental law of your true self. Compare these objects, see how one completes, enlarges, exceeds, transforms the other, how they form a ladder on which you have so far climbed up toward yourself. For your true nature does not lie hidden deep inside you but immeasurably high above you, or at least above that which you customarily consider to be your ego. Your true educators and molders reveal to you the true original meaning and basic stuff of your nature, something absolutely incapable of being educated and molded, but in any case something fettered and paralyzed and difficult of access. Your teachers can be nobody but your liberators. And that is the secret of all education; it does not provide artificial limbs, wax noses, or corrective lenses—on the contrary, what might provide such things is merely a parody of education. Education is rather liberation, the clearing away of all weeds, rubble, and vermin that might harm the delicate shoots, a radiance of light and warmth, the kind rustling fall of rain at night; it is imitation and adoration of nature where nature is maternal and mercifully minded; it is perfection of nature when it prevents nature's fits of cruelty and mercilessness and converts them to good, when it throws a veil over nature's stepmotherly disposition and sad incomprehension.

Admittedly, there are other means of finding oneself, of coming to oneself out of that stupor in which we customarily float as though in a dark cloud. But I know of no better way than to reflect on one's own educators and molders. And this is why I want to bring to mind the one teacher and severe taskmaster of whom I boast: *Arthur Schopenhauer.* And after him to recall others.

2   To describe what an event it was for me when I first looked at Schopenhauer's writings, I might linger briefly on an idea that in younger days occurred more frequently and touched me more urgently than almost any other. When in earlier years I used to indulge in wishful thinking, I thought that fate would spare me the dreadful task and effort of educating myself: at the right moment I would find a philosopher to be my teacher, a true philosopher whom I could obey without further thought because I could trust him more than myself. And I would ask myself:

by what principles would he educate? And I mused on what he might say of the two educational precepts in vogue today. The first of these requires the teacher to recognize his student's particular forte quickly, and then to direct all his energies, all his sunlight and sap, to just that point in order to help that unique excellence ripen and bear. In contrast, the other precept requires the educator to elicit and foster all existing abilities and bring them into harmonious rapport. Are we then to force a boy with a decided bent for the goldsmith's art into music? Are we to side with Benvenuto Cellini's father, who constantly drove his son back to that "delicious little horn"— or "that damned piping," as the boy called it?[4] In the case of natural gifts as vigorous and clearly defined as Cellini's, such a tack is obviously wrong; and it may be that the maxim of harmonious education applies only to weaker natures, in which there is a whole swarming hive of needs and bents, but which, taken singly or collectively, do not amount to much. But where do we find harmonious wholeness and polyphonic unity in a single nature, if not in men like Cellini, men in whom everything—all insight, desire, love, hatred—converge toward a single career, a single radical strength, where, because of the compelling and ruling power of this center, a harmonic system of movements—movements radiating out in every direction, back and forth, upwards and downwards—is created.

And so the two precepts are perhaps not contradictory? Perhaps the first merely declares that man should have a center, the second that he should have a circumference? The teacher-philosopher of my daydreams would, then, not only discover the focal strength but would also know how to keep it from destroying the other talents. His educational task, as I imagined it, would rather be to transform the whole man into a solar and planetary system with its own life and movement, and to discover the laws of its higher mechanics.

But in the meantime my philosopher failed to put in an appearance, and I tried one thing after another. I discovered how pathetic we moderns are in comparison with the Greeks and Romans, even in this matter of taking the aims of education seriously and strictly. With a need like this in your heart, you can visit all Germany, and in particular German universities, and not find what you are seeking. Much simpler, much humbler wants than these go unfulfilled here. For instance, if a German wants to become an orator, or to enter a school for writers, he will nowhere find either master or school; it does not yet seem to have dawned on anyone in Germany that speaking and writing are arts that cannot be acquired without the most rigorous discipline and years of painstaking apprenticeship. Yet nothing more plainly and shamefully reveals the arrogant complacency of our contemporaries than the shabbiness—half stinginess, half mindlessness—of the

4. Benvenuto Cellini, *Life*, chaps. 1 and 2. Nietzsche is quoting from Goethe's translation.

demands they make of teachers and educators. Even among our most re-
spectable and best-informed people, absolutely anybody will do as a family
tutor, and how common it is for some motley conclave of noddies and fossils
to be called a gymnasium and found *good.*

And consider what we settle for in the highest institution of learning, the
university! What leaders, what institutions, when we compare them with the
difficulty of their task of educating a man to be a man! Even the celebrated
way in which German scholars attack their discipline clearly reveals that
they think more of their scholarship than of humanity; that they have been
trained like a lost battalion to sacrifice themselves to their disciplines in
order to lure new generations to make the same sacrifice. If the practice of
scholarship is neither guided nor controlled by any higher educational principle but granted always greater freedom on the grounds of "the more, the
better," it is surely just as pernicious to the scholar as the economic doctrine
of laissez-faire is to the morality of whole nations. Who nowadays recognizes
that the scholar's education, if we are not to sacrifice or desiccate his humanity in the process, poses an extremely ticklish problem? But if we merely
note the countless numbers of men whose natures, by a mindless and premature surrender to scholarship, have been warped or endowed with a
hump, the problem leaps to the eye. But there is more important evidence
of the total absence of higher education—more important, more perilous,
above all more general. If it is immediately apparent why at present no
orator, no writer can be educated—because there are no teachers for them;
if it is almost as clear why a scholar is nowadays doomed to being warped
or deformed—because he is to be educated by scholarship, an inhuman
abstraction; if this is so, then we must ask ourselves: Where among our
contemporaries can we—educated and uneducated, noble and humble—
find moral examples and men of true distinction, visible embodiments of
all creative morality in this age? That meditation on moral questions which
in every age has been the concern of every noble society—what has become
of it? There are no longer men of that distinction, meditation of that sort
no longer exists. The truth is that we are living off the inherited moral
capital accumulated by our forefathers, a capital we no longer know how to
increase but only to squander. Such matters are in our society either not
discussed or discussed with revolting naturalistic amateurishness and inexperience. We have reached the point at which our schools and teachers
simply ignore moral education or content themselves with mere formalities.
And *virtue* is a word that finds no echo among the thoughts of teachers and
students, a musty word at which people smile—and woe to you if you fail
to smile, since that makes you a hypocrite!

Explanation of this faintheartedness, this low watermark of all moral
forces, is difficult and involved. But certainly nobody who considers the
influence of victorious Christianity on the morals of the ancient world can

ignore the counter-reaction of Christianity in its time of decline—and further decline is its likely fate in our time. Through its lofty idealism Christianity so far surpassed the moral systems of antiquity and the naturalness prevalent in all of them, that mankind grew indifferent to that naturalness and became disgusted with it. But afterwards, when men still knew the higher and the better, but could no longer achieve it, they found they could no longer return to the high and the good—to that ancient moral virtue—despite their desire to do so. Modern man lives in this oscillation between Christianity and antiquity, between a cowardly and deceitful Christian approach to morals and a classicizing approach equally timid and self-conscious, and he suffers by so doing. The inherited fear of the natural and, on the other side, its renewed fascination for him; his longing for stability somewhere; the impotence of his intellect as it stumbles back and forth between the good and the better—all this produces a restlessness, a confusion in the modern soul, that condemns it to joyless sterility. Never were moral teachers more needed, and never was there smaller likelihood of finding them. The time when doctors are most needed, the age of great epidemics, is also the time when doctors themselves are in the greatest danger; and where are the doctors of modern man who are sufficiently strong and sure-footed to support another man and lead him by the hand? Over the best men of our time there hangs a somber, paralyzing gloom, an everlasting discontent over the battle between pretense and honesty that is being fought in their breasts, a restless failure of self-confidence, and for this reason they are quite incapable of showing others the way and, as teachers, providing a stern discipline.

In short, it was a debauchery in wishful thinking when I imagined that I could find a true philosopher as my teacher, a man who could raise me above the inadequacy of the age and once again teach me to be *simple and honest* in thought and life—that is, to be *unmodern,* in the deepest sense of the word. For modern man has become so multiple and complex that he is necessarily dishonest every time he speaks, asserts an opinion, and wants to act accordingly.

These were the distress, the needs, and desires I was feeling when I first encountered Schopenhauer.

I am among those readers of Schopenhauer who, from the moment they finish the first page, know for certain that they will read every page he wrote, listen to every word he uttered. My faith in him was immediate, and it is no less today than it was nine years ago. I understood him as though he had written expressly for me, to put it arrogantly and foolishly, but understandably. This is why I have never found a paradox in Schopenhauer, though here and there a minor error. For what are paradoxes but assertions that inspire no confidence because the author made them without conviction, because he wants to glitter, or mislead, and in general *seem*? Schopenhauer never wants to shine in this showy way. He writes for himself, and no man wants to be self-deceived, least of all a philosopher who has made this his law: Deceive nobody, not even yourself! Do not deceive even with those polite social deceptions which are part of almost every conversation, and which our writers almost unconsciously imitate; still less with the more conscious deceits of the public platform, and the artificial techniques of rhetoric. But Schopenhauer speaks to himself; or, if we have to imagine an audience, imagine a son being advised by his father. It is a straightforward, brusque, good-natured speech, addressed to someone who listens lovingly. We lack writers of this sort. The vigorous well-being of the speaker surrounds us at the first sound of his voice; it is like entering a forest of tall trees; we breathe deeply and suddenly we feel well again. Here, we feel, the air is always bracing; here is that inimitable naturalness and lack of affectation of men at home with themselves, and masters of a very rich home at that—the exact opposite of those writers who are stunned if they somehow manage something witty, and whose style is therefore somewhat nervous and unnatural. So, when Schopenhauer speaks, there is literally nothing to remind us of the scholar with his natural stiffness and awkwardness, his hollow chest, and his jerky, embarrassed, or pompous gait. On the other hand, Schopenhauer's rough, almost bearish spirit teaches us not so much to regret as to abhor the smoothness and polished grace of the good French writers; certainly nobody will find in him that pseudo-French tinsel on which German writers so preen themselves. In places, Schopenhauer's way of expressing himself reminds me somewhat of Goethe, but of no other German model whatever. For he knows how to say profound things simply, to be moving without rhetoric, to speak technically without pedantry; and from what German could we have learned this lesson? He is also quite free of Lessing's mannered subtlety, excessive sprightliness, and—if I may use the word—quite un-German style; and this is a great merit in him, since Lessing is, of all writers in prose, the most seductive model. The highest praise I can give his style is to apply to it his own saying: "A philosopher must be very honest in order to dispense with poetical and rhetorical devices."[5]

That honesty matters and may even be a virtue is one of those private

5. For the gist, though not the exact words of this quotation (which I cannot locate), see Schopenhauer's penetrating stylistic observations in "On Authorship and Style" and "On Philosophy and Its Methods" in *Parerga and Paralipomena*. The tension between poetry as a complex, coherent metaphorical whole and philosophy as the cold scientific pursuit of truth, between myth and metaphor on one hand and discursive reason on the other, is of course central in the thought of Nietzsche, whose work oscillates between one and the other. In *Schopenhauer as Educator*, Nietzsche exalts Schopenhauer's mythical and metaphorical power as that of a living pre-Socratic; in *Human, All-Too-Human*, the stress is upon reason, science, etc. For enlightening discussion, see the essays by Pütz, Pasley, and others in Malcolm Pasley, ed., *Nietzsche: Imagery and Thought* (Berkeley, 1978).

opinions prohibited in this age of public opinion. So I shall not have praised Schopenhauer, but merely characterized him, if I say once more that he is honest, even as a writer. So few writers are honest that we should really distrust all writers. I know of only one writer whom, in point of honesty, I can rank with Schopenhauer, and even above him, and that is Montaigne. The fact that such a man has written truly adds to the joy of living on this earth. At any rate, since my first encounter with this freest and most vigorous of spirits, I feel moved to say of him what he said of Plutarch: "No sooner do I look at him than I sprout a leg or a wing."[6] If my task were to make myself at home on this earth, it is to him that I would cleave.

Schopenhauer shares with Montaigne another quality besides honesty: a genuinely cheering cheerfulness. *Aliis laetus, sibi sapiens.*[7] There are two very different kinds of cheer. The true thinker invariably cheers and quickens, whether he expresses his seriousness or his playfulness, his human insight or divine indulgence; he does this not with gloomy gestures, trembling hands, and tearful eyes, but surely and simply, with courage and strength, perhaps somewhat cavalierly and harshly, but in any event as a conqueror. And it is this that provides the most profound and intense cheer—to see the victorious god amid all the monsters he has fought. By contrast, the cheerfulness we sometimes meet in mediocre writers and small-time thinkers makes us miserable on reading them: the way I felt, for instance, with the "cheerfulness" of David Strauss. There is truly something shameful in having such cheerful contemporaries, because they expose to posterity the nakedness of our age and the people in it. These cheerlings[8] do not even see the suffering and monsters which, as thinkers, they pretend to see and fight. And because their cheerfulness is deceptive, it provokes irritation; it tends to mislead us into believing that a victory has been won. Basically, there is good cheer only where there is victory, and this applies just as much to the works of true thinkers as to any work of art. Even if the subject is as grave and terrible as the problem of existence, the work will have a depressing and painful effect only when the half-thinker and the half-artist have smothered it in the fumes of their own inadequacy. On the other hand, nothing more joyful, nothing better, can happen to a man than to be close to one of those victorious spirits who, because they have thought most deeply, must therefore love precisely what is most alive, and who, because

6. Montaigne, *Essais*, ed. Pierre Villey (Paris, 1923), 3:121. Montaigne's "Je n'en tire cuisse ou aisle" has been wrongly rendered (as a marginal note in the manuscript indicates) by Nietzsche as "I spread a leg or a wing." See W. D. Williams, *Nietzsche and the French* (Oxford, 1952), 20.
7. "Cheerful to others, sensible to himself."
8. The German is "solche Heiterling." *Heiterling* is Nietzsche's own coinage, meant to conjure up a man who is ostentatiously, professionally "cheerful" or "hearty."

they are wise, are finally disposed to what is beautiful. They really speak.
They neither stammer nor parrot; they truly move and live, not in the sinister
masquerade in which men are accustomed to live. And so, when we are
close to them, we feel human and natural at last, and would like to cry out
with Goethe, "How wonderful and precious is a living thing! How suited
to its condition, how truly, how vividly it *is!*"[9]

I am describing only the first, almost physiological, impression Schopenhauer made on me, the uncanny outflowing of inner power from one living
thing to another that takes place at the first, gentlest contact. And analyzing
that impact in retrospect, I find it composed of three elements: the impression of his honesty, his cheerfulness, and his steadfastness. He is honest
because he speaks and writes to himself and for himself; cheerful because
he has conquered with his thought the most difficult thing of all; and steadfast because that was his nature. His power rises like a flame on a windless
day, straight up, easily and undisturbed, steady, unflickering. Wherever he
is, he finds his way, without our ever noticing that he had sought it; he
moves along as steadily and nimbly and inevitably as though propelled by
the law of gravity. And anyone who has felt what it means, in this age of
stunted freaks and hybrid humanity,[10] to discover a completely integrated,
harmonious, free, and uninhibited nature—a man who, like a door, swings
freely on his hinges—will understand my joy and astonishment on discovering Schopenhauer. In him I felt that I had found that teacher and philosopher I had so long been searching for. Granted, he existed only as a
book, and this was a great deprivation. And so I made greater efforts to
look behind the book and imagine the living man whose great testament I
was reading, and who promised that his heirs would be only those who
wanted to be and were able to be more than readers—that is, his sons and
disciples.

3   A philosopher matters to me according to his
ability to be an example. There is no doubt that by force of his example he
can draw whole nations after him; the history of India, which is virtually the
history of Indian philosophy, proves it. But the example must be evinced
not merely in his books, but in his visible life, in the way the Greek philosophers taught—through their facial expressions, demeanor, dress, food,
and habits, rather than through what they said or wrote. How utterly we
Germans still lack this courageous manifestation in our philosophical life!

9. Goethe, *Travels in Italy*. Entry dated: Venice, Oct. 9, 1786.
10. In the German, *Tragelaphen-Menschheit*, formed from Greek *trag-elaphos*, a "goat-
stag," i.e., a fabulous composite animal analogous to the hybrid chimera. Cf. Aristophanes
Frogs 937; Plato *Republic* 6.488a.

Here the body is very gradually being liberated,[11] whereas the mind was long ago emancipated; and yet it is an illusion to think that the mind can be free and independent unless this acquired freedom from limitation—which is basically a creative limitation, self-imposed—is manifested from morning till night in every glance and footstep. Kant clung to the university, submitted to authority, sustained the pretense of religious faith, put up with colleagues and students; so it is only natural that his example has begotten university professors and professorial philosophy. Schopenhauer thinks very little of the learned classes; he keeps aloof; he strives for independence from state and society—this is his example, the model he sets—to start with the most superficial aspects. But many stages in the emancipation of the philosophical life are still unknown among the Germans, and they cannot for long remain that way. Our artists live more boldly and honestly; and the mightiest example presented to our eyes—that of Richard Wagner—shows that, if the genius wants to bring to light the higher order and the truth that live in him, he must not flinch from a fight to the death with established forms and rules. That "truth," however, of which our professors chatter so much, appears a mousy little creature from whom nothing unruly or exceptional need be feared—a cozy, good-natured little thing who constantly assures all the established powers that she will cause nobody any trouble; after all, she is only "pure knowledge." In sum, I would say that philosophy in Germany must more and more forget about being "pure knowledge." And this is precisely the example set by the man Schopenhauer.

But it is a miracle, nothing less, that Schopenhauer should have become

---

11. For Nietzsche, the body's liberation is the essential condition of man and the desired transvaluation of Christian and bourgeois culture founded on hypocrisy and the body's suppression. As Walter Kaufmann observes (*The Portable Nietzsche* [New York, 1954], 262), "Nietzsche's early impact was in some ways comparable to that of Freud and Havelock Ellis. But prudery was for him at most one of three great evils, one kind of hypocrisy, one aspect of man's betrayal of the earth and of himself." Cf. "On the Despisers of the Body" (*Z*, part 1) and "On the Three Evils" (*Z*, part 3). Only by accepting his body can the new man be loyal to the earth, to the "Mensch und Menschen-Erde": "Remain faithful to the earth, my brothers, with the power of your virtue. Let your earth-giving love and your knowledge serve the meaning of the earth. . . . Lead back to the earth the virtue that flew away, as I do—back to the body, back to life, that it may give the earth a meaning, a human meaning" (*Z*, part 1, "On the Gift-Giving Virtue," 2).

It is not always realized that in this matter as in so many others Nietzsche's mentor is Schopenhauer, for whom the body is simply the "objectification of the Will to Live"; in all its parts the body is defined by the Will, and on this objectified Will—the body's *Ding-an-Sich*—identity and character depend. Intellect is secondary, designed (like Bergson's Memory) to serve the needs of the body—like claws and teeth. See *The World as Will and Representation*, trans. E. F. J. Payne (Indian Hills, Colo., 1958), 1:326ff.; also 2:xix, "On the Primacy of the Will in Self-Consciousness," and 2:xx, "Objectification of the Will in the Animal Organism."

this human example. Outwardly and inwardly he was assailed by pressures and dangers so frightful that they would have crushed or broken a weaker nature. There was, it seems to me, a strong likelihood that the man Schopenhauer might have perished, leaving at best a residue of "pure knowledge," and this only in the best of circumstances. More likely, neither man nor knowledge.

The dangers that most commonly threaten exceptional men who live in a society bound to convention have been described by a modern Englishman in these words: "Unusual characters of this kind are at first cowed, then they turn melancholy, then sicken, and finally die. A Shelley could not have lived in England, and a race of Shelleys would have been impossible."[12] Our own Hölderlin and Kleist, and countless others, died of their own unconventionality and could not endure the climate of what is called "German culture"; only natures of iron—like Beethoven, Goethe, Schopenhauer, and Wagner—can stick it out. But even these natures reveal, in any number of traits and wrinkles, the effect of this utterly exhausting agony and struggle: their breathing becomes labored, their tone too easily tends to be violent. A knowledgeable diplomat, who had barely set eyes on Goethe and exchanged a few words with him, observed to a friend: "Voilà un homme qui a eu de grands chagrins!"—which Goethe translated as, "There's a man who worked himself to death." And he adds, "If there is no way we can erase from our features the marks of the sufferings we endured and the activities we brought to conclusion, it is no wonder that every surviving remnant of us and our struggles should bear the same traces." And this is Goethe, whom our culture-philistines point out as the happiest of Germans in order to prove from his example that it must be possible to be happy in their midst—with the implied corollary that it is unforgivable for a man to feel unhappy and alone among them. For this reason they have, with great cruelty, advanced and put into practice the theory that every case of loneliness implies a secret guilt.

Poor Schopenhauer too, of course, has a secret guilt on his conscience and in his heart, the guilt of valuing his philosophy more highly than he valued his contemporaries. Besides, he was unfortunate enough to have learned from Goethe that in order to save the life of his philosophy he had to protect it at any cost from the indifference of his contemporaries. For there is a kind of inquisitorial censorship which, according to Goethe, the Germans have brought to perfection: glacial silence. At least it was for this reason that most of the first edition of Schopenhauer's masterpiece had to be pulped. The looming danger that his great project might be doomed by indifference produced in Schopenhauer a terrible, almost uncontrollable

12. Walter Bagehot (1826–77), *Physics and Politics* (Boston, 1956), 107 (chap. 4, "On Nation-Making"). Nietzsche has "England" where Bagehot wrote "New England."

anxiety; not one worthy supporter made an appearance. It is saddening to watch him searching for any sign of recognition; and his final piercing cry of triumph that he was actually being read (*legor et legar*)[13] is somehow painfully moving. It is precisely those traits in which the philosopher's dignity is absent that reveal the suffering man, in anguish over his most precious possession; he is tormented by the fear of losing his small fortune and, along with it perhaps, his ability to maintain his pure, classical attitude toward philosophy. And so, in his yearning for trusting and sympathetic companions, he frequently made mistakes, only to return sadly to his faithful dog. He was in every respect a solitary; not a single truly like-minded friend consoled him; and here, between one and none, as between something and nothing, lies an infinity. No one who has real friends knows what real loneliness is, not even if the whole world is against him.

But I see my reader does not know what solitude is.[14] Wherever powerful societies, governments, public opinion, and religions have existed—in short, wherever tyranny existed—the solitary philosopher has been hated. For philosophy offers an asylum where no tyranny can penetrate, the cavern of inwardness and the labyrinth of the heart.[15] And this angers the tyrants. There the solitary ones take refuge; but there too lies their greatest danger. These men who have internalized their freedom must also live in the external world, must be visible, must let themselves be seen. By virtue of birth, domicile, country, chance, and the importunity of others, they are bound by countless human ties. Similarly, all sorts of opinions are attributed to them simply because these are the dominant opinions; every attitude that is not denial is construed as assent; every gesture that does not destroy is taken as approval. They know, these solitary, free-spirited people, that in some way they always appear different from their own sense of themselves. Whereas all they want is truth and honesty, they are tangled in a web of

---

13. "I am read, and I will be read."

14. For Schopenhauer and Nietzsche the essential requirements of genius were: solitude, intellect, leisure. Zarathustra's solitude on his icy height, Nietzsche's lifelong passion for an ascetic, hermit-like existence in the solitude of Sils Maria and elsewhere—these found their initial example and text in Schopenhauer's life and writings. See *The World as Will and Representation* (hereafter cited as *WWR*), passim, but esp. 1:203–04; 2:383, 390. The following passage (*Parerga and Paralipomena* [hereafter *PP*], 1:419–20) is typical: "In solitude the wretch feels the whole of his wretchedness, the great mind the full extent of his greatness; in short, everyone feels himself to be what he is. Further, the higher a man stands in nature's order of precedence, the more lonely he is; and this is essential and inevitable."

15. A glance at Goethe's beautiful lyric "An den Mond": "Happy the man who can withdraw without hatred from the world, keep a friend beside him, and enjoy with him what, unknown or neglected by man, walks in the night through the labyrinth of the heart."

misunderstandings; and despite their own passionate desires they cannot keep a dense fog of wrong opinions, compromises, half-truths, charitable silences, and misinterpretations from settling over everything they do. And so a cloud of melancholy gathers on their brows, for these natures hate the necessity of pretense worse than death;[16] and this continuous bitterness makes them volcanic and menacing. Every so often they take revenge for their enforced self-concealment and the reserve imposed upon them. They emerge from their caves with a ferocious look; their words and actions are explosions, and they can destroy themselves. Schopenhauer lived in this way, dangerously.

Solitaries of this kind need love above everything else; they must have companions with whom they can be as open and simple as they are with themselves, in whose presence the strain caused by silence and hypocrisy is absent. Remove their companions and you create a growing danger. Heinrich von Kleist was destroyed by this lack of love, and the most dreadful antidote that can be applied to exceptional men is to drive them so deeply into themselves that their re-emergence is invariably a volcanic eruption. And yet there is always some demigod who can bear to live under such frightful conditions, and to live victoriously. If you want to hear his solitary song, listen to Beethoven's music.

Solitude: this is the first danger in whose shadow Schopenhauer developed. The second danger is called despair of truth. To this danger every thinker who takes the philosophy of Kant as his starting point is susceptible, providing that in his sufferings and desires he is a whole and vigorous man and not merely a clacking machine for thinking and calculating. We all know very well the shameful situation implied by this assumption; in my opinion, anyway, Kant vitally affected and radically transformed only a very few people. True, the work of this quiet scholar is said, as we can read on all sides, to have revolutionized every field of intellectual life. But I cannot believe it. For I see no signs of it in people themselves, who would have had to be revolutionized before any whole field of inquiry. And if Kant began to have a popular effect, we would be aware of it in the form of a corrosive and destructive skepticism and relativism. Only in the case of the noblest and most active spirits—those who could never persist in doubt—would there come that shattering upheaval and despair of all truth which, in the case of Kleist, were the effect of Kant's philosophy. "It was only recently," writes Kleist in his moving way, "that I encountered the philosophy of Kant, and now I must tell you one of its ideas, without indulging my fear that it will shatter you as deeply and as painfully as it did me. 'We cannot decide whether what we call truth really is truth, or whether it only seems so. If

16. An echo of Achilles' words to Odysseus at *Iliad* 9:312–13: "Worse than the gates of hell I hate that man who hides one thing in his heart and says another."

the latter, then the truth we gather here is nothing after we die, and all our efforts to win a property that can follow us to the grave are useless. If this pointed thought does not pierce your heart, do not smile at another man who feels himself wounded in the sacred inmost depths of his being. My highest, my only purpose has vanished, and I have no other left.' "[17] Alas, when will men again feel things with the naturalness of Kleist? When will they learn again to measure the meaning of a philosophy in "the sacred inmost depths of their being"?

Yet this is what is above all needed if we are to evaluate what, after Kant, Schopenhauer might mean to us—that is, the leader who guides us up from the cave of skeptical disillusion or critical renunciation to the peaks of tragic contemplation, the night sky with its infinity of stars overhead, and who first trod this path himself. This is his greatness, that he confronts the picture of life as a whole in order to interpret it in its wholeness,[18] whereas the acutest intellects cannot liberate themselves from the mistaken notion that this interpretation is best mediated by a painstaking analysis of the colors and canvas on which the picture is painted—only to conclude perhaps that the texture of the canvas is extremely intricate and that the chemistry of the paints resists analysis! To understand the picture, you must first divine the painter: this Schopenhauer knew. But now the whole scholarly guild is engaged in understanding that canvas and those colors, but not the painting. In fact, one could say that only he who has the overall picture of life and existence firmly in view can make use of the individual fields of learning without suffering damage; and that without a comprehensive view as a controlling norm, the disciplines are merely guidelines leading nowhere, which makes the course of our life even more confused and labyrinthine. It is in this, as I observed earlier, that Schopenhauer's greatness lies; he pursues the picture as Hamlet pursues the ghost, without letting himself be diverted like the scholars, or tangled in a web of scholastic abstractions, which is the fate of uncontrolled dialecticians. If the study of these stunted philosophers is appealing, it is because they immediately stumble on just those points in

17. See von Kleist's letter to Wilhelmine and Ulrike, March 22–23, 1801.
18. For Schopenhauer one of the essential distinctions between the genius and the ordinary man—as between the genius and the merely talented man or the scholar—is that the genius takes all of nature or reality, the *totality* of existence, as his subject or concern. As he wrote in *WWR* (2:129): "Empirical sciences, pursued purely for their own sake and without philosophical tendency, are like a face without eyes. They are, however, a suitable occupation for people of good capacity, who nevertheless lack the highest faculties. ... Such persons concentrate their whole strength and all their knowledge on a single limited field. Therefore in that field they can reach the most complete knowledge possible, on condition that they remain in complete ignorance of everything else, whereas the philosopher must survey all fields, and indeed to a certain extent be at home in them all." See also *WWR*, 2:338, and *PP*, 1:340 and 2:77.

the structure of a great philosophy where scholarly pros and cons, commentary, doubts, and contradictions are permitted, and thereby evade the demand made by every great philosophy, which as a whole says only and always: This is the picture of all life; learn from it the meaning of your own life. And conversely too: Read your own life and, by so doing, understand the hieroglyphs of universal life.

And this is how, from the outset, Schopenhauer's philosophy should be interpreted: individually, by each individual for himself alone, to acquire insight into his own misery, and need, and limitations, and to know the remedies and consolations—that is, the sacrifice of the ego, submission to the noblest goals, above all to justice and compassion. He teaches us to distinguish between real and apparent means of promoting human happiness: how the acquisition of wealth, respectability, or erudition cannot pluck the individual out of his deep disgust at the worthlessness of his existence; and how the aspiration towards all these good things acquires meaning only by a lofty and transfiguring common goal—to acquire power in order to assist our own *physis*[19] and correct somewhat its folly and awkwardness. At first, only for oneself; but through one's self, finally for all. Admittedly, this is an aspiration that leads, profoundly and cheerfully, to resignation. For what, and how much, after all, can still be improved, in the individual and in general!

Applying these words directly to Schopenhauer, we touch upon the third danger, the one most peculiar to him, imbedded in the whole structure and makeup of his nature. Every man usually discovers a limitation in himself, in both his talents and his moral will, which fills him with longing and melancholy. And just as consciousness of sin makes him yearn for what is holy, so, as an intellectual creature, he has a deep longing for his own personal genius.[20] All true culture is rooted in this longing. And if I equate

19. Greek for "nature." Nietzsche uses this word not in order to be pretentious, but to distinguish what he means from German *Wesen* (i.e., "nature" as "entity," "being," "behavior"). When, in the first section of this essay, Nietzsche says that one's educators reveal "the true original being and basic stuff of your nature" (Urstoff und Grundstoff deines Wesen), he is speaking of *physis* as the raw material (Greek *hylē*), the "bedrock," as it were, of one's being. This physis is given, it cannot be changed; all an educator can do is to discover it and liberate it so it can realize itself, according to its possibilities. This is the ineradicable, almost inaccessible core—"The obstinate, the tougher self, who does not speak, / Who never talks, who cannot argue"—synonymous with the latent daimon, waiting its opportunity to unfold itself and *become*, according to the Pindaric maxim: "Become the thing you are." Cf. "The Tomb Song" in *Z*, part 2: "Indeed, in me there is something invulnerable and unburiable, something that explodes rock. That is my will. Silent and unchanged, it strides through the years."
20. Nietzsche's conception of self-realization—that true self which "does not lie hidden deep inside you but immeasurably high above you, or at least above that which you

culture with man's yearning to be *reborn* as saint and genius, I know that one need not be a Buddhist to understand this myth. Where we come across talent without this longing, in scholarly circles or among those who call themselves cultured, we feel revulsion and disgust. For we suspect that these people, with all their intelligence, do not foster, but impede a developing culture and the generating of genius—which is the aim of all culture. They exhibit a hardening, of no greater value than the cold arrogance of conventional righteousness, which is so far removed from true holiness and drives men away from it.

Schopenhauer's nature contained an unusual and extremely dangerous duality. Few thinkers have felt so strongly, with such incomparable certainty, their own in-dwelling genius; and his genius made him the supreme promise—that the furrow cut by his ploughshare in the soil of modern mankind would be the deepest furrow of all. So he knew that half of his nature was fulfilled and satisfied, conscious of its power and without other cravings; and he therefore carried out his calling with the greatness and dignity of a man who had victoriously fulfilled himself. In the other half of his nature there was a violent yearning; we intuit it at once when we hear how he turned away, pain in his eyes, from the portrait of Rancé, the great founder of the Trappist order, with these words: "It is a matter of grace."[21] For the genius yearns more deeply for holiness because he has seen, from his high vantage point, farther and more clearly than any other man into the reconciliation of knowledge and being, into the realm of peace and the denial of the will, across to the shore beyond, of which the Hindu sages speak. But this is precisely the miracle: how inconceivably whole and unbreakable Schopenhauer's nature must have been, that this yearning could neither destroy nor harden it! Each man will comprehend this according to his stature and nature; none of us will grasp it all, in all its gravity.

---

customarily consider to be your ego"—is, like Plato's doctrine of Eros, founded on the necessary imperfection of human nature. All human aspiration is in direct proportion to what a man *lacks* or *needs* or *wants*. Therefore, culture—*Bildung* as self-*molding,* treating oneself as a statue to be sculpted—is rooted in this lack and corresponding yearning to remedy it. Man wants, out of this very imperfection of nature, to transcend himself, to be himself a bridge between the beast of his past and the hero (or Overman or even god) of his ideal future. On this principle Nietzsche's later doctrine of "backward inference" is in fact founded. One intuits the ideal or desired value or virtue of an individual or a culture from the felt absence of that virtue or value; it is the lack that creates the ideal. The Greeks, for instance, valued *sophrosynē* over everything else because they were temperamentally and culturally disposed to *hybris.* So, too, Schopenhauer's passionate yearning for the life of Rancé, founder of the Trappist order, is, for Nietzsche, an instance of successfully emancipating the service of the intellect from that of the Will, though at terrible cost (see n. 23 below; also *WWR,* 2:388–89).

21. Cf. W. Gwinner, *Arthur Schopenhauer aus persönlichen Umgange dargestellt* (Leipzig, 1862), 108.

The more one ponders the three dangers I have described, the more astonishing appears Schopenhauer's vigor in defending himself from them, and the fact that he emerged from the struggle healthy and unbroken. With many scars and open wounds to be sure, and in a mood that may seem overly harsh and at times excessively pugnacious. Even the greatest man is shorter than his own ideal. But despite scars and flaws, Schopenhauer can surely stand as a model to men. We might even say that what in him was imperfect and all too human brings us closer to him in the most human sense, since we view him as a sufferer and fellow-sufferer, not merely on the remote heights of genius.

These three constitutional dangers that threatened Schopenhauer threaten us all. Every man carries within him a creative uniqueness, as the core of his being; and when he becomes aware of this uniqueness, a strange radiance surrounds him, the aura of the unusual. To most men this awareness is intolerable because, as I observed earlier, they are lazy, and because each man's uniqueness shackles him to burdens and troubles. For the exceptional man who burdens himself with these shackles, there is no doubt that life loses almost everything we hope to have from it when we are young—joy, security, amusement, honors. The fate of solitude is the gift he receives from other men; live where he will, the desert and the cave are instantly with him. So let him take care that he is not forced to submit, that he does not become depressed and melancholy. And let him therefore surround himself with the examples of good, courageous warriors, like Schopenhauer.

But the second danger that threatened Schopenhauer is not uncommon. It sometimes happens that nature equips a man with keenness of vision; his thoughts readily take the ambiguous way of dialectic. How easy it is for him, by giving free rein to his talent, to perish as a human being and lead merely a ghostly existence in the realm of "pure knowledge." Or alternatively, because he is accustomed to seeking the pros and cons of things, he begins to doubt the truth itself and to live without courage or confidence, denying and doubting, gnawed by remorse, discontented, in half-hopes and anticipated disappointment. "Even a dog wouldn't want a life like that!"[22]

The third danger is moral and intellectual hardening. Man breaks the bond that linked him to his ideal. He ceases to be productive in this or that field, to reproduce himself; culturally speaking, he is either a menace or useless. The uniqueness of his nature has become an indivisible, isolated atom, a frozen stone. In this manner a man can be destroyed through his uniqueness just as he can perish through fear of his uniqueness; he can perish through his self as he can by surrendering himself, through yearning as by hardening. And living means, in short, to be in danger.

22. See Goethe, *Faust*, part 1, 376.

Besides these constitutional dangers to which Schopenhauer would have been exposed in whatever century he lived, there are also dangers that beset him from his *own time*. And this distinction between constitutional and historical dangers is essential if we are to grasp what is exemplary and educational in Schopenhauer. Imagine the philosopher's gaze as it muses on existence: he wants to make a fresh assessment of its value. For this has always been the peculiar work of all great thinkers, to be the legislators of the weights and measures and coinage of things. What an obstacle to his work when the humanity he sees before him is in fact a blighted, worm-eaten fruit! What a great supplement of value must be added to the worthlessness of our times, if he is to do justice to existence in general. If there is any value in studying the history of past or foreign peoples, it is especially valuable to the philosopher who wants to deliver an accurate judgment on the whole destiny of man—not merely on the average lot of man, but also and above all on the highest fate that can befall a single individual or whole peoples. But the present is importunate; it manipulates and determines the philosopher's eye, despite his resistance; and it is unintentionally overvalued in the final reckoning. This is why the philosopher must take pains to assess his own time in comparison with others; and by overcoming the present for himself, also overcome the present in the picture he draws of life, making it inconspicuous and, as it were, painting it over.

This is a difficult, indeed almost impossible, assignment. The judgment of the ancient Greek philosophers on the value of existence means so much more than a modern judgment because all around them and before their eyes they had life itself in luxuriant realization, and because with them the thinker's intuition was not troubled, as it is with us, in the conflict between the craving for freedom, beauty, and greatness of life, and the drive for truth which asks only: What is the cumulative value of existence? It is important for every age to know what Empedocles, living in an age when Greek culture was in full exuberant flush and lust for life, has to say about existence. His judgment carries great weight, especially since he is not contradicted by a single contrary judgment by any other great philosopher of that same great period. He speaks more clearly than the rest, but basically—that is, if we keep our ears open a little—they are all saying the same thing. A modern thinker, as I said, will always suffer from an unfulfilled desire: he will insist first on being shown life again, real, red-blooded, healthy life, in order to pass judgment on it. He will think it necessary, at least for himself, to be a living man before he can dare to think that he will be a good judge. It is for this reason that the modern philosophers are among the staunchest champions of life and the will to live, and that they long to escape from their own enervated age and yearn for culture, a transfigured physis. This yearning, however, is also their *danger*; in them the reformer of life and the philosopher, that is, the judge of life, are in conflict. Whichever way the victory goes, it is a victory that implies a defeat. And how did Schopenhauer escape this danger too?

If we like to think of every great man as a true child of his times, and he clearly suffers from all its maladies more strongly and sensitively than smaller men, then the struggle of such a great man *against* his times is apparently only a senselessly self-destructive struggle against himself. But only apparently. For his war is with that quality in his own age which prevents him from being great, which for him means simply being free and wholly himself. It follows that his hostility is actually directed against something that is clearly in him but which is not truly himself; that is, against the impure, chaotic confusion of forever irreconcilable and uncombinable things, against the false fusion in him of the contemporary and the timeless.[23] And in the end the putative child of the age proves himself to be only its stepchild. Thus Schopenhauer, from early youth on, struggled against that false, vain, and unworthy mother—his own age—and by expelling her from himself, he purified and healed his nature and recovered the health and purity that were properly his. For this reason Schopenhauer's writings should be used as a mirror of the age; and it is surely no flaw in the mirror

23. The essential texts for Nietzsche's argument here are Schopenhauerian, as Nietzsche duly observes. See *WWR*, 2, "On Genius," esp. 384–91. Nietzsche's belief that the great man wars against himself, against the false fusion in himself of "the contemporary and the timeless' (die falsche Anlötung des *Zeitgemässen* an sein Unzeitgemässen), derives from Schopenhauer's account (*WWR*, 2:384–85) of the genius's sacrifice of his own interests on behalf of the "timeless":

> Therefore only extremely rare and abnormal men, whose true seriousness lies not in the personal and practical, but in the objective and theoretical, are in a position to apprehend the essential element of things and of the world, and hence the highest truths. . . . For such a seriousness of the individual, falling outside him in the *objective*, is something foreign to human nature, something unnatural. . . . But only through it is man *great*. . . . For such a man, his painting, poetry, thinking is an *end*; for the other, it is a *means*. Those others look to it for *their own interest* and, as a rule, know how to promote it, for they insinuate themselves into the favor of contemporaries, and are ready to serve their wants and whims. They therefore usually live in happy circumstances; whereas the genius exists under very wretched conditions. For he sacrifices his personal welfare to the *objective* end; he simply cannot do otherwise, because there lies his seriousness. They act conversely; therefore they are *small*, but he is *great*. His work usually is for all times and ages . . . they live and die with their time. In general, he alone is *great* who in his work, be it practical or theoretical, *seeks not his own interest*, but pursues only an *objective* end.

Nietzsche describes Schopenhauer in terms drawn from Schopenhauer's own thesis. By struggling to emancipate his philosophical intellect from the service of the Will to Live, by persistently seeking the *totality* of things, at the sacrifice of his own self-interest, Schopenhauer finally freed himself from the tyranny of the contemporary, i.e., the locally temporal and parochial, from the idols of the age, its conventions and "public opinion." He became, in short, an "unmodern" (*unzeitgemässe*) man.

if everything modern appears in it only as a disfiguring sickness, as emaciated pallor, sunken eyes, and worn features, as the recognizable maladies of the stepchild. His yearning for a vigorous nature, for sane and simple humanity, was a yearning for himself; and as soon as he had overcome his own times within himself, he was bound to look with astonishment upon the genius within himself. Now the secret of his being was disclosed to him; the aim of his stepmotherly age to conceal his genius from him was thwarted, and the realm of transfigured physis was revealed. Now, when he turned with fearless eyes to the question "What is life finally worth?" he no longer had to pass judgment on a chaotic and anemic age and its life of hypocritical obscurity. He really knew that there was something far higher and purer than contemporary life to be found and achieved on this earth, and that he who knows and appraises existence only in its hateful contemporary guise does it a bitter injustice. No, genius itself is now called to witness, so we may hear whether it, the supreme fruit of existence, can perhaps justify life as a whole. The man, magnificent and creative, must answer the question: "Do you affirm this life in the depths of your being? Does it suffice you? Will you be its advocate and redeemer? A single sincere 'Yes!' from you— and life, now so terribly accused, will be set free." What answer will he give? The answer given by Empedocles.

4   Let this last hint remain unexplained for the moment. I am now concerned with a very comprehensible matter, namely, to explain how all of us *can*, with Schopenhauer's help, educate ourselves *against* the age—because through him we have the advantage of really *knowing* this age of ours. That is, if knowing our age is an advantage! In any case it may no longer be even possible a few centuries from now. I take pleasure in the thought that man may soon grow sick and tired of books and writers as well, and that one day the scholar may take stock, write his will, and leave orders for his corpse to be cremated amidst his books—especially his own. And if the forests keep on thinning away, might there not be an age in which libraries will be treated like wood, straw, and brush? Most books, after all, are born from the smoking heads of scholars, and to smoke they shall return. If they lack fire, then fire will punish them for it. A later century may perhaps view this age of ours as a *saeculum obscurum*[24] because its products served to keep the furnaces constantly burning. In that case, how fortunate we are that we can know this age of ours. For if there is any sense at all in studying our own times, it is a fortunate thing to study it as thoroughly as possible, so that no further doubt will remain. And it is just this opportunity that Schopenhauer provides.

Admittedly, our good fortune would be a hundred times greater if this

24. "dark age"

inquiry showed that there had never been a period as proud and promising as our own. And even now in some corner of the world, like Germany, there are people so naive that they are ready to believe such things, and even to declare in all seriousness that the world has been set right in the last two years, and that anyone who has grave and grim misgivings about existence has been refuted by the "facts." And the "fact" is that the founding of the new German Reich is the decisive blow that demolishes all "pessimistic" philosophizing—this simply can't be denied! Opinions of this sort, widely held and fostered above all in the universities, must be dealt with by anyone who asks about the significance of the philosopher as educator in our times. And this is our answer: It is a shame and a disgrace that such nauseatingly obsequious flattery of the idols of the age could be uttered and repeated by presumably decent and intelligent people—proof that we no longer grasp the vast difference in seriousness between philosophy and a newspaper. People of this sort have lost every last shred of religious and philosophical conviction, and have exchanged them, not for optimism, but for journalism, the wit and unwisdom of the day—and the dailies. Any philosophy founded on the belief that the problem of existence has been changed or solved by a political event is a parody of philosophy and a sham. Many states have been founded since the world began; it is an old story. How could a political innovation suffice to make men contented dwellers on this earth at last? If anyone sincerely believes this to be possible, let him make himself heard. He truly deserves to be appointed professor of philosophy at a German university, like Harms[25] at Berlin, Jürgen Meyer[26] at Bonn, and Carrière[27] at Munich.

In this matter we are experiencing the consequences of a doctrine lately

---

25. Hans Joachim Friedrich Harms (1816–80), professor of philosophy at the University of Berlin from 1867 until his death. His work reveals him as still another Idealist epigone, interested in advancing and broadening the domain of Reason, but at the same time committed to the empiricism and positivism of the "scientific" disciplines. Essentially, his work is an uneasy and unsuccessful effort to reconcile the dominant academic Idealism, post-Kantian and post-Hegelian, with the increasingly scientific and antimetaphysical outlook of the age. As such, Friedrich's work seemed to Nietzsche patently, and deplorably, contemporary (*zeitgemässe*) and conventional.

26. Jürgen Meyer (1829–97), from 1868 professor of philosophy at Bonn, where both as teacher and writer he attempted to interpret Kant's transcendentalism in psychological terms. His works include *Kants Psychologie* (1869) and *Schopenhauer* (1871), a widely read critique which, it may be assumed, aroused Nietzsche's indignation and scorn.

27. Phillip Moriz Carrière (1817–95), post-Hegelian philosopher, historian, and esthetician, professor at Munich from 1853. Politically a champion of German unification, he was an avowed enemy of Ultramontanism and labored to make German unity acceptable to Catholic South Germany. Culturally and philosophically, his work is a blend of late Idealism and Fichtean Christianity with liberal ideas of progress; it enjoyed a wide readership.

preached from every rooftop, that the state is the highest purpose of mankind, and that man has no higher duty than service to the state. In this I
see a relapse, not into paganism, but into stupidity. It may be that a man
who views service to the state as his highest duty actually knows no higher
duty. Still, this is precisely why there are higher men and higher duties, and
one of these duties (which to me at least seems higher than service to the
state) calls for the destruction of stupidity in every form, which means this
stupidity too. I am therefore concerned here with those men whose teleology
extends farther than the welfare of the state, that is, with philosophers, and
with them only as regards a world fairly independent of the welfare of the
state—namely, the world of culture. Of the many links in the mesh com-
posing the human community, some are gold, others gilt.

How, then, does our philosopher view culture in this age? Very differently,
of course, from those professors of philosophy who are so delighted with
the state and the present state of affairs. If he reflects on the universal frenzy
and the accelerating tempo, the disappearance of contemplation and simplicity, it almost seems to him as though he were seeing the symptoms of
the complete destruction, the total extirpation of culture. The flood of religion recedes, leaving swamps or puddles behind; the nations veer apart
once again in the most violent hostility, impatient to massacre one another.
The various fields of learning, pursued without moderation and in the blind-
est laissez-faire, are fragmenting and dissolving every established belief.
Educated classes and nations alike are being swept away by a gigantic and
contemptible economy of money. Never has the world been more worldly,
never has it been poorer in love and goodness. In all this secular turmoil,
the educated are no longer a beacon or sanctuary; day by day they become
increasingly restless, mindless, and loveless. Everything, contemporary art
and scholarship included, serves the approaching barbarism. The educated
man has degenerated into culture's greatest enemy by denying the general
malaise with lies and thereby impeding the physicians. They take offense,
these poor, spineless rascals, when you speak of their weakness and oppose
their pernicious falsehood. They would very much like to persuade you that
they have surpassed all past centuries, and so they walk about with affected
gaiety. Their manner of pretending happiness has something touching about
it, since their happiness is so utterly incomprehensible. We have to resist
the temptation to ask them what Tannhäuser asked Bitterolf: "Poor thing,
what pleasure have you ever known?"[28] But, alas, we know better, we know
otherwise. Over our heads lies a wintry sky, and we live on a high mountain,
in danger and in need. Every pleasure is brief, and the pale sunlight steals
down to us from the white peaks. Then a burst of music, an old man cranks
a hurdy-gurdy, the dancers whirl around—the wanderer looks and shud-

28. Richard Wagner, *Tannhäuser*, ii, 4.

ders. Everything is so wild, confining, bleak, and hopeless. And then, suddenly, a note of joy, of pure, thoughtless joy! But the early evening mist is already closing in, the music dies, the wanderer's steps crunching on the snow. As far as his eye can reach, there is nothing to be seen but the bleak and terrible face of Nature.[29]

But if it is one-sided to stress the faintness of line and dullness of color in this picture of modern life, the other side is no more comforting but, if anything, more alarming. True, there are forces here, tremendous forces, but wild, primitive, and completely pitiless. One looks at them as one might look at the cauldron in the witches' kitchen, with terrible suspense. At any moment it may erupt in flame and thunder, announcing horrible apparitions. For a century now we have been expecting radical upheavals. And although an attempt has recently been made to offset the modern world's profound tendency to explosion or collapse through the cohesive power of the so-called national state, yet for a long time to come the effect of the state will be to increase the general insecurity and danger. The fact that individuals behave as though they were ignorant of these anxieties does not mislead us; their very restlessness shows how much they are aware of them. They think about themselves more obsessively and exclusively than men have ever done before. They build and plant only for their own day; and the quest for happiness will never be greater than when its quarry must be taken today or tomorrow, because the day after tomorrow the hunting season may be over forever.

We live in the age of atoms, of atomistic chaos. In the Middle Ages the opposing forces were more or less held together, and to some degree assimilated to each other, through the strong pressure exercised by the Church. But when the bond breaks and the pressure slackens, each force rises up against the other. The Reformation declared many matters to be *diaphora*[30]—areas exempt from control by religious considerations. This was

---

29. A typically lyrical Nietzschean "translation" of Schopenhauer's account of the recurrent cycle—fear-joy-despair-boredom—in human life (*WWR*, 1:58). But the knowledgeable reader of Nietzsche will also notice, even in this poetic paraphrase of Schopenhauer, the characteristic images and motifs of Nietzsche's own mythopoeia: the figure of the wanderer, the Dionysiac dance, the bleak, wintry mountain landscape, even the hurdy-gurdy (which will reappear in *Zarathustra*). Here we see Nietzsche in the act of assimilating Schopenhauer imaginatively as the first step in *surpassing*—getting *past*—his pessimistic resignation and negative heroism and moving on to a positive statement of heroism, such as we find in Nietzsche's later work. In its earliest form the vision of Eternal Recurrence which the Nietzschean Overman must confront at its peak intensity of horror and nausea is identical with this Schopenhauerian *cycling* of human feeling between joy and despair, need and fulfillment, constraint and freedom. Here too is the first anticipation of "the death of Nature."

30. Greek for "indifferent," i.e., "unrelated," "irrelevant."

the price religion had to pay for its existence, just as Christianity itself, threatened by a far more religious ancient world, paid a similar price to ensure its survival. Since then the gulf has steadily widened. At present almost everything on earth is determined by the grossest and most malignant forces, by the selfishness of financial profiteers and by military despots. The state, controlled by the latter, attempts—as does the egotism of the money-makers—to reorganize everything, beginning with itself, and to become the bond and pressure linking all those opposed forces. It wants, that is, the same idolatry that men once accorded the Church. With what success? We will know before too long. For today at any rate we are still in the icy, glacial stream of the Middle Ages; the thaw has begun, and a disastrously powerful movement is under way. Floe piles on floe, the shores are flooded and endangered. The revolution, the atomistic revolution, cannot be avoided. But what are the smallest indivisible particles of human society?

There is no doubt that humanity is in almost greater danger during the advent of periods like this than during the actual collapse and chaos of revolution, and that the terrible suspense and greedy exploitation of the moment stimulate every vileness and selfish instinct in the human soul, whereas a real danger, above all a great universal calamity, usually makes men braver and better. Who then, amidst these dangers besetting our age, will pledge his services as sentinel and champion of *humanity,* to the sacred and inviolable temple-treasure gradually amassed by so many different generations? Who will raise the *image of man* when everyone feels in himself the worm of selfishness and a jackal terror, and has fallen from that image into bestiality or even robot automatism?

There are three images of man that modern times have successively raised, whose contemplation will for a long time inspire mortals to transfigure their own lives. These are Rousseau's Man, Goethe's Man, and Schopenhauer's Man. The first of these has the greatest luster and is certain to have the widest popular influence; the second is only for the few, that is, for contemplative thinkers in the grand style, and is misunderstood by the mob. The third can only be contemplated by truly active men; only they can gaze at it without coming to grief, since it undoes contemplative men and terrifies the mob. From the first image came a force that incited, and still incites, violent revolutions. For in every socialist tremor and upheaval, it is always Rousseau's Man who is stirring, like old Typhon underneath Etna. Oppressed and half-crushed by class arrogance and the cruelty of wealth, corrupted by priests and bad education, humiliated in his own eyes by absurd customs, man in his misery calls out to "holy Nature," and suddenly he feels that she is as remote from him as any Epicurean god. So deeply has he sunk into the chaos of the unnatural that his prayers fail to reach her. Scornfully, he casts off all the showy finery—his arts and sciences, the refinements of his life, which he had only recently regarded as his most human possessions. He beats his fists against the wall in whose shadow he has degenerated; he cries out for light, sunshine, the forests, the mountains. And as he exclaims, "Only Nature is good, only the natural is human," he despises himself and yearns to transcend himself—a condition in which the soul is ready for frightful decisions, but which also summons from the depths her noblest and rarest powers.

Goethe's Man is a less threatening force; in some sense he is even the corrective and sedative antidote to just those dangerous excitements to which Rousseau's Man is exposed. Goethe himself in his younger days passionately embraced the gospel of kindly Nature; his Faust was the highest and boldest image of Rousseau's Man, at least insofar as it portrayed the former's lust for life, his discontent and yearning, his converse with the demons of the heart. But look now what emerges from all those gathering clouds—certainly no lightning! In this fact the new image of Man, Goethe's Man, stands revealed. One would have thought that Faust would be led through life, menaced on all sides, the tireless rebel and liberator, the power that negates out of love; he would be the true and proper genius, as it were religious and daemonic, of revolution, in sharp contrast to his quite undaemonic companion; and this, despite the fact that he cannot rid himself of his companion and makes use of him even while loathing the latter's evil and destructive skepticism—which is the tragic destiny of every rebel and liberator. But we are wrong to expect anything of the kind. In this respect Goethe's Man diverges from Rousseau's Man, for he hates all violence, any sudden leap—which means any action; and in this way Faust the world-liberator turns into something like a mere world-traveler. Before the eyes of this insatiable observer every domain of life and nature goes floating by, all past epochs, arts, mythologies, all the sciences. His deepest desire is aroused and satisfied; even Helen can no longer hold him. And now must come the moment for which his mocking companion has been furtively waiting. At a certain place on earth the flight comes to an end, the wings fall away, and Mephistopheles stands at his side. When the German ceases to be Faust, his greatest danger is that of becoming a philistine and falling into the clutches of the devil, from which only heavenly powers can save him. Goethe's Man is, as I said earlier, a contemplative in the grand manner; he survives in this world only by gathering for his nourishment everything great and memorable in the past and the present, so he lives on, even though living only from one desire to another. He is not the active man. On the contrary, if at some point he adapts himself to existing categories of activity, we can be certain that nothing will come of it, as nothing came of Goethe's passion for the theater. Above all, we can be certain that no "order" will be overthrown. Goethe's Man is a conservative and conciliatory force—but in danger, as I said, of degenerating into a philistine, just as Rousseau's

Man can easily become a Catilinarian.[31] Add just a little more muscularity and natural wildness to Goethe's Man, and all his virtues would be greater. It looks as though Goethe knew where the danger and the weakness of his man lay, and he hints at it in Jarno's words to Wilhelm Meister: "You are disgruntled and bitter, and that is all to the good; if someday you got really angry, that would be better still."[32]

And so, to put it bluntly, we must for once be really wicked, in order to make things better. And the image of Schopenhauer's Man should encourage us in this task. *Schopenhauer's Man voluntarily imposes upon himself the suffering of truthfulness,* and this suffering serves to destroy his individual will and to prepare him for that total upheaval and reversal of his nature whose attainment is the real meaning of life. To others, this blunt, outspoken truthfulness looks like the effect of malice, for they think it is their humanitarian duty to preserve their mediocrity and half-truths, and that those who wreck their childish little games in this way must be wicked. To such a man they are tempted to say what Faustus said to Mephistopheles: "To the eternally active, healing, and creative energy, you oppose your devil's fist,"[33] and the man who wants to live, according to Schopenhauer, must resemble Faustus more than Mephistopheles—that is, to the myopic modern eye which detects signs of wickedness in any negation. But there is a species of negation and destruction which is the exact expression of that powerful yearning for holiness and salvation of which Schopenhauer has been, to profane and secularized people like ourselves, the first philosophical teacher. All existence that can be denied deserves to be denied; and being truthful means believing in an existence which could not in any way be denied, which is true in itself and exempt from falsehood. This is why the truthful man feels that his activity has a metaphysical meaning, explicable according to the laws of another, higher life; and, in a deeper sense, affirmative, even

---

31. Lucius Sergius Catiline (ca. 108–62 BC), Roman politician who, disappointed in his quest of the consulship, turned conspirator and revolutionary, the leader of an abortive coup in which the consuls were to be killed, Rome fired, and all debts canceled. Catiline posed as the champion of the proletariat, though the extant sources, all hostile, view him as self-serving, both vicious and ruthless. In *TI*, 45, Nietzsche later wrote: "All innovators of the spirit must for a time bear the pallid and fatal mark of the Chandala [a Vishnavite, regarded by orthodox Brahmins as a pariah or outcast] on their brow—*not* because they are considered that way by others, but because they themselves feel the terrible cleavage separating them from everything that is customary or reputable. Almost every genius knows, as one stage of his development, the 'Catilinarian existence'—a feeling of hatred, revenge, and rebellion against everything which already *is*, which no longer *becomes*. Catiline—the form of pre-existence of *every* Caesar."
32. Goethe, *Wilhelm Meisters Lehrjahre*, 8.5.
33. *Faust*, part 1, 1,379–81.

though everything he does appears to be destructive and a violation of the laws of that higher life. In this respect, his activity necessarily means constant suffering. But, like Meister Eckehart, he knows that "suffering is the swiftest steed to carry you to perfection."[34]

I like to think that anyone whose soul was confronted by such an ideal of life would feel his heart expand and within him a burning desire well up to become such a Schopenhauerian man. That is, to be disinterested and wonderfully serene as regards himself and his personal welfare; in intellectual pursuits, filled with a fierce, consuming fire, far removed from the cold and contemptuous neutrality of what is called "pure scholarship"; exalted high above sulky and peevish contemplation; always ready to sacrifice himself as the first victim of the truth he has discovered; and deeply conscious of the sufferings that must necessarily result from his truthfulness. Admittedly, he destroys his own earthly happiness through his courage; he must be an enemy to those he loves and to the institutions that gave him birth; he is permitted to spare neither men nor things, even though he suffers with them in their injuries. He will be misunderstood and for a long time regarded as an ally of forces he despises; and despite his aspiration to justice, he will have to be unjust when judged by human standards. But he can comfort and encourage himself with these words which Schopenhauer, his great educator, once used: "A happy life is impossible; the highest life attainable by man is *a heroic life.* This is the life of the man who, for whatever motive and in any way, fights against immense difficulties for the benefit of all and who finally conquers but receives little or no reward. So, at the end, he finds himself like the prince in Gozzi's *Re Corvo,* turned to stone, but in a noble stance and with magnanimous features. His memory lives on, and it is honored like that of a hero; his will, mortified by a lifetime of toil and trouble, by lack of success and the world's ingratitude, is absorbed into Nirvana."[35]

This heroic life, with the complete mortification it implies, clearly bears no relation whatever to the petty ideas of those who discuss it most. They celebrate the memory of great men and imagine that the great man is great in the same way that they are small, quite as though greatness were a gift designed for one's own pleasure, or through some mechanism and in blind obedience to this inner compulsion, with the implication that the man who has not received the gift, or who feels no compulsion, has just as much right to be small as the other man to be great. But *gift* and *compulsion*—these are contemptible words by whose means one tries to escape an inner voice and which are insulting to the man who has heeded this voice, that is, to the

34. Meister Eckehart, *Werke,* ed. Franz Pfeiffer (Leipzig, 1857), 1:492. Cited by Schopenhauer in *WWR,* 2:439.
35. *PP,* 2:322.

great man, since he is the last person in the world to accept gifts or suffer compulsion, even though he knows as well as any little man that he could find an easy life and a soft berth if only he took the conventional, courteous way with himself and his fellow man. For all human arrangements are directed towards this end—that, through constant distraction of thinking, life may not be *felt*. Why does the hero so passionately desire the opposite, namely, to feel life, which is the same thing as suffering from life? Because he sees that others would like to defraud him of himself, that there is a kind of conspiracy to lure him out of his cave. And so he balks, pricks up his ears, and decides: "I will remain my own!" It is a frightful decision; only gradually does he come to realize this. For now, in fact, he must descend into the depths of existence with a string of curious questions on his lips. Why am I alive? What lesson am I to learn from life? How did I become what I am, and why do I suffer from being what I am? He tortures himself, and observes that nobody else tortures himself in this way. On the contrary, the hands of his fellow men are stretched passionately towards the fantastic events provided by the political theater where men strut about in a hundred masks—young men, old men, fathers, citizens, priests, officials, and merchants, all utterly preoccupied with their common comedy and not at all with themselves. To the question "Why are you alive?" they would answer, proudly and promptly, "To *become* a citizen, or a scholar, or a statesman." And yet they *are* something which can never become anything else, and why are they precisely this? And alas, why not something better?

The man who regards his life as merely a point in the evolution of a race, a state, or a field of knowledge, the man who therefore wants to belong wholly to the history of Becoming, has not mastered the lesson given him by existence and must therefore set about learning it over. This eternal Becoming is a fiction, a puppet-play[36] over which man forgets himself, a distraction in the true sense of the word, which disperses the individual to the four winds; the endless silly game which Time, the great baby, plays before our eyes, and with us. The heroism of truthfulness lies in our some-day refusing to be Time's toy. In Becoming, everything is hollow, false, shallow, and contemptible; the riddle which man must solve, he can only

---

36. One of Schopenhauer's favorite images, designed to convey the distinction between the *freedom* of the pessimistic genius (who recognizes the universal operation of the Will to Live and therefore denies it) and the *unfreedom* and *automatism* of the majority of mankind, manipulated by the wires and strings of Nature and the World-as-Will. In *WWR* (1:453), he writes of "the threads that set in motion the many-colored puppet-show of the world of perception." And again: "In consequence of [determinism] . . . the world becomes a puppet-show worked by wires without it being possible to see for whose amusement. If the piece has a plan, then a *fate* is the director" (2:321). And: "On the other hand, the genius, with his unfettered intellect, could be compared to a living person playing among the huge puppets of the famous Milan puppet-show" (2:386).

solve in Being, in being what he is and not something else, in the immutable. Now he begins to investigate how deeply he is involved with Becoming, and how deeply with Being, and a fearful task confronts his soul—that of destroying all Becoming, of exposing to the light all falseness in things. He too wants to know everything, but to know it in a different way from Goethe's Man, not for the sake of a noble delicacy, or to preserve himself and delight in the multiplicity of things. On the contrary, he himself is the first sacrifice he offers. The heroic man scorns his own misery or well-being, his virtues and vices; he scorns to make himself the measure of things. He no longer hopes for anything more from himself, and in all things wants to look down into this hopeless abyss. His strength lies in forgetting himself; when he thinks of himself, it is to measure the distance between himself and his goal, and it is as though what he saw behind and below him were a wretched pile of rubble. With all their might the ancient thinkers sought for happiness and truth—and what a man must seek, he will never find: such is the malicious law of Nature. But he who seeks untruth in everything and willingly makes unhappiness his companion, will perhaps experience another miracle of disillusionment. Something inexpressible, of which happiness and truth are merely idolatrous imitations, approaches him, the earth loses its gravity, the events and powers of the world seem like a dream, and everything, as on a summer evening, sheds a radiance around him. It seems to the beholder as though he were just waking, and the cloudy wisps of a fading dream were playing around him. But these too will drift away. And then it is day.

5   But I promised to depict Schopenhauer as *educator,* according to my own experience. Hence, it is simply not enough to offer an image, and an inadequate one at that, of the ideal man who holds sway in Schopenhauer and around him, his Platonic Idea, as it were. The most difficult task remains, that is, to show how a new round of duties is to be derived from this ideal, and how we can make contact with this boundless ideal through ordinary activity; in short, to show that this ideal *educates.* Otherwise, we might suppose it was nothing more than an enchanting, even intoxicating vision vouchsafed us in isolated moments, only to abandon us immediately, leaving us even more alone and prey to even deeper disgust. Now it is clear that our acquaintance with this ideal *begins* in this way, with these startling alternations of light and darkness, intoxication and disgust, and that in this respect we are repeating an experience as old as the ideals themselves. But we must not remain standing at the threshold, but proceed quickly past the initial stages.

We must therefore ask, seriously and purposively, whether it is possible to bring that incredibly lofty goal so close to us that it educates us while drawing us upwards. By so doing, we may avoid fulfilling in our own respect

Goethe's great words: "Man is born to a limited position; he is able to grasp simple, proximate, and definite goals, and he gets used to employing those means that are immediately available to him. But when he escapes his limits, he knows neither what he wants nor what he ought to do. And it makes no difference whether he is distracted by the multiplicity of objects or driven into ecstasy by their loftiness and nobility. For him it is always a misfortune when he is impelled to strive for something with which he cannot connect himself by means of ordinary activities originating in himself."[37] And with a good semblance of justice, this same objection might be brought against Schopenhauer's Man, whose nobility and loftiness may carry us beyond ourselves, with the result that we are once again removed from all communities of active men; the coherence of duties, the flow of life vanish. One man may perhaps accustom himself to unhappy self-division and to living by a double standard, that is, in conflict with himself, insecure in either part of himself, and hence becoming daily more weak and sterile; whereas another man on principle rejects all activity in common with others and scarcely notices when others act. The risks are always great when excessive hardship is imposed upon a man and he can *fulfill* no duties at all. Stronger natures may be destroyed in this way; weaker men—that is, the majority—sink into contemplative laziness and finally, through laziness, lose even the habit of contemplation.

In reply to these objections, I admit that our work here has barely begun, and that from my own experience there is only one fact that I perceive and know for certain. And that is that, starting out from that ideal image, it is possible to impose on you and me a chain of duties capable of being fulfilled, and that some of us already feel the weight of that chain. But before I can state categorically the formula under which I would like to subsume this new round of duties, certain preliminary considerations are in order.

At all times men of greater profundity have felt compassion for animals, since animals suffer from life yet lack the strength to turn the sting of suffering against themselves and thereby achieve a metaphysical understanding of their existence. Moreover, the sight of senseless suffering is deeply revolting. This is why in many places on earth the belief arose that the souls of guilty men had been implanted in these animal bodies, and that senseless suffering, at first sight so outrageous, resolves itself intelligently and meaningfully as punishment and penance under eternal justice. Obviously it is a harsh punishment to live like an animal, in hunger and desire, and yet to achieve no awareness of this life. And no harsher fate can be imagined than that of the beasts of prey who are driven through the desert by the most devouring torment, seldom ever satisfied; and even when it is, the satisfaction turns into pain in the flesh-tearing struggle with other an-

37. See *Wilhelm Meisters Lehrjahre*, 6.5.

imals, or in nauseating greed and satiety. To cling to life wildly and blindly with no prospect of higher reward; and far from knowing that one is being punished and why, but rather craving this punishment as if it were a happiness, with the stupidity of a frightful desire—this is what it means to be an animal.[38] And if all nature aspires to man, it is to show us that man is necessary in order to redeem nature from the curse of animal existence; and that in man existence at last owns a mirror in whose depths life no longer appears as senseless, but in its metaphysical meaning.

But consider this question carefully: Where does the animal stop, where does man begin? That man who is Nature's sole concern? So long as we crave life as if it were happiness, we have not succeeded in lifting our gaze above the animal's horizon; we merely desire with greater awareness what the animal pursues from blind instinct. But this is how it is with most of us for the greater part of our lives. We rarely transcend our animal existence; we ourselves are the animals that seem to suffer senselessly.

But there are moments *when we understand this.* The clouds break, and we see how we, together with all of nature, aspire toward Man as something standing high above us. In that sudden blaze of light, we look with terror around us and behind us. There they go, the delicate beasts of prey, and we are there among them. The immense commotion of men over the great desert of the earth, the cities and states men found and the wars they wage, their restless conclaves and dispersions, their chaotic collisions and mutual imitations, their reciprocal overreachings and down-treadings, their shrieks of pain and howls of triumph[39]—all this is a continuation of our animal existence; almost as though man had been deliberately created to regress and cheated of his metaphysical disposition; as if Nature, having for so long yearned and labored for man, now recoiled from him with a shudder, preferring to return to the unconsciousness of instinct. Alas, Nature needs knowledge, and is terrified of the knowledge she needs; and so the flame flickers uncertainly as though afraid of itself, seizing on a thousand things before seizing on the one thing which above all else Nature needs to know.

In isolated moments we all know that we have deliberately complicated the arrangements of our lives only in order to evade our real task. We know how happy we would be to hide our heads somewhere—as though our

38. A paraphrase of Schopenhauer's remarks in *WWR*, 2:354ff.
39. Another glance at the same passage of Schopenhauer as in the preceding note: "We see . . . universal need, restless exertion, constant pressure, endless strife, forced activity, with extreme exertion of all bodily and mental powers. Many millions, united into nations, strive for the common good, each individual for his own sake, but many thousands fall a sacrifice to it. Now senseless delusion, now intriguing politics, incite them to wars with one another; then the sweat and blood of the great multitude must flow. . . . All push and drive, some plotting and planning, others acting; the tumult is indescribable."

hundred-eyed conscience could not find us there; and how ready we are to surrender our selves to the state or money-making, to social life or scholarship, only in order to get rid of them; and that even in our everyday work we slave more fiercely and busily than necessary in order to earn a living because it seems even more necessary to avoid reflection. The haste is universal because everyone is running from himself. And because we want to seem contented and to disguise our misery from the more acute observers, the timid concealing of this haste is no less universal. Also universal is the need for fresh-sounding words in order to adorn life with a kind of riotous festivity. We all know that peculiar state when disagreeable memories suddenly invade our minds, and we try to expel them by violent sounds and gestures. But the sounds and gestures of common life allow us to perceive that we are always in such a state, fearful of memory and inward experience. What bothers us so, what is this mosquito that will not let us sleep? The air around us is filled with spirits; every instant of life wants to tell us something, but we refuse to listen to this ghostly voice. When we are alone and quiet, we fear that something will be whispered into our ear, and for this reason we hate the quiet and drug ourselves with social life.

As I said earlier, there are moments when we understand all this, and we look with astonishment at the dizzy haste, and anguish, and the whole dreamlike quality of our life, which seems to be afraid of waking, which dreams more intensely and restlessly as the moment of waking approaches. But at the same time we feel that we are too weak to bear these moments of deep introspection, and that we are not the men toward whom all of Nature presses for her redemption. It is no small achievement that we can now and then lift our heads and see the stream into which we have sunk so deeply. And even this—this emerging and waking for a fleeting instant—we cannot manage by our own strength. We have to be lifted up—and who are those who lift us up?

They are those true *men, those no-longer animals, the philosophers, artists, and saints.* In their appearance and through their appearance, Nature, who makes no leaps, makes her only leap, a leap of joy! For the first time she feels that she has reached her goal, the point at which she intuits that she will have to unlearn her goals, and that she has staked too much on the game of life and Becoming. She is transfigured by this knowledge, and a gentle twilight weariness which men call "beauty" suffuses her face. What these transfigured features now express is the great *illumination* of existence, and the highest wish possible to mortals is to share, constantly and with open ears, in this illumination. When we think of everything that Schopenhauer, for instance, must have *heard* in the course of his life, we may well say to ourselves later: "Oh, these deaf ears of mine, this dull head, this feeble intellect of mine, this shrunken heart, how I despise everything I call my own! I cannot fly, only flutter my wings! To look up without the capacity to rise! To know, almost to take, the way that leads to the philosopher's immeasurably free vision, and then to reel back after a few steps! If only that greatest of all wishes could be fulfilled for one day, how gladly would we give the rest of our lives in exchange for it! To climb as high as any thinker ever climbed, into the icy purity of the Alpine air where there is no longer any fog or veiling mist, where the underlying structure of things is revealed, stark and rigid, but in absolute clarity! Merely at the thought the soul becomes solitary, infinite. But if the soul's great wish were granted; if its gaze fell on things below, sheer and radiant as a ray of light; if shame, anxiety, and desire could vanish—what words could describe the state of mind, that new, enigmatic, motionless emotion with which the soul—like Schopenhauer's soul—would settle and diffuse itself over the whole immense hieroglyph of existence and the petrified doctrine of Becoming—not as black night but as a blazing crimson light[40] streaming out over the world? And obversely, what a fate it would be to have so clear an intuition of the philosopher's special destiny and blessedness that one might sense the uncertainty and despair of the nonphilosopher, the man who desires but has no hope! To feel that one is fruit on the tree, fruit that cannot ripen because there is too much shade, and to see only a little way off the sunlight that one lacks!"

The torture would be enough to make such a mis-gifted man envious and malicious, if he were capable of envy and malice. More probably, it will end by his turning his soul in another direction so that it will not be devoured by vain desire. And it is at this point that he will *discover* a new round of duties.

I am now in a position to reply to the question I raised earlier: whether it is possible, through ordinary, self-originating activity, to establish a relation with the great ideal represented by Schopenhauer's Man. Above all, one fact is certain: these new duties are not the duties of a single individual; rather, by their means, one belongs to a mighty community welded together not by external forms and laws, but by a fundamental idea. This is the fundamental idea of *culture*, insofar as culture imposes only one duty on each of us: *to promote the production of the philosopher, the artist, and the saint, within us and in the world, and thereby to labor for the perfection of Nature.* Just as Nature needs the philosopher, so she also needs the artist, for a metaphysical purpose, that is, for her own illumination, so that she may at last be presented with a pure and perfected image of what she never sees in the confusion of Becoming—and by so doing achieve self-consciousness. It was Goethe who, with arrogant profundity, observed that all of Nature's efforts

---

40. The germinal idea behind Nietzsche's *Dawn* (*Morgenröte*), as well as the dawn imagery associated with Zarathustra's triumphant destruction and transvaluation of absolute values.

are useful only insofar as the artist finally guesses the meaning of her stammering, meets her half-way, and expresses the real meaning of her efforts. "I have often said," he once exclaimed, "and I will say it again and again, that the *causa finalis* of the world's business and human affairs is dramatic poetry. For otherwise the stuff is completely useless."

And for this reason Nature finally has need of the saint, in whom the individual ego has entirely melted away and whose life of suffering is no longer, or hardly any longer, felt individually, but rather as a profound sensation of likeness, compassion, and unity with every living thing; the saint in whom the miracle of transformation takes place, and on whom the play of Becoming leaves no trace—that last, supreme humanization for which all Nature, in search of its redemption, strives. There is no doubt that we are all bound by kinship to the saint as we are bound by kinship to the philosopher and the artist. There are moments and sparklings, as it were, struck from that most brilliant and amorous fire, by whose light we no longer understand the word *I*. Beyond our being there lies something which in those moments becomes here and now, and this is why we desire from the bottom of our hearts to make bridges between here and that which lies beyond.

In our customary state we can of course contribute nothing to the production of the redeeming man, and we therefore *hate* ourselves in this state—a hatred which is the root of that pessimism which Schopenhauer had to reteach our age, but which is as ancient as the aspiration to culture. The root, but not the flower; the foundation, but not the gable; the start of the road, not the goal: for someday we must learn to hate something else, something larger than our individual self with its wretched limitations and its restless turmoil. In that exalted state we shall have learned to love something different from what we now love. Only when, either in this life or in some later incarnation, we have been welcomed into that exalted order of philosophers, artists, and saints, will there be new goals assigned to our love and hatred. In the meantime we have our tasks and our round of duties, our hatred and our love. For we know what culture is. Applied culture requires us to prepare for and promote the production of Schopenhauer's Man by learning what impedes his coming and removing it from his path— in sum, requires us to fight tirelessly against everything that has held us back from the highest fulfillment of our existence, preventing us from becoming such Schopenhauerian men.

6   It is at times harder to concede a point than to understand it. And this may be the effect on most readers when they reflect on this proposition: "Mankind must labor unceasingly to produce great individuals. This and nothing else is its function." One would gladly apply to society and its goals the lesson to be drawn from the study of all species

of plant and animal life—the only thing that matters is the higher specimen, the more unusual, the stronger, more complex and creative individual. One would gladly apply it, if only inbred illusions about the purpose of society did not so stubbornly resist it. In point of fact, it is easy to see that a species' evolutionary goal is the point at which it reaches its limits and makes its transition to a higher species. The goal is not the number of specimens or their material well-being. Nor is it the most recently evolved specimens that count but rather those apparently random and fortuitous individual existences which, under favorable conditions, now and then arise. And it should be just as easy to understand that, since mankind is capable of achieving consciousness of its goal, its duty lies in searching out and realizing the favorable conditions under which those great, redeeming human beings can appear.

But innumerable objections arise. According to one theory, the ultimate goal is to be found in the happiness of all or of the greatest number. Another theory holds that it lies in the development of great communities. But however readily a man may sacrifice his life to the state, for instance, he would be equally slow and reluctant to do so if an individual rather than the state demanded the sacrifice. It seems nonsensical that one man should exist for the sake of another. "No, rather for the sake of all others, or at least for the greatest possible number!" But come, come, my dear fellow. As though it were more reasonable to let numbers decide when matters of value and meaning are the issue! The real question is surely this: In what way is your life least wasted? Surely only by your living for the benefit of the rarest and most valuable specimens, not for that majority which, considered as individuals, is the least valuable. And it is precisely this conviction that should be implanted and nourished in every young man. He should view himself as a botched product of Nature's artistry, but at the same time as a witness to the greatest and most miraculous projects of that artist. "In my case she made a bad job of it," he should tell himself, "but I will honor her great purpose by being at her service so that she will someday prove more successful."

Fired by this resolve, he takes his place in the world of *culture*. For culture is the offspring of every man's self-knowledge and dissatisfaction with himself. Every partisan of culture is implicitly saying: "I see something above me, nobler and more human than myself. Help me, all of you, to attain it, as I will help anyone who shares my vision and suffering and aim: the appearance of that man who feels in himself the fullness and infinity of knowledge and love, of vision and power, who with his whole being loves Nature and belongs to her, as judge and measure of all things." It is difficult to awaken in others this state of fearless self-knowledge, since love cannot be taught; and it is by love alone that the soul attains not only its clear, incisive, scornful view of itself, but the desire to look beyond the self and to search with all its strength for a higher self not yet revealed. Hence, only he who is committed heart and soul to a great man receives the *first sacrament of culture*. The sign of it is shame without chagrin, hatred of one's own shriveled narrowness, sympathy with the genius who has repeatedly lifted himself above our hollowness and aridity, an anticipatory feeling for whatever is struggling to emerge, and a deep conviction that, almost everywhere he goes, he encounters Nature in distress—in her striving toward Man, in her pain at seeing her work once again miscarry, yet everywhere successfully producing beginnings, features, forms. With the result that the people among whom we live are like a sculptor's yard, full of precious fragments, all crying out: "Come help us! Complete us! Put together what belongs together. You cannot imagine how we hunger to become whole!"

I called this complex of inner states the first sacrament of culture. Now I must describe the effects of the *second* sacrament, and this, I am quite aware, is a much more difficult task. For now we have to make the transition from the inner event to the judgment of external events; our gaze must move outwards in order to discover in the vast, turbulent world that yearning for culture known to us from childhood experience. The individual must use his aspirations and struggles as the alphabet with which to spell out the strivings of mankind. But he cannot stop here; he must proceed to the next higher stage. Culture requires of him not only inner experience, not only the judgment of the external world around him, but finally, and above all, action, that is, to do battle for culture and oppose those influences, customs, laws, and institutions in which he cannot recognize this goal—the production of genius.

Anyone capable of reaching the second stage immediately recognizes that *knowledge of this goal is extraordinarily scant and rare*, and, conversely, that the striving for culture is universal and that its service consumes quite unbelievable amounts of energy. Astonished, he asks himself: "Perhaps this knowledge is unnecessary? Perhaps Nature achieves her goal anyway, even though most men misunderstand the purpose of their exertions?" Those inclined to respect Nature's unconscious purposiveness will doubtless immediately reply: "Yes, that's how it is. No matter what men say or think about their ultimate goal, in their blind urges they are thoroughly conscious of the right way."[41] To refute this statement, some experience of life is required. But if we are convinced that the sole and exclusive goal of culture is to foster the production of the true *man*, and if we observe that even nowadays, despite all the pomp and circumstance of culture, the production of this man is not much different from the protracted torturing of a helpless animal, then we will find it absolutely necessary to replace "blind instinct" with conscious willing. And this for a second reason, namely, to prevent our

41. A glance at Goethe, *Faust*, part 1, 328–29.

diverting that famous "blind instinct," so uncertain of its goal, to entirely
different ends, and setting it on a course in which the supreme goal, the
production of genius, cannot be achieved. For there exists a kind of *culture
which has been misapplied and prostituted*—one need merely glance around
him! And the very forces that at present most vigorously promote culture
do so for ulterior reasons and not from pure and disinterested motives.

There is, first of all, *the selfishness of the money-makers.* This requires the
support of culture, which it gratefully supports in return, but at the price
of prescribing culture's aims and standards. From this quarter comes that
fashionable doctrine whose intricate logic goes something like this: "The
more knowledge and education we have, the more needs there are to supply;
whence greater production; whence greater profit and prosperity." The partisans of this seductive formula would define education as the discernment
by which a man becomes completely contemporary in his desires and their
satisfaction, but by whose means he effectively controls all the ways of
making money with the maximum facility. The aims of this education would
be to make men contemporary and "current"—in the same sense as one
might speak of the "currency" of money. And on this view, the more of
these "current" men a country possesses, the more happy and prosperous
it will be. Hence, the goal of modern educational institutions should be to
make the individual as "current" as his abilities allow; to educate each man
so that he may get the greatest possible profit and happiness from the degree
of skill and knowledge he possesses. Thanks to his liberal education, the
theory goes, the individual is expected to be able to appraise himself so well
that he will know what to exact of life. Lastly, it is maintained that there is
a natural and necessary connection between "intelligence and property" and
between "wealth and culture," and that this connection is a *moral* necessity.
Any education which makes men solitary, which proposes goals beyond
money and profit, which takes time, is hated. More serious forms of education are disparaged as "refined egoism" or "immoral cultural Epicurean-
ism." Naturally, given the morality by which they live, these people honor
the precise opposite—that is, a speedy education designed to make its re-
cipient a money-maker as speedily as possible, but liberal enough to allow
him to make liberal amounts of money. A man is permitted only as much
culture as benefits the general economy and world trade—and that much
he is required to have. In short: "Man necessarily aspires to worldly happiness, and therefore education is necessary, but only for this reason!"

Second, there is *the selfishness of the state,* which also desires the greatest
possible diffusion and generalization of culture and has at its disposal the
most effective instruments for satisfying its desire. Providing that the state
is confident that it has the strength not only to liberate but, at the proper
moment, to impose its yoke; providing that it is so securely and broadly
based that it can support the whole cultural edifice, then the diffusion of

education among its citizenry is useful to it only in its rivalry with other states. Wherever there is talk these days of "state culture," we see that the state is charged with liberating a generation's intellectual powers only insofar as they can serve established institutions; but only to that degree. In this respect, it is like a mountain stream partially diverted by dams and sluices in order to drive a mill with its diminished power—whereas its full power would be more dangerous than useful to the mill. That liberation is at the same time, and to a greater degree, a shackling. Merely recollect what gradually happened to Christianity under the selfishness of the state. Christianity is certainly one of the purest manifestations of the impulse to culture and, above all, of the constant re-creation of the saint. But because it was exploited in hundreds of ways to drive the mills of state power, it had gradually become hypocritical and dishonest, diseased to the marrow, and degenerate to the point where it disavowed its original purpose. Even its latest event, the German Reformation, would have been nothing more than a sudden dying blaze, had it not borrowed fresh fuel and flames from the conflagration of the national states.

In the third place, culture is supported by all those who are conscious of an *ugly or boring content* and who want to disguise it with what is called *"formal beauty."* Such externals as words, gestures, decor, ostentation, and mannerism compel the spectator to draw false conclusions about the content on the assumption that content is usually inferred from outward appearance. At times it seems to me that modern men find one another so infinitely boring that they are forced to use every conceivable art and artifice to make themselves interesting. So they allow themselves to be served up by their artists as piquant and spicy dishes; they splash themselves with all the spices of East and West and, no doubt about it, they *do* have a most interesting smell that combines both East and West in their entirety. They are prepared to please all palates, and everyone must be served, whether he hankers for good smells or bad, for sublimity or country coarseness, for tragedy or theatrical filth. The most celebrated of these master chefs of modern man, who want to be interesting and interested at any cost, are to be found, as we all know, among the French; the worst are found among the Germans. Basically, this is more comforting for the latter than for the former, and we should not be offended with the French if they scoff at us for being uninteresting and inelegant, and if the craving of some Germans for elegance and polished manners reminds them of the Indian who wants a ring in his nose and clamors to be tatooed.

At this point I cannot resist a digression. Since the recent war with France, much in Germany has changed or shifted, and it is clear that our soldiers have brought back with them a number of new desires as regards German culture. For many the war was their first venture into the more elegant half of the world; and how can the conqueror display more handsome simplicity than in not disdaining to acquire a little culture from the conquered? Craftsmen in particular are constantly being urged to compete with our more cultivated neighbor. The design of the German house is to be modeled on that of the French. Through an academy established on the French model, even the German language is to acquire "sound taste" and cast off Goethe's dangerous influence, according to the recent pronouncement of Dubois-Reymond, the Berlin academician. Our theater has for a long time, quietly and with dignity, pursued the same objective. We have even invented the elegant German scholar. And, as matters now stand, the only likely prospect is that everything that has not yet conformed to the law of elegance—German music, tragedy, and philosophy—will be written off as un-German.

In fact, I would not lift a finger on behalf of German culture if the German saw in the culture which he still lacks and today craves to acquire, anything more than the arts and artifices by which life is to be embellished, including the arts of the dancing-master and the upholsterer; or if in language he aimed at academically sanctioned norms and a general tone of gentility. But the last war and the personal confrontation with the French seem to have aroused no higher aspirations. On the contrary, I frequently suspect that the German is violently eager to escape the ancient duties imposed on him by his wonderful gifts, his temperamental talent for seriousness and profundity. He would much rather play the buffoon or ape, and master those arts and amenities that make life amusing. But the greatest insult to the German spirit is to treat it as though it were so much wax which might someday be molded into elegance. And while it is regrettably true that many Germans let themselves be molded and kneaded in this way, we must keep on repeating our point until they hear us. "Listen," we should tell them, "that old German nature is no longer innate in you." Admittedly, it was hard, rough, and obstinate. Nonetheless, it was very precious material on which only the greatest sculptors should work because only they are worthy of it. You, on the other hand, are made of soft, doughy stuff. However you mold it into elegant puppets and interesting idols, Richard Wagner's statement still holds true: "When the German pretends to elegance, he is angular and gauche. But when he catches fire, he is sublime and surpasses the whole world." And elegant folk have every reason to be wary of this German fire, since it may someday devour them alive, along with their puppets and waxen masks.

We might, of course, find that the prevalent vogue of "formal beauty" has its roots in other and deeper causes. In haste, for instance, in that breathless grasping of the moment and the impatience that prematurely plucks all the fruit from the branch, in the frantic competitive race that cuts deep lines in men's brows and, as it were, tatoos everything they do. Tortured slaves of the three *M*'s—Mode, Moment, and Majority Opinion—

they storm along in undignified anxiety as though they had taken some potion that would not let them breathe normally. The resulting lack of dignity and decorum leaps all too painfully to the eye, and a false elegance is once again required to disguise the sickness of their undignified haste. This, in fact, is the connection between the fashionable craving for formal beauty and the hateful content of modern man: the form is meant to conceal, the content to be concealed. To be cultured nowadays means concealing from others how vile and wretched we are, how animal-like in our desires, how insatiable in acquisition, how shameless and selfish in enjoyment. When I point out that Germany lacks a culture, I frequently meet with this objection: "But until now Germans have been too poor and modest, so their lack of culture is only natural. Let our fellow countrymen acquire wealth and self-confidence, and they will have a culture too." Faith brings happiness, but *this* particular faith makes me unhappy, since I feel that the future culture on which this faith is founded—that of wealth, polish, and elegant hypocrisy—is the exact antithesis and enemy of the German culture in which I have faith. Clearly, anyone who has to live among Germans suffers considerably from the notorious drabness of German life and feeling, its shapelessness, apathy, and dullness, its coarseness in the more tender relations of life, and still more so from their envy and a certain slyness and uncleanliness of character. He is pained and offended by their rooted love of the false and counterfeit, of shoddy imitation, of the conversion of good foreign products into bad German ones. But if to this we add their frantic restlessness, their pursuit of profit and success, and the excessive value set on the moment, it is shocking to think that there is no satisfactory cure for all these weaknesses and diseases. They can only be touched up with a cosmetic "culture of interesting form"! And this from a people who produced *Schopenhauer* and *Wagner*, and who will produce such men in the future! Or are we desperately deceiving ourselves? Aren't men like these a guarantee that such forces are inherent in the German mind and spirit? Could they be exceptions, the last offshoots and heirs of qualities we once considered German?

At this point I confess my bafflement and so return to the main argument from which my restless doubts distracted me. I have not yet enumerated all the forces that promote culture while failing to recognize its true purpose—the production of genius. Three have been described: the selfishness of the money-makers, the selfishness of the state, and the selfishness of all those who purposely disguise themselves and hide beneath the cloak of form. In fourth place I put the *selfishness of scientific scholarship* and the peculiar nature of its servants, the *scholars*.

Scholarship and knowledge stand to wisdom as morality to holiness. Scholarship is cold and dry, it has no love, and it is ignorant, and it has no deep feeling of inadequacy and yearning. It is as beneficial to itself as it is harmful to its servants, since it transfers its own character to them and thereby ossifies their humanity. So long as culture is essentially equated with the advance of knowledge, scholarship will pass by the great man and his suffering with callous indifference. For it has no eyes for anything but problems of knowledge, and in the world of scholarship suffering is an incomprehensible irrelevance, which is to say, at best another problem.

Let a man once acquire the habit of turning every experience into a purely intellectual affair, a dialectical game of question and answer, and it is amazing how quickly he will shrivel in the process until reduced to a rattling skeleton. We all know it, we all see it. How is it possible then for young men not to shy away in terror from these human skeletons and go right on blindly, recklessly, and involuntarily sacrificing themselves to scholarship? But the cause cannot be the "instinct for truth." How, after all, could there be any such thing as an instinct for pure, cold, inconsequential knowledge? On the contrary, the impartial observer can see only too plainly the real motivating forces of the servants of knowledge. And there is clearly every good reason for investigating and analyzing scholars, since they themselves are in the habit of boldly seizing upon and dissecting absolutely everything, no matter how venerable.

Therefore let me speak my mind frankly. This is my premise: The scholar is a complex tangle of very different drives and stimuli; he is an alloy in every sense of the word. The first component is a strong and constantly intensifying curiosity, a craving for intellectual adventures, the perpetually attractive power of the new and rare as opposed to the old and boring. Add to this a certain bent for dialectical blood sports, the hunter's joy in tracking the crafty fox of thought, where the object of the chase is not the truth but the chase, and the chief pleasure lies in skillfully stalking, surrounding, and killing according to the rules of the game. Next add the instinct for contradiction; the personality wants to assert itself, to make itself felt, against all others. The battle becomes a pleasure, and the aim is personal victory, the battle for truth a pretext. The scholar also contains a strong admixture of the impulse to discover *certain* "truths," which comes from his servility to certain powerful persons, classes, opinions, churches, and governments, since he feels that he profits by bringing "truth" to their side.

The following qualities occur less frequently in the scholar, but still fairly commonly. First, rectitude and a feeling for simplicity, qualities to be esteemed if anything more than gaucheness and inexperience in dissimulation, for which some mother-wit is required. In fact, wherever wit and smoothness are much in evidence, we should be wary and question the man's sincerity. On the other hand, that rectitude is in most cases of little value; being stubbornly conventional, it is rarely helpful even in scholarship; and it usually tells the truth only in simple matters or in *adiaphoris*,[42] since it is

42. "immaterial matters"

more in keeping with laziness to tell the truth than to suppress it. And whereas every new fact imposes relearning, rectitude venerates received opinion and charges the innovator with a lack of *sensus recti*.[43] Certainly it was men of rectitude who opposed Copernicus's theory, since they had visual commonsense as well as tradition on their side. The hatred of philosophy—not at all uncommon among scholars—is primarily a hatred of long chains of reasoning and the artificiality of proof. Basically, every generation of scholars has unconsciously established a limit for *permissible* ingenuity; whatever exceeds this limit is questioned and used almost as evidence against the offender's integrity.

Second, keenness of sight for near objects, combined with great myopia for the remote and universal. The scholar's visual field is usually very restricted, and his eyes must be kept closely focused on the object. If he wants to move from a point under investigation to another point, he must shift his whole visual apparatus to that point. He divides the picture into sections, like a man focusing his opera glasses on the stage and seeing now a head, now a piece of clothing, but never anything as a whole.[44] He never sees how the individual parts are combined, he only infers their connection; hence he has no strong impression of the whole. He judges a piece of writing, for instance, on the basis of individual passages, or sentences, or errors, because he is incapable of forming a complex overall impression. He would be tempted to hold that an oil painting was nothing but a barbarous mess of splotches.

Third, staid conventionality in his likes and dislikes. This trait serves him well, especially in the study of history, since he can track down the motives of past men in terms of motives he understands. A mole is most comfortable in a molehill. He is wary of all ingenious and extravagant hypotheses; if he is persistent, he digs up all the common motives of the past because he feels an affinity for them. This, of course, is precisely why he is incapable of understanding what is rare, great, and exceptional—that is, what is important and essential.

Fourth, poverty of feeling and insensitivity. These traits qualify him to perform vivisections. He has no idea of the suffering that often accompanies insight, and so he has no fear of treading in places where other men shudder to walk. He is cold and therefore easily passes for cruel. He is thought to be courageous, but he has no more courage than the mule who doesn't feel dizzy.

Fifth, low self-esteem, even modesty. Even when banished to some wretched corner, these scholars have no feeling of being sacrificed or

---

43. "sense of propriety," "rectitude"
44. See *PP*, 2:479–90, esp. 485.

wasted. Deep in their hearts, they often seem to realize that they are not flying but crawling creatures. This quality makes them seem pathetic.

Sixth, loyalty to their teachers and mentors. With all his heart, the scholar wants to be helpful to them, and he knows quite well that he can best do this with the truth. He is disposed to be grateful, because only through his teachers has he obtained admission to the august halls of scholarship, which he never would have entered on his own. At present any teacher who opens up a new field in which even smaller minds can work with some success will very rapidly become a famous man, so large is the crowd that swarms in after him. Admittedly, every one of these faithful and grateful disciples is at the same time a misfortune for his master, since they all imitate him, and his shortcomings seem disproportionately large and exaggerated because they appear in such petty individuals, whereas his virtues, mediated by these same individuals, are correspondingly diminished.

Seventh, the habit of steadily plodding down the same road on which he first set out, and a feeling for truth stemming from a lack of ideas, in accordance with his acquired habit. Scholars of this sort become compilers, commentators, makers of indices and herbaria; their studies are specialized because it never occurs to them that there might be other areas. Their industry has something of the monstrous stupidity of gravity, and for this reason they often accomplish a great deal.

Eighth, fear of boredom. While the real thinker wants nothing more than leisure, the ordinary scholar, not knowing what to do with it, dreads it. Books are his comfort; that is, he listens to other men thinking and by so doing manages to amuse himself all day long. Above all, he chooses books that somehow involve him personally, that to some small degree stir him by engaging his likes and dislikes; books, that is, that have to do with the scholar himself, or with his class, or his political, or esthetic, or merely grammatical convictions. If he has a special discipline of his own, he never lacks means of amusing himself or swatting away the flies of boredom.

Ninth, his motivation to make a living, at bottom the famous "borborugmos of an empty belly."[45] Truth is served, if it can lead directly to salaries and promotions, or at least to the favor of those who have bread and honors to confer. But only *this* truth is served; hence, a line can be drawn between the profitable truths served by many scholars, and the unprofitable truths served by that small handful whose motto is not *ingenii largitor venter.*[46]

---

45. A quotation from Goethe's translation of the (then) unpublished manuscript of *Rameau's Nephew* by Diderot. See Goethe, *Werke* (1805–06), 45:70.

46. See the prologue to the *Satires* of Persius: "Picumque docuit verba nostra conari? / magister artis ingenique largitor / venter . . ." [Who taught the magpie to imitate our words? It was that Master of Arts, that dispenser of Genius, the Belly . . .].

Tenth, respect for fellow scholars, dread of their disapproval—a rarer and higher motive than the preceding, but not uncommon. All the members of the guild keep very strict and jealous watch over one another, so that the truth on which so much depends—bread, office, honor—can be accurately baptized in the name of its discoverer. One scholar pays strict tribute to another for the truth he has discovered, in order to exact the same tribute in return in case he should someday discover a truth of his own. Untruth and error are loudly exploded in order to reduce the number of competitors. But sometimes even the real truth is exploded in order to make temporary room for stubborn and daring errors. And so there is always a plentiful supply of those "moral idiocies" which are elsewhere called pranks.

Eleventh, the scholar from vanity, now a rather rare species. He wants, if possible, to have an area all to himself, and he therefore chooses curiosities, especially if they require unusual expenditures, travel, excavations, and numerous connections in different countries. He is usually quite content with the honor of being regarded as a curiosity himself, and he never dreams of earning a living by means of his research.

Twelfth, the scholar who likes to play. His delight is finding and untying the knots in knowledge. But he is careful to avoid over-exertion, lest he lose the feeling of a game. This is why he fails to go very deeply into things, though he often succeeds in discovering a detail which the laboriously crawling eye of the bread-and-butter scholar never sees.

If now, thirteenth and last, I suggest the passion for justice as a scholarly motive, someone may object that this noble—no, this almost metaphysical— passion is only with difficulty to be distinguished from the others, and is essentially invisible and incomprehensible to the human eye. So I add this final quality in the pious hope that the passion for justice may be more common and more effective among scholars than it appears to be. For if a single spark from the flame of justice falls into the scholar's soul, it is enough to set his life and aspirations afire, purifying them by consuming them, so that he can no longer find peace and is forever expelled from that icy or lukewarm state in which ordinary scholars do their daily work.

Now imagine all these elements, or some, or a few, vigorously blended and scrambled: this is the origin of the servant of truth. It is an amazing thing. In the service of a basically nonhuman and superhuman enterprise— pure knowledge, without consequence and therefore without passion—a mass of very human passions and drives have been combined and fused in chemical combination. And the resulting scholar appears so transfigured in the light of that sublimely pure and unworldly enterprise that the mixing and adding that went into his making are quite forgotten. But there are moments when we really must heed and remember all this; when, that is, we raise the question of the scholar's significance for culture. Any perceptive observer can see that the scholar is by nature *sterile*—the result of his origin!—and that he feels a quite natural hatred for the creative man.[47] Hence, in every age there has been a feud between scholars and men of genius. The scholar wants to kill nature, to dissect it and understand it; the man of genius wants to augment nature with freshly living nature, whence a conflict of convictions and activities. Completely happy ages neither needed the scholar nor knew him; it is sick and peevish ages that have valued him as the noblest and worthiest of men and assigned him the highest rank.

Who is physician enough to diagnose the health and sickness of our own age? Certainly the scholar these days is too highly valued, and this has harmful results, above all for the emerging genius. The scholar has no feeling for the distress of the genius. He speaks of him in a cold and cutting voice, dismissively; and he swiftly shrugs him off, as though he were dealing with some malformed monster for whom he has neither time nor inclination. In the scholar, then, no awareness of the aim of culture can be found.

But what, in summary, do all these reflections teach us? Recognition of the fact that, wherever culture seems to be most vigorously promoted, its true purpose is unknown. However loudly the state may advertise its services to culture, it promotes it only in order to promote itself; and it understands no higher goal than its own welfare and existence. What the moneyed interests want when they clamor constantly for education and culture is ultimately nothing but money. When the votaries of form claim that they deserve the credit for being the champions of culture and tell us, for instance, that all art belongs to them and must serve their needs, it is obvious that in affirming culture they are only affirming themselves. They too, in short, are the victims of a misconception. Of the scholar, enough has been said already. All these four powers, then, are just as assiduous in scheming to benefit *themselves* with the aid of culture as they are sluggish and devoid of ideas when their self-interest is not involved. I conclude therefore that conditions for the production of genius have *not improved* in modern times, and that aversion to originality has so increased that Socrates could not have lived among us and clearly would never have reached the age of seventy.

At this point let me recall my thesis in the third section—that our whole modern world is not, it seems, so solidly built and enduring as to augur everlasting life for its idea of culture. It is, in fact, quite likely that the next millennium will produce several new ideas that might make the hair of our contemporaries stand on end. *The belief that culture has a metaphysical*

---

47. Cf. *PP*, 2:44, and also 2:77: "The simple scholar in the real sense, say the philosopher-in-ordinary of Göttingen, regards the genius in much the same way as we look at a hare, namely, as something palatable only after it has been killed and prepared for dinner. Thus he regards the genius as one who must be shot at, so long as he is alive."

meaning might not terrify them, but some of the conclusions we might draw from it for education and our system of schooling could prove daunting.

Clearly, no ordinary mode of reflection is required for us to look away from contemporary educational institutions and to see beyond them to those strangely different institutions that in two or three generations will perhaps be thought necessary. As things stand now, our higher education endeavors to produce either scholars, or officials, or businessmen, or educated philistines, or more often, a potpourri of all four; those future institutions, still to be established, would obviously have a harder task. Clearly not harder in itself, since in any case it would be a more natural and therefore a lighter task. And what, for example, could be harder than defying Nature, as we now do, by training a young man to be a scholar? What makes it hard lies in relearning and establishing a new goal. It will take unspeakable effort to replace the basic principle of our present pedagogy—whose roots go back to the Middle Ages and whose paradigm of a perfect education is the medieval scholar—with a new basic principle. Now is the time to face this antithesis; one generation or another must undertake the struggle in which a future generation will be victorious.

Even now the individual who has grasped the new concept of culture stands at the crossroads. If he takes one fork, his age welcomes him, heaps him with laurels and honors. He is supported by powerful parties; throngs of sympathizers crowd around him, following or leading the way; and when the leader says the word of command, it echoes through the ranks. His first duty here is "to fight in rank and file"; the second, to treat as enemies all those who will not join the ranks. The second fork gives him fewer traveling companions; the road is harder, steeper, more tortuous. The people traveling on the first road jeer at him because the going is rougher and more dangerous, and try to lure him over to their side. If the two roads happen to intersect, he is mistreated and shoved aside or subtly shunned and isolated.

What, then, is the meaning of a cultural institution to these two very different travelers? To that vast crowd pressing toward its destination on the first road, culture means the laws and institutions by whose agency it is organized and advances, and by which all the solitary rebels—those who aim at higher and more distant goals—are banished. To the smaller group on the other road, a cultural institution would have a quite different function to perform. Through the protection of a strong organization, they want to prevent their being swept away and dispersed by the crowd; they want to prevent individual members from wearing themselves out prematurely or being diverted from their great task. These individuals must finish their work—that is the meaning of their solidarity; and all those who share in that institution must strive, through continual purification and mutual care, to provide for the birth of the genius and the fruition of his work, in themselves and in those around them. Many men—even those whose talents are of the second and third order—are destined to be helpers in this task; only by submitting to this destiny do they come to feel that they are living for a duty and that their lives have meaning and a purpose. But at present it is precisely these who are diverted from their path by the seductive voices of fashionable "culture" and alienated from their own instincts. The temptation is addressed to their selfishness, their weaknesses and vanities; the spirit of the age whispers to them, persistently insinuating: "Follow me and avoid the other road. There you are only servants, helpers, instruments; eclipsed by higher natures, never happy in your own identity; puppets manipulated by strings, slaves fettered with chains, robots even! But with me you are happy, masters of your own free identities, your talents shine with their own radiance; you yourselves will stand in the front ranks, a huge following will surround you. And the plaudits of public opinion will surely delight you far more than an aristocratic nod vouchsafed from above, from the cold, ethereal heights of genius."

To such blandishments even the best succumb. And fundamentally the decisive factor is not the rarity or vigor of talent but the influence of a certain basic heroic attitude and the degree of real organic affinity with genius. For there *are* men who suffer *personally* when they see genius painfully struggling and in danger of destroying itself, or its works coldly ignored by the shortsighted selfishness of the state, the shallowness of the money-makers, or the arid smugness of the scholars. So I hope that there are some who understand what I mean by this account of Schopenhauer's fate and for what goal, according to my notions, Schopenhauer as educator must actually *educate.*

7   But leaving aside all thoughts of distant future and a possible revolution in our educational system, let me ask: What *present* conditions should we aim at, and if necessary procure, for our philosopher-to-be? How can we help him breathe and, in the luckiest cases, at least lead a life like Schopenhauer's (admittedly not an easy one, but not quite impossible)? How should matters be contrived to make his impact on contemporaries greater? And what obstacles would have to be removed for his example to take full effect, so the philosopher might once again educate philosophers? At this point our reflections are diverted into painful practicality.

Nature always wants to be generally useful, but she cannot find the ways and means best suited to her purpose. This is her great grief, the cause of her melancholia.[48] That she intends to make life intelligible and meaningful

---

48. For Nature's menancholy, see n. 29 above and related passage of text. According to Schopenhauer, both Nature and genius are indelibly stamped with melancholy. Genius

to men by producing the artist and philosopher is unmistakably implied in her own strongly redemptive instinct. But the effect she obtains with philosophers and artists is again and again dubious, pale, weak. Often there is no effect at all. Her efforts to use philosophers for the good of all are particularly embarrassing. Because her means are groping attempts and casual ideas, she persistently fails, and most philosophers are of no general utility. Nature's ways seem wasteful, not from wanton prodigality, but from inexperience. If Nature were a man, she would presumably find her own incompetence a source of continual annoyance. Nature shoots the philosopher like an arrow into the midst of mankind. She does not aim, she simply hopes that her shaft will find a target somewhere. In this way she makes

---

is pessimistic because it sees Nature and the world as they actually are, no longer veiled by the glowingly optimistic self-praise of the Will to Live: "This world is the battleground of tormented and agonized beings who continue to exist only by each devouring the other. Therefore, every beast of prey in it is the living grave of thousands of others. . . . In this world the capacity to feel pain increases with knowledge, and therefore reaches its highest degree in man, a degree that is higher, the more intelligent the man. . . . The gloomy disposition of highly gifted minds . . . has its emblem in Mont Blanc, whose summit is often hidden in the clouds" (*WWR*, 2:383). Genius implies suffering and pain, both founded upon accurate insight into the misery of Nature and the world.

It was the spirit of Schopenhauer as genius of pessimism that presided over the first meeting between Wagner and Nietzsche, each of whom recognized in the other the features of the Schopenhauerian genius. Nietzsche described his first meeting with Wagner in a letter to Rohde (Nov. 9, 1868) in this way: "During the course of the evening, we had a long conversation about Schopenhauer, and you can imagine my unbounded joy at hearing him [Wagner] say, with indescribable enthusiasm, how much he owed to Schopenhauer, and to hear him called the only philosopher who had recognized the real nature of music." Subsequently, throughout the course of their friendship and in their joint dedication to the reform of German culture, it was Schopenhauer's spirit that bonded and affined them. In Wagner, Nietzsche described "the melancholy features of Schopenhauer's genius," and Melancholy, as mediated by Dürer (of whose work Wagner was inordinately fond), became the tutelary divinity of their "holy alliance." This is why in 1870—the heyday of his "Tribschen idyll" with Cosima and Wagner, his "seraphic father"—Nietzsche presented Wagner on his birthday with a dozen flowering rose-*bushes* (the *rooted* flower) and, above all, a fine print of Dürer's *Melancholia*, which, as Cosima's letter of thanks makes clear, was viewed as a Schopenhauerian emblem. (During the birthday festivities, Cosima's daughter honored "Uncle Richard" by releasing five caged birds. The last bird, however, refused to leave the cage and had to be set on a branch, from which it fell and was immediately savaged and devoured by a dog. Altogether a Schopenhauerian birthday!)

If Nietzsche was convinced of Wagner's Schopenhauerian genius, Schopenhauer was not. Wagner, it is said, had sent Schopenhauer a presentation copy of *Tristan und Isolde* with a note of gratitude to the great philosophical master whose writings had made the opera possible. Schopenhauer, clearly recognizing that Wagner's opera, however tragic, was essentially a paean in praise of the Will to Live, not a denial of it, replied drily by saying that, in his opinion, the composer who best embodied his theory of art was Rossini.

countless mistakes, and this vexes her. Culturally, she is as wasteful as she is in planting and sowing. She attains her ends in a gross and heavy-handed way, using too much energy in the process. Her artist confronts his audience and admirers the way a howitzer confronts a flock of sparrows. Only a simpleton would start an avalanche to remove a pile of snow, or kill a man to swat the fly on his nose. Artists and philosophers are proof that Nature's means are not perfectly adapted to her ends, though they are the best proof of the wisdom of those ends. They strike only a few when they should strike all—and even those they strike are not struck with the force with which artist and philosopher shot.

It is saddening to have to distinguish between art's value as cause and its effective value. How immense it is as cause, how crippled and echo-like in its effect! It is Nature's will that the artist do his work for the good of other men; of this there can be no doubt. Nonetheless, he knows that none of them will love and understand his work as he loves and understands it. This higher and lonely degree of love is necessary, given Nature's clumsy arrangements, in order to produce a lower degree. The greater and the nobler are the means of producing the smaller and less noble. Nature is not a clever manager: her expenses far exceed her income and, despite her wealth, she will someday be a pauper. Her household arrangements would be more sensible if she made it her rule to reduce her expenses and increase her income a hundredfold. Imagine, for instance, that there were only a handful of artists of much more modest talent, but a large and receptive audience composed of livelier and more talented people than the artists themselves. In this case the effect of a work of art would correspond to its cause, an echo magnified a hundredfold. Or at least we could expect cause and effect to be of equal power; but how far Nature falls short of answering our hopes!

It often seems as though an artist and a fortiori a philosopher are in their age *by accident*, as hermits and wanderers who have straggled away and been left behind. Simply try to understand, with real sympathy, how great, personally and in everything, Schopenhauer is—and how absurdly small his effect has been. Nothing can be more humiliating to an honest contemporary than to see the casual position which Schopenhauer occupies in this age, and by what forces—and nonforces—his impact has until now been curtailed. The first obstacle, to the everlasting shame of our literary age, was his longstanding lack of readers; then, when readers came, the inadequacy of his first public supporters. Even worse, I think, was the insensitivity of modern men to books, which they absolutely refuse to take seriously. And now, gradually, a new danger has appeared, arising from various efforts to adapt Schopenhauer to this insipid period by applying him as a seductive, exotic spice, a sort of metaphysical pepper. It was in this way that he gradually won renown and fame so that at present, I believe, his name among some people is better known than Hegel's. Nonetheless, he is still a hermit;

he still has had no real effect. Those who can least claim the honor of having presented his influence are the yapping literary jackals who opposed him, first of all because so few people have the patience to read them, and, secondly, because those who do are immediately led to Schopenhauer. Who, after all, would let a mule-driver prevent him from riding a fine horse, no matter how loudly the driver praised his mule at the horse's expense?

Those who are conscious of the folly afflicting the age might consider how to come to its assistance. But their task will be to make Schopenhauer's work known among free spirits and those who suffer deeply from the age, and to organize them into a coherent force that will counteract Nature's past and present inability to put her philosophers to use. They will come to see that the obstacles that prevent a great philosophy from having an effect are one and the same as those that impede the appearance of a great philosopher. So their task might be defined as preparing for the rebirth of Schopenhauer, that is, of the philosophical genius. From the beginning what has slowed the spread of his work and influence, and what will in every possible way oppose the rebirth of the philosopher, is, in a word, the imbecility of modern human nature. And so all those destined for greatness must waste incredible energy in order to save themselves from this imbecility. The world into which they now come is smothered in cant. By which I do not necessarily mean religious dogmas only, but such claptrap notions as "progress," "general education," "nationalism," "modern state," "struggle of church and state." We might, in fact, observe that all general terms nowadays are prinked out with such arty unnaturalness that a more enlightened posterity will charge our age in particular with being twisted and deformed, quite despite our noisy boasting about our "health." According to Schopenhauer, the beauty of ancient vases is that they express with such simplicity exactly what they are meant to be and do. And the same holds true of all other ancient utensils. We feel that if Nature had created vases, amphoras, lamps, tables, chairs, helmets, breastplates, armor, and so on, *this* is how they would look. If, however, we consider how everybody these days handles his utensils—politics, art, religion, and education (not to mention, for obvious reason, our "pots" and vases)—we find that men express themselves with a certain barbaric capriciousness and excess, and that such crackbrained ideas and moronic needs are the great vogue of the age. *These* are the leaden pressures which, invisibly and inexplicably, so often force down the hand of the genius while he tries to guide his plow, with the result that even his highest achievements bear to some degree the marks of the violent upward straining required by their creation.

If I turn now to the conditions under which, in the luckiest cases, the born philosopher might avoid being overwhelmed by the imbecility of the age, I am struck by a remarkable fact. It is that these are, at least partly, the same general conditions in which Schopenhauer grew up. There were, of course, unfavorable conditions. The lunatic quality of the age, for instance, came frightfully close to him in his mother's vanity and literary pretentiousness. But his father's proud, free, republican character saved him, as it were, from his mother and gave him the chief thing a philosopher needs: dogged, rugged virility. His father was neither a civil servant nor a scholar; he traveled with his young son in numerous foreign countries, all very helpful to someone destined to know men, not books, and to revere the truth, not governments. Schopenhauer quickly became insensitive to, or too sensible for, national limitations. He was at home in England, France, Italy, and he felt marked sympathy with the spirit of Spain. On the whole, he did not consider it an honor to be born in Germany; I cannot say whether he would have felt differently under our new political conditions. He believed, as everyone knows, that the sole purpose of the state was to provide defense from abroad, defense from within, and defense from the defenders; and that to assign the state any other purpose might easily endanger its true purpose. And for this reason, to the horror of so-called liberals, he bequeathed his property to the orphans and widows of the Prussian soldiers who had fallen in 1848 in the struggle to maintain order. Henceforth, the ability to understand the state and its duties in simple terms is more and more likely to be seen as a sign of superior intelligence. For the man with the *furor philosophicus* will have no time for the *furor politicus*, and will wisely refrain from reading newspapers every day, and above all serving in a party, though he will not for an instant hesitate to take his place when real danger threatens his country. All states in which men other than politicians must concern themselves with politics are badly organized and deserve to perish of too many politicians.

Schopenhauer was also extremely fortunate in not being destined and educated for scholarship. For some time, although reluctantly, he actually worked in a commercial office, and throughout his youth he breathed the freer air of a large trading house. A scholar can never become a philosopher. Even Kant could not manage it and, despite the innate power of his genius, remained to the very end in chrysalis state. Those who think these words are unfair to Kant do not know what a philosopher is—not only a great thinker but a genuine human being. And when has a scholar ever turned into a genuine human being? Anyone who lets concepts, opinions, past events, and books come between himself and things, who in the broadest sense is born to history, will never see things for the first time and will never himself be one of those prodigies that have never been seen before. But both these traits must be present in the philosopher, since most of what he teaches he has to draw from himself and because he himself is his own image and compendium of the whole world. If a man sees himself through the opinions of others, it is no surprise if he sees in himself nothing but— other people's opinions! And this is how scholars live, see, and are.

Schopenhauer, in contrast, had the indescribable good fortune not only to observe genius at close range, in himself, but also outside himself, in Goethe. And this double reflection instructed him and made him wise with regard to all scholarly goals and culture. Through this experience, he knew how the strong, free man to whom every artistic culture aspires should be formed. How, after a vision like this, could he have still wanted to deal with what is called "art" in the learned or hypocritical way of modern man? He had, after all, glimpsed something far higher: an awful scene of otherworldly judgment in which all life, even the highest and most perfected, was laid in the scales and found wanting. He had seen the saint as the judge of existence. We cannot determine at what age Schopenhauer saw this vision of life in the form in which he tried to describe it in his later writing. We can show that the young man, and perhaps even the child, had already seen this tremendous vision. Everything he later acquired from life, and books, and every field of knowledge, was for him little more than color and means by which to express it. Even Kant's philosophy he used mainly as an extraordinary rhetorical device for expressing that vision more clearly. Buddhist and Christian mythology at times served the same purpose. For Schopenhauer there was only one task, and a thousand ways of accomplishing it. There was one meaning and countless hieroglyphs to express it.

It was one of the splendid conditions of his existence that he could really live for such a task, according to his motto—*vitam impendere vero*[49]—and that he was never weighed down by the vulgarities associated with poverty. It is well known how magnificently he thanked his father for this. But without such good fortune, the contemplative man in Germany pursues his spiritual vocation usually at the expense of the purity of his character, as a "deferential tramp," greedy for honor and position, circumspect and pliable, obsequious to influential people and his betters. Regrettably, Schopenhauer insulted them in nothing quite so much as his failure to resemble them.

8 I have cited some of the conditions required if the philosophical genius, harmful factors notwithstanding, is to make an appearance in our times. They are: freedom and vitality of character; early knowledge of human nature; a nonscholarly education; exemption from the constraints of patriotism, from the necessity of earning a living, from any connection with the state. In short, freedom; always freedom—that same wonderful and dangerous element[50] in which the Greek philosophers flour-

---

49. Juvenal *Satires* 4.91: "To stake life on truth." Motto on the title page of Schopenhauer's *Parerga and Paralipomena*.

50. The ideas of *danger* and *wonder* are constantly and dynamically linked in Nietzsche's thought where, as in this account of Schopenhauer's life, "living dangerously" and the consequent suffering are the necessary antecedent to great accomplishment. Risk your

ished. Anyone who wants to reproach our genius with being a bad citizen, as Niebuhr reproached Plato, is welcome to do so provided he is a good citizen himself. In that case he will be right, and so will Plato. Others will construe such great freedom as presumption, but since they would not know what use to make of their freedom, and would clearly be guilty of great presumption if they claimed it, they are right too. The freedom is really a heavy burden of guilt that can only be expiated by great actions. Every ordinary son of earth has of course the right to resent anyone so favored, but may some god preserve him from being so favored himself, that is, so terribly obligated. He would immediately die of his freedom and loneliness; he would become a fool, a vicious fool, out of boredom.

Some father may perhaps learn something of value from our discussion which can be applied to his son's private education, though it cannot of course be expected that fathers should want only philosophical sons. In all ages fathers have probably resisted a philosophical vocation for their sons as the supreme imbecility. Everyone knows that Socrates fell victim to paternal wrath for "corrupting the youth," and that Plato, for the same reasons, thought it necessary to establish a radically new state in which the making of the philosopher would not be subject to paternal folly. And now it almost looks as though Plato had accomplished something. For the fact is that the modern state currently views the promotion of philosophy as one of *its* tasks and constantly tries to provide a number of men with that "freedom" we regard as the crucial condition for creating the philosopher. But historically Plato has been singularly unlucky. No sooner does a concrete structure basically conforming to his proposals arise than it turns out on closer inspection to be a changeling, an ugly goblin-child substituted for the real one. Merely compare, for instance, the priest-state of the Middle Ages with Plato's dream of a state ruled by "the sons of the gods." Obviously the modern state could not possibly be farther from appointing philosophers as rulers—"Thank God for that!" the Christian will say. But we have to ask whether even that encouragement of philosophy, as the modern state understands it, has been *Platonically* understood—by which I mean seriously and sincerely, as though its highest purpose were to produce new Platos. In most

---

genius, Nietzsche admonishes, if you have genius; if you don't, the risk taken will instruct and humanize you. Every man risks his uniqueness, and "living means to be in danger." "Therefore don't make philosophers the flunkeys of the state; persecute them—and miracles will happen." Out of danger, wonder.

Whether Nietzsche projected this dynamic onto the Greeks or found it embodied in the pre-Socratic philosophers, there is no way of saying. But this is, nonetheless, the dynamic implied by the Greek word *deinotēs* (formidability), which according to context means either "wonderful" or "terrible"—or, as in the great choral ode of Sophocles' *Antigone, both*: "Many things are wonderful-terrible [*deina*] / But nothing is more wonderful-terrible [*deinoteron*] than Man."

cases, the philosopher's appearance in his own time is accidental. But perhaps the state is now actually proposing to assume the task of conscientiously
translating that accident into a necessity and even here lending nature a
hand?

Experience, alas, teaches us better—or worse. It tells us that there is no
greater obstacle to producing and reproducing naturally great philosophers
than bad philosophers produced by the state. A painful subject, no? The
same subject, it is well known, to which Schopenhauer first directed attention in his famous essay on university philosophy.[51] I return to this topic
because men must be required to take it seriously, by which I mean they
must be moved to action. All words, I believe, are futile unless they imply
such a call to action. In any case, it is good to show that Schopenhauer's
permanently valid observations once again apply to our closest contemporaries. Otherwise, some good-natured soul will imagine that after Schopenhauer's fierce accusations everything in Germany has taken a turn for the
better. Even in this respect, admittedly a small one, his work has not yet
been completed.

Examined more closely, that "freedom" which governments, as I said,
now confer on certain men in order to promote philosophy is not really
freedom at all but a post which feeds its occupant. That is, the promotion
of philosophy merely means that the state enables a few men to *live* their
philosophy, by which I mean, to make a livelihood from it, in complete
contrast to the ancient Greek sages, who were not paid by the state but at
best, like Zeno, honored with a golden crown and a grave in the Ceramicus.[52]
Whether it is generally a service to the truth to show how a man can make
a living from it, I cannot say, since everything depends on the quality and
worth of the man who takes this path. I could easily imagine the degree of
pride and self-respect with which a man might say to his contemporaries:
"Take care of me, since I have something better to do—that is, to take care
of you." Such greatness of feeling and expression would not be surprising
in Plato and Schopenhauer, who might therefore serve as university philosophers, much as Plato served for a time as a court philosopher without
lowering the dignity of philosophy. Even Kant, like many of us scholars,
was respectful, obsequious, and, in his relations with the state, lacking in
greatness. So, if academic philosophy were ever put on trial, Kant would
clearly not be able to justify it. If, however, there are men who might justify
it—just such men as Schopenhauer and Plato—I fear only one thing, that
they will never have the chance, since no state would ever dare to show
favor to such men by appointing them to university posts. Why? Because

51. See "On Philosophy at the Universities," *PP*, 1:137ff.
52. Famous Athenian cemetery situated not far from the Agora, just outside the Dipylon
gates.

every state fears them and will show favor only to those philosophers of whom it is not afraid.

So the state is afraid of philosophy in general. That being the case, it will always try to recruit as many philosophers as possible in order to create the illusion that philosophy is on its side. It therefore enlists men who are called "philosophers," from whom it has nothing whatever to fear. If, however, a man appeared who really proposed to attack everything with the knife of truth—in that case the state, which above all else affirms its own existence, would be justified in excluding this man and treating him as an enemy in the same way that it excludes and declares war against any religion that sets itself above the state and acts as its judge. So if a man can bear to become a philosopher by means of state favor, then he must also bear with hearing it said that he has renounced the unconditional pursuit of truth. So long as he is state-favored and state-employed, he necessarily acknowledges something higher than the truth—that is, the state. And not only the state, but everything that the interest of the state demands, for instance, a certain form of religion, social order, and military organization. Over all these things is written: *Noli me tangere.*[53] Has any academic philosopher ever faced the full extent of his bondage and constraints? I do not know the answer. But if anyone has done so and still remains the servant of the state, he is clearly a poor friend of truth. And if he has not done so—well, in that case I suppose he is no friend of the truth either.

This is the most general of my objections, but as such, our contemporaries, being what they are, will regard it as the weakest and most irrelevant. Most will merely shrug: "As though anything great and pure could ever live, or live long, on this earth, without making concessions to human baseness! Which would you prefer? A state that persecuted the philosopher or one that paid him for services rendered?" Leaving this question unanswered for now, I will add only that the concessions made to the state by philosophers have gone too far. First of all, the state chooses its philosophical flunkeys according to its institutional requirements. By so doing, it not only pretends that it can distinguish between good and bad philosophers, but that there are always enough *good* philosophers around to fill all the professorial chairs. The state now effectively decides not only on their quality but on the number needed. Second, it requires its appointees to stay in a specific place, among specific people, for a specific activity. They are required to instruct every undergraduate who wants instruction, and to do so every day, and at fixed hours. Question: Can a philosopher conscientiously engage to teach something every day? And to teach anyone who cares to listen? Perhaps he shouldn't be addressing an unfamiliar audience on mat-

53. Proverbial for "Do not touch," derived from John 20:17: "Jesus saith unto her [Mary Magdalene] *touch me not,* for I am not yet ascended to my Father."

ters which he could safely discuss only with his closest friends? And in general isn't he robbing himself of his splendid freedom to follow his genius wherever it calls him, if he is obliged to think in public, at fixed hours, on prearranged topics? And in front of young people too? Isn't such thinking emasculated from the start? And what would happen if one fine day he felt, "I can't think today. I don't have an intelligent thought in my head"—but he still had to stand up and go through the motions of thinking?

But someone may object: "The academic philosopher is not meant to be a thinker. At most he is a minor epigone and rethinker of other men's thought. Above all, he is an expert on all the thinkers of the past, and he will always have something to say of which his students are ignorant." This is the third, and extremely dangerous, concession which philosophy makes to the state—this commitment to present itself as scholarship first and foremost, and above all as knowledge of the history of philosophy. The genius, in contrast, is like the poet. He has a pure and loving view of things, in which he cannot immerse himself deeply enough. Nothing is more tedious or repulsive to him than rummaging through innumerable odd and mistaken notions. The scholarly history of the past has never concerned a real philosopher, either in India nor Greece; and if a professor of philosophy concerns himself with such things, he must be content to hear it said that he is at best a good philologist, antiquarian, linguist, or historian—but not a philosopher. And that only at best, as I said. For with scholarly work done by academic philosophers, the philologist feels that it is done badly, without scientific rigor and is, for the most part, intolerably boring. Who, for instance, can rescue the history of Greek philosophy from the narcotic haze produced by the learned (but none too scientific and, alas, all too tedious) labors of Ritter,[54] Brandis,[55] and Zeller?[56] At any rate I would rather read Diogenes Laertius[57] than Zeller, since the spirit of the ancient philosophers

---

54. Heinrich Ritter (1791–1869), German historian of philosophy, professor at Göttingen, and author of a twelve-volume *History of Philosophy* (Hamburg, 1829–53).

55. Christian August Brandis (1790–1867), philologist and historian of philosophy at Bonn, the author of a history of Greek and Roman philosophy, and of a history of the development of Greek philosophy.

56. Eduard Zeller (1814–1908), German historian of ancient philosophy, author of a much admired and nearly "standard" *Philosophie der Griechen* (1844–52), translated into English as *Outline of the History of Greek Philosophy*. Because of Zeller's Hegelian bias and interpretation of Greek philosophy, he incurred Nietzsche's dislike and censure. He was also one of the founders of the *Theologische Jahrbücher*, a journal devoted to propagating the historical methods of David Strauss.

57. Diogenes Laertius (floruit AD 225–40), author of *Lives of the Eminent Philosophers*, a largely anecdotal compilation of personal biographies of eighty-two Greek thinkers from Thales to Epicurus. Encouraged by his mentor Ritschl at Leipzig, Nietzsche wrote a prize essay on Diogenes' sources (*De Diogenis Laertii fontibus*), published in *Rheinisches Museum* 23 and 24 (1868–69).

is at least alive in Diogenes, whereas Zeller lacks that spirit as well as every other. And, finally, what in the world does the history of philosophy matter to our young people? Should the chaos of scholarly opinion discourage them from having opinions of their own? Should they be taught to join in the celebration over our own stupendous progress? Should they even learn to hate and despise philosophy? One might think they did just that, if we recall how our students torture themselves preparing for examinations in philosophy, trying to cram pell-mell into their poor heads the most lunatic subtleties ever devised by the human mind, together with the greatest and most complex ideas.

The only possible criticism of a philosophy, the only criticism that proves anything at all, is trying to see if one can live by it. But that criticism has never been taught in any of our universities; all we ever teach is the criticism of words by words. And now imagine that fifty of these verbal systems, along with fifty verbal critiques of those systems, are scrambled and stuffed into a youthful mind. What a wilderness, what a jungle, what a caricature of a philosophical education! And the fact is that our students are not educated for philosophy, but for an examination in philosophy. And the usual result, as we know, is that the young man who has been examined and tested—all too sorely tested!—confesses to himself with a sigh of relief, "Thank God I'm not a philosopher, only a Christian and a citizen of my state!"

But suppose that this loud sigh of relief were the state's real purpose, and "educating *for* philosophy" actually meant diverting *from* philosophy? Ask yourself. But if so, there is only one thing to be feared—that young people will someday detect the real purpose behind this abuse of philosophy. Is the highest goal, the making of the philosophical genius, merely a pretext? Is the true goal perhaps to prevent him from appearing? Meaning converted into its opposite? Woe, then, to the whole complex of political and professorial fraud!

Is such a scheme perhaps already in the air? I don't know. University philosophy in any case has fallen into universal doubt and disrepute. The reason is partly that a feeble generation presently occupies the university chairs; if Schopenhauer were to write his essay on university philosophy today, he would no longer need his club, he could conquer it with a reed. The present generation are the sons and heirs of those bogus thinkers whose warped heads he battered. Their appearance is so dwarfed and infantile that we are reminded of the Indian proverb: "Men are born according to their deeds: dull, deaf, dumb, deformed." Fathers of this sort deserve a posterity like this, according to their "deeds," as the proverb has it. No doubt about it, undergraduates will soon manage to do without the philosophy taught in the universities, and nonacademic men manage without it now. Merely recall your own student days. To me, for instance, academic philosophers were utterly irrelevant men. I thought of them as people who concocted a little something from the results of other disciplines, read the newspapers in their leisure hours, went to concerts, and were treated by their colleagues with politely veiled contempt. They were reputed to know very little, and never to be at a loss for obscure phrases to disguise their ignorance. They therefore had a special liking for those twilight zones which a man with keen sight cannot tolerate for long. One of them objected to the natural sciences that "none of them can adequately explain the simplest physical process, so what do they matter to me?" Another said of history: "To a man with ideas, history has nothing new to say." In short, they always found a reason why it was more philosophical to know nothing than to learn something. If they did condescend to learn, their hidden motive was to escape the learned disciplines by establishing an obscure empire in some nook or dark little cranny. And so they keep ahead of their discipline *only* in the way in which the fox keeps ahead of the hunters. Lately they have taken to amusing themselves by saying that they merely control and police the frontiers of knowledge, a task in which they make special use of Kant, whose doctrines they are busy trying to convert to an idle skepticism, of which nobody will soon take the slightest account.

Every so often one of them rises to a little metaphysics, with the usual results—dizziness, headaches, bloody noses. Whenever their journey into the mist and the clouds miscarries, whenever some rough, tough-minded student of real scholarship catches them by the hair and pulls them down to earth, their faces assume the habitual simper of the exposed liar. They have so completely lost their cheerful confidence that not one of them enjoys living his philosophy in the slightest. In past days a few of them believed that they could invent new religions or replace old religions with their own philosophical systems. This exuberance has now abandoned them, and they are mostly pious, timid, and muddled people, quite lacking in Lucretius's courage and outrage at the oppressions afflicting mankind. Even logic can no longer be learned from them, and an accurate sense of their own strengths has made them discontinue their traditional exercises in disputation. There can be no doubt that among the scholars in other disciplines there is nowadays more logic, prudence, modesty, creativity, in short, more philosophy than among those who are called philosophers. Everyone will therefore agree with the remarks of that impartial Englishman, Bagehot, on our contemporary system builders:

> Who is not almost sure beforehand that they will contain a strange mixture of truth and error, and therefore that it will not be worthwhile to spend life in reasoning over their consequences? The mass of a system attracts the young and impresses the unwary; but cultivated people are very dubious about it. They are ready to receive hints and

suggestions, and the smallest real truth is ever welcome. But a large book of deductive philosophy is much to be suspected. Unproved abstract principles without number have been eagerly caught up by sanguine men and then carefully spun out into books and theories which were to explain the whole world. But the world goes clear against these abstractions, and it must do so, as they require it to go in antagonistic directions.[58]

In former days, in Germany especially, philosophers were immersed in such profound speculations that they were in constant danger of bumping their heads on every beam. Nowadays they go around accompanied, like Swift's Laputans, by a whole flock of beadles or "flappers" who every so often give them a gentle whack on the eyes or elsewhere. At times the slaps become a little too hearty, and those dreamers forget themselves and slap back—which always ends in their embarrassment. "Look out for that beam, you nitwit!" the flapper cries, at which the philosopher sometimes actually sees the beam and calms down. These flappers are the natural sciences and history, which have gradually so intimidated that German Dream-Thinkery[59] —long confused with philosophy—that its proprietors would be only too happy to give up trying to walk on their own two feet. If, however, they suddenly collapse into their flappers' arms or try to put them into leading-strings so they can be led themselves, the flappers immediately set up the most dreadful din imaginable, as though to say, "That's all we needed, one of those Thinkery types messing up our natural sciences or history! Away with him!" Whereupon the philosophers go tottering back to their uncertainty and helplessness. All they want is just to get their hands on a little scrap of natural science—maybe some empirical psychology, like the Herbartians[60]—or a snippet of history. Then they could create the public illusion of pursuing knowledge, while privately hoping that philosophy and scholarship would go to the devil.

But granted that this flock of bad philosophers is ludicrous—and who wouldn't grant it?—to what degree is it also pernicious? Brief answer: *to the extent that it makes philosophy ludicrous.* So long as these bogus philosophers

---

58. Walter Bagehot, *Physics and Politics* (Boston, 1956), 139. Nietzsche has slightly rearranged the word order of the sentences, but the meaning is unchanged.

59. A glance at Socrates' "Thinkery" (*phrontistērion*) in Aristophanes' *Clouds*.

60. Followers of Johann Friedrich Herbart (1776–1841), German philosopher and educationist of vehemently empirical and anti-Idealist conviction. In his psychological views, Herbart rejected all the older theories of "faculties" or multiple causes immanent in a person, accepting in place of them only "representations" (analogous to the physiologist's "fibers"). In sum, Herbart was a realist who believed that reality was not immediately "given," and that we only come to know its general characteristics, or laws, through the medium of phenomena.

are recognized by the state, a genuine philosophy will be prevented or at least hindered from having any great impact, and for no other reason than the curse of ridicule which the representatives of that great cause have drawn upon themselves, but which strikes philosophy itself. This is why I consider it a cultural necessity to withdraw all political and academic recognition from philosophy, and to relieve both state and university of the task—for them insoluble—of distinguishing between true and sham philosophy. Let philosophers grow in a wild state, undomesticated. Deny them every prospect of civic position and assimilation; stop titillating them with salaries. Better still, persecute them, frown upon them—and miracles will happen! They will immediately scatter in search of a shelter somewhere, these wretched make-believe philosophers. A parsonage will open up for one, a schoolmaster's job for another, a third will disappear into a newspaper's editorial office; a fourth will write textbooks for girls' finishing schools. The wisest of the lot will take up plowing, the vainest will be a courtier. Suddenly the whole place is deserted, the birds have flown the nest. There is nothing to getting rid of bad philosophers—all one has to do is withdraw support. That at any rate is a more advisable course than politically motivated support of any philosophy, *no matter what.*

The state is not concerned with truth, but only with the truth useful to it, that is, with anything that serves its interests, whether truth, half-truth, or plain falsehood. Hence, an alliance between philosophy and state makes sense only when philosophy can promise to serve the state unconditionally, which means a philosophy that sets a higher value on the state's interests than on the truth. Of course, it would be wonderful for the state to have the truth at its service and on its payroll, except that it knows very well that the *nature* of truth is that it serves nobody and never accepts payment. So all it ever obtains is the false "truth," a masked figure regrettably incapable of providing what the state craves from the real truth—the legitimation and canonization of the state. When a medieval prince wanted to be crowned by the pope but was unable to secure papal assent, he appointed an antipope to perform that service. Up to a certain point, this is quite proper. But it is not proper when a state appoints an antiphilosophy to legitimate its power, since philosophy is still opposed to it, and if anything more opposed than before. I seriously believe that it is better for the state to have nothing to do with philosophy, to make no demands of it, and to ignore it as something neutral and irrelevant. If philosophy loses its neutrality and turns dangerously aggressive, then let the state persecute it. Since the state's only interest in the university is the training of useful and obedient citizens, it should be wary of raising doubts about this function by requiring young men to take an examination in philosophy. I admit that the specter of an examination may be the right device for scaring the lazy and incompetent from academic studies, but the advantage cannot offset the harm done the more daring and restless young men. They make an acquaintance with forbidden books, they start to criticize their instructors, and finally they get a glimpse of the real purpose of university philosophy and its examinations—not to mention the doubts this produces in young theologians who, for this reason, have become, like the ibex in the Tyrol, a threatened species in Germany.

I am quite aware of the objection which the state might have made to this line of argument while it still had a fine bumper crop of green Hegelian corn standing in the fields. But now that harvest with its disappointed hopes and promises has been ruined by the hail and all the ricks stand empty— no objection can be made, only a rejection of philosophy. Today we have the power to reject it; in Hegel's time we lacked the power. There is a great difference. Since the state no longer needs the sanction of philosophy, philosophy is dispensable. If the state no longer maintains professorial chairs in philosophy or, as I predict for the future, maintains them only in appearance and perfunctorily, this is the state's good fortune. But it strikes me as even more important that the university should discern its own advantage in this matter. At least it seems to me that a center of genuine academic disciplines might detect some advantage in being relieved of the company of half-subjects and quarter-disciplines. Besides, the university's reputation is far too dubious for it not to welcome the abolition of fields enjoying scant respect even among academic colleagues. Nonacademic people rightly feel a certain universal contempt for the universities. They charge them with being effete, saying that the smaller ones are afraid of the larger ones, and the larger ones are afraid of public opinion; that, in all matters of higher culture, they do not lead but rather limp slowly behind; and that the essential, the fundamental orientation of those studies worthy of respect is no longer maintained.

Philological studies, for instance, are being cultivated more strenuously than ever before, yet no philologist regards rigorous training in writing and speaking as a requirement for himself. Ancient India throws open its doors to students, and the experts have as much relationship to the immortal works of the Indians, to their philosophies, as a dumb animal to a lyre[61]—and this, despite the fact that Schopenhauer thought our new knowledge of Indian philosophy was one of the greatest advantages our century enjoyed over others. Classical antiquity has become no different from any other antiquity, neither classical nor exemplary in its effect, as its votaries, in no way exemplary men, demonstrate. Where has the spirit of Friedrich August Wolf[62] vanished? Wolf, of whom Franz Passow[63] could say that he seemed a genuine

61. According to the Pythagoreans, the ass was deaf to the music of the lyre.
62. See *WC*, esp. n. 10 and relevant passages of the text.
63. Franz Ludwig Carl Friedrich Passow (1786–1833), German classicist and lexicographer. His chief work was his *Handwörterbuch der griechischen Sprache* (1819–24), which eventually culminated in the great lexicon of Liddell and Scott.

patriot, a truly human spirit, with the sort of power that could set a continent in ferment and in flames? Where has Wolf's spirit gone? In its place, the spirit of journalism more and more pervades the university, frequently under the name of philosophy. Slick, showy delivery; constant allusions to Faust and Nathan the Wise; the ideas and diction of our revolting literary journals; and more recently, chitter-chatter about our sacred German music, even a demand for special chairs in Schiller and Goethe studies: these symptoms tell us that the academic spirit is now being mistaken for the spirit of the times.

So it seems to me of immense importance that there should be a higher tribunal, outside the universities, to protect and criticize those institutions with regard to the education they promote. And philosophy has only to sever its connections with the university, purge itself of all unworthy motives and pretenses, and it will quickly become just such a tribunal. Separated from the power of the state, lacking honors and stipends, it will be able to perform its task, liberated from the spirit of the age as well as the fear of that spirit— in short, living as Schopenhauer lived, as judge of the so-called culture around him. In the same way, the philosopher may also be of service to his university by refusing to become a part of it and observing it from a dignified distance.

But, ultimately, what does the state's existence or university progress matter when the very survival of philosophy on this earth is at stake? Or when, to leave no doubt of my meaning, the appearance of a philosopher on this earth matters infinitely more than the survival of a university or a state? To the same degree that deference to public opinion increases and the threat to freedom grows, the dignity of philosophy may be raised. It was highest during the upheavals of the dying Roman republic and in the imperial period, when both philosophy and history became *ingrata principibus nomina*.[64] Brutus is greater proof of the dignity of philosophy than Plato; he lived in an age when ethics ceased to be platitudes. If philosophy is not highly regarded at present, ask yourself why it is that it has no following among generals or statesmen. The answer can only be that when they went in search of philosophy, they found only a pathetic specter that called itself philosophy—the pedantic and circumspect wisdom of the professorial chair. In short, because philosophy quickly became an absurdity, at least for them. It should have been a terrible apparition; and men who are called to power should know what a torrent of heroism flows from this source. Let an American tell them what it means when a great thinker appears on this earth, what a fresh source of tremendous power he is. "Beware," says Emerson, "when the great God lets loose a thinker on this planet. Then all things are at risk. It is as when a conflagration has broken out in a great city, and

64. Tacitean phrase: "names unwelcome to princes."

no man knows what is safe, or where it will end. There is not a piece of science, but its flank may be turned tomorrow; there is not any literary reputation, not the so-called eternal names of fame, that may not be revised and condemned. The things which are dear to men at this hour are so on account of the ideas which have emerged on their mental horizon, and which cause the present order of things as a tree bears its apples. *A new degree of culture would instantly revolutionize the entire system of human pursuits.*"[65]

Now if thinkers of this sort are dangerous, it is obvious why our academic thinkers are harmless; their thoughts grow as tranquilly in the soil of tradition as ever a tree bore apples. They inspire no terror, they throw open no doors; and to all their hustle and bustle we might raise the same objection Diogenes made when he heard a philosopher praised: "What great deed has he ever done? All his life he practiced philosophy and never yet *disturbed* a soul." And surely this should be the epitaph of a university philosophy: "It never disturbed a soul." But this is the sort of praise we might give an old woman, not the goddess of truth. So it is hardly surprising that those who know the goddess only as an old woman are hardly men themselves and are rightly ignored by men of power.

But if this is how matters stand in our times, then the dignity of Philosophy is trampled in the dust, and she seems in fact to have become absurd or irrelevant. For this reason all her true friends are obliged to bear witness against this confusion and to prove that it is not Philosophy but her false servants and unworthy worthies who are absurd and irrelevant. Better yet, let them prove in their actions that the love of truth is mighty and terrible.

Schopenhauer proved it—and he will go on proving it more and more with every passing day.

---

65. See "Circles" in *Essays: First Series* (Boston, 1892), 289.

Introduction
and translation
by Gary Brown

Notes to
translation by
William Arrowsmith

Richard
Wagner in
Bayreuth

Introduction

Hardly a month after the publication of *Richard Wagner in Bayreuth* in July 1876, Nietzsche had recovered sufficiently from illness and strain to attend the festival and composer in whose honor the present essay was written. His correspondence reveals joyful anticipation; what he actually experienced at Bayreuth was shock and disillusionment. The performances were disastrous, the costumes ludicrous, the voices unnatural and overwrought. Petty squabbles backstage, the patrons' conceit, boredom, and unmusicality, and the superficiality of the spectators, interested more in fashion than in art, merely enhanced the carnival atmosphere. Nietzsche, who had ardently envisaged something very different, witnessed the triumph of philistinism and the confirmation of his worst fears.

After three almost unbearable days of persistent, severe headaches, he took refuge in the Bavarian forest at Klingenbrunn. Rest and work on an improvisational essay (later to become *Human, All-Too-Human*, making a decisive break with Wagner) gave him the strength to return to Bayreuth. At issue was not simply a disastrous opening, but the validity of Wagner's artistic ideals. Bayreuth was to have been a cultural revolution, setting a new standard of performance in all the arts, which would attract serious speculators ready to welcome the modern rebirth of the archaic Greek ideal; an outright declaration of war on the mendacity and superficiality of contemporary culture. The fact that Bayreuth was the obverse of these ideals was, however, less painful to Nietzsche than the knowledge that he had years ago predicted this outcome; that he had long known Bayreuth would be the death agony of the last great art—and that he had perhaps lacked the courage to accept the fact.

When he came face to face with the awful reality, he felt startled out of a dream. Suddenly nothing was familiar to him, not even Wagner. He seemed to have created the passionately idealized Wagner from his own imagination, and he now saw his beau ideal lying shattered in the dust. Unwilling to separate friendship from shared ideals, he felt he could no longer sustain the old relationship. They seemed wasted now, all those years in which he had kept his devastating criticisms of Wagner's art in his notebooks and carefully edited them out of his published writings. He had done so because of Wagner's friendship and the hope of success at Bayreuth; perhaps even for himself, to forestall what appeared to him his own inevitable drift into the isolation of his later life, an isolation that had fascinated and frightened him since early youth. This was how he later explained it to himself: "Does anybody doubt that I, old artillerist that I am, could easily have deployed my *heavy* guns against Wagner? Everything decisive in this matter I held back—I have loved Wagner."[1] After Bayreuth Nietzsche was to see Wagner only once more, but the meaning, the *idea* of Wagner obsessed him for the rest of his life.

He had been reluctant to publish *Wagner in Bayreuth* because of his ambivalence towards Wagner at the time he was writing it. He had privately condemned Wagner's art, but he still loved it, still found in it his Dionysian ideal. He wrote to Rohde, "Perhaps I have a bad flaw in me, my longing and my need are of a different kind. I can scarcely express it."[2] Unless he could crystallize his attitude toward Wagner, he would prefer not trying to help other people.[3] It was only when a young musician named Köselitz (later to become Peter Gast) took an enthusiastic interest in the essay that Nietzsche decided to complete it and sent it to press. In the exhilaration of the actual rewriting, he seemed to have re-experienced his old great hopes for Wagner; hence his excitement en route to Bayreuth; hence his bitter disappointment. Any adequate reading of the essay requires the reader to grasp Nietzsche's ambivalence while writing it. Indeed, this ambivalence makes the essay especially rewarding for the light it throws not only on Wagner but on Nietzsche and his life's task.

Nietzsche's struggle with himself over Wagner's art began at least as early as 1874. The Bayreuth enterprise was then in serious financial jeopardy. A year earlier, at Wagner's request, Nietzsche had already drafted an appeal urging the German nation to support Bayreuth, an appeal which, even in the form released by the committee, went unheeded. Knowing that Wagner was about to announce the shipwreck of his plans, Nietzsche, who had been greatly disturbed about the resistance met by Wagner's art, eased his mind in a remarkable way. To Rohde he wrote: "I set to work to investigate the reasons for the failure of the undertaking: this I did in the most cold-blooded manner, and in so doing I learned a great deal and arrived at a far better understanding of Wagner than I ever had before."[4] He entered these discoveries into his notebooks as an outline for his "Unmodern Observation" of Wagner. German unresponsiveness, he observes, has driven Wagner to excess; lacking discipline, he employs everything to achieve effects—the magnificent, the intoxicating, the bewitching, the grandiose, the mythical, the neurotic. Such painting for effect is extremely dangerous for an artist. Equally alarming are his dictatorial nature and actor's instincts for using

1. *CW,* 1, trans. Kaufmann (New York, 1969), 317.
2. Nietzsche to Rohde, July 18, 1876.
3. Nietzsche to Rohde, Sept. 26, 1875.
4. Elisabeth Förster-Nietzsche, *Wagner und Nietzsche zur Zeit ihrer Freundschaft* (Munich, 1915), chap. 18; trans. C. V. Kerr, *The Nietzsche-Wagner Correspondence* (London, 1922), 198.

drama and music merely as rhetoric and self-expression. Despite all this, his powers of unification make him a culture bearer.[5]

When later asked by his sister whether he had really analyzed the matter so coolly at least two years before *Wagner in Bayreuth*, Nietzsche replied, "Not always, it was only now and then that I forced myself to look truth squarely in the face."[6] But these criticisms in his notebooks of 1874 were merely the signs of a profounder, even earlier analysis which he had largely suppressed. While still enjoying the pleasure of Wagner's friendship within reach of Tribschen, Nietzsche had early made a discovery that began to gnaw into his happiness like a cankerworm.

In November 1868, the twenty-four-year-old Nietzsche had received a note inviting him to meet Richard Wagner. This unexpected, thrilling event was remarkably timely. Freshly released from military service, Nietzsche was reluctant to resume the philological drudgery of his student years, despite the success he had achieved. Mere learning without purpose depressed him. Since Schopenhauer had reawakened his interest in larger issues, he was now determined to divide his loyalties between philology and philosophy. Exploring the fresh possibilities of civilian life, he became a reviewer for the *Deutsche Allgemeine* and had the opportunity to hear an orchestral production of the Overture to *Die Meistersinger* and the Prelude to *Tristan und Isolde.* Just after the concert, he wrote to Rohde: "I cannot bring myself to take a critically cool view of this music. It sends a thrill through every fiber, every nerve, and for a long time I have not had such a sustained feeling of being carried away as the Overture gave me."[7] Beneath his pleasure there is already a hint of reticence, as though his judgment, could he bring it to bear, would mar this pleasure. This reticence did not cool his ardor, however, when, less than two weeks later, he had the opportunity to meet the Master.

Even to this meeting Nietzsche would bring a long history of ambivalence toward Wagner. He relates that he became a confirmed Wagnerian from the moment he received a piano transcription of *Tristan.* At seventeen he and his friend Krug had performed this new piece for hours a day with what his sister has described as frightful howling. But even then he resisted the overwhelming appeal of this music: "In my student days I said, 'Wagner is a romanticist, not of the art in its zenith, but in its last quarter, soon it will be night!' Despite this insight, I was a Wagnerian; I *knew* better, but I could not do otherwise."[8]

5. Ibid.
6. Ibid.
7. Ronald Hayman, *Nietzsche: A Critical Life* (New York, 1980), 97.
8. Förster-Nietzsche, *Wagner und Nietzsche*, chap. 18. This precocious judgment was probably inspired by Goethe, in whose work Nietzsche had been steeped since boyhood. To Eckermann Goethe had proclaimed, "The classical is healthy, the romantic is sick."

Wagner, who was secretly in Leipzig to visit his sister, had been the author of Nietzsche's opportunity. Craving admiration, eager for followers, especially among the younger generation, Wagner sent for Nietzsche after learning of the young student's enthusiasm for his music. On this one guest Wagner lavished all his charm and virtuosity. He played parts of *Die Meistersinger* on the piano, taking all the roles; he read from his autobiography in progress and spoke of his enthusiasm for Schopenhauer, whom he called the only philosopher who understood music, even claiming (falsely) that Schopenhauer approved his music. He spoke, too, of the inspiration he found in the Greeks. For Nietzsche, oppressed by the narrowness of classical philology and uneasy with Schopenhauer's pessimism, this vivacious musical genius, of the same age as his dead father, fired him like a torch in tinder. He wrote to Rohde with the exalted lyricism of a fresh convert: "Together we could march to the bold, indeed giddying rhythm of his revolutionary and constructive esthetic. We could finally let ourselves be torn away from the passionate surge of his music, from this Schopenhaurian sea of sound. I feel so involved in the beating of its most secret waves that for me listening to Wagner's music is a jubilant intuition, indeed an astonishing self-discovery."[9] Again, the strange ambivalence. He wanted to free himself from the music in order to assess it, and he hoped that Wagner would provide him with the requisite esthetic instruments to resist its compelling power—a power to which something within him too eagerly responded.

Less than a month after this meeting, Nietzsche, still uncertain of his direction, was unexpectedly appointed professor at Basel, just fifty miles from Wagner's villa at Tribschen. Although he dreaded this enforced commitment to philology, the proximity to Wagner was strong compensation. Once established at Basel, he quickly grew somewhat contemptuous of his narrow colleagues with their limited specialities; but from Wagner he learned of forgotten classicists, and from Wagner's writings on esthetics and philosophy he acquired an ambitious sense of mission. Nietzsche was especially responsive to certain of Wagner's favorite topics: the insufficiency of modern life to satisfy the artist who can, in the present regime, address only a sect instead of the wider public; the debasement of modern civilization by Christianity, science, and commerce, with the attendant rejection of the instincts, fragmentation of culture, enslavement of the individual, and reduction of art to profit and entertainment; the poverty of modern life and art as compared with that of ancient Greece (the incarnation of unified culture); and above all the power of true art which, allied to nature and genuine feeling, might destroy a false culture by recreating a true culture.[10]

9. Nietzsche to Rohde, Dec. 9, 1868.
10. E. Newman, *A Study of Wagner* (London, 1889), 53–64.

Against this background of shared ideas, Nietzsche's particular sense of mission was the determination to revive the Greek ideal of art as a force in the modern world.

This sense of mission, catalyzed by Wagner, fueled his first great creative period and culminated in *Wagner in Bayreuth*. Wagner's ideas had an especially powerful impact on Nietzsche because they chimed so well with a number of his boyhood influences: Goethe, Schiller, Hölderlin, Byron, and so on, all of whom felt the fascination of Greece, its superiority to bourgeois culture, and the restoring power of art. But among these Schiller was thrust retroactively into special prominence, partly because he seemed a precursor of Wagner,[11] but mostly because of the uncanny parallel with Nietzsche's own situation. As Thomas Mann has pointed out, the young Schiller's relation to the older Goethe was "the most famous of all intellectual alliances, which was to bear such rich fruit out of the reciprocal relation of two great spirits."[12] Schiller's famous works on esthetics grew mostly out of his friendship with Goethe, under the influence of Kant, and were attempts not only to understand Goethe, but to define his position against Goethe. This similarity to Nietzsche's relation with Wagner was enhanced by similarity of temperament. In words that might have been Nietzsche's own, Schiller said of himself, "Whatever I am, I have become by an often unnatural tensing of all my powers."[13] Furthermore, Schiller's scope—he was poet, philosopher, esthetician, historian, essayist, and aphorist—was both example and challenge to the young Nietzsche, whose approach to those he admired was to absorb and more or less consciously emulate them, a process which not only restored these elements of the past to contemporary significance, but elicited them as tradition in which his own work was rooted.

Even a casual reading of Schiller's *On the Esthetic Education of Man, Naive and Sentimental Poetry,* and *On the Sublime* will reveal how thoroughly Nietzsche has absorbed into his *Unmodern Observations*[14] not only Schiller's

11. In a letter to Gersdorff during this period, Nietzsche had written that Wagner's idealistic manner "gives him his strongest affinity with Schiller: this glowing, high-minded struggle for the 'day of nobility' finally to arrive" (Hayman, *Nietzsche,* 125). Schiller had also envisioned the recreation of Greek tragedy as a composite art of singing, instrumental music, and dancing.

12. Thomas Mann, "On Schiller," in *Last Essays,* trans. R. and C. Winston and T. and J. Stern (New York, 1957), 15.

13. Ibid., 85.

14. Even the title of this group of essays echoes a comment Schiller makes in his second letter that to seek the laws of esthetics when interest is much greater in morality and political theory is to be uncontemporary (*ausser der Zeit*) (*Über die ästhetische Erziehung des Menschen,* in *Sämtliche Werke: Säkular Ausgabe* [Stuttgart and Berlin, 1904–05], 12:7; trans. E. M. Wilkinson and L. A. Willoughby, *On the Aesthetic Education of Man* [Oxford, 1967], 2:1).

critique of modern culture, its degeneration into the two extremes of barbarity and enervation, its worship of power and utility, its debilitating fragmentation of modern man into intellect and sensuousness, but also, especially in Bayreuth itself, his emphasis on the capacity of true art to destroy this false culture by reuniting the two sides of man. In fact Nietzsche's sketch of Wagner's evolution, his artistic awakening and emancipation from his surroundings, the fusing of the two sides of his nature, the clear unison of all his powers at maturity, is heavily indebted to *On the Esthetic Education of Man*, just as his comparison of Wagner to Aeschylus implies Schiller's perception, echoed in *The Birth of Tragedy*, that the loss of the Greek union with nature was already evident in Euripides.[15] Schiller, rejecting the uniformity and one-sidedness of Kant's logic, greatly extended the scope of esthetics, only recently declared a separate branch of philosophy by Baumgartner, by regarding synthetic a priori judgments not as fixed for all time, but as free, creative acts of reason to impose order on chaos.[16] This reversal in mid-career—he had initially sought the laws of esthetics—was supremely important for Nietzsche, for it now followed that laws, whether in science, morality, or political theory, had an esthetic basis. Schiller could speak of Lycurgus the lawgiver, for example, as an artist whose material was mankind[17]—an example certainly not lost on Nietzsche. This esthetic metaphysics was the starting point and central core of Nietzsche's entire oeuvre, and represents his greatest debt to Schiller.

But if Nietzsche took up the torch from Schiller in the domain of esthetics, there was another area in which Schiller's example could only taunt him—that of friendship. For Nietzsche's task of defining his own esthetic jeopardized and finally destroyed his friendship with Wagner. Unlike Goethe, who could tell Schiller, "You have given me a second youth, made me a poet again,"[18] Wagner regarded his young friend simply as a brilliant follower, and became jealous not only of the time Nietzsche spent away from Tribschen, but of any projects that strayed from his own interests. Nietzsche, burdened with his teaching duties and elaborating his esthetics in public lectures, gradually began to chafe under the restrictions created by his loyalty to Wagner, especially after he discovered the insurmountable philosophical gulf between them.

15. Schiller, *Über naive und sentimentalische Dichtung*, in *Schillers sämtliche Schriften* (Stuttgart, 1867–76), 4:666; trans. J. A. Elias, *Naive and Sentimental Poetry* (New York, 1980), 105.

16. *Über die ästhetische Erziehung*, 27:4. See also *Über das Erhabene*, in *Schillers sämtliche Schriften*, 4:735; trans. J. A. Elias, *On the Sublime* (New York, 1980), 206.

17. *Die Gesetzgebung der Lykurgus und Solon*, in *Schillers sämtliche Schriften*, 4:267; trans. J. B. Greene, *The Legislation of Lycurgus and Solon* (New York, 1959), 219.

18. Mann, "On Schiller," 81.

The initial problem was that Wagner's and Schopenhauer's esthetics were diametrically opposed. They simply could not be meaningfully reconciled. Wagner had discovered Schopenhauer late in life, after his own quite different esthetics had already been worked out. His major effort had been to replace opera with music drama, because opera had committed the error of employing music as the expressive end rather than the means. This led to passages of absolute music interspersed with unmusical dialogue; Wagner's own method was to employ music solely as an expressive means by keeping it always subordinate to the libretto, to which it supplied emotional coloring and significance.[19] In marked contrast, Schopenhauer had invested music with a metaphysical significance as the expression of the Will, or thing-in-itself, which made it the most powerful of the arts. Other arts were, in his view, reflections of the phenomenal world, itself an expression of the Will, hence copies of a copy. Consequently, in a musical drama the primary role must be assigned to the music, which expresses the unfathomable depths of universality, for which words and actions can merely provide a specific analogy or gloss, and are therefore secondary. Schopenhauer of course condemned the subordination of music to libretto, and offered as an example of their proper relation the operas of Rossini,[20] which Wagner despised.

Nietzsche appeared unaware of this incompatibility when he began a series of lectures at Basel following his inaugural address on Homer (May 1869). This series included "The Greek Music Drama" (January 1870), "Socrates and Tragedy" (February 1870), "Oedipus the King" (summer 1870), "The Dionysian Attitude" (summer 1870), "Socrates and Greek Tragedy" (April 1871), and culminated in *The Birth of Tragedy from the Spirit of Music* (April 1871).[21] Initially Nietzsche espoused Wagner's conception of a composite art and the use of music as a means to an end; he also linked tragedy to the ecstatic liberation of individuality experienced at folk festivals, a linkage consonant with Schopenhauer's theory of the Will. As the series progressed, Nietzsche continued this easy blend of ideas from his two mentors. But while merely asserting the ancillary relation of music to words, he actively elaborated within the domain of music the notion of suspended individuation and metaphysical identification with the terrors of existence; he differed with Schopenhauer, however, by disavowing the renunciation of the Will. By summer he had elaborated piecemeal the Dionysian-Apollinian polarity that figured centrally in *The Birth of Tragedy*,[22] enabling him to

19. Newman, *A Study of Wagner*, 81ff.

20. *Parerga and Paralipomena*, §§218–20.

21. T. Moody Campbell, "Nietzsche-Wagner, to January, 1872," *PMLA* 56 (1941): 552–72.

22. As Jung points out, Nietzsche here takes up in a new and original way the problem of types that was discerned and partially worked out by Schiller (Carl Jung, *Psychological*

define, in contrast with Schopenhauer, the achievement of tragedy as a life-affirming, rather than a life-denying, pessimism. The terrors of life are acknowledged, but the sense of Apollinian art, which focuses the Dionysian ecstasy, renders them bearable. Having rethought in modern terms the ancient heroic embrace of the tragic life, Nietzsche then turned to the music-word problem, breaking down words, as Wagner might do, into gesture and tone, and tone into rhythm, dynamics and harmony, a procedure which left music and words tightly wedded. But at this point Nietzsche recognized the incompatibility inherent in his mentor's ideas. In his next essay, "Socrates and Greek Tragedy," this analysis of the word is omitted; furthermore, Nietzsche now declares the absolute priority of music over words, thereby effectively breaking with Wagner. Music provides the metaphysical power and ecstatic liberation of the drama; words merely hint at a depth beyond them.

The revised form of this essay, now entitled *The Birth of Tragedy from the Spirit of Music*, makes public Nietzsche's new, fundamentally Schopenhauerian view of the relation of music to words: "Language can never adequately render the cosmic symbolism of music, because music stands in symbolic relation to the primordial contradiction and primordial pain in the heart of the primal unity, and therefore symbolizes a sphere which is beyond and prior to all phenomena.... Language ... can only be in superficial contact with music."[23] The title of the book implicitly rejects Wagner's approach, and this analysis undermines any possibility of a composite art. But in the act of generating *The Birth of Tragedy* out of the previous essay, Nietzsche excised some very explicit elaborations of his new position, which emphasized how destructive of Wagner's theory of music drama it really is. From the excised segments, which in the superseded essay had followed the paragraph just cited, and from notes of the same period, Nietzsche's view of Wagner's art when *The Birth of Tragedy* was published can be reconstructed.

Nietzsche's mission of reviving the Greek ideal referred precisely to that metaphysical, life-affirming tragic sense cited above. The alternatives to this position—Platonic Idealism and the devaluation of life in favor of Paradise or Nirvana, advocated by Christianity, Buddhism, and Schopenhauer—were to Nietzsche radically inferior life-modes. But Wagner's dramas of this period could not attain the Dionysian ideal, since they reduced music to a mere auxiliary of the logical idea; therefore, they could not awaken the penetrating metaphysical insight into the unity of existence and the suffering

Types, trans. R. F. C. Hull [Princeton, 1971], 6:136). Nietzsche absorbed the naive into the Apollinian, and the Dionysian, heavily influenced by Schopenhauer's Will, resembles the sentimental under the aspect of the sublime.
23. *BT*, 6 (trans. Kaufmann).

which this entailed. His music could express only emotions, and this placed his dramas squarely within the romantic, rather than the tragic, tradition. Moreover, lack of response had driven his work toward emotional excess. Wagner was working, therefore, in the inferior, operatic genre, despite his claim to have transcended it. The Greek world was lost. Wagner's achievement, as Nietzsche now saw it, was to have brought the degenerative tendencies—which had begun with Euripides and Socrates—to fulfillment, thereby clearing the way for something new. Only Bach, Shakespeare, and Beethoven had taken the right path. Wagner occasionally, almost unconsciously, strayed into it, as in *Tristan*, where music was allowed to soar according to its own laws. But even here the message was Schopenhauerian resignation, a nostalgia for a better life—idyllic opera—rather than affirmation.[24] With this assessment, Nietzsche had returned to the attitude of his student days: soon it would be night.

His investigations placed Nietzsche in an untenable relation to Wagner, and precipitated a long spiritual crisis. The publication of *The Birth of Tragedy* was therefore a traumatic event for Nietzsche. Friendship, gratitude, and loyalty required him to suppress certain details, but the apostasy was still glaring and might provoke Wagner's wrath. While the book was in press, Nietzsche for the first time declined a Christmas invitation to Tribschen; when in January he sent Wagner a copy, the effusive gratitude of his accompanying note must have compensated for nervousness and guilt. Wagner, however, was full of exuberant praise for a book that closed with a paean to his art and compared his operas to Greek tragedy. Excitedly he summoned Nietzsche to Tribschen. But the strain had taken its toll. Nietzsche was suffering from insomnia, stomach pains, headaches, and exhaustion—and he declined this invitation as well. Both times he was rebuked; the second time Wagner hinted that Nietzsche's independent behavior threatened their friendship; he attributed Nietzsche's illness to emotional distress, and wondered whether Nietzsche regretted publishing this book. Later Wagner penetrated Nietzsche's flattery and understood the book's message better. He wrote, "Nothing but *Tristan* will still interest you. But take off your glasses! You must pay attention only to the orchestra."[25] But to Nietzsche's relief, Wagner still demanded his loyalty, which Nietzsche continued to show by drafting the appeal to the German nation, soliciting from an old schoolfriend, Baron von Gersdorff, hospitality for Wagner, and providing his sister as babysitter. At great financial sacrifice he became a patron of Bayreuth; he even offered to resign his professorship to work for the festival, and attacked Davis Strauss at Wagner's request in the first of the *Unmodern Observations*. But the inner conflict was exacting its price. He

24. Campbell, "Nietzsche-Wagner," passim.
25. Förster-Nietzsche, *Wagner und Nietzsche*, chap. 14.

considered resigning his professorship for other reasons—to take a chair in philosophy, to travel the world as an aide to a young prince. Although intermittently depressed and ill, he uncharacteristically surrendered at times to Dionysian excess. He celebrated the publication of *The Birth of Tragedy* by socializing and dancing at balls until his suit was worn out, and his sister once described him disappearing, dancing wildly into a carnival crowd. Perhaps the ambiguity and desperation of his hopes at this time—ungrounded but persistent—are best revealed by a statement he made to Rohde. After hearing that the King of Bavaria had financially secured the success of Bayreuth, he wrote his friend: "If this miracle is true, the results of my investigations will nonetheless remain. But if it really is true, let us rejoice and make it a feast day."[26]

In the early days the polarity between Tribschen and Basel had been creative for Nietzsche; Wagner's esthetic perspective had allowed Nietzsche to escape philology and take a larger stance toward the Greeks. But after rejecting Wagner's esthetics, and seeing his own book in turn rejected by philologists, deprived, that is, of both mission and profession, all he could do was to continue with his own rapidly progressing work—the essays, prefaces, and projects born of his doomed efforts to reconcile the ideals of his mentors—which was now making its own original claims. He pursued this work almost clandestinely at times, meanwhile performing his duties at Basel and maintaining his loyalty to Wagner. From Bayreuth Nietzsche could still hope for a meeting place of creative minds, the development of a significant cultural center. But even here there were misgivings. He slowly began to realize that Wagner had eyes only for his own work, while others interested him primarily as instruments of his purposes. Wagner, for instance, was disturbed whenever Nietzsche wrote anything in which he was not mentioned, such as the book on early Greek philology, or the second of the *Unmodern Observations* on history. This realization could only increase Nietzsche's painful ambivalence and widen the conflict already raging within him. His illness was growing steadily worse. He sought doctors, cures, and diets, but by the summer of 1875 he was convinced that his symptoms "were deeply intertwined with spiritual crisis";[27] he doubted whether medicine and diet could ever restore his health. Everything he wrote during this period spoke of emancipation: "'Wake up,' cries Philosophy";[28] "philosophers are the arbiters of art";[29] "falsehood must be cut out with a knife";[30] "conscience cries, 'Be Yourself!'"[31] A time of decision was at hand; apart from his

26. Ibid., chap. 18.
27. Nietzsche to Malwida von Meysenburg, Aug. 11, 1875.
28. *Über das Parthos der Wahrheit, NWKG*, 3.254.
29. *NF*, summer 1872–beginning 1873, paraphrased.
30. *HSDL*, 3, paraphrased.
31. *SE*, 1, paraphrased.

irresolution over Wagner, there were personal considerations: friends were getting married, he was getting deeper into his thirties, teaching was exhausting him. But his intermittent vomiting attacks were also getting worse, and by Christmas of 1875 he collapsed; the following February he took a leave of absence from teaching, thereby acquiring the freedom he sought. But he also complained of becoming daily more disillusioned. His lack of resolve only deepened his personal and professional crisis.

It was during this dispirited period, in which he later claimed to have believed in nothing at all, that Nietzsche wrote *Wagner in Bayreuth*. In tenor, despite Nietzsche's inner doubts, the essay is unmistakably laudatory; it portrays an artist whom he wished, and once sincerely believed, to be the real Wagner. But for the reader aware of Nietzsche's private doubts, it takes on a stereographic quality. The criticisms of 1874 are woven into the text, but explained as dangerous tendencies which Wagner in the course of his development has overcome. As Hayman rightly observes, Nietzsche slips "his stowaway criticism on board the vessel of praise."[32] Hence he can speak of Wagner's immoderation, boundless ambition, lust for power, use of spurious artistic techniques, and the absurd, demeaning burlesque of great portions of his life, and yet assert that these tendencies have all been transcended at a higher level. He speaks of the mendacity of modern success, but points out that once Wagner's eyes were opened to this mendacity, he had disowned it as unworthy of him. On other points of difference, Nietzsche simply interprets matters in the loftiest possible way; he sublimates, for instance, Wagner's idea of the "folk." Instead of a creative mass of people (*Volk*) for whom the artist is spokesman, Nietzsche translates the concept of a people into that group called into being by shared suffering through Wagner's healing art; this "people," with its fresh awareness, will therefore compose a cultural elite which will reform society on the basis of authentic feeling and psychic health. He even praises as a virtue, without obvious irony, Wagner's restraint in subordinating music to words, when music longs to cast off its shackles and soar into freedom. Elsewhere he speaks of the relation of music to words only in the context of the highest level of dithyrambic art, in which words and music are inseparably bonded.

The entire essay is thus an equilibrist's act. Topics are chosen so that Nietzsche's commitment to truth, loyalty to Wagner, and sense of the Greek ideal can all legitimately intersect. But to the initiated reader, the essay offers two Wagners: on the one hand, the ideal Wagner, a profoundly metaphysical, dithyrambic artist in whom the young Nietzsche had once believed; and on the other, the all-too-human Wagner whom he had privately discovered. We are also offered two arts: first, a dithyrambic art, presumably Wagner's, which grants its viewers the courage to face life; and, second, the

32. Hayman, *Nietzsche*, 186.

debased art of the modern period, actually Wagner's, which rescues its viewers from their boredom—an art, that is, which looses a braying herd of passions and atrocities on its doltish audience, which craves them. Read backwards, the essay is a palimpsest in which the entire history of Nietzsche's relationship to Wagner (except for the worst of the 1871 comments) is latently layered—the early rapturous idealization, the later insight into Wagner's darker sides, and the ideal against which Wagner is measured and condemned.

As we noted earlier, Nietzsche's work on the essay, combined with the enthusiasm of his young amanuensis (and perhaps a dash of guilt), brought him back in touch with his highest Wagnerian aspirations and the memory of those wonderful Tribschen days with Wagner and Cosima. For years he had heard Wagner complain of the inadequate production of his works, the poor techniques of singing and conducting, the wretched staging. And he looked forward to seeing the newly completed operas presented properly by Wagner himself at Bayreuth.[33] But this resurgence of hope was hopelessly defeated at the 1876 festival, a transparent apotheosis of modern "success" in the most vulgar sense. The mendacity, the sham effects, the lack of moderation, and the uninformed audience were all too plainly apparent. When headaches forced Nietzsche to close his eyes, he recognized how unbearable, apart from the scenic aspect, Wagner's music was; that instead of developing according to its own laws, it was everywhere merely explication of the conceptual frame of the opera. Where he had sought the cleansing powers of nature, he found only grotesque unnaturalness and exaggeration. The shock of observing these failures broke much of Wagner's spell. When asked at the festival about his essay on Wagner, he refused to speak of it: "Why don't people let those old stories rest?" he complained to his sister. When she reminded him of its appearance only five weeks prior, he replied, "It seems like five years."[34]

The protracted disillusionment made Nietzsche's next book seem a savage break with the past. As he himself said later: "What reached a decision in me at that time was not a break with Wagner; I noted a total aberration of my instincts of which particular blunders, whether Wagner or the professorship at Basel, were mere symptoms. I was overcome with impatience with myself. All at once it became clear to me in a terrifying way how much time I had already wasted."[35] As an antidote, Nietzsche forbade himself all romantic music, all emotional excess, and concentrated instead on cold analysis. His next book, *Human, All-Too-Human,* born at the Bayreuth Festival and a monument to his crisis, was so different from what preceded it that

33. Förster-Nietzsche, *Wagner und Nietzsche,* chap. 23.
34. Ibid.
35. *HAH,* 3, trans. Kaufmann (New York, 1969), 286.

Rohde accused him of having exchanged his soul for another's. But at this point Nietzsche's task required a correction of instinct and eradication of error. "One error after another is coolly placed on ice,"[36] he later said of this book.

His turn away from his emotional, artistically inspired, aberrant self paralleled a similar decision early in his life. As a child he had not only improvised on the piano (a skill acquired from his father), but had composed motets, ballads, religious songs, and plays, and drawn excellently. He had written fifty poems in his tenth year alone; by his fourteenth, he was dividing his oeuvre into three periods. But instead of a career in art, he studied first theology, then classical philology. He wrote in a youthful autobiography that he wanted a science that would not "seize the heart."[37] But after the constraints imposed by his commitment to philology, his suppressed artistic nature began to rebel. The precipitant was Wagner, who galvanized Nietzsche's diverse impulses and gave him purpose and direction. For a while intellect and emotion had functioned in tandem, and the two sides of his nature coalesced, a fusing similar to that praised in *The Birth of Tragedy* and in *Wagner in Bayreuth*. But now, after disillusionment at Bayreuth, he once again turned away from the resurgent Dionysian emotion which had overwhelmed him in Wagner's art. Just as he thought that Socratic rationality had helped to destroy tragedy, so he now appealed a second time to science to curtail his own Dionysian excess. But the process of emotional eruption after rational suppression, which had occurred in his youth, was now repeated at a higher level; over the next six years his re-repressed emotions gradually sought new release. The very titles reveal the metamorphosis: *Human, All-Too-Human, The Wanderer and His Shadow, Dawn, The Gay Science*, and *Thus Spoke Zarathustra*.

Zarathustra swept over Nietzsche like a possessing demon, seizing his heart—an event which he had once feared. But he now had the intellectual and artistic maturity to give this seizure form, to contain it in an Apollonian structure. The entire first part he wrote in ten days, in a state of rapture— the birth within Nietzsche of the dithyrambic poet, the dancing philosopher. This book, Nietzsche tells us, was born out of a rebirth of the power of hearing, that is, out of music. The ideal that he had announced in *The Birth of Tragedy*, and believed he had found in Wagner—he now recovered for himself. The dithyrambic poet was not Wagner after all, but the author of *Zarathustra*, the book which Nietzsche regarded as his best, and the synthesis of everything that went before.[38]

36. Ibid., 1.
37. Hayman, *Nietzsche*, 56.
38. Among the many reflections in *Zarathustra*, a careful reader can catch glimmers of Schiller, especially in images such as the storm-tossed boat, receding horizons, companion animals, preferences for the slopes of Vesuvius, etc.

With *Zarathustra* well behind him, *Wagner in Bayreuth* took on yet another significance. In *Ecce Homo* (1888) he saw his earlier essays as a portrait of himself, as an image of his future—a description from within of the ideal dithyrambic artist:

> A psychologist might still add that what I heard as a young man listening to Wagnerian music really had nothing to do with Wagner, that when I described Dionysian music I described what I had heard—that instinctively I had to transpose and transfigure everything into the new spirit that I carried in me. The proof of that, *as strong as any proof can be*, is my essay on *Wagner in Bayreuth*: in all psychologically decisive places I alone am discussed—and one need not hesitate to put down my name or the word "Zarathustra" where the text has the word "Wagner." The entire picture of the dithyrambic artist is a picture of profundity and without touching even for a moment the Wagnerian reality.[39]

He elaborates the points of contact between *Wagner in Bayreuth* and *Zarathustra* (1883–84).

> The pathos of the first pages is world-historical; the glance spoken of on the seventh page is Zarathustra's distinctive glance; Wagner, Bayreuth, the whole wretched German pettiness are a cloud in which an infinite mirage of the future is reflected. Even psychologically all decisive traits of my own nature are projected into Wagner's—the close proximity of the brightest and the most calamitous forces, the will to power as no man ever possessed it, the ruthless courage in matters of the spirit, the unlimited power to learn without damage to the will to act. Everything in this essay points to the future: the impending return of the Greek spirit, the necessity of counter-Alexanders who will retie the Gordian knot of Greek culture.[40]

Consequently, in Nietzsche's judgment, *Wagner in Bayreuth* must be viewed as in the direct line of development from *The Birth of Tragedy* to *Zarathustra*; that is, the evolution of an artist toward Dionysian depths of creativity and tragic perception is strategically located between the depiction of Dionysian art in *The Birth of Tragedy* and its demonstration in *Zarathustra*, and understanding this sequence deepens our reading of all three.[41]

39. *ET*, 4 (trans. Kaufmann).
40. Ibid.
41. By this time Nietzsche's conception of the Dionysian was no longer the unleashed, chaotic energy of *The Birth of Tragedy*, which required the counterforce of Apollinian formative power, but had its own formative power. Dionysian art, then, was no longer an ensemble of two forces, but an inward unity, an art of wholeness, a conception influenced

The retrospective view also demonstrates Nietzsche's continuing obsession with his friendship with Wagner. Even immediately after the Bayreuth Festival of 1876, after claiming that he saw Wagner shrink to nothing, he still made no firm break with Wagner. He had given up the esthetics, then Bayreuth, but still clung to the friendship. Even in Italy, where he wrestled with the Wagner question,[42] Nietzsche was glad, after an initial shock, to learn that he and Wagner were to be neighbors in Sorrento. They rushed together there whenever they met, but their pleasure was short-lived. On their last evening together, Wagner told Nietzsche of his work on *Parsifal*, elaborating the religious experiences guiding his work while Nietzsche listened in stunned silence. Wagner—avowed atheist, enemy of Christianity, admirer of ancient Greece, lover of power, baroque luxury, perfumed baths, and women—this Wagner was now praising the chastity, humility, simplicity, and naiveté of the "pure fool." In Nietzsche's eyes Wagner's conversion was not genuine, but a cynical strategy calculated to win adulation and profit for Bayreuth. This catering to the taste of Bismarck and the German public robbed Wagner, he felt, of all greatness.[43] Furthermore, this new religious tack destroyed Nietzsche's last hope that he might somehow exercise a positive influence on Wagner's art.[44] He now realized that he and Wagner were fated by nature to part company. Nearly a year later he received a copy of the completed score of *Parsifal*—bound and signed "Richard Wagner, High Ecclesiastical Consistory." Nietzsche saw no humor in this device; to him the opera marked Wagner's allegiance to the Counter-Reformation, which in his opinion had impeded all the progressive forces of the Renaissance and frustrated the creative fusion of antiquity and the modern spirit. He found it incredible to contemplate: "Wagner has become pious."[45] And after Wagner had received *Human, All-Too-Human*, which contained disparaging references to him, he attacked, without naming, Nietzsche in the Bayreuth paper. Nietzsche claimed to be more upset by the vindictive clumsiness of the polemic, but by the end of the month he was in a state of near collapse. In *Ecce Homo* a decade later, he claimed that these two works had crossed each other like two swords.

Despite the crossed swords, his shattered friendship with Wagner preoccupied Nietzsche for the rest of his life. The old split between judgment

---

by Goethe's perception of nature: "independent and alive and ever productive in accordance with its own laws in all depths and all heights" (Goethe, "Erste Bekanntschaft mit Schiller," in *Gedenkausgabe der Werke, Briefe und Gespräche* [Zurich, 1961] 12:620).

42. Förster-Nietzsche, *Wagner und Nietzsche*, chap. 24.

43. Ibid.

44. It was as though Wagner had gained nothing from Nietzsche, who in *The Birth of Tragedy* had attacked Schiller's notion of the naive and Rousseau's *Émile* as falsities of the romantic age; behind these, of course, lay Christianity's veneration of innocence.

45. *HAH*, 5 (trans. Kaufmann).

and feeling persisted as a perpetual sense of loss and mourning, which no other relationship—not with Paul Rée, Peter Gast, Franz Overbeck, nor even Lou Salomé—could alleviate: "Nothing can compensate me for the fact that I lost Wagner's goodwill during the past years. . . . Not a single disagreeable word was ever spoken between us, not even in my dreams, but very many encouraging and happy ones, and perhaps I never did laugh so much in anybody's company. That's all over now—and what is the use of being right against him in many points! As though one could in this way wipe this lost friendship from memory."[46] In the following years his writings are filled with poignant references to Wagner:

Wagner was by far the most complete man I ever met.[47]

This has been my most severe test as regards justice toward men— this whole association and no further association with Wagner.[48]

Know that I believe even today as much as before in the ideal in which Wagner believed—what difference does it make that I stumbled over so much of the human, all-too-human, that Richard Wagner placed in the path of his ideal?[49]

Except for Wagner nobody so far has met me with one thousandth the passion and suffering necessary to understand me.[50]

The rest of my human associations I count lightly, but for no price would I omit from my life the days of Tribschen, days of trust, of gladness, of sublime incidents, of *profound* moments.[51]

I had nobody except Richard Wagner.[52]

This painful turning away from Wagner involved an obvious rejection of Nietzsche's own feelings, a rejection of that part of himself which he believed to be allied to modern debasement. It was therefore necessitated by his own judgment and sense of his mission. As he wrote to Gersdorff: "Not one step toward accommodation, not for anything in the world! Great success can be gained only by remaining faithful to oneself."[53] But the pain involved in this radical commitment to authentic inner truth led him to imagine ever greater refinements of the idea of friendship. Even if he could

46. Nietzsche to Gast, Aug. 20, 1880.
47. Nietzsche to Overbeck, March 22, 1883.
48. Nietzsche to Gast, April 27, 1883.
49. Nietzsche to Overbeck, Oct. 29, 1886.
50. Nietzsche to Overbeck, Nov. 12, 1887.
51. *EH,* "Why I Am So Clever," 5 (trans. Kaufmann).
52. *NAW,* "How I Broke away from Wagner," 1.
53. Nietzsche to Gersdorff, April 15, 1886.

not himself experience it, he could perhaps at least make such friendship possible for others: "Here and there on earth we may encounter a kind of continuation of love in which this possessive craving of two people for each other gives way to a new desire and lust for possession—a shared higher thirst for an ideal above them. But who knows such love? Who has experienced it? Its right name is Friendship"[54] But he wanted a concept of friendship that transcended even this passion of a shared ideal: "That we have become estranged is the law above us; by the same token we should also become more venerable for each other—and the memory of our former friendship more sacred. There is probably a tremendous but invisible stellar orbit in which our very different ways and goals may be *included* as small parts of this path; let us rise up to this thought … Let us then *believe* in our stellar friendship even if we should be compelled to be enemies on earth."[55]

Still, Nietzsche had actually sacrificed friendship to an even higher ideal, which he reads finally into Brutus's relation to Caesar: "Independence of the soul!—that is at stake here. No sacrifice can be too great for that: one must be capable of sacrificing one's dearest friend for it, even if he should also be the most glorious human being, an ornament of the world, a genius without peer."[56] By *Zarathustra*, he was ready to assert the necessity that friends should part, and views such parting as an essential aspect of discipleship:

Now I go alone, my disciples. You too go now, alone. Thus I want it.

The man of knowledge must not only love his enemies, he must also be able to hate his friends.

One repays a teacher badly if one always remains nothing but a pupil. And why do you not want to pluck at my wreath?

Now I bid you lose me and find yourselves; and only when you have all denied me will I return to you.[57]

While he was writing *Zarathustra*, *Beyond Good and Evil*, and *The Genealogy of Morals*, a new element complicated Nietzsche's relation to Wagner. His sister Elisabeth, who saw no practical use for his philosophy, married a

---

54. *GS*, 1.14.
55. *GS*, 4.279. One of the countless points of contact with Emerson, whom he was reading as he wrote *The Gay Science*, and who had written: "Ah! seest thou not, O brother, that we thus part only to meet again on a higher platform, and only be more each other's because we are more our own?" (R. W. Emerson, "On Friendship," *Essays: First Series* [Boston, 1865], 204).
56. *GS*, 2.98 (trans. Kaufmann).
57. *Z*, part 1, "On the Gift-Giving Virtue," 3.

certain Dr. Bernard Förster, a well-known Wagnerian and anti-Semite, a malcontent who wanted to form racially pure colonies in Paraguay. "We feast," she wrote, "on compassion, heroic self-denial, Christianity, vegetarianism, Aryanism and South American colonies."[58] Nietzsche regarded this liaison as highly embarrassing; it also clarified to him the kind of cultural danger posed by Bayreuth, and the nature of German regeneration which Wagner envisioned: "A pure race," Wagner had written, "of which Germany could be the shining exemplar if only it could rid itself of the Jews."[59] Nietzsche made his feelings clear to his sister, whose wedding he refused to attend: "You have gone over to my antipodes. . . . I will not conceal that I consider this engagement an insult—or a stupidity which will harm you as much as me."[60] Further: "One of the greatest stupidities you have committed—for yourself and for me! Your association with an anti-Semitic chief expresses a foreignness to my whole way of life . . . it is a matter of honor to me to be absolutely clean and unequivocal regarding anti-Semites, namely *opposed*, as I am in all of my writings . . . The relation to Förster . . . always brings the adherents of this disgusting party back to the idea that I must after all belong to them . . . That in every Anti-Semitic Correspondence sheet the name *Zarathustra* is used has already made me almost sick several times."[61]

It was now clear to Nietzsche that Bayreuth represented not only Wagner's worst elements, but those of the German Reich which it celebrated. In 1883, having just prepared Part 1 of *Zarathustra* for the printer, he discovered that Wagner had died that previous day. After several days ill in bed, he was able to write: "It was hard, having for six years to be against the man one has most revered. . . . Finally it was the senescent Wagner that I had to resist; as for the real Wagner, I shall to some extent become his *heir*."[62] But there were other men now who claimed to be Wagner's heirs. Nietzsche, who had spent years fighting toward the freedom required for his greatest works, had now the additional task of clarifying his position toward Wagner. Everything he had hitherto suppressed had to be made public. The latent hints in *Wagner in Bayreuth* were not enough to prevent it from being read as anything but a paean. He accordingly shifted his attention from the historical perspectives of his recent works back to Wagner, on whom he wrote two additional books.

In *The Case of Wagner*, the criticisms of 1874 along with those of 1871

58. Unpublished letter, Naumburg/S., Jan. 7, 1883, cited in H. F. Peters, *Zarathustra's Sister* (New York, 1977), 71.
59. E. Newman, *The Life of Richard Wagner* (New York, 1946), 4:616.
60. Walter Kaufmann, *Nietzsche* (New York, 1968), 43.
61. Ibid., 45.
62. Nietzsche to Gast, Feb. 19, 1883.

have gathered into a wrathful storm. Nietzsche holds nothing back, his virulence presumably justified by his claim that his polemic is aimed not at individuals but at the causes they represent.[63] He describes Wagner as one of his sicknesses, a decadent artist who has made even music sick. Not only has Wagner written operas instead of dramas, but they are especially bad operas. His works, in fact, are nothing but theater, which is to Nietzsche not art at all, but merely a revolt of the masses, which lack the dignity of art. Wagner is not even a musician, but a semiologist and rhetorician; he has destroyed music as melody and become the Victor Hugo of music as language. Worse, Wagner is an actor whose "art" is a mere rhetorical trick. His work has no unity; he serves up chaos, calculated composites, and patchwork. He creates not clarity, but fog, obscurity, and imitations for the titillation of the fundamentally unmusical. His plots are slack and ridiculous; his heroines, stripped of their mythic garb, are nothing but Emma Bovarys and neurotic Parisiennes. Wagner is a seducer to the joys of sickness; he casts a shadow over health. His work is counterfeit; it belongs to the Reich, to mass man, to Teutonic obedience and the impending age of war. As though unconvinced of the thoroughness of his assault, Nietzsche added two postscripts and an epilogue in much the same vein.

Later, he must have worried whether there was still a possibility of being misunderstood; so he wrote a brief second book, *Nietzsche against Wagner*, composed of selections from earlier writings beginning with *Human, All-Too-Human* in 1877. His aim was clearly to prevent the former work from being discounted as a sudden paroxysm of malice. After all, he had been referred to, after the publication of *The Birth of Tragedy*, as one of Wagner's literary lackeys. But he could prove that, eleven years before *The Case of Wagner*, he had written in *Human, All-Too-Human*: "Since Wagner had moved to Germany, he had condescended step by step to everything that I despise—even to anti-Semitism."[64] He could also show that by 1882, in *The Gay Science*, he had understood Wagner as an actor: "If it was Wagner's theory that 'the drama is the end, the music is always a mere means,' his *practice* was always, from beginning to end, 'the pose is the end, the drama, also the music, is always a mere means.'"[65] In the Epilogue of *Nietzsche against Wagner*, he directs attention away from Wagner, romantic art, and the modern pursuit of pleasure, even away from the search for truth at any price to describe his new taste and his need—born of pain and suffering— for surfaces and *cheer*, above all *Greek* cheer. The Greeks (like himself) were "superficial out of profundity," he wrote. "And is not this precisely what we are again coming back to, we daredevils of the spirit who have

63. *EH*, "Why I Am So Wise," 7 (trans. Kaufmann).
64. *NAW*, "How I Broke away from Wagner," 1.
65. *NAW*, "Where I Offer Objections," 1.

climbed the highest and most dangerous peak of present thought . . . ? Are we not precisely in this respect Greeks? Adorers of forms, of tones, of words? And therefore—artists?"[66] He here announces the return of the spirit of Hellenism, which he had predicted in *Wagner in Bayreuth*, and he openly claims this mantle, previously accorded to Wagner, for himself.

This view of himself as in some respects Wagner's heir touches a human, all-too-human aspect of their relationship. For not only was Wagner something of a father figure for Nietzsche,[67] but Nietzsche had been Wagner's inspiration for the music of Siegfried, Wotan's son. And although the break in their friendship affected Nietzsche more, Wagner, while at the height of his power and success, confessed to Nietzsche's sister six months before his death: "Tell your brother that I am quite alone since he went away and left me."[68] The psychological ties established at Tribschen not only complicated the relationship between the two men, but affected Nietzsche's relation to Wagner's wife, Cosima, as well. He had dedicated several of his early literary productions and much of his attention to Cosima, but after the master had died, he wrote her. "The only way I know of pouring out my feelings is by directing them entirely and exclusively to you. I regard you today, even from far away, as I have always regarded you—as the woman my heart most honors."[69] After Nietzsche's collapse into insanity in 1889, Cosima received one of his lucidly mad postcards: "Ariadne, I love you. Dionysus."[70] Later, at the asylum of Jena, Nietzsche said: "My wife, Cosima Wagner, has brought me here."[71]

But Nietzsche's assault on Wagner's work cannot be reduced to Oedipal promptings. These attacks were skirmishes within a larger campaign against the entire moral-religious age—of which Wagner's work was a late product. In *Beyond Good and Evil, The Genealogy of Morals,* and *The Antichrist,* Nietzsche attempts to overturn everything that the majority of mankind has valued for millennia: God, immortality, the true and apparent world, release from suffering, the good—a list easily extended. Hence, not Wagner alone, but a host of great figures from Plato to Pascal were attacked. But since so few withstood the trenchancy of his criticism, the question of what Nietzsche actually admired looms large. Was he truly the herald of a fresh, life-enhancing, Dionysian vision? Or merely a megalomaniac nihilist? A naysayer who attacked everything previously great with a deconstructive urge?

66. *NAW*, Epilogue, 2.
67. Even Wagner's piano playing must have awakened on their first meeting at least subliminal memories of Nietzsche's childhood hours beside his father's piano.
68. Förster-Nietzsche, *Wagner und Nietzsche*, chap. 24.
69. Hayman, *Nietzsche*, 261.
70. Nietzsche to Cosima Wagner, Jan. 1889.
71. Quoted in records of clinic, March 27, 1889.

"That I have hitherto been a thoroughgoing nihilist I have admitted to myself only recently: the energy and radicalism with which I advanced as a nihilist deceived me about this basic fact."[72]

The key word here is *hitherto*. The groundlessness that followed his loss of faith in Wagner had been overcome by *Zarathustra*, that modern epiphany of Dionysus. Nietzsche could now view his attack against the millennial Christian slander of man as a positive task according to the formula: "Dionysus versus the Crucified."[73] His goal was to accomplish for European history that inevitable breakdown into nihilism (the final stage of Christianity) and subsequent recovery through Dionysus which he had already experienced personally. This countermovement to nihilism was to be consummated by his four-part magnum opus, the *Revaluation of All Values*, to which *Zarathustra* was to be merely prologue: "Overcoming of philosophers through the destruction of the world of being: intermediary period of nihilism: before there is yet present the strength to reverse values and to deify Becoming and the apparent world as the only world, and to call them good."[74]

Nietzsche's belief that this deification of the actual world could be achieved only through art produced his starkest divergence from Wagner, whose *Tristan*, *Ring*, and now *Parsifal* were celebrations of the Will to Nothingness. Such romantic art as Wagner's, like contemporary religion, philosophy, and morality, had been corrupted by Christian otherworldliness and the ascetic ideal—whereas true art, as Nietzsche now envisions it, is fundamentally sensual, "essentially affirmation, blessing, deification of existence."[75] Where values have vanished into chaos, the authentic artist, through self-mastery, masters even this meaninglessness by imposing upon chaos a significant unity of form, a process which binds art "to the great conception of man."[76] The greatest artists, the tragic, are able to embrace within artistic unity even the terrifying and evil, which renders their art the strongest opponent of the ascetic ideal. Hence Nietzsche's praise of art:

Art and nothing but art! It is the great means of making life possible, the great seduction to life, the great stimulant of life.[77]

Art [is] the only superior counterforce to all will-to-denial of life, as

72. *WP*, 25.
73. *EH*, "Why I Am a Destiny," 9.
74. *WP*, 585a.
75. *WP*, 821.
76. *WP*, 820. Such imposition of meaning on chaos was first adumbrated by Schiller (*Über das Erhabene*, then elaborated by Hegel (*Science of Logic*, trans. W. H. Johnston and L. G. Struthers [London, 1961], 2:46off.); Nietzsche is most emphatic about calling this exercise of freedom artistic.
77. *WP*, 853.

that which is anti-Christian, anti-Buddhist, anti-nihilist par excellence.[78]

Plato versus Homer: That is the complete, the genuine antagonism—there the sincerest advocate of the "beyond," the great slanderer of life, here the instinctive deifier, the golden nature.[79]

Having rejected the artist whose music was once his greatest joy, whose works he used to "conduct" on lonely forest paths, Nietzsche's notes elaborate a broader notion of the Dionysian, which includes not only art per se, but all creative activity of self-mastered men. Napoleon, for instance, he regarded as a posthumous brother of Dante and Michelangelo, and compared him with Goethe. Indeed, he elevates such visionary men of power above mere artists, because the marble upon which they work is mankind. But at the peak of his hierarchy of power, he places "the artistic-philosopher. Higher concept of art."[80] This is a revival of the artistic Socrates of *The Birth of Tragedy*, who is capable of creating what the philosopher within him reveals is needed. The whole line of thought also reveals how strongly he still feels the early influence of Schiller. This artistic Socrates becomes artist of the world; he legislates values, imposes his will upon millennia, and stamps Becoming with the character of Being. Although certain rhetorical questions in Nietzsche's late work might suggest that he was preparing the way for such an artistic Socrates, evidence points to the intended projection of himself into the role:

Before long I must confront humanity with the most difficult demands ever made of it.[81]

The truth speaks out of me—but my truth is terrible; for so far one has called lies truth.[82]

Since the old God is abolished, I am prepared to *rule the world*.[83]

Unfortunately for Nietzsche, his rare moments of total vision, which would purportedly have vindicated such statements, remain unarticulated.

78. Ibid.
79. *GM*, 3.25.
80. *WP*, 95 (trans. Kaufmann).
81. *EH*, Preface (trans. Kaufmann).
82. *EH*, 1.
83. *EH*, discarded draft, "Final Consideration," cited in Kaufmann's translation, p. 344. One of Nietzsche's related comments makes this idea appear less preposterous: "Thoughts which come on Dove's feet rule the world." But from another point of view it exemplifies what Thomas Mann calls Nietzsche's typically Germanic, ruinous, romantic passion: "the drive to eternal expansion of the self into space without a fixed object; a will which is free because it has no goal and aspires to the infinite" (*Last Essays*, 174).

His irreversible fragmentation into insanity prevented the completion of all but one volume of his projected *Revaluation*, the last volume of which would have been devoted to his central concept, the Dionysian. The tragic consequence of this failure is the eternally problematic nature of his work; the preparatory critique will forever threaten to overshadow that elusive esthetic vision which guided his life and fueled his dreams of supreme mastery— only to vanish, leaving him to scream his inarticulate rage from a tiny cell: "I can conceive of no greater aim in life than to perish while attempting a great and impossible task."[84]

But his failure to complete the task that unites his work from beginning to end—the esthetic justification of existence and the world—is not absolute. His unfortunate collapse, fated perhaps from the beginning, forces us to re-examine the earlier work in light of this intention. One reward of such scrutiny is the enhanced significance of *Wagner in Bayreuth*, his longest exposition of the evolution and function of a Dionysian artist. The essay has long been slighted by commentators, who have taken Nietzsche's subsequent rejection of Wagner as their cue. But if we ignore Wagner's name, most of the important perspectives of Nietzsche's late work appear already in place: the critique of Christianity and the modern world as corruptions of life; the falseness of current feeling, language, and art; the impending return of the Hellenic spirit as a countermovement to Christian-oriental values; the restorative power of great art, which is capable of initiating a new age; and so on. Indeed, the essay sustains a retrospective reading which regards it almost as subsequent to the *Revaluation*.

Nietzsche himself wanted to call attention to the essay's persisting validity by suggesting in *Ecce Homo* that Wagner's name be replaced by his own. But although this substitution makes an important point about the intensity of his self-projection, it is ultimately an inappropriate reading of what, in effect, is a paradigmatic study of great Dionysian creators.[85] Since Nietzsche was far more philosophical than artistic (a bit of self-knowledge he early but grudgingly accepted), and since the artistic philosopher is higher in his hierarchy of power than the artist, substitution of his name for Wagner's devalues large portions of the essay. A better suggestion would be for the reader to imagine in place of Wagner a future dramatic artist of the first rank whose relation to Nietzsche parallels that of Euripides to Socrates in *The Birth of Tragedy*; an artist, that is, who is actively engaged in expressing through music drama the Dionysian age which Nietzsche had initiated.

---

84. *HSDL*, 9.
85. Which justifies the constant comparative reference to such exceptional men as Heraclitus, Aeschylus, Demosthenes, Alexander the Great, Shakespeare, Goethe, Napoleon, and Jesus (the latter most suggested by images describing the suffering Wagner).

This, after all, appears to be the relation which Nietzsche privately wished he could have achieved with Wagner. And best of all would be an artist who could also say to Nietzsche, as Goethe did to Schiller, "After so unexpected a meeting, we must travel on together."[86]

86. Goethe to Schiller, Aug. 27, 1794.

Richard Wagner in Bayreuth

I   The greatness of an event depends upon the conjunction of two factors: the unusual discernment of those who create it, and the unusual discernment of those who witness it. In itself no event is great; even if whole constellations disappear, nations collapse, powerful states are founded, and incredibly violent and destructive wars are waged, the breath of history may scatter them like down. A strong man may sometimes strike a useless blow against an unyielding rock; the sharp retort is followed only by silence. History seldom remembers such nonevents. Hence, over anyone observing an approaching event there steals the concern that those destined to witness it be worthy of it. When one acts, in the most momentary and most trivial matters, one always aims for and counts on this reciprocity between an act and its reception. The man who has something to offer must carefully choose recipients equal to the significance of his gift. For this reason a single action by a single great man has no greatness if it is brief, blunted, and inconsequential. He has acted without the insight that his action was necessary at precisely that moment. He failed to take aim enough and to seize the moment accurately. He was made subject to chance. Greatness and an eye for necessity are closely allied.

We are justified in leaving the doubts and worries about the timing and necessity of the present events at Bayreuth to those who still entertain doubts of Wagner's eye for necessity. To those of us who are more confident, he seems to have just as much faith in the greatness of his achievement as in the exceptional discernment of those who should experience it. Hence, all those to whom Wagner's confidence is ascribed should feel pride, whether many or few—for it is not everyone to whom it can be ascribed, not to the age as a whole, nor even to the German people as presently constituted. Of this Wagner informed us in his dedicatory address of May 22, 1872, and in this matter nobody among us could possibly console him with a rebuttal. "Only you," he told us at the time, "the friends of my particular art, my most personal works and creations, were in sympathy with my sketches; only from you could I obtain the support I needed in order to present this work, pure and undistorted, to those who have shown their sincere affinity for my art, despite the impure and uncontrolled from in which they have hitherto found it."[1]

At Bayreuth the spectators are without doubt worth considering. A wise and observant spirit, wandering from one century to another and comparing the significant cultural movements, would have much to observe. At Bay-

---

1. Wagner, *Das Bühnenfestspielhaus zu Bayreuth*, in *Gesammelte Schriften und Dichtungen* (Leipzig, 1871–73), 9:392.

reuth he would certainly feel that he had suddenly encountered warmer water, like the swimmer in a lake coming upon the current from a hot spring: he tells himself that this must be rising from another, greater depth. The surrounding water does not account for it, and doubtless comes from a shallower source. Hence, all those who celebrate the festival at Bayreuth will seem to be unmodern men: they belong to a different age than the present; their explanation and justification lie elsewhere. It has become increasingly clear to me that the "cultured man," insofar as he is completely and solely a product of this present, can approach all that Wagner has thought and done only through parody—and what has not already been parodied?—and that he prefers to be enlightened about the event at Bayreuth through the very mundane lantern of our jeering journalists. Luckily, they are content with parody! For through parody the feelings of hostility and alienation, which could be, and sometimes have been, vented by other means, are discharged. That observer of culture would also note this extraordinary animosity and tension. That an individual could, in the course of an ordinary human life, create something wholly new, arouses the indignation of everyone who swears by the gradualness of all change as a kind of moral law, because, being lethargic themselves, they demand lethargy. Now, seeing a man of such swiftness, they do not know how he does it, and are therefore angry with him. There was no portent, no transition, no mediation for an enterprise like Bayreuth; only Wagner knew the long road to the goal, or the goal itself. It is the first circumnavigation of the world in the field of art; whereby, as it appears, not only a new art, but art itself has been discovered. Consequently, all modern arts to date, stunted by isolation or use as decoration, are robbed of half their value. Even the groping, disconnected memories of a true art that we moderns have from the Greeks, must now fall silent insofar as they cannot at present offer any enlightenment. For a great many things, the final hour has come; this fresh art is prophetic of the doom that threatens more than the arts. The warning finger that it points will appear quite sinister to our entire contemporary culture, as soon as the laughter at its parodies has died away—but let people have time to laugh and enjoy themselves a little longer!

In contrast, we, the disciples of a regenerated art, have time and will for seriousness—a deep, holy seriousness. The rhetoric and noise produced by contemporary culture on the subject of art—we must now view it as shameless meddling; it obliges us all to silence, to a five-year Pythagorean silence.[2]

2. According to Diogenes Laertius (*Lives of the Eminent Philosophers* 7.10), Pythagoras's students listened to his lectures at night when they could not see him and were required "to keep silence for five whole years without seeing him, until they passed an examination and were thereafter admitted to his house and permitted to see him." During his university years at Leipzig, Nietzsche published two remarkable philological studies in Latin

Who among us has not soiled his hands and thoughts on the loathsome idolatry of modern culture? Who does not need cleansing waters, or hear a voice warning him, "Silence and cleanliness! Silence and cleanliness!" Only as those who listen to this voice will we have the *great insight* to witness the event at Bayreuth, and the *great future* of that event depends solely upon this insight.

On that May day in 1872, when the cornerstone had been laid on the knoll at Bayreuth, in pouring rain and lowering skies, Wagner drove back to the city with a few of us. He was silent and retreated into his own thoughts with a look that would be impossible to put into words. On this day he had begun his sixtieth year, and everything he had done before this day had been a preparation for this moment. We know that during times of exceptional danger, or even during an important decision in their lives, people condense all their experience with an extremely swift introspection, and with the rarest acuity they once again recognize the nearest and most distant things. What might Alexander the Great have seen in that instant when he let Asia and Europe drink from the same cup? But what Wagner saw inwardly on that day—how he had become, what he was, what he would be— we who are closest to him can to some degree visualize. And only from this Wagnerian perspective will we be able to grasp the greatness of his achievement—*and with this understanding testify to its fruitfulness.*

2   It would be strange if what a man knows best and most loves doing were not also evident in the overall pattern of his life. Rather, in men of exceptional talent, their life becomes the image not only of their character, as with everyone else, but also and above all the image of their intellect and special abilities. The life of the epic poet will contain an epic quality—this, I add parenthetically, was true in the case of Goethe, unjustly perceived by Germans as primarily a lyric poet. So too the life of the dramatist will take dramatic form.

The dramatic quality of Wagner's development is hardly to be denied from the moment when his ruling passion became conscious of itself and crystallized his whole nature.[3] He immediately forsook his previous grouping, his drifting, his wild tangents. The most tortuous paths and transformations, the often quixotic arc of his plans, were subjected to a single inward law, a will that makes them explicable, however odd the explanations may often sound. There was, however, a predramatic period in Wagner's life, his childhood and youth, which cannot be examined without stumbling on

---

on the sources of Diogenes (*De Laertii Diogenis fontibus*) in *Rheinisches Museum* for 1868 and 1869.

3. Nietzsche to Wagner (May 24, 1875): "When I think of your life, I always have the feeling of its dramatic development."

riddles. He *himself* seems as yet unannounced; and that which one could, in retrospect, regard as announcement proves to be a bundle of traits that would have aroused more misgivings than hopes: a restless, irritable spirit, a nervous haste in understanding a hundred things, an intense delight in almost pathologically exaggerated states of mind, abrupt swings from moments of serenity to violence and noise. There was no stern artistic discipline by family tradition to limit him; poetry, painting, drama, or music were all as close to him as a future in scholarship; a superficial glance might suggest that he was born to be a dilettante. The small world under whose influence he grew up was not the sort of home one would wish upon an artist. Around him he saw that dangerous propensity for things of the mind, combined with the pretense of knowing a little about everything, which one encounters in university towns. His feelings were easily aroused, yet insatiable; wherever the boy looked, he was surrounded by a singularly pretentious but busy society, with which the colorful theatrical world and the ravishing sound of music stood in ludicrous and incomprehensible contrast. Comparison makes it apparent how rare it is that modern man, if endowed with great talent, possesses in childhood and youth the quality of naiveté, simple originality, and individuality. Those rare men who, like Goethe and Wagner, achieve naiveté, nowadays possess more of it in their maturity than in childhood and youth. The artist in particular, whose innate mimetic power is uncommonly strong, is sure to be ravaged by the slothful diversity of modern life as by a violent childhood illness; as child and youth he will more resemble an old man than his true self. Only one man could have created that remarkably austere archetype of youth, the Siegfried of the *Ring of Nibelungen*, indeed one who had discovered his own youth only late in life. As youth came late to Wagner, so did his maturity, and in this respect he is the opposite of a precocious talent.

As soon as he attained his intellectual and moral manhood, the drama of his life also began. And how changed that is! His nature appears formidably simplified, divided into two drives or spheres. From deep down inside him there erupts, in an impetuous torrent, a violent will that explores every path, crevice, and ravine, struggling to find light, aspiring to power. Only a force of the utmost purity and freedom could have directed this will toward good and useful action; combined with narrowness of spirit, such a will, with its unlimited, tyrannical desire, could have been disastrous; and in any event it required an immediate outlet to freedom, to bright air and sunshine. Such powerful striving, constantly confronted with failure, is aggravating; the inadequacy may at times lie in circumstances, in the inflexibility of fate, not in lack of strength. But the man who, despite his inadequacies, cannot stop striving, takes as it were a kind of contagion, and hence becomes irritable and unjust. He may perhaps attribute his failure to others; he may even, in passionate hatred, hold the entire world responsible. He may even use corrupt and underhanded means, or resort to violence—which is precisely how good men turn savage in pursuit of excellence. Even among those men who were pursuing their own moral purification, among hermits and monks, one finds men who have reverted to savagery, sickened through and through, drained and devoured by failure. But the spirit that spoke to Wagner was a spirit rich in love, which spoke a language overflowing with kindness and sweet persuasiveness, to which violence and self-destruction were hateful, and which detested the sight of any man in chains. It descended upon him, folded him in its consoling wings, pointed him the way.[4] We shall now glance at this other sphere of Wagner's nature. But how shall we describe it?

The figures an author creates are not himself; but clearly the series of figures to whom he apparently attaches himself with innermost love tells us something about the artist. Imagine the figures of Rienzi, of the Flying Dutchman and Senta, Tannhäuser and Elisabeth, Lohengrin and Elsa, Tristan and Mark, Hans Sachs, Wotan and Brünnhilde; through all of them there flows an underground current of moral grandeur and nobility, linking them, becoming increasingly purer and more refined. And here we stand with shameful hesitation, confronted with the most intimate evolution of Wagner's spirit. In what other artist can we discern anything similar, of comparable dimensions? Schiller's figures, from *Die Räuber* through *Wallenstein* and *Tell*, run a similar path of ennoblement and also reveal something of their creator's evolution, but in Wagner the scale is much larger, the distance greater. Everything participates in and expresses this purification, not only the myth, but the music as well; the *Ring of the Nibelungen* contains the most moral music I know. For example, in the scene where Brünnhilde is awakened by Siegfried, Wagner attains such loftiness and sanctity of mood that we think of the glowing ice and snowcaps of the Alps— so pure, isolated, remote, and still is the emergence here of Nature, bathed in the light of love, overtopping clouds and storms, even the sublime.

Looking back from this vantage on *Tannhäuser* and *The Flying Dutchman*, we sense how the man Wagner evolved: how he began in darkness and turbulence; how he vehemently strove for satisfaction, power, and intoxicating pleasure; how he withdrew in disgust; how he learned to throw off his burden; how he longed to forget, deny, renounce—how the whole current of the man plunged into first one valley, then another, how it plummeted down the darkest ravines. Then, in the night of this half-subterranean frenzy, high overhead appeared a star of melancholy luster. As soon as he saw it, he named it *Fidelity, selfless Fidelity!* Why did this star shine brighter and purer than everything; what secret did the word fidelity have for his

---

4. See Wagner, *Eine Mittheilung an meine Freunde*: "On the essence of music I have recently expressed myself with sufficient clarity; here I want to recall it only as my guardian angel who saved me as an artist, even made me an artist" (*Gesammelte Schriften*, 4:325).

whole being? For, in everything he thought and wrote, he emphasized the image and problem of fidelity. In his works there is an almost complete series of every possible form of fidelity, and among them instances of the rarest and most splendid kind: fidelity of brother to sister, of friend to friend, of servant to lord; of Elisabeth to Tannhäuser; of Senta to the Dutchman; of Elsa to Lohengrin; of Isolde, Kurvenal, and Mark to Tristan; of Brünnhilde to Wotan's innermost wish—and this is simply the beginning. It is his most unique and fundamental experience, one which Wagner himself lives, and honors as a religious mystery and expresses it with the word *fidelity*. He never tires of demonstrating it in a hundred different forms. Investing it with the utmost splendor he possesses and can realize—that marvelous knowledge and experience by which one sphere of his being remained faithful to the other. Through free, utterly selfless love, it preserved fidelity. The creative sphere, luminous and innocent, remained faithful to the dark, indomitable, and tyrannical sphere.

3   In the mutual relationship of these two deepest forces, in the devotion of one to the other, lay the great necessity through which alone he could remain whole and himself. At the same time it was the only thing that was beyond his power, that he had to observe and accept, while he saw himself constantly approached by the temptation to infidelity and its terrible dangers for him. For the evolving man, here was a fertile source of suffering—uncertainty. Each of his instincts sought the unknown, each talent for enjoying life wanted to break away on its own and satisfy itself; the greater their breadth, the greater the tumult, the greater the hostility of their confrontation. Moreover, life and chance stimulated him to win power, splendor, feverish pleasure; still more often he was tormented by the pitiless necessity of having to live it all. Everywhere there were chains and pitfalls. How was it possible to keep the faith, to stay whole?

This doubt often overwhelmed him and was expressed as an artist would express it, in artistic forms: Elisabeth can only suffer, pray, and die for Tannhäuser; she saves the inconstant and excessive man through her fidelity, but not for this life. There is danger and despair in the life of every true artist who is thrown into modern times. There are many ways he can arrive at honor and power; peace and satisfaction offer themselves to him repeatedly, but always and only in the form in which modern man knows them, and in which, for the honest artist, they necessarily become a suffocating vapor. In this temptation, and especially in his dismissal of this temptation, lie the artist's dangers: in the nausea over the modern ways of gaining pleasure and prestige, and in the rage which turns against all the egotistical pleasure of modern man as a type. If one imagines him in an official position (just as Wagner filled the position of concertmaster in state and court theaters), one realizes how the most serious artist wants to impose seriousness by force precisely where modern institutions are constructed with almost systematic frivolity and demand frivolity; how in part he succeeds but on the whole always fails; how he feels the approach of nausea and wants to flee; how he can find no place to run to, and must return again and again to the gypsies and outcasts of our culture as one of them. If such an artist extricates himself from one position, he can rarely find a better one for himself; sometimes he sinks into the direst need. Hence, Wagner changed cities, companions, countries, and one can hardly imagine what sort of exacting demands and surroundings he constantly had to endure for so long.

Over the greater part of Wagner's life to this point lay a heavy cloud; it appears he no longer had hopes for things in general, but only from day to day, and although he did not despair, neither had he faith. He must often have felt like a wanderer in the night, heavily burdened, utterly exhausted, yet agitated with fatigue. A sudden death was then, in his eyes, not a horror but a seductive, charming apparition.[5] Burden, path, and night, everything suddenly to disappear!—that sounded tempting. A hundred times with that short-winded hope he threw himself afresh into life, and left all apparitions behind. But the way he went about this was almost always excessive, a signal that he did not believe in that hope deeply and firmly, but was simply intoxicated by it. The conflict between his desire and his usual partial or total inability to satisfy it tormented him like thorns. Provoked by continuing deprivation, his imagination lost itself in extravagance when his needs were temporarily gratified. Life became increasingly twisted, but the means and expedients which he, the dramatist, discovered were also increasingly bold and creative, even though they were merely dramatic makeshifts, artificial motives, which deceived for a moment, and were only intended for a moment. He had these at hand with lightning speed, and just as quickly exhausted them. Wagner's life, seen completely close-up and without love, has, to recall a thought of Schopenhauer,[6] a good deal of comedy about it, and, to be sure, of the peculiarly grotesque. How the feeling about this, the admission of a grotesque worthlessness of whole segments of his life, must have affected the artist, who more than anyone else can only breathe freely in the sublime and ultrasublime—this is for thinkers to think about.

In the middle of such drifting, of which only the most exact description could arouse the degree of compassion, terror, and wonder it deserves, there

---

5. "Never," Wagner wrote, "as in that period did I grasp with greater clarity the odious constriction with which the inexorable system of life and modern art succeed in subduing a free heart and transforming him into an evil man. What way out was offered to the individual except—death?" (*Gesammelte Schriften*, 4:371ff.).

6. See *The World as Will and Representation*, 1:58: "The life of every individual, considered in its entirety and viewed above all in its most significant aspects, is in truth always a tragedy; if, however, one dwells on its particulars, it assumes the character of a comedy."

unfolds a *talent for learning* which, even among Germans, the true people of learning, is totally extraordinary. And from this gift again sprang a new danger, even greater than that of an uprooted, apparently unstable life, driven hither and thither by conflicting illusions. Wagner developed from a struggling novice into a consummate master of music and the stage, and, in all preliminary technical matters, an inventor and improver. Nobody can dispute his renown any more for having set, in greatness of delivery, the supreme standard for all art. But he became much more still, and in order to become that and more, he was as little spared as anyone else the acquisition of the highest culture through learning. It is a pleasure to see this! From all sides it grew on him and in him, and indeed the greater and heavier the structure, the greater became the tension on the arch of his ordering and commanding thought. And yet rarely has the access to knowledge and proficiency been made so difficult; often he had to improve such access. The renewer of simple dramas, the discoverer of the place of the arts in the true human society, the poet and interpreter of forgotten views of life, the philosopher, historian, esthetician, and critic, the master of language, the mythologist and mythic poet who for the first time described a ring around those splendid, ancient, enormous creations, and engraved on it the runes of his mind—what a wealth of knowledge he had to accumulate and encompass in order to become all of this! And yet neither did this sum overwhelm his will to act, nor did the particular and most attractive elements lead him astray.

To gauge the singularity of such behavior, we may take Goethe, for example, as a great antitype who as scholar and sage resembles a river system with many multiple branches, one that does not, however, discharge all its strength into the sea, but loses and disperses at least as much along its meandering course as at its source. It is true that a being such as Goethe possesses and produces more pleasure; there is a mild and noble extravagance about him, whereas the violence of Wagner's course and current can startle and intimidate. But let those tremble who must: the rest of us want to become all the more courageous, that we may see with our own eyes a hero who, even with regard to modern culture, "has not learned to fear."[7]

He has also never learned through history and philosophy to pacify himself or to acquire the marvelous softness and disinclination to action which they induce. Neither the creative nor the militant artist in him was deflected from its course by scholarship and culture. The moment his creative power takes hold of him, history becomes malleable as clay in his hands; he then suddenly has a different relation to it from any scholar, a relation much closer to that of the Greek to his myth, to something that one molds and poeticizes, with love and a certain humble devotion to be sure, but yet with

7. An allusion to the character of Wagner's heroic Siegfried.

the sovereign right of the creator. And precisely because it is to him more pliant and variable than any dream, he can make the isolated event typical of the whole age, and hence achieve a truth of representation which the historian never achieves. Where has the chivalry of the Middle Ages assumed a form with such flesh and spirit as in *Lohengrin*? And won't *Die Meistersinger* express the German spirit until the end of time? Indeed, more than express it? Won't it be one of the ripest fruits of that spirit which always wants reform, not revolution,[8] and which has not forgotten, despite the broad base of its content, that noblest of all discontents, the renewing action?

Again and again Wagner was forced into precisely this kind of discontent by his engagement with history and philosophy; in these he found not only weapons and armor, but above all felt that breath of inspiration which rises above the graves of all great combatants, sufferers, and thinkers. Nothing can distinguish one further from the whole present age than the use he makes of history and philosophy. On the former, as it is usually understood, the task now seems to have fallen of allowing modern man, who runs panting and struggling towards his goal, to catch his breath for once, so that for a moment he can feel, as it were, out of harness. What Montaigne the individual means in the spiritual agitation of the Reformation, a coming to peace with oneself, a serene being-for-self, and a sigh of relief—as he was certainly regarded by his best reader, Shakespeare—that is the meaning of history today. If for a century the Germans have devoted themselves especially to the study of history, this shows that within the movement of the modern world, they are the holding, inhibiting, quieting power, which some might construe to their credit. But on the whole it is a dangerous sign when the spiritual struggle of a people is directed primarily toward the past, a characteristic of enervation, regression, and weakness, since it leaves them vulnerable in the most dangerous way to every fever to which they are exposed—political fever, for example.

Such a condition of weakness, in contrast to all reforming and revolutionary movements, is represented in the history of the modern spirit by our scholars; they have not set themselves the proudest task, but secured themselves their own sort of tranquil happiness. Every free and more manly step clearly leads beyond them—but by no means beyond history itself. This in itself has wholly different forces, precisely those which natures like Wagner intuit; only it must first be written with a far more serious and rigorous sensibility, by a powerful spirit, and above all no longer optimistically, that

8. In his essay on Beethoven (*Gesammelte Schriften*, 9:105), Wagner wrote: "Here is revealed the peculiar trait of the German nature, which is inwardly so rich and talented ... that it knows how to stamp every form with its own essence, renewing such a form from within without having to subvert it. So the German is not a revolutionary, but a reformer."

is, done quite differently than German scholars have done until now. There is something prettified, submissive, and smug in all of their works; they are satisfied with the course of events. It is already a good deal if one of them reveals that, if he is contented, it is precisely and only because things might have been still worse; most of them instinctively believe that a thing is very good just because it has finally come to be. If history were not still always a camouflaged Christian theodicy,[9] if it were written with more justice and fervent sympathy, then it would truly be least capable of performing the service it now performs: as an opiate against everything revolutionary or reforming.

It is similar with philosophy, from which indeed most men want to learn nothing other than a rough—very rough!—understanding of things, in order then to adapt themselves to them. And even its noblest advocates so powerfully stress its tranquillizing and comforting power that the slothful and indolent must believe they seek the same thing that philosophy seeks. To me, in contrast, the most important question in all of philosophy seems to be this: how far things have an unchangeable nature and form, so that, once this question is resolved, we can begin, with relentless courage, the *improvement of that part of the world recognized as capable of being changed.* The true philosophers teach this through action, by having worked towards the improvement of the extremely changeable insight of men, and by not having kept their wisdom to themselves. The true disciples of true philosophers also teach this—those who, like Wagner, know precisely how to extract from them a growing determination and resolution of will, but no sleeping potions. Wagner is most philosophical where he is most active and heroic. And precisely as a philosopher he has gone not only through the fire of the various philosophical systems without fear, but also through the vapor of knowledge[10] and scholarship and remained true to his higher self, which demanded of him *unified action from his polyphonic being* and which commanded him to suffer and learn in order that he might accomplish those acts.

4   The history of the development of culture since the ancient Greeks is very brief if we consider the actual distance covered and disregard entirely the stoppings, retreats, hesitations, and evasions. The Hellenizing of the world—and, to make this possible, the Orientalizing of the Hellenic, the twofold task of Alexander the Great—remains the last great event. The old question as to whether an alien culture

9. A variation on Feuerbach's observation that "philosophy is disguised theology," a remark several times cited by Wagner in his writings.
10. A glance at Goethe's *Faust*, part 1, 395.

can be assimilated at all is still the problem over which modern men labor. The rhythmic interplay of these two factors has determined the course of history to date. Christianity, for instance, appears as a fragment of Oriental antiquity, on which men have meditated and acted with extravagant thoroughness. As its influence wanes, the power of Hellenic culture once again waxes; we are now witnessing phenomena so alien that they would float inexplicably in the air if one could not link them across a vast interval of time to Greek analogies. Hence, between Kant and the Eleatics, between Schopenhauer and Empedocles, between Aeschylus and Richard Wagner, there exist such kinships and connections that one is clearly warned how extremely relative is every conception of time: it seems almost that many things belong together and time is merely a cloud, which makes it hard for us to see their connection.

The history of the exact sciences, in particular, also gives the impression that we find ourselves even now closely related to the Greek Alexandrian world, as though the pendulum of history were again veering back toward the point from which it began its swing into the enigmatic distance and dissipation. The image of our present world is by no means novel; more and more the man who knows history feels as though he is recognizing the familiar features of a face. The spirit of Hellenic culture is infinitely dispersed in the present; while forces of every kind are jostling each other, and the fruits of modern science and technology are offered as commodities, the pale features of the Hellenic image are once again dawning faintly, though distant and ghostly. The earth, which has by now been sufficiently Orientalized, yearns once again for Hellenization; those who want to help her will certainly need speed and winged feet to unite the most various and distant points of knowledge, the remotest continents of talent, and to explore and dominate the incredible expanse of territory. Hence, a succession of *counter-Alexanders* has now become necessary, men who possess the supreme power to consolidate and bind things, to recover the remotest strands and protect the fabric from tattering. Not to unloose the Gordian knot of Greek culture as Alexander did, leaving the ends to flutter in every direction, but rather *to bind it together after it has been loosed*—that is the present task. In Wagner I recognize such a counter-Alexander, he charms and binds together what was isolated, weak, and indolent; he possesses, if I may use a medical term, an *astringent power*: to this extent he belongs to the great forces of civilization. He has mastered the arts, the religions, and the various folk histories; yet he is the opposite of a polyhistor whose mind merely compiles and organizes: for he sculpts and breathes life into the material he has brought together, he *simplifies the world*. We must keep such an idea clearly in mind when comparing this comprehensive task imposed on him by his genius with the much narrower, more immediate task usually first linked at present to Wagner's name. We expect him to reform the theater, but if he had been successful at this, what would have been accomplished toward that higher, farther task?

Of course, even this would have changed and reformed modern man: each thing is so necessarily related to the other in our modern world that anyone who removes a single nail causes the structure to tremble and fall. Even from any other true reform one might expect the same thing that we now attribute to Wagner's, with only apparent exaggeration. It is utterly impossible to produce the highest and purest effect of theatrical art without changing things everywhere—in mores and government, in education and commerce. Love and justice become potent at one point, namely, here, in the domain of art, and must spread outward according to the law of their inner necessity and cannot regress into the immobility of their earlier chrysalis. Even to comprehend how far the relation of our arts to life is symbolic of the deterioration of this life, how far our theaters are a disgrace to those who build and support them, we must be able to readjust our views completely and regard the conventional and commonplace as very unconventional and complex. A strange obscuring of judgment, a poorly concealed addiction to amusement, to entertainment at any price (on the part of the audience); the pedantry, pomposity, and affectation with the seriousness of art on the part of the performers; the brutal greed for profit on the part of the impresarios; the vacuity and mindlessness of society that heeds the common people only insofar as they are useful or dangerous to it, a society that frequents theaters and concerts without being reminded of its obligations—all this together forms the oppressive and fatal atmosphere of our contemporary artistic situation. But once a man is accustomed to this atmosphere, as our educated classes are, he fancies it essential to his health and feels unwell if some constraint or other forces him temporarily to do without it. There is really only *one* brief way to persuade oneself how vulgar, indeed how peculiarly and complexly vulgar, our theatrical institutions are; simply compare them to the reality of the ancient Greek theater!

Granted, if we knew nothing of the Greeks, our conditions would probably seem unassailable and we would regard such objections as those first raised in grand style by Wagner as the daydreams of a people at home in utopia. As men are now, we would probably say, such art is fitting and proper—and people have never been any different! —But they certainly were different, and even now there are men for whom our present institutions are inadequate—precisely this is demonstrated by the theater at Bayreuth. Here you encounter prepared and devoted spectators, the emotional state of men at the peak of their happiness, who feel their whole being seized by this happiness, strengthening them for further and higher aspirations; here, too, you encounter the most devoted self-sacrifice of the artist, and that spectacle of all spectacles, the creator of a work that is itself the compendia of innumerable artistic victories. It almost seems magical, doesn't it, to be able to encounter in the present day such a phenomenon? Aren't those who were able to collaborate and observe already transformed and rejuvenated, and thereby empowered to transform and rejuvenate other areas of life afterward?

Haven't we found a haven from the desolate expanse of the sea? Hasn't stillness here spread over the water? —He who returns from these sovereign depths and solitude of mood to the totally different shallows and marshes of life, won't he ask himself hereafter, like Isolde, "Oh, how have I endured this? How can I go on enduring it?"[11] And if he cannot bear to hide his happiness and unhappiness selfishly inside him, he will thereafter seize every opportunity to bear it witness through action. "Where are those who suffer from the present establishment?" he will ask. "Where are our natural allies in the fight against the rampant and suffocating spread of modern culture?" For at present we have only one enemy—at present!—precisely the "cultivated" class for whom the word *Bayreuth* signals the profoundest defeat. They offered no help, and were savagely opposed; they demonstrated that even more effective deafness which has become the common weapon of the most calculating hostility. But precisely because they could not destroy the essence of Wagner or obstruct his work through hatred and malice, we know something else: they have revealed that they are weak, and that the resistance of those presently in power can no longer withstand many attacks. The time has come for those who really want to conquer and vanquish; the greatest kingdom stands waiting, and a question mark stands after the names of its proprietor, insofar as property exists.

The educational structure, for instance, is known to be in decay, and everywhere we find individuals who have already, in utter silence, abandoned it. If only, just once, we could push those who are even now deeply dissatisfied with it into open revolt and outrage! If only we could liberate them from their despairing cowardice! This I know: if that tacit contribution of such natures to the making of our collective educational institutions were removed, the resultant bloodletting would be so grievous as to weaken the institutions. Among scholars, for instance, those remaining in the old system would be only literary dilettantes of every sort and those professors afflicted by the political madness. That sickening system, which now draws strength from its reliance on spheres of violence and injustice, that is, from state and society, and whose interest lies in making these more evil and ruthless still, would, without this reliance, be a feeble and exhausted business. It need only be despised for it to collapse into rubble. The man who fights for justice and love among mankind has least to fear from it; his true enemy

11. An echo of *Tristan und Isolde*, ii, 2.

will rise to meet him only after he has concluded his present struggle with its vanguard, modern culture.

For us Bayreuth signifies the dawn ritual on the day of battle. No greater injustice could be done us than to assume that our concern is with art alone, as though art were some remedy or narcotic, designed to spare us all other conditions of misery. In the image of that tragic art of Bayreuth we witness precisely this battle of the individual against everything that confronts him with apparently invincible necessity: against authority, law, tradition, convention, the whole order of things. The individual could not live a fuller life than by preparing for death and sacrificing himself in the battle for love and justice. The gaze with which the secret eye of tragedy looks at us is no tranquillizing or paralyzing spell. It does, however, demand stillness as long as it looks at us—because art is not for the battle itself but for the pauses before and during it, for those moments when, looking backward and forward, we understand the symbolic, when with the feeling of mild fatigue a refreshing dream comes to us. Day and battle begin together, the holy shadows vanish, and art is again remote from us—yet its comfort remains with men all day.

Indeed, in everything else the individual encounters his personal inadequacy, his partial or complete powerlessness: with what courage could he fight if he were not previously consecrated to something supra-personal? The greatest suffering that exists for the individual is the absence of common knowledge among all men, the uncertainty of ultimate truth, the disparity of ability; all this puts him in need of art. We cannot be happy so long as everything around us suffers and inflicts suffering; we cannot be moral so long as the course of human events is determined by force, fraud, and injustice; we cannot even be wise so long as the whole of mankind has not entered the competition for wisdom and does not lead the individual to the wisest mode of life and knowledge. How could a man endure this threefold feeling of inadequacy unless he could already recognize something sublime and meaningful in his struggle, aspiration, and defeat, unless he had learned from tragedy to take pleasure in the rhythm of the great passions and in the sacrifice of these?

Art is assuredly no teacher or governess of immediate action; the artist is never in this sense an educator and counselor; the objects for which the tragic heroes strive are not in and of themselves things worth striving for. As long as we feel transfixed by the spell of art, the value of things is, as in a dream, changed; what we deem for the moment so worthy of the endeavor that we applaud the tragic hero when he chooses death rather than renouncing it—it is in real life seldom of the same value or worthy of the same effort: hence, art is the activity precisely of the man in repose. The struggles that it depicts are simplifications of the real struggles of life; its problems are abbreviations of the endlessly complicated reckoning of human action and aspiration. But the greatness and indispensability of art lies precisely in this evocation of the *appearance* of a simpler world, of a quicker solution to the puzzles of life. Nobody who suffers from life can do without this appearance, just as nobody can do without sleep. Indeed, the more difficult becomes the knowledge of the laws of life, so much more ardently we desire the appearance of simplicity, if only for an instant; so much greater becomes the tension between the general knowledge of things and the spiritual and moral capacity of the individual. Art exists *in order that the bow not break.*

The individual must be consecrated to something supra-personal—that is what tragedy wants; he must forget the terrible anxiety that death and time create in him: for even in the most fleeting instant, the tiniest particles of his lifetime, he may encounter something holy that abundantly compensates him for all his struggle and need—this means *to have the tragic sense.* And if mankind as a whole must ultimately perish—who could doubt this!— then the goal, as the supreme task for all future ages, has been set: to fuse in such a unity, such a community that mankind *as a whole* can confront its impending destruction with a *tragic sense.* Implicit in this supreme task is every ennobling of man; the decisive rejection of this would produce the most dismal image a friend of men might imagine. This I feel! There is only one hope and one guarantee for the future of what is human: it consists in this, *that the tragic sense not die out.* A cry of woe without equal would resound over the world if men were ever to lose this sense completely. And, on the other hand, there is no more thrilling joy than to know, what we do know, that tragic thought has been reborn in the world. For this joy is completely supra-personal and universal, a rejoicing of mankind in the certainty that the cohesion and progress of what is essentially human are guaranteed.

5   Over contemporary life and the past, Wagner casts the searchlight of a knowledge so strong that he can see with unprecedented scope; this is why he is a simplifier of the world. For the simplification of the world has always meant that the gaze of the knower has once again mastered the prodigious profusion and disorder of an apparent chaos, and compressed into a unity what once lay irreconcilably fragmented. Wagner achieved this by discovering a relationship between two things which seemed to live foreign and cold to each other, in disparate spheres: between *music and life,* and also between *music and drama.* Not that he invented or created these relationships; they exist and lie literally at everyone's feet, for as always the great problem is like a precious stone over which thousands walk until one man someday picks it up. What does it mean, Wagner asks himself, that in the life of modern men just such an art as music has emerged with such incomparable power? It requires no contempt for modern life to

see this as a problem; on the contrary, if we consider all the great forces characteristic of this life and confront ourselves with the image of a human being striving powerfully and battling for *conscious freedom* and *independence of thought,* then the appearance of music in this world suddenly seems a puzzle. Must we not say: in such times music *could not* arise? But then how account for its existence? As a fluke? Certainly a single great composer could be a fluke, but the appearance of such a series of great artists as the history of modern music shows, an event only paralleled once before, in the age of the Greeks, leads us to believe that necessity governs here, not chance. This necessity is precisely the problem to which Wagner provides an answer.

Wagner was the first to recognize a crisis which has by now spread throughout the civilized world: *language* is everywhere diseased, and the pressure of this monstrous sickness weighs on the whole of human evolution. Because language has constantly been pushed to the highest peaks it could reach, as far removed as possible from the strong emotions it was originally able to arouse with greatest simplicity, in order to express the domain of thought—the antithesis of feeling—it has exhausted itself in the effort in the brief span of modern civilization. Hence, it can no longer now perform the function for which alone it was made: to enable suffering men to communicate with each other about the elementary necessities of life. In his distress man can no longer make himself understood by means of language, nor truly communicate with others. In this dimly perceived circumstance, language everywhere becomes an autonomous power which seizes men with ghostly arms and forces them where they do not really wish to go. As soon as men try to communicate and to unite in a common enterprise, the madness of general concepts, indeed, of pure verbal sounds, possess them; as a result of this inability to communicate, the collective creations of their spirit in turn carry the marks of their mutual misunderstanding, insofar as these do not correspond to true needs, but only to the emptiness of those despotic words and concepts. So to all its other problems mankind adds the problem of *convention,* that is, agreement of words and actions without agreement of feelings. Just as in the decline of any art a point is reached where the morbid proliferation of techniques and forms acquires a tyrannical power over the young souls of artists and enslaves them, so, too, in the present destruction of language men have become the slaves of words. Under this pressure, no one can reveal himself as he is or any longer speak naturally, and few can preserve their individuality in the struggle against a culture which regards as proof of its success not fostering the individual's clear feelings and needs, but entangling him in the net of "clear and distinct ideas"[12] and teaching him to think correctly—as though there were any

---

12. An obviously disparaging allusion to Descartes' rationalism and the Enlightenment's tendency to overvalue ratiocination at the expense of the affective domain.

value in shaping someone into a being who thinks and discriminates rightly, if he has not first learned how to feel rightly! When now, amidst all this crippled humanity, the music of our German masters sounds, what exactly is it that we hear? Quite simply, *right feeling*, the foe of all convention, of all artificial alienation and unintelligibility between man and man. This music is return to nature, but at the same time purification and transformation; for in the souls of the most loving men the need for this return arises, and *what sounds in their art is nature transformed into love.*

Let us accept this as one of Wagner's answers to the question "What is the meaning of music in our age?" But he also has a second answer. The relation between music and life is not only that of one kind of language to another, it is also the relation of the entire auditory world to the whole visual world. But as a visual spectacle, when compared to earlier manifestations of life, modern man's existence reveals an exhaustion and unspeakable poverty, quite despite the indescribable variety of colors, which can satisfy only the most superficial glance. Look a little more closely and analyze the impression produced by this churning play of color. Is all this anything more than the shimmer and sparkle of countless pebbles and shards borrowed from earlier cultures? Isn't everything here vulgar ostentation, the aping of movement, affected superficiality? A cloak of motley rags for the naked and shivering? A seemingly joyful dance imposed upon the suffering? Arrogant looks on the faces of the mortally wounded? And in between, disguised and concealed only by the swiftness of movement and whirling drab impotence, corrosive agony, laboring boredom, dishonorable misery.

The phenomenon of modern man has become nothing but illusion; he himself is not visible in the image he now presents, but hidden; and the residue of artistic capacity still preserved in a people—for instance, among the French and Italians—is employed in this game of hide-and-seek. Wherever "form" is demanded, in society and conversation, in literary expression, in international relations, this automatically implies making a pleasant impression—the exact opposite of the true concept of form as a necessary formation having nothing to do with "pleasant" and "unpleasant," precisely because it is necessary and not optional. But even where form is now expressly exacted among civilized peoples, we not only don't possess that necessary formation, but we are much less happy in our striving for a pleasant appearance, despite our eagerness. To what point appearance can at times succeed in being *pleasant*, and why it pleases everyone that modern man at least tries to realize this appearance, is felt to the degree that each one is himself a modern man. "Only the galley slaves know themselves," says Tasso, "and therefore we deny that we *recognize* others with the hope that they in turn will deny they recognize us."[13]

13. See Goethe's *Torquato Tasso*, v, 5.

In this world of forms and invited denial there suddenly appear souls full of music—to what purpose? They move in time to the large, free rhythm, in noble honesty, in a passion which is supra-personal. They glow with the powerfully calm fire of the music which issues into the light from the inexhaustible depths within them—all this to what purpose?

Through the soul of these men, music demands its sister and equal, *gymnastic*, as its necessary formulation in the realm of the visible; this seeking and yearning has made music the judge of the whole pretentious sham-world of the present. This is Wagner's second answer to the question of the meaning of music in our time.[14] "Help me!" he cries out to all who can hear. "Help me discover that culture which my music, the recovered language of genuine feeling, predicts. Realize that the soul of music now wants to create a body, that through all of you it seeks its path toward visibility in movement, action, institution, and morals!" There are men who understand this call, always more and more of them; they too understand as though for the first time what it would mean to found the state upon music, something which the ancient Greeks not only understood but which they demanded from themselves. And these same understanding men will condemn the modern state as unconditionally as most people today already condemn the Church.

The path toward such a goal so new and yet not unprecedented leads us to acknowledge the area of the most shameful lack in our education, and the real reason for our inability to emerge from barbarism—education lacks the inspiring and informing soul of music. On the other hand, the needs and institutions of our educational system are the product of an age in which the music we invest with such significant trust had not yet been born. Our eduction is the most backward contemporary structure, and backward precisely as regards the only fresh educational force in which modern men have the advantage over earlier centuries—or might have the advantage, if they were willing to stop living so mindlessly, on the spur of the moment, as they

14. See Wagner, *Über musikalische Kritik*: "If our music must emerge from the false position imposed upon it by the literary mediation of its understanding, this can only take place by reapplying to music the much larger meaning which its *name* originally contains. . . . In fact the people which invented the name 'music' meant by this not merely *poetic and musical art*, but every artistic manifestation of man's inner life. . . . Hence the education of the Athenian youth was divided into two parts—into *music* and *gymnastic*, that is, the quintessence of all those arts that refer to the most perfect expression by means of representing the body itself. Through 'music,' then, the Athenian communicated with the *hearing*, by means of 'gymnastic' with the *eye*, and only the man who had been at one and the same time formed by music and gymnastic could for them be a truly educated person. . . . To be whole artists, we must therefore turn from 'music' to 'gymnastic,' that is, to the true art of physically sensible representation, to the only art that transvalues what we want into what we are capable of" (*Gesammelte Schriften*, 5:74–78).

do now. Because until now modern men refuse to shelter in themselves the spirit of music, they also lack the slightest notion of gymnastic in the Greek and Wagnerian sense of the world. And this is also why our plastic artists are condemned to hopelessness so long as they are willing, as they now are, to ignore music as the guide to a new world of vision. However abundant talent may be, it is always too late, or too early, and in any case out of season, since it is superfluous and ineffectual, since even the supremely perfect of earlier ages, the models of modern artists, are superfluous, almost ineffectual, and scarcely add one stone to the building. If artists cannot inwardly perceive fresh forms appearing but merely old forms of the past, they serve history but not life, and they are dead before they have died. But how could anybody who feels within himself a genuine, fruitful life—which at present means precisely music—be seduced even momentarily to further hope by anything concerned with figures, forms, and styles? He is above all vanities of this sort; and he no more thinks of finding artistic miracles outside his world of ideal sound than he expects to find more great writers in our leached and discolored language. Rather than lend ear to who knows what foolish hopes, he endures the deeply dissatisfying spectacle of our modern spirit; if his heart lacks enough warmth for compassion, better for him to be full of bitterness and hate. Even anger and scorn are better than abandoning himself to illusory pleasure and quiet drunkenness in the manner of our "art-lovers." But even if he is capable of more than negation and scorn, if he can love, sympathize, and assist, he must begin with negation in order to prepare the way for his desire to be helpful.

In order that music may someday arouse the devotion of many men and inspire their confidence in its highest purposes, there must be an end to the whole hedonistic trafficking with so sacred an art. The foundation on which our artistic institutions, theaters, museums, and concerts rest is that "art-lover" who must be proscribed; the political favor tendered to his wishes must be converted into disfavor; public opinion, which sets such inordinate value on encouraging this dilettante patronage, must be swept away by a better judgment. Meanwhile, we must view the *avowed enemy of art* as a more true and more useful ally, since the art against which he avows hatred is exactly that which is understood to be art by the "art-lover"— indeed, he knows no other. Let him tally the foolish waste of money by the art-lovers in building their theaters and public monuments, engaging their "famous" singers and actors, supporting their utterly sterile art schools and collections of paintings, not to mention all the energy, time, and money squandered in every household on the education of so-called esthetic interests. There is no hunger here, no satisfaction, only a dull charade with the illusion of both, and serving as a futile exhibition to confound the regard of others. Or worse still are those who take art relatively seriously and demand that it arouse in them a kind of hunger and desire, and who think that the role of art is to produce this artificial excitement. Quite as though one feared destruction through disgust and apathy, and appealed to all the evil demons to let him be driven about like a wild animal by these hunters. Men yearn for suffering, anger, hatred, passion, sudden terror, and breathtaking suspense, and they summon the artist to be the conjurer of this devilish chase. Present art, in the spiritual housekeeping of our educated classes, is either an utterly spurious, or an ignoble, debased need; either nothing at all, or an evil something!

The artist—the better, the uncommon artist, as though caught in an intoxicating dream—sees nothing of this; with hesitant and uncertain voice he repeats mysteriously beautiful words he thinks he hears from a distant source but cannot perceive distinctly. On the other hand, the artist of very modern stamp feels an extreme aversion for the dreamlike gropings and speech of his nobler colleagues, and drags along with him, on a leash, the whole braying pack of passions and atrocities in order to loose them at will on modern man. For modern man would indeed rather be chased, wounded, and savaged than have to live with himself in solitude. With himself! This thought jolts the modern spirit, and is *its* anxiety and ghastly terror.

When I watch thronging crowds in a teeming city, with expressions of stupor or haste, I constantly tell myself: they must be inwardly miserable. But for all of them art exists only to make them even more miserable, apathetic, and unaware, or more impatient and greedy. For they are endlessly goaded and driven by *false feeling*, which prevents them from even admitting their own squalor. If they want to speak, convention whispers in their ears until they forget what they really wanted to say. If they want to communicate, their understanding is so paralyzed, as it were by witchcraft, that they call their unhappiness happiness and diligently collaborate in their own damnation. In this way they are wholly transformed and reduced to involuntary slaves of false feeling.

6   I shall offer only two examples of how perverted feeling has become in our time and how unconscious of this perversion it remains. Previously one looked with genuine superiority upon moneylenders, even when one needed them. It was understood that every society requires such viscera. At present they are the dominant power in the modern mentality, the group most envied. In the past men were warned especially against taking the day, or the moment, too seriously, and were recommended the *nil admirari*[15] and concern for things eternal. The only remaining form of seriousness in the modern mentality today is reverence for the news delivered by the daily paper or telegraph. "Use every second,"

15. The famous Horatian precept (*Ep.* 1.6.1): "*To wonder at nothing* is perhaps the one and only thing . . . that can make a man happy and keep him so."

and so that you can use it, "evaluate it as quickly as possible"—one might think contemporary men have only one virtue: present-mindedness. Unfortunately, the truth is rather the omnipresence of vile, insatiable greed, and an intrusive curiosity in everybody about everything. Whether the *mind* today is at all *present* is an inquiry we want to leave to the future judges who will sift through the detritus of modern man. But this age is vulgar, we can see it now, because it honors what earlier noble ages despised. But if it nonetheless appropriates all the precious wisdom and art of the past and capers about in this most priceless of garments, this shows an uncanny awareness of its own vulgarity—since it requires this cloak not for warmth but for self-deception.

The need to disguise and conceal itself seems to our age more imperative than not freezing to death. Hence, contemporary scholars and philosophers do not employ the wisdom of India and Greece to become wiser and tranquil; their work is intended simply to procure for the present age an illusory reputation for wisdom. Researchers in natural history are laboring to rank and classify the brutal outbreaks of violence, cunning, and revenge in the contemporary relations of men and nations as immutable laws of nature. Historians are diligently engaged in demonstrating the proposition that every age has its own legitimacy, its own conditions—in order to prepare the fundamental defense for the future tribunal which our age must face. Our theories of the state, the people, economy, commerce, and law have all an *anticipatory apologetic character.* Indeed, it seems as though that portion of the mind that is still active, not consumed in the great bustling mechanism of acquisition and power, has the unique task of defending and excusing the present.

"Against what accuser?" we ask in astonishment.

"Against our own bad conscience."

And here the task of contemporary art suddenly becomes clear, that is, to stupefy or intoxicate! To narcotize or deaden! One way or another to force our conscience into unconsciousness! To help the modern soul escape its feeling of guilt—at least for a moment!—rather than assist its return to innocence! To defend man from himself by forcing him to remain silent and by stopping his ears! . . . The few who have, even once, experienced this supremely humiliating task, this horrible degradation of art, will be forever filled with misery and compassion, but will also feel a fresh, overpowering yearning. Anybody who wants to liberate art and restore its unprofaned sanctity must first liberate himself from the modern mentality. Only as an innocent can he discover the innocence of art; hence, he must first complete two harrowing rites of purification and initiation. If he is successful, and can speak to men from a liberated self in his liberated art, he will then be exposed for the first time to his gravest danger, his supreme battle—men would rather tear him and his art to shreds than admit that they must slink away in shame before him. It is possible that the emancipation of art, the only promising spark of light and hope in the modern age, will remain an event for only a few rare individuals, while the majority will persist in viewing the flickering, smoking flame of their current art. They do not *want* light, but rather blinding; they even *hate* the light[16]—on themselves.

So men avoid the new light-bringer, but he pursues them, compelled by the love from which he was born, and wants to compel them. "You *must* undergo my mysteries," he calls out to them. "You need the purification and shock. Take this risk for your own benefit. Abandon for once that dimly lit corner of nature and life which is all you seem to know. I lead you into a kingdom no less real; you yourselves will say so when you return from my cave to what you call the light of day, you will say which life is more real, where the daylight really is, and which is the cave.[17] Nature is inwardly far richer, far more powerful, blissful, and terrible; you cannot know this from the way in which you normally live. Learn it, to become Nature once more, and let yourself be transformed with it and into it through my magic of love and fire." It is the voice of *Wagner's art* that speaks to men in this way. That we, children of a wretched age, are the first permitted to hear its sound shows how worthy of compassion our age must be. It also shows that genuine music is, in general, a parcel of fate and primal law since it is virtually impossible to derive its emergence, at precisely this time, from empty, meaningless chance. An accidental Wagner would have been overwhelmed and crushed by the other elements amidst which he was thrown. But the evolution of the actual Wagner is governed by a revealing and justifying necessity. The genesis of his art provides a wonderful spectacle, however painful its evolution may have been, since reason, law, and goal are everywhere manifested. Like observers enthralled by this spectacle, we enjoy even these painful developments, we delight in seeing how everything contributes to the health and success of his predestined nature and talent, no matter how difficult its schooling must have been. We delight in the fact that every danger enhanced its courage, that every success made it more deliberate, that poisons and misfortunes made it healthy and strong. The mockery and hostility of the world around it goaded and stimulated his talent; if it strayed from the path, it returns home from error and wandering with marvelous quarry; if it sleeps, "it sleeps only to find new strength." His talent hardens and tempers his body, affording him more vigor; it does not consume his

16. Typically Nietzschean echo of the language of John 3:19–20: "And this is the condemnation, that light is come into the world, and men loved darkness rather than light, because their deeds were evil. For one that doeth evil hateth the light . . . lest his deeds should be reproved."

17. An allusion to Plato's famous allegory of the cave, *Republic* 7.514–17.

life, but increases it and watches over the man like a winged passion that swept him aloft whenever his feet wearied in the sand or were bruised by stone. It can do nothing but communicate, the whole world must collaborate in its work, it is unstinting with its gifts. Rejected, it gives more lavishly; despised by those to whom it had given, it adds to its gifts its most precious jewel—and never have the recipients of its gifts been wholly worthy of them, as the earliest and most recent experience confirm. This is why the predestined nature through which music speaks to the world of phenomena is the most enigmatic thing under the sun, an abyss in which strength and bounty are united, a bridge spanning self and not-self.

"Who could say precisely for what end such a nature exists, even if he could guess what sort of purposiveness brought it into being?" By a lucky hunch one might ask: Could the greater really exist only for the sake of the less great, the greatest talent for the good of the least talented, the supreme virtue and holiness for the most fallible? Must true music be heard because *men least deserve it, but most need it?* Immerse yourself just once in the boundless wonder of this possibility: if from this viewpoint you look back over life, however dreary and confused it may seem to this point, it is bright.

7   Nothing else is possible: in the presence of a nature like Wagner's the observer must every so often be thrown back involuntarily on himself, on his own frailty and insignificance, and he asks himself: "What is he to you? What's your reason for your existence?" He is likely to receive no answer and remains embarrassed and bewildered by his own being. He will perhaps be content that he has had this experience; he may even find the answer to his questing in this *feeling of alienation from his own being.* For precisely through this feeling he shares in the strongest expression of Wagner's life, in the very focus of his power, that daimonic *infectiousness* and self-renunciation of his nature which enables him to impart himself to others just as he absorbs other natures into his own, and which has its greatness in giving and receiving. The observer who appears to surrender to the flood-tide of Wagner's nature shares in its power and is thereby made powerful *through* Wagner *against* Wagner. And every painstakingly serious observer knows that contemplation entails a mysterious opposition, that of confrontation.[18]

If Wagner's art lets us experience all that a soul, in its wandering, might experience by sharing other lives and other destinies, thereby learning to see the world through many different eyes, so we ourselves, given this estrangement and remoteness, are able to see Wagner as he is after we have experienced him. We then feel utterly certain that in Wagner everything

18. See the preface to the second book of Nietzsche's *Human, All-Too-Human,* where Nietzsche reinterprets his words here.

visible in the world tends to deepen and intensify itself by becoming audible, and seeks its own lost soul; and that, equally, everything in the audible world seeks to emerge into the light in visible form, seeks, that is, its own incarnation. His art carries him always in two directions, out of a world of auditory drama into a mysteriously kindred world of visual drama, and vice versa. He is continually compelled—and the observer with him—to translate visible movement back into pure spirit and primal life, and in turn to see the hidden fabric of the inner world made manifest, and clothed in the semblance of a body.[19] All this is the very essence of the *dithyrambic dramatist,* if we use this term in its fullest sense to include at once actor, poet, and musician—a term we must take from the single perfect manifestation of the dithyrambic dramatist before Wagner, that is, from Aeschylus and his Greek rivals.

If the attempt has been made to trace evolution back to inner barriers or deficiencies; if for Goethe, for instance, poetry was a kind of compensation for a thwarted vocation for painting; if it can be said that Schiller's plays indicate a deflected talent for popular oratory; if Wagner himself has tried to attribute the musical advance made by the Germans to, among other things, the fact that, because Germans lacked the seductive impulse provided by a naturally melodic singing voice, they were obliged to apply to their music the same profound seriousness which the men of the Reformation applied to Christianity; if, similarly, we wanted to link Wagner's evolution with some such interior barrier, we would clearly have to assume in him a profound theatrical talent. This talent, denied the most conventionally trivial means of satisfaction, found release and salvation by merging all the arts into a magnificent theatrical revelation. But then we might just as easily say that the strongest musical nature, in despair of having to speak to half- and nonmusical audiences, violently forced access to the other arts in order to express itself at last with hundredfold clarity, and to elicit comprehension, the broadest national comprehension. But no matter how we might imagine the evolution of the original dramatist, his constitution at maturity and prime is free of all inner obstacles and defects. He is the truly free artist, who cannot help thinking in all the arts simultaneously, who mediates and conciliates between spheres apparently sundered, who restores the unity and wholeness of the artistic faculty, a wholeness which can be neither intuited nor deduced, but only revealed in the act.

But the man for whom this act is suddenly performed will quickly succumb to its extremely seductive and troubling spell; he suddenly finds himself confronted by a force that overcomes the resistance of reason, that in

19. See, for instance, Wagner's remarks in *Das Kunstwerk der Zukunft* (*Gesammelte Schriften,* 3:114): "Only there, where eye and ear can be mutually certain of their manifestation, is the artist present in his entirety."

fact makes everything he has lived to date seem irrational and incomprehensible. Lifted out of ourselves, we float in a mysterious, fiery element, we no longer know ourselves, we don't recognize the most familiar things. We have no available reference point; everything lawful, every fixed point begins to shift; everything glows in fresh color, speaks to us in new characters. Ravished by this blend of intense rapture and fear, one could have to be a Plato to decide, as Plato did, to tell the dramatist: "In our republic we will honor any man as a wonderful and holy being who as a consequence of his wisdom can become anything at all and imitate everything; we will anoint his head with myrrh, and garland him with fillets of wool, but seek to persuade him to move to some other city."[20] Perhaps a citizen of Plato's republic could, and must, exert such self-control; all the rest of us, who live in cities quite unlike his republic, crave and demand that the magician come to us, even though we fear him—precisely so that our community and the evil reason and power that it embodies might suddenly seem to vanish. A condition of mankind—with its societies, morals, habits, and institutions—which could do without mimetic artists is perhaps not wholly impossible, but this possibility is surely very ludicrous, and next to impossible. The only man who should speak freely of such a possibility is one with the creative power to intuit and anticipate the ultimate moment of everything to come, and who then, like Faust, must—and may well—be stricken with blindness.[21] For we have no right to this blindness, whereas Plato, for example, after his unique glimpse into the Hellenic ideal, had the right to become blind to all Hellenic reality.

The rest of us, however, have much greater need for art because we have learned *to see from the actual*; and precisely what we need is the total dramatist who can release us, if only for a few hours, from the terrible tension which those with such eyes now feel between themselves and the tasks imposed upon them. With him we attain the highest reaches of feeling, and there we fancy that we have at last returned to free nature and the domain of freedom. From there too, as in a vast mirror of air, we can see, as a sublime and meaningful spectacle, ourselves and those like us in our struggles, victories, and defeats; we take pleasure in the rhythm of passion and sacrifice, we hear under the hero's masterful footsteps the dull echo of death, and understand in its proximity the supreme stimulus of life. Thereby transformed into tragic men, we return to life in a strangely confident mood; with a fresh feeling of security, as though, after the greatest perils, excesses, and ecstasies, we had found our way back to the limited and domestic, where we can behave with consideration, or at least more nobly than before. For everything that here seems serious and necessary, as a course directed to a goal, re-

20. See *Republic* 3.398a.
21. See Goethe's *Faust*, part 2, 5, "Midnight."

sembles—compared to the journey we have just taken, if only in a dream—
merely strangely isolated fragments of that total experience of which we are,
when terrified, aware. Indeed, when we encounter danger, we will run the
risk of taking life too lightly simply because in art we clung to it with such
desperate seriousness—as Wagner remarked of his own life and destiny.[22]
For if those of us who only experience and do not create this dithyrambic
drama feel that the dream is almost more real than waking reality, how
much more the artist must feel this contrast. There he stands, surrounded
by all the clamoring demands and intrusions of the day, the necessities of
life, of society, and state—and what is he? Perhaps the only waking man,
the only one sensitive to the true and the real, surrounded by dazed and
tormented sleepers, by the deluded, the sufferers. And there he feels himself
the victim of chronic insomnia, as though doomed now to live out his life
with exhausting clarity and awareness in the company of sleepwalkers and
solemn, ghostly beings; everything which other men regard as ordinary
seems unearthly to him, and he feels tempted to dismiss the impression of
this phenomenon with arrogant derision.

But what a strange contrast to this feeling when the clarity of his shuddering arrogance is joined by a completely different impulse, the yearning
of the heights for the depths, the passionate longing for the earth, for the
happiness of community. For if he thinks of all the privations that his solitary
creativity costs him, then he must immediately, like a god descending to
earth, "exalt with fiery arms to heaven"[23] everything weak, human, and
forlorn, that he may finally have love instead of being idolized, and in love
utterly relinquish himself. But precisely this assumed conflict is the miracle
that really happens in the soul of the dithyrambic dramatist; if his essence
could be expressed in words, it must be precisely here. For these are the
creative moments of his art—when this conflict of feelings is taut, when his
gloomy arrogance and horrified distaste for the world fuse with his passionate urgency to approach the world as a lover. When he now casts his
eyes on earth and life, his eyes are like the rays of the sun which "draw up
the water," collect mist, and accumulate towering thunderheads. *Cautiously
lucid and selflessly loving* at the same time, his gazing eyes touch earth, and
everything illuminated by this binocular vision is compelled by Nature with
frightful rapidity to discharge all its powers, and to reveal its most hidden
secrets—and surely, moreover, from modesty.

It is more than a metaphor to say that Wagner's gaze has caught Nature
by surprise while she was naked, and that she wants to flee modestly into
her own contradictions. Previously unseen, the interior now flees into the

---

22. See Wagner, *Über Staat und Religion* (*Gesammelte Schriften*, 7:7–9).
23. Nietzsche's (slightly less than literal) citation from Goethe's poem "Der Gott und
die Bejadere."

sphere of the visible and becomes appearance, what was previously only visible escapes into the dark sea of sounds. *In the effort to conceal herself Nature reveals the essence of her contradictions.* Through a violently rhythmical yet floating dance, through ecstatic gestures, the primal dramatist expresses what is within him and within Nature; the dithyramb of his movements is as much shuddering understanding and arrogant insight as it is his passionate drawing near, his ecstatic self-surrender. The intoxicated speech follows the movement of these rhythms; paired with words the melody rings out; and melody in turn casts its flames deeper into the domain of images and ideas. A dreamlike appearance, like and yet unlike the image of Nature and her liberator, floats down toward us; it condenses into more human shapes, it broadens out as a consequence of a proud heroic will, an ecstatic ruin and extinction of that will. Thence arises tragedy; thence life receives its most splendid wisdom, the gift of tragic thought; thence at last the greatest magician and benefactor awakens among mortal men—the dithyrambic dramatist.[24]

8　　　　　　　　　　Wagner's essential life—that is, the gradual emergence of the dithyrambic dramatist—was at the same time an endless battle with himself, insofar as he was not solely this dithyrambic dramatist. The battle against the opposition of the world was for him so fierce and grim only because he could hear this "world," this seductive foe, speak from within himself, and because he harbored a powerful demon of opposition within him. When the *governing idea* of his life emerged, that through the theater one could exert incomparable influence, an influence greater than that of all the other arts, this aroused in him the most violent ferment. This did not mean that he immediately reached a clear, clean decision about his subsequent desires and actions; this idea appeared at first almost exclusively in the form of a temptation, as the expression of that ominous, insatiable, personal will that yearns for *power* and *glory*. Influence, incomparable influence—but how? Over whom? From then on that was the question and search which gave his head and heart no rest.

Wagner wanted to conquer and captivate as no other artist had, and, if possible, to attain at a single blow that tyrannical supremacy toward which his will so darkly urged him. With a jealous, profoundly watchful eye he gauged everything that was successful, and he paid special attention to those

24. Cf. Wagner, *Deutsche Kunst und deutsche Politik* (*Gesammelte Schriften*, 8:8off.): "If we enter a theater, we look ... into a demonic abyss of base and sublime possibility. ... Always the greatest poets of peoples have approached this abyss in terror; they have discovered wise rules and sacred magic formulas in order to exorcise by genius the demon hidden there, and Aeschylus even conducted the Furies to the place of their redemption. The melodic musicians of musical art approach this abyss."

he wanted to influence. Through the wizard eye of the dramatist who can read soul as fluently as the simplest text, he explored the spectator and audience, and although he was often disturbed by what he discovered, he nonetheless immediately seized the means to subdue them. These means were at his fingertips; whatever strongly affected him he wanted and was also able to produce; from his predecessors he understood at every stage just as much as he himself could create, and he never doubted his ability to achieve what pleased him. Perhaps in this respect his nature was even more "presumptuous" than Goethe's, who said of himself, "I have always thought I had everything; had I been offered a crown, I would have thought it reasonable." Wagner's talent, his "taste," and, equally, his intention—all these always fitted each other as snugly as a key fits a lock; combined, they *became* great and free, but at this time they were not.

What did it matter to him—that weak but nobler, and yet selfishly solitary emotion felt by this or that lover of the arts, trained in literature and esthetics, remote from the great multitude? But those powerful storms of the soul generated in the great multitude by individual intensifications of dramatic song, those sudden, contagious intoxications of the heart, thoroughly honest and selfless—those were the echoes of his own experience and feeling, and with them he was permeated by an ardent hope of supreme power and influence! He thus understood *grand opera* as the means by which he could express his governing idea; urged into opera by his desire, he turned his eyes toward its homeland.[25] A lengthy period of his life, including the boldest changes of plans, studies, residences, and friends, can be explained only by this desire, and by the external resistance which this shabby, restless, passionately naive German artist was bound to encounter. How one became a master in this field another artist understood better; and now that it has gradually been recognized how extremely intricate was the mesh of varied influences to which Meyerbeer resorted in order to ready and realize each of his great triumphs, and the scrupulousness he devoted to the sequence of "effects" in the opera itself, we will also understand the degree of shame and humiliation that overwhelmed Wagner when his eyes were opened to these "artistic devices" so essential to public success. I doubt that there has ever been a great artist in history who started out with such an enormous mistake and who so resolutely and trustingly accepted the most revolting forms of an art. And yet there was greatness in the way he approached it, and it was therefore astonishingly fruitful. For, out of this despair on recognizing his mistake, he understood modern success, the modern public, and the whole mendacious nature of modern art. While becoming critical of "effects," he was thrilled by the anticipation of his own purification. It

25. That is, Paris, where Meyerbeer's grand opera was in the ascendant and where Wagner lived from 1839 until 1842.

was as though the spirit of music spoke to him hereafter with a charm wholly new to his soul. Like someone returning to the light of day after a long illness, he scarcely trusted hand and eye anymore. He groped his way, and so he regarded it a wonderful discovery that he was still a musician, still an artist; indeed, that he had only just now become one.

Each additional step in Wagner's evolution is characterized by the fact that the two basic forces of his nature join ever more closely together; the aversion of one for the other is diminished; the higher self no longer condescends to be of service to its violent, earthly brother; it *loves* him and must serve him. The most delicate and purest qualities are finally, by the end of this development, also absorbed into the most powerful; the turbulent drive pursues its course as before, but along other paths where the higher self is at home; this self, in turn, descends to earth and recognizes its own likeness in everything earthly. If we could speak in this way of the ultimate goal and outcome of such a development and still remain intelligible, then we might also find a graphic expression to designate a long intermediate stage; but, doubting the former, I decline to attempt the latter. This intermediate stage can be differentiated historically from the earlier and later stages by two facts—Wagner becomes a *revolutionary of society*;[26] Wagner recognizes that the only artist who has ever lived is the *people-as-poet*. His governing idea, which after his great despair and recovery appeared before him in a fresh form, more potent than before, led him to both. Influence, incomparable influence through the theater! —But over whom? He shuddered at the memory of those whom he had previously wanted to influence.

From experience Wagner understood the whole humiliating position in which art and the artist find themselves, how a soulless or callous society, which calls itself good and is really evil, includes art and artists in its slavish entourage for gratification of its *imagined needs*. Modern art is a luxury; this he understood as thoroughly as the corollary that it will stand or fall with the legitimacy of this luxury society. This society knows nothing beyond the most callous and cunning use of its power to render those who are powerless, the people, ever more abject, subservient, and unlike a people, and to transform them into the modern "worker." It has also deprived the people of their greatest and purest things—things they have created out of profoundest necessity, and through which they—the true, the only, artist— gently communicate their spirit: their myth, song, dance, and innovation in language, in order to distill a sensuous antidote to the exhaustion and bore-

---

26. See Wagner, *Eine Mittheilung an meine Freunde* (*Gesammelte Schriften*, 4:325): "Here I want to recall music as my guardian angel, which saved me as an artist . . . just when, with ever greater determination, my rebellious feeling revolted against the whole condition of a civilization."

dom of their own existence—modern art.[27] How this society originated, how it learned to draw fresh strength from apparently conflicting spheres of power, how, for example, a declining Christianity allowed itself through hypocrisy and mediocrity to be used as a shield against the people for the protection of this society and its possessions, how science and scholarship surrendered only too docilely into its service—all of this Wagner has traced through the ages, until, by the end of his considerations, he leapt to his feet full of nausea and rage: out of sympathy for the people he became a revolutionary. From that point on he loved the people and yearned for them as he yearned for his art; for, alas! only in the people, in that vanishing, hardly detectable, artificially scattered people, could he now see the spectators and listeners worthy of, and equal to, the power of his artistic works as he envisioned them. So he concentrated his reflections on the question "How is a people generated? How regenerated?"

Always he found only one answer. If a multitude suffer the same need that he suffers, he told himself, they would be the people.[28] And where the same need leads to the same urgency and desire, the same mode of gratification would also be sought, and the same happiness found in this gratification. If then he looked around for what in his need most profoundly consoled and comforted him, for what most spiritually met his need, he knew with blissful certainty that this could only be myth and music. Myth he knew as the creation and language of the people's need; music had a similar yet more mysterious origin. He bathed and healed his soul in both of these elements; he needed them most fervently—from this he could infer how his need was related to the people as it arose, and how the people must again rise if there were to be *many Wagners*. But how then do myth and music survive in our modern society, insofar as they have not been its victims? A similar fate has befallen them, which testifies to their secret kinship. Myth has been profoundly degraded and deformed into "fairy tales," devalued into a pleasantly playful possession of children and women of the stunted people, its wonderful character, serious, sacred, virile, completely stripped away. Music has survived among the poor and humble, among the solitary; the German musician has not succeeded in happily incorporating himself in the luxury industry of art, and has himself become a monstrous, cryptic fairy tale, full of pathetic sounds and omens, a helpless questioner, something completely bewitched and in need of liberation.

27. See Wagner, *Das Kunstwerk der Zukunft* (*Gesammelte Schriften*, 3:61): "The satisfying of an imaginary need, however, is *luxury*. . . . Luxury is heartless, inhuman, insatiable, and egotistical insofar as provoked by need. . . . This demon rules the world; it is the spirit of this industry that murders man in order to make use of him like a machine. . . . It is, alas—the spirit, the condition of our—*art*!"
28. Ibid.: "Who is the people? The people is the quintessence of all those who *feel a common affliction*."

Here the artist clearly heard the mandate given to him alone: restore virility to myth, and liberate music from its enchantment that it might speak. He felt a sudden release of his strength for *drama*, the establishment of his mastery over a hitherto unexplored middle realm between myth and music. His new artwork, in which he fused together everything he could of what was powerful, affective, and exhilarating, he now presented to men with his great, painfully penetrating *question*: "Where are you who feel the same suffering and need as I? Where is the multitude in whom I aspire to find a people? I want to know you, that you might share the same happiness, the same consolation with me; by your joy you shall reveal to me your suffering." With *Tannhäuser* and *Lohengrin* he posed this question; in this way he looked around for kindred souls; the solitary thirsted for multitudes.

But how must he have felt? Nobody gave an answer, nobody had understood the question. Not that all remained silent; on the contrary, there were answers to a thousand questions which he had never asked; people chattered about the new works as though they were created expressly for verbal dissection. The whole esthetic mania for scribbling and chattering broke out like a fever among Germans; they measured and fingered the works of art and the artist's person with that shamelessness no less characteristic of German scholars than German journalists. With his writings Wagner tried to help them understand his question: more confusion, more buzzing—a musician who writes and thinks was regarded by everyone in those days as an absurdity. They cried out, "He's a theoretician who wants to reform art with his intellectual cleverness; stone him!" Wagner was stupefied; his question was not understood, his need was not felt, his art seemed a communication to the deaf and blind, and his "people" seemed an allusion. He staggered and stumbled. The possibility of a total overthrow of all things suddenly confronted his eyes, he no longer shrank from this possibility. Perhaps a new hope could be founded on the upheaval and destruction, and perhaps not—in any event nothing is better than the repugnant something. Soon he was a political refugee, and in misery.[29]

And only now, precisely with the frightful reversal of his inner and outer destinies, does that period in the life of the great man begin, over which the light of supreme mastery shone with the splendor of liquid gold! Only now does the genius of dithyrambic drama cast off its last veil! He is alone, the age seems meaningless to him,[30] he has lost hope; so, once again, he turns his world-vision into the depths, this time penetrating to the bottom.

29. Despairing of social and political life in Germany and of an art founded on a new society, Wagner, in May 1849, following the failure of the Dresden uprising, decisively turned his back on Germany and sought refuge abroad.
30. Cf. Wagner, *Epilogischer Bericht* (*Gesammelte Schriften*, 6:369): "The age seemed to me devoid of meaning, and real existence for me lay outside the laws of the time."

There he sees suffering in the nature of things, and now, having become impersonal, as it were, he accepts his portion of suffering with serenity. The craving for supreme power, the heritage of earlier circumstances, is now channeled wholly into artistic creation. With his art he now speaks only to himself, no longer to a "public" or a people, and he strives to achieve the greatest clarity and adequacy that such a powerful dialogue requires. Even in the artworks of the preceding period it was quite otherwise; even in these he had aimed, although in a delicate and noble way, at the immediate impression. As a question this work was indeed meant to elicit an immediate answer. And Wagner had so often wanted to help those he questioned to understand him that he met them and their awkwardness at being questioned halfway, adapting his art to older forms and modes of expression. Where he had reason to fear that his most intimate language would be unconvincing or unintelligible, he had tried to persuade and render his questions more public by choosing a tongue half foreign to himself but more familiar to his listeners. Now nothing could have disposed him to such considerations; now he wanted only one thing, to come to terms with himself, to think about the essence of the world in terms of events, to philosophize in sound; what remains to him of *intentions* aims at ultimate *insights*.

Those worthy of knowing what took place in Wagner during this period when, in the dark sanctuary of his soul, he carried out that dialogue with himself—not many are worthy—should hear, watch, and experience *Tristan und Isolde*, the true *opus metaphysicum* of all art, a work over which lies the shattered gaze of a dying man, with its insatiable, sweet longing for the mysteries of night and death, utterly removed from life, which appears evil, deceptive, and divisive in the harsh light of a horrible, ghostly dawn. Hence, it is a drama with the starkest austerity of form, overwhelming in its simple greatness, and precisely adapted to the mystery of which it speaks: the experience of death by the living body, unity of being in duality. And yet there is something still more wonderful than this work: the artist himself who, in a short period of time, was able to create a world-image of utterly different color, *Die Meistersinger von Nürnberg*; who, moreover, in both merely paused and refreshed himself as it were, in order to complete with measured haste that enormous four-part structure, planned and begun before them, the product of twenty years of meditation and writing, his Bayreuth masterpiece, the *Ring of the Nibelungen*. Whoever feels surprised by the proximity of *Tristan* to *Die Meistersinger* has failed to grasp a crucial aspect of the life and essence of all truly great Germans. He does not know the ground from which alone that fundamentally and uniquely *German gaiety* of Luther, Beethoven, and Wagner can grow—a gaiety inexplicable to other nations, and which seems to have been lost by contemporary Germans— that bright, golden, yeasty blend of simplicity, the penetrating gaze of love, contemplative simplicity, and mischief that Wagner offers as the most de-

licious drink to all those who have suffered deeply from life, but have returned to face it once more with convalescent smile.

And while Wagner himself looked at the world in a more conciliatory
spirit, less frequently seized by nausea and rage, more likely to renounce
power out of sadness and love than to recoil from the world in horror; while
he was furthering his greatest work in tranquility, accumulating score upon
score,[31] something happened which made him take notice. *Friends* came and
announced to him an underground movement of many hearts—it was still
a far cry from the "people" that was here stirring and announced, but
perhaps the germ and life-source of a truly human society, realizable in the
distant future; for the present it was merely the guarantee that his great
work could be entrusted to the caring hands of loyal men, who would have
to guard, and be worthy of guarding, this most magnificent legacy to posterity. With the love of friends the colors in his life's day grew brighter and
warmer; his noblest concern, that before evening he could conclude his
work and find a haven for it, would no longer depend upon him alone. Then
there occurred an event which he could only interpret symbolically, and
which to him meant a fresh consolation, a propitious sign. A great war waged
by the Germans[32] opened his eyes, a war by those same Germans whom he
knew to be so profoundly degenerate, so inferior to that high German spirit
that he recognized and explored in himself and other great Germans of
history—Germans whom he saw displaying, in a quite abnormal situation,
two authentic virtues, simple courage and discretion, and he began to believe
with deep inward happiness that perhaps he was not, after all, the last
German. And that, standing beside his work there might be a power greater
than that devoted yet modest strength of a few friends, for that long period
during which it must await its predestined future as the art of that future.
It may be that this belief could not have protected him from doubt indefi-
nitely, all the more since he sought strenuously to raise his own immediate
hopes; suffice it that he felt a powerful impulse to recall a high *obligation*
he had still not fulfilled. His work would not have been completed nor fully
realized if he had merely entrusted it to posterity as a sheaf of silent scores.
He had to teach and demonstrate publicly what no one could have intuited,
and what was above all reserved for him, the innovative style of his execution,
his presentation—in order to provide an example which nobody else could
give, and thus establish a *stylistic tradition* which exists not as marks on paper
but as impressions on human souls. This obligation had become all the
more serious for him as his other works had meanwhile suffered the most

31. Ibid.: "And while I was writing one score after another, without even turning to open
them, it seemed to me at times that I was a sleepwalker without consciousness of his own
actions."
32. The Franco-Prussian War of 1870–71.

intolerable and absurd fate precisely as regards their style of execution. They were celebrated, admired, and—botched; and nobody seemed shocked. For, strange as it might sound, whereas he had rejected thoughts of power and more and more radically renounced success among his contemporaries, according to his very judicious assessment of them, nonetheless "success" and "power" came to him; at least so everyone told him. To no avail he repeatedly and obstinately made it clear that this "success" was an utter misunderstanding, and indeed humiliated him. People were so unaccustomed to seeing an artist sternly discriminate between his effects that even his most solemn protests were not really heeded.

After Wagner understood the connection between theatrical life and theatrical success, and the character of contemporary man, he detached himself spiritually from this theater; with esthetic raptures and the acclaim of excited masses, he had nothing further to do. Indeed, it must have infuriated him to see his art vanish so indiscriminately into the yawning maw of insatiable boredom and the craving for amusement. How shallow and mindless every effect here had to be, how much depended on gorging the insatiable rather than feeding the hungry, he above all inferred from a recurrent phenomenon: everyone, even producers and performers, regarded his works as no different from any other theatrical music composed according to vulgar handbooks of operatic style. Moreover, thanks to cultivated conductors, his works were immediately cut and chopped up into standard form, in the same way that the singer believed he could approach them only after they had been emptied of their spirit. And where there was a desire to do them properly, Wagner's prescriptions were followed with great clumsiness and the kind of prudish timidity with which one might have depicted, by means of the artificial choreography of ballet, the staging of the gathering in the streets of Nuremberg at night in the second act of *Die Meistersinger.* And all the while they imagined themselves to be acting in good faith, without malicious second thoughts.

Wagner's generous efforts, through action and example, to indicate at the very least the simple correctness and integrity of performance, and to coach individual singers in his wholly novel style of delivery, were repeatedly swept away and swamped by the reigning mindlessness and old habit. Moreover, these efforts constrained him to devote himself to just that kind of theater whose whole milieu had become nauseating to him. Even Goethe himself lost all desire to attend performances of his *Iphigenie*: "I suffer terribly," he said in explanation, "when I have to grapple with these apparitions which never succeeded in taking the shape they should."[33] Nonetheless, Wagner's "success" in this theater he loathed continued to grow; it finally reached the point where precisely the large theaters survived almost exclusively on

33. See entry for April 1, 1827, in Goethe's *Conversations with Eckermann.*

the fat profits that Wagnerian opera, deformed into conventional opera, brought in. The confusion over this growing passion of the theatrical public touched even some of Wagner's friends; he—the great martyr!—had to endure the extreme bitterness of seeing his friends become intoxicated with his "successes" and "triumphs" precisely when his thought, single and noble, had been shattered and rejected. It almost seemed as though this people, in many ways grave and serious, were usually, with regard to their most serious artist, unwilling to spoil a fundamental frivolity, and as though, for precisely this reason, it had to direct against him everything that was vulgar, mindless, clumsy, and spiteful in the German spirit.

Later when, during the German war, a greater, more liberal current of feeling seemed to rule men's minds, Wagner recalled his duty to fidelity, in order at least to preserve his greatest work from spurious success and insult, and to present it in its most authentic rhythm as an example for all time. Thus the *idea of Bayreuth* was born. As a result of that current of feeling, he also believed that among those to whom he wanted to entrust his most precious possession, he could see the awakening of a more enhanced sense of duty. From these two aspects of duty grew the event which, like a strange blaze of sunlight, illuminates the sequence of years before and after—this event devised for the health of a distant future, possible but not demonstrable, which for the present and for merely contemporary men means little more than a riddle or a scandal. But for the few who could contribute to it, it is a foretaste of joy, of life, of the highest kind, through which they are conscious of receiving and bestowing happiness and fruitfulness far beyond their span of years. For Wagner himself the event is a dark cloud of toil, worry, brooding, and grief; a renewed outbreak of conflicting elements, but all irradiated by the star of *selfless fidelity* and, in this light, transformed into unspeakable joy.

One hardly needs to say it: the breath of tragedy envelops life. And everyone whose soul can intuit something of this, all those who are familiar with the constraint of a tragic illusion about the purpose of life, with the warping and shattering of his intentions, with renunciation and purification by love, must feel in what Wagner in his art now reveals to us a dreamlike remembrance of the heroic personal existence of the great man. As from a far distance we feel that Siegfried is narrating his deeds: with the touching joy of memory is woven the deep sorrow of waning summer, and all Nature lies quiet in a yellow twilight.[34]

9   To contemplate *Wagner as an artist*, to review and reflect on the drama of talent and daring becoming truly free: this is necessary for the healing and comfort of anyone who has thought and suf-

---

34. A glancing allusion to the second scene of Wagner's *Götterdämmerung*.

fered over the evolution of *the man Wagner*. If art in general is nothing more than the ability to communicate to another what one has experienced, every work of art contradicts itself if it cannot be understood; hence, Wagner's greatness as an artist must consist precisely in that demonic *communicability* of his nature, which speaks of itself as it were in every language, and allows his inner, most personal experience to be recognized with supreme clarity. His entry into the history of art is like a volcanic eruption of all the undivided artistic powers of Nature herself after mankind has grown used to perceiving the separation of the arts as a law. One may therefore hesitate over what name should be applied to him, whether he should be called poet, sculptor, or musician, taking each term in an unusually broad sense, or whether a new word must be coined for him first.

The *poetic* in Wagner reveals itself in the fact that he thinks in visible and tangible events, not in concepts; that is, he thinks mythically, as the people have always thought. Myth is not founded on a thought, as the children of an overly refined culture suppose, but is itself a thinking; it conveys an image of the world through the sequence of events, actions, and sufferings. The *Ring of the Nibelungen* is an enormous system of thought without the conceptual form of thought. A philosopher could perhaps juxtapose it with something wholly corresponding to it, which was completely devoid of image and action and spoke to us purely in concepts; we would then have the same thing presented in two separate domains, one for the people, and the other for the people's opposite, the theoretical man. Wagner therefore does not appeal to him, for the theoretical man understands precisely as much of true poetry, of myth, as a deaf mute does of music, that is, they both see an apparently meaningless movement. One cannot look from one of these separate compartments into the other; so long as one is under the poet's spell, he thinks with the poet as though he were merely a creature of feeling, seeing, and hearing; the conclusions he draws are links between the events he sees, hence real, not logical, causalities.

If the gods and heroes of such mythical drama, as composed by Wagner, must also express themselves in words, no danger is more immediate than that this *language* awaken the theoretical man in us and thereby transport us into another, nonmythical domain. So that finally, far from understanding through these words what was happening before our eyes, we would have understood nothing at all. That is why Wagner has forced language back to its primal state, where it almost does not think in concepts, where it is still poetry, image, and feeling itself. The fearlessness with which Wagner tackled this whole frightening task shows how powerfully he was driven by the poetic spirit, like someone who must follow wherever his ghostly guide took him. Every word in these dramas had to be singable, and gods and heroes had to be able to speak them; this was the enormous demand imposed by Wagner on his verbal imagination. Anyone else would have despaired, since

our language seems almost too old and devastated to make the same demands of it that Wagner made; and yet where he struck the rock, a rich
spring came pouring forth.[35]

Wagner, precisely because he loved this language more and demanded
more from it, suffers even more than any other German from its debility
and degeneration; hence from the countless formal losses and mutilations,
from the ponderous particles that trouble our syntax, from the unsingable
auxiliary verbs, from all those things that have entered our language through
our sins and omissions. On the other hand, he felt with deep pride the
spontaneity and inexhaustibility still present in this language, the resonant
vigor of its roots, in which he sensed, in contrast to the highly derivative,
artificial rhetoric of the Romance languages, a wonderful proclivity and
readiness for music, for true music.[36] A love of German pervades Wagner's
poetry, a hardness and frankness in his relation to it which can be felt in
no other German except Goethe. Concrete expression, bold concision,
rhythmical variety and vigor, a remarkable richness of strong and meaningful
diction, syntactical simplicity, an almost unique inventiveness in the language of fluctuating feeling and intuition, an aphoristic and colloquial power
flowing at times with extreme purity—such qualities should be enumerated,
and even then the greatest and most wonderful of all would have been
overlooked.

Anyone who reads successively two such poems as *Tristan* and *Die Meistersinger* will feel toward the language the same astonishment and incredulity
he feels toward the music: namely, how was it possible to master creatively
two worlds as diverse in form, color, and structure as they are in spirit? This
is the most potent thing in Wagner's talent, something which only the great
master can accomplish: to fashion for each work a new language, also to
give the new inwardness a new body, a new sound. Where this rarest of
powers expresses itself, the censure which applies to sporadic exuberance
and oddities or the more common obscurities of expression and vagueness
of thought will always remain merely petty and sterile. Besides, those who

35. A pointed echo of the miraculous feasts performed by Dionysus's Maenads on Mt.
Cithaeron, as reported by the Messenger in Euripides' *Bacchae* 706–07.
36. Cf. Wagner, *Oper und Drama* (*Gesammelte Schriften*, 4:263ff.): "If we now cast a glance
at the languages of the European nations that until now have contributed in an original
way to the development of musical drama, to opera—and only the Italians, French, and
Germans have done so—we find that of these three, only the *Germans* possess a language
which in everyday use is still clearly and directly linked to its roots. Italians and French
speak a language whose etymological richness became comprehensible to them only
through the study of ancient languages, the so-called dead languages; it is their language
which speaks for them, and not they who speak in their own language. . . . Among all the
languages of modern opera only the German is susceptible . . . to being used in order to
revive artistic expression."

have until now been the loudest in their condemnation objected not so much to the language as to the soul of the work, to the whole mode of feeling and suffering, which they found offensive and shocking. We will wait until they themselves have another soul, for then they will speak another language themselves, and the German language will be better off, I think, than it now is.

But, above all, nobody who contemplates Wagner, poet and sculptor of language, should forget that none of Wagner's dramas was meant for reading; hence, they should not be burdened with the same demands we make of spoken drama. Spoken drama wants to affect our feelings solely through words and concepts, an aim which subordinates it to the laws of rhetoric. Although passion in life is seldom eloquent, in such drama it must be eloquent for any sort of communication to occur. But if the language of a people is already in a state of decay and exhaustion, the verbal dramatist will be tempted to give unusual color and form to his language and thought; he wants to heighten the language so as to allow it to express heightened feeling, and thereby runs the risk of not being understood. So too if he seeks to impart a certain grandeur to passion by employing lofty phrases and sudden sublimity, he runs another risk: he seems false and artificial. Life's real passion does not speak sententiously, and poeticized passion easily arouses suspicion about its sincerity when it differs substantially from this reality. In contrast, Wagner, who first recognized the inner deficiency of spoken drama, gives each dramatic sequence a threefold illustration, through word, gesture, and music. And it is precisely the music that transmits the basic emotions of the characters of the drama directly to the soul of the listener, who now witnesses in the gestures of the same characters the first visible sign of those inner events, and hears in the language a second, paler manifestation of these, translated into the conscious will. All of these effects take place simultaneously, without mutual disturbance, and force the spectator of such a drama into a wholly fresh understanding and shared experience, as though his senses were suddenly more spiritual and his spirit more sensual, as though everything which wants to emerge from man and thirsts for knowledge, found itself free and blessed in a jubilation of knowing.

Since each sequence in a Wagnerian drama is communicated with supreme clarity to the spectator, that is, illuminated and inwardly inflamed by the music, the composer can dispense with all the means required by the verbal poet to give warmth and luminous strength to what he represents. The whole economy of the drama can be simpler, the architect's rhythmic sense can again venture to express itself in the grand, complex proportions of the edifice; for there is no longer any motive for that deliberate intricacy and bewildering variety of architectural styles by which the poet endeavors, for the sake of his work, to arouse the feeling of wonder and straining interest, so as to elevate these into ecstatic admiration. The impression of idealizing distance and height is no longer dependent on artifice. The language abandons the wordiness of rhetoric for the concision and energy of a language of feeling; and although the performing artist speaks much less than before of what he did and felt in the play, the inner events, hitherto barred from the stage by the poet's anxiety toward what was allegedly undramatic, now compel the listener into passionate empathy, while the accompanying language of gesture needs only to express the most delicate modulation. The sung passion, however, is in general of somewhat longer duration than the spoken passion; music as it were stretches out feelings; from which it follows in general that the performing artist, who is at the same time a singer, must overcome the excessively great, unplastic arousal of movement from which the performance of spoken drama suffers. He sees himself obliged to confer nobility on his gesture, the more so as the music, bathing his feelings in a pure ether, thereby spontaneously brought beauty closer.

The extraordinary tasks that Wagner has imposed upon actors and singers will for whole generations ignite among them a competition to present at last the image, in the fullest visibility and perfection, of each Wagnerian hero, just as this consummate physicality is already prefigured in the dramatic music. Following this lead, plastic artists will finally open their eyes to the wonder of a fresh visual world, beheld for the first time only by him, the creator of such works as the *Ring of the Nibelungen*—a supreme *sculptor* who, like Aeschylus, points the way to an art of the future. Won't great talents be quickly awakened by jealousy when the plastic artist will compare the effect of his art to that of a music like Wagner's? A music of the purest, sunniest happiness, so that those who hear it feel as though almost all music of the past had spoken an alienated, enslaved language, as though it had been intended as a game for those unworthy of seriousness, or as a means of teaching and demonstrating for those unworthy even of the game! Only for a few brief hours does this music of the past fill us with that happiness we always feel in Wagnerian music; it seems to be seized by rare moments of oblivion when it speaks only to itself, and directs its gaze upward like Raphael's Saint Cecilia, far from its listeners who demand from it diversion, entertainment, or edification.

Of Wagner the *musician* we may say in general that he has linguistically endowed with language everything in nature which until now has not desired to speak: he did not believe that anything had to be dumb. He immersed himself in the dawn, the forest, in the mist, the ravine, in the mountain peak, the night shiver, the moonlight, and he noted in these a secret desire: they too wanted to sound. If the philosopher[37] says that there is *one Will* in

37. That is, Schopenhauer in *The World as Will and Representation*.

Nature, animate and inanimate, which thirsts for existence, the musician adds: At every stage this Will wants an audible existence.

On the whole, music before Wagner had narrow boundaries; it referred to man's abiding conditions, to what the Greeks termed *ethos*, and only with Beethoven had it begun to discover the language of *pathos*, of the passionate will, of dramatic events within man. Formerly, a mood, a calmer, brighter, more devout, or more penitent state—had to be expressed by sound: through a certain prominent homogeneity of form, and through a sustained duration of this homogeneity, the listener was to be compelled to interpret the music, and eventually put into the same mood. All such images of moods and states required distinct forms; others were established by convention. The duration was left to the discretion of the musician, who wanted, of course, to put the listener in a mood, but not to bore him by extending this too long. A further step was taken when images of contrasting moods were sketched in succession and the pleasure of contrast was discovered; and still another step when the same musical piece contained a contradiction of the ethos, for example, the conflict of a masculine and a feminine theme. All of these are still the gross and primitive stages of music. Fear of passion dictated one principle, fear of boredom the other; all deepenings and excesses of feeling were considered "unethical." But after the art of ethos had itself presented man's familiar continuing states and moods in hundreds of repetitions, it finally, despite the wonderful ingenuity of its masters, exhausted itself. Beethoven was the first to let music speak a new language, the hitherto forbidden language of passion; but because his art sprang from the laws and conventions of the art of ethos, and had to seek its justification in its own eyes, as it were, his artistic development was beset by a peculiar difficulty and obscurity. An interior dramatic process—for every passion has a dramatic course—wanted to break through to a new form, but the traditional schema of mood music opposed this and spoke almost with the attitude of morality toward an outbreak of immorality. At times it seems as though Beethoven has assumed the contradictory task of letting pathos express itself through ethos. But for the last and greatest of Beethoven's works, this notion is inadequate. To render the great soaring arc of passion, he actually discovered a new means: isolating certain points of his trajectory, he defined them with the maximum precision in order to allow the listener to *intuit* from these the whole line. From an external perspective, the new form resembles an arrangement of various musical fragments, each of which seems to represent a continuing state, but is actually a moment in the dramatic course of a passion. The listener might believe he was hearing the old music of mood, except that the relation of the individual parts to one another had become incomprehensible, and he could no longer interpret it according to the canon of opposites. Even among lesser musicians there arose a contempt for the demands of a coherent artistic structure; the sequence of parts in their works became arbitrary. The discovery of the great form of passion led back, through a misunderstanding, to the single phrase of arbitrary content, and the mutual tension of the parts vanished entirely. Hence, the symphony after Beethoven is such an astonishingly indistinct language of Beethovenian pathos. The means are not suited to the intention, and the intention on the whole is not clear to the listener, because it was never clear in the mind of the composer. Yet precisely the demand that one have something absolutely definite to say, and that one say it in the clearest possible way, is more imperative as the genre is higher, more difficult, and more exacting.

Wagner's whole effort, therefore, was to find every means of serving *clarity*;[38] this required him above all to detach himself from all the self-conscious demands of the old music of states-of-mind, and to give his music—the process of feeling and passion made audible—completely un-ambiguous utterance. If we examine what he has achieved, it seems to us that in the field of music he has done what the discoverer of figure in the round did in the field of sculpture. Compared to Wagner's, all prior music seems stiff and anxious, as though it could not be viewed from all sides and were ashamed of itself. Wagner seizes every grade and every color of feeling with absolute firmness and determination; he takes the most delicate, re-mote, and primal emotion in hand without fear of losing it, and holds onto it like something hard and solid, even though everyone else must regard it as an impossibly elusive butterfly. His music is never vague or sentimental; everything that speaks through it, human or natural, possesses a powerfully individualized passion; storm and fire acquire in him the coercive power of a personal will.

Suspended over all the sonorous individuals and the conflict of their passions, over the whole vortex of contradictions, supremely self-possessed, is an overpowering symphonic intellect which, out of war, continually gives birth to concord. Wagner's music as a whole is a reflection of the world as this was understood by the great Ephesian philosopher,[39] as a harmony

---

38. Cf. Wagner, *Eine Mittheilung an meine Freunde* (*Gesammelte Schriften*, 4:367ff.): "But even in this direction I was always guided by a single impulse, that of communicating to the intuition of others, in the clearest and most intelligible possible way, what I had myself seen; the greatest clarity in realization was therefore my chief aspiration, but precisely anything but that superficial clarity with which one communicates a theme empty of significance; rather, that infinitely rich and complex clarity, in which alone a vast and meaningful content can be represented intelligibly: something which, certainly to those accustomed to superficiality and stupidity, must frequently in fact seem to be clear in no way whatever."

39. Heraclitus of Ephesus Fr. 80: "It is necessary to know that war is common and that justice is strife, and that all things happen by strife and necessity." See also Fr. 51 on the revealing tension of bow and lyre.

generated out of strife, a unity of justice and strife. I admire the ability to work out, from a multitude of passions running in various directions, the grand line of a collective passion; that such a thing is possible is proven to me by every single act of a Wagnerian drama, in which, side by side, are narrated the personal histories of various individuals and a collective history of all. From the very beginning we sense that we have before us divergent individual currents, but also, dominating everything, a current with one powerful direction. This current at first flows turbulently over the hidden, jagged rocks; the torrent seems at times to break apart, trying to flow in different directions. Gradually, we notice that the whole inner movement has become stronger, more sweeping; the convulsive frenzy is absorbed in the serenity of the broad, terrible rush toward a still unknown goal; and suddenly, at the conclusion, the whole huge expanse of the river plunges down into the depths with a demonic yearning for the abyss and the breakers.

Never is Wagner more Wagner than when the difficulties multiply tenfold, and he can dominate truly great relationships with the joy of the lawgiver. To subdue turbulent, resisting masses to simple rhythms, to convey a single will through a bewildering multiplicity of claims and aspirations—these are the tasks to which he feels he was born, in which he feels his freedom. Never does he lose his breath over them, never does he arrive panting at his goal. He has striven as relentlessly to impose the strictest laws on himself as others do to lighten their burden; life and art oppress him when he cannot play with their most difficult problems. If one ponders even once the relation of the sung melody to the melody of unsung speech—how Wagner used the pitch, force, and tempo of the passionately speaking human voice as the natural model he transposed into art; if then one also ponders the incorporation of such passionate singing into the context of symphonic music—he will know that a miracle of obstacles has been surmounted. Wagner's ingenuity in things great and small, the ubiquity of his spirit and industry are such that anyone viewing a Wagnerian score would like to believe that, until Wagner, true work and exertion have never really existed. It seems that Wagner might even have said, with respect to the toil of art, that the true virtue of the dramatist consists of self-denial; but he probably would have replied: "There is only one toil, that of the man who is still unfree; virtue and goodness are easy."

In sum, considered as an artist, Wagner has in him, to recall a famous type, something of *Demosthenes*—the terrible seriousness toward his object and the powerful grip that invariably grasps the object; he instantly wraps his hand around it and holds it as firmly as if it were bronze. Wagner, like Demosthenes, conceals his art and makes us forget it by forcing us to think of the object; yet he is, like Demosthenes, the last and supreme manifestation of a whole line of potent artistic spirits. Consequently, he has more to conceal than his predecessors: his art acts as nature, a nature rediscovered and restored. He tolerates nothing epideictic[40] in himself, unlike all previous composers who occasionally even play games with their art and display their virtuosity. In the presence of Wagner's art, one does not think of the interesting, of the diverting, of Wagner himself, nor of art in general; one feels only the *necessary*. What austerity and constancy of will, what self-conquest were required of the artist during the period of his development in order ultimately, at maturity, at each creative moment, with joyful freedom, to do the necessary, no one could calculate: enough if we sense in individual cases how he subordinates his music to the course of the drama with a certain cruelty of resolution, which, like fate, is inexorable, while the fiery soul of his art yearns to wander for once without restraint in freedom and wild places.

10   An artist who has this power over himself subjugates, even without wanting to, all other artists. On the other hand, only he is not endangered or limited by those he has subjected, his friends and followers; whereas artists of smaller character, because they seek to depend on friends, tend to forfeit their freedom. It is utterly wonderful to see how Wagner, throughout his life, shunned every form of political faction, although after every phase of his art a circle of adherents had formed, apparently in order to hold him to that phase. He always broke directly through their midst, and refused to be bound. Moreover, his path has been much too long for an individual easily to have accompanied him from the beginning, and so unusual and steep that even the most faithful follower would probably have lost his breath. Nearly all of Wagner's life, his friends—and, for different reasons, his enemies as well—have readily sought to make him dogmatic. Had the purity of his artistic character been even a shade less resolute, he could much earlier have become the arbiter of the contemporary situation of art and music—which he has now at last become, but in the far higher sense that whatever happens in the domain of art is automatically brought before the tribunal of his art and his artistic character. Wagner has subjugated even the most reluctant. There is no longer any musician of talent who does not inwardly listen to him, and who does not find him more

40. Epideictic oratory, as practiced by such orators as Gorgias and Isocrates, was essentially nonforensic. The epideictic orator did not usually intend his work for actual delivery, but to demonstrate some novel or familiar point in a striking way, and his emphasis was typically not so much on the point to be demonstrated as on the display of rhetorical virtuosity in making it. Demosthenes' orations, in contrast, dealt, through immense rhetorical power fueled by passion, with the most urgent political and cultural questions of the day. For further discussion, see George Kennedy, *The Art of Persuasion in Greece* (Princeton, 1963), 152ff.

worthy of hearing than his own or any other music. Many who desperately want to be of some significance struggle directly with this inner attraction, which they find overpowering; they confine themselves anxiously and diligently to the circle of the older masters and prefer to base their "independence" on Schubert or Handel rather than on Wagner. In vain! By struggling against their own better conscience, they themselves become slighter and pettier as artists; they destroy their own character by having to keep bad company and friends; and, after all these sacrifices, it still happens, perhaps in a dream, that their ear hearkens to Wagner. These adversaries are pitiful; they believe that much is lost if they lose themselves, and in this they are mistaken.

Obviously, it makes very little difference to Wagner whether musicians compose henceforth in a Wagnerian manner or whether they compose at all; indeed, he does all he can to destroy the miserable belief that a new school of composers should form around him. Insofar as he directly influences musicians, he tries to train them in the art of great execution; it seems to him that a point has been reached in the development of art where the goodwill to become a skilled master of performance and execution is far more praiseworthy than the yearning to "create" at any price. For at the state that art has now reached, this creating has the fatal effect of reducing true greatness to triteness by reproducing it so well and, by daily attrition, exhausting the means and devices of genius. Even the good in art is superfluous and harmful when it derives from imitation of the best. Wagner's ends and means belong together; it requires nothing more than artistic honesty to feel this, and it is dishonest to copy the means and apply them to wholly different, meaner ends.

If, then, Wagner declines to live among a troop of musicians who compose in the Wagnerian manner, he even more urgently imposes on all men of talent the fresh task of discovering, with him, the *laws of style for dramatic performance.* The deepest need drives him to establish for his art the *tradition of a style* through which, in pure form, his work can survive from one age to another until it reaches that *future* for which it was predestined by its creator.

Wagner possesses an insatiable drive to communicate everything that pertains to that establishment of a style and, similarly, to the enduring of his work. To make this work, in Schopenhauer's words, "a sacred *depositum* and real fruit of his existence, the property of mankind, and to hand it on to a posterity with better judgment, this is his aim which is more important than all other ends and for which he wears a crown of thorns that shall one day sprout into a wreath of laurel. His efforts are just as decidedly concentrated on the completion and security of his work as are those of the insect in its final form on the security of its eggs and provision for the brood it will never see. It deposits the eggs where, as it well knows, they will one day find life and nourishment, and then dies fearlessly and with resignation."[41]

This end, which surpasses all other ends, impels him toward always fresh discoveries; indeed, the more acutely he is aware of struggling against the extreme aversion of the age, which is accompanied by the poorest will to listen, the more deeply he draws from the will of his demonic power of communication. But gradually even this age begins to yield to his tireless efforts, his supple insistence, and lends him its ear. Wherever a distant opportunity, small or significant, arose for explaining his thoughts by an example, Wagner was ready for it: he adapted his thoughts to present circumstances, and succeeded in expressing them even through the most mediocre embodiments. Where a halfway receptive soul opened to him, he cast his seed. He grows hopeful in situations where a cold observer could only shrug his shoulders; he deludes himself a hundred times over in order just once to be justified against such an observer. As the wise man, at bottom, associates with living men only insofar as through them he can augment his store of knowledge, so it almost seems as though the artist should have no further association with those men of his age from whom he cannot obtain the immortality of his art. One can love him only by loving his immortality, and so he feels only one form of the hatred directed against him, the hate, that is, which would destroy the bridge to that future of his art.

The students whom Wagner himself trained, the individual musicians and actors to whom he uttered a word or demonstrated a gesture, the large and small orchestras he directed, the cities that witnessed the seriousness of his activity, the nobles and ladies who, half with dread, half with love, took part in his plans, the various European countries to which he belonged for a while as judge and bad conscience of their art—everything became an echo of his thought, his insatiable striving toward a future fruitfulness. If this echo also frequently returned to him distorted and confused, yet the irresistible power of the great voice with which he cried out a hundred times to the world must also evoke an echo no less powerful; it will soon be impossible not to hear him any longer or to misunderstand him. It is this echo which is already now causing the artistic institutions of modern man to tremble; each time the breath of his spirit has blown through these gardens, it has shaken all the overripe fruit and deadwood. A sudden appearance of universal doubt speaks even more eloquently than this shaking; nobody now can say where or when Wagner's unexpected influence might still break out. Wagner is completely incapable of considering the salvation of art in isolation from any other kind of salvation and damnation; wherever the modern spirit harbors danger within it, there he scrutinizes it with the

41. Schopenhauer, *Parerga and Paralipomena*, 2:60. Except for the italics, the passage is cited verbatim from Schopenhauer.

eye of the most vigilant mistrust as being the danger to art also. In his imagination he dismantles the structure of our civilization and allows nothing rotten, nothing frivolously constructed, to escape him. If in so doing he comes up against a weatherproof wall on a solid foundation, he immediately thinks of a way to exploit it as a bulwark and protective shelter for his art. He lives like a fugitive who tries to preserve not himself but a secret, or like an unfortunate woman who wants to save not her own life, but that of the child in her womb: she lives, like Sieglinde, "for the sake of love."[42]

Certainly it is a life full of every kind of torment and shame to be a homeless wanderer in a world and yet have to address that world and make demands on it, to despise a world and yet be unable to do without it—this is the true affliction of the artist of the future. Unlike the philosopher, he cannot pursue knowledge alone in some dark corner, for he needs human souls as mediators to the future, public institutions as guarantors of this future, as bridges between the present and the future. His art cannot set sail on a skiff of written record as can the philosopher's; art wants *capable men*, not letters and notations, as transmitters. For whole periods in Wagner's life there rings the note of fear that these capable men will not arrive in time, that, in the place of the example he might give them, he will see himself limited perforce to written indications, and that, instead of demonstrating his achievement, he will exhibit its palest reflection to those who read books, which means, in a word, to those who are not artists.

As a *writer* Wagner exhibits the construction of a brave man with a shattered right hand who must fight with his left: when he writes, he always suffers because he is temporarily deprived by an insurmountable necessity of his proper mode of communication, in the form of a luminous and triumphant example. His writings contain nothing canonical or rigorous, but the canon lies in his works. They are attempts to understand the instinct that motivated his work, to look himself in the eye, as it were. He hopes that, if only he could succeed in transforming his instincts into knowledge, the opposite process would occur in the souls of his readers: he writes with this expectation. If it should turn out that he was perhaps here attempting something impossible, then Wagner would be sharing the same fate as all those who reflect on art; and his advantage over most of these is that the most powerful, total instinct for art is lodged within him. I know of no writings on esthetics that shed so much light as Wagner's; whatever can be learned about the birth of a work of art can be learned from him. He is one of the supremely great artists to appear here as a witness, and whose testimony, over a long sequence of years, has been constantly bettered, liberated, clarified, and more precise; even when he stumbles as a man of knowledge, he

---

42. An allusion to Brünnhilde's injunction to Sieglinde in act 3 of *Die Walküre*: "Live, O woman, for love!"

kicks up sparks. Certain writings such as *Beethoven, On Conducting, On Actors and Singers,* and *State and Religion*[43] quiet any desire for contradiction and confer an inward calm and attentive contemplation, such as might suit the opening of a precious casket.

Other articles, especially those of the earlier period, including *Opera and Drama*,[44] are exciting and disquieting; it is the uneven rhythm in them that, as prose, creates the confusion. In them the dialectic is repeatedly broken; the pace is hampered rather than augmented by bursts of feeling; a kind of reluctance on the writer's part looms over them like a shadow as though the artist were ashamed of the conceptual demonstrations. Perhaps the greatest difficulty for those not wholly initiated is the expression of authoritative dignity, which is totally peculiar to Wagner and hard to describe. It strikes me that Wagner frequently *speaks as though confronted with enemies*—for all these writings are in an oral, not a written, style, and one would find them much clearer if read aloud before enemies with whom one has no familiarity; hence their restraint and reticence. But not infrequently the unrestrained vehemence of his feeling breaks through this deliberate curtain; then the heavy, artificial periods, richly swollen with compound words, vanish, and there escape from him sentences and whole pages which are among the most beautiful in German prose. But even while admitting that in these sections of his writing he is speaking to his friends and therefore his enemy's ghost is no longer standing next to his chair, all the friends and enemies that concern Wagner as a writer have something in common which radically separates them from the people for whom he, as an artist, creates. They are, in the polish and sterility of their culture, thoroughly *unpopular*, and he who wants them to understand him must speak *unpopularly*: so our best writers have always done, and so Wagner does. What the constraint is, we can guess. But the power of that nurturing, almost maternal, instinct to which he sacrifices everything leads him back into the ambience of scholars and cultivated men to whom, as a creator, he has forever bade farewell. He submits to the language of culture, and all the laws of its expression, although he was the first to feel the profound inadequacy of this expression.

For if anything at all distinguishes his art from all art of the modern age, it is this: it no longer speaks the language of caste culture, and in general no longer recognizes the difference between cultivated and uncultivated. It thereby stands in opposition to all Renaissance culture which has until now enveloped us moderns in its light and shadow. Because Wagner's art momentarily carries us out of this culture, we are now able to make a general survey of its uniform character. Goethe and Leopardi now appear to us as the last great followers of the Italian poet-scholars; *Faust* appears as the

43. All written in the period 1869–72.
44. Published in 1851.

dramatization of the most unpopular riddle posed by the modern age, in the form of the theoretical man who thirsts for life; even the Goethean lyric derives from, and does not inspire, the folksong. The poet knew this, which is why he confided the thought so seriously to an adherent: "My things can never become popular; whoever thinks so and strives to realize it, is in error."[45]

That in general there could be an art so sunny, bright, and warm, so capable of enlightening with its rays the humble and poor in spirit as of melting the arrogance of the learned—this had to be experienced and could not have been divined. In the mind of anyone who now experiences it, this art must overturn all ideas of education and culture; it will seem to him that the curtain has been parted to reveal a future in which there exists no supreme good and happiness that is not common to all hearts. The stigma until now attached to the word *common* will be erased.

When prescience ventures into the distance like this, conscious insight trains its eye on the dismal social insecurity of our present and does not hide from itself the dangers to an art which seems to have no roots at all except in that distant future, and which lets us see its blooming branches before the ground from which it grows. How do we save this homeless art, until that future? How check the flood of revolution which seems everywhere inevitable, so that with much that is doomed, and deservingly doomed, to destruction, the happy anticipation and assurance of a better future, a freer humanity, is not also swept away?

Whoever asks and cares about such questions has shared Wagner's concern. With Wagner he will feel compelled to seek out those existing powers which have the goodwill, in the time of earthquakes and upheaval, to be the guardian spirit of man's noblest possessions. Only in this sense does Wagner, through his writings, ask of cultured men whether they want to protect his legacy, the precious ring of his art, in their treasures. Even the splendid confidence which Wagner has placed in the German spirit, even in its political goals, seems to me to originate in the fact that he credits the people of the Reformation with that strength, gentleness, and courage necessary to "channel the sea of revolution into the serenely flowing stream of humanity."[46] I would almost like to believe that he wanted to express this and nothing else with the symbolism of his *Imperial March*.[47]

45. See the entry for Oct. 11, 1828, in Goethe's *Conversations with Eckermann*.
46. Cf. Wagner's introduction to the third and fourth volumes of his *Gesammelte Schriften*: "To present to life itself this work of art as a prophetic vision of its future, the most important contribution seemed to me to lie in the enterprise of checking in the streambed of mankind's placidly flowing river the sea of revolution. . . . According to the lofty opinion which that historian of genius [Thomas Carlyle] expresses on the mission of the German people and its spirit of truth, the fact that we recognized that those 'heroic wise men'

But, in general, the generous impulse of the creative artist is too great, the horizon of his love of man too extensive for his sight to remain enclosed within the national reality. His thoughts are, like those of every good and great German, *supra-German,* and the language of his art speaks not to nations but to men.

But to men of the future!

That is his uniquely personal belief, his torment and his distinction: no artist of whatever past has received such a remarkable dowry with his genius, nobody but he has had to drink these utterly bitter drops with every draught of nectar that enthusiasm proffered him. He is not, as one might believe, the rejected, mistreated artist, a fugitive as it were in his own age, who acquired this belief for self-defense: success or failure among his contemporaries could not destroy or confirm it. He does not belong to this generation, whether it praise or condemn him: this is his instinctive judgment. And whether a generation will ever belong to him is also something that cannot be demonstrated to anyone who is unwilling to believe it. But even this unbeliever may well ask the question: What sort of generation must it be in which Wagner would recognize his "people" as the incarnation of all those who feel a common affliction and want to liberate themselves from it through a common art? Schiller was certainly more believing and hopeful. He did not ask how the future would look if the artist's instinctive prediction of it were right; instead, he *demanded* of the artist:

> Lift yourself on wings of daring
> High above your age's course!
> And let your mirror catch the distant light
> Of the new century's dawning![48]

11   Good sense should preserve us from the belief that someday or other mankind will discover a definitive, ideal order, and that happiness will then always shine down on such an ordered state with constant rays, like the sun of tropical lands. Wagner has nothing to do with such beliefs; he is no Utopian. If he cannot dispense with belief in the future, this simply means that he observes qualities in modern men that do not belong to the human being's immutable character and skeletal frame,

---

whom he [Carlyle] invokes in order to shorten the period of horrible universal anarchy, are destined to spring from this German people—who, thanks to their Reformation, seem to have been spared the necessity of sharing in revolution—should not seem an empty consolation."

47. The march was written by Wagner in 1871 to celebrate the German victory in the Franco-Prussian War.

48. A stanza from Schiller's poem "The Artists."

but are mutable, indeed transient, and that precisely *because of these qualities* art must be without a home among them and he himself must be the messenger and forerunner of another age. No golden age, no cloudless sky is allotted to those future generations to which his instinct directs him and whose general features can be surmised in the hieroglyphs of his art, insofar as it is possible to fathom the type of the need from the type of satisfaction. Even superhuman goodness and justice will not arch over the fields of this future like a motionless rainbow. Perhaps that generation will seem generally even worse than the present one—for it will be, in evil as in good, more *open*; indeed, it is possible that if its soul were once to express itself in free, full sound, it would shake and startle our souls, as though we were suddenly to hear the voice of some hitherto hidden evil spirit of Nature.

Or as these sentences sound in our ear: that passion is better than stoicism and hypocrisy; that honesty, even in evil, is better than losing oneself with traditional morality; that the free man can be good as well as evil, but the unfree man is a disgrace to Nature and shares in neither heavenly nor earthly consolation; finally, that everyone who wants to become free must do so by himself and that freedom falls into nobody's lap like a miraculous gift. However shrill and incredible these phrases may seem, they are the sounds of that future world, a world that *truly needs art* and can also expect true satisfaction from art. It is the language of Nature restored within man as well, precisely what I earlier called right feeling, in contrast to the wrong feeling that now prevails.

But now there are true satisfactions and release only for Nature, not for unnaturalness and wrong feeling. All that remains of the unnatural once it becomes conscious of itself is the yearning for nothingness; Nature, on the other hand, desires to be transformed through love. The former wants not to be, the latter wants to be *different*. Whoever has grasped this should bring the simple themes of Wagnerian art silently before his soul to ask himself whether it is Nature or the unnatural that with them pursues its goals, as these have just been defined.

The unstable, the desperate man finds release from his torment through the compassionate love of a woman who would rather die than be unfaithful to him: the theme of *The Flying Dutchman.* A loving woman, renouncing all her own happiness, becomes a saint, in a heavenly transformation of *amor* into *caritas,* and saves the soul of her beloved: the theme of *Tannhäuser.* The noblest and most sublime spirit descends in longing among men and does not want to be asked whence he came; when the fatal question is put, he returns under painful necessity to his higher life: the theme of *Lohengrin.* The loving soul of a woman, and also of the people, willingly takes in the new genius who bestows happiness, although the guardians of tradition and convention expel and slander him: the theme of *Die Meistersinger.* Two lovers, not knowing they are loved, believing themselves instead deeply wounded and despised, desire to drink the deadly potion from each other's hand, apparently to expiate the offense, but actually out of an unconscious urge: through death they want to be freed from all separation and pretense. The death they believe near liberates their souls and leads them into a brief and terrible happiness, as though they had really escaped the day, illusion, and life itself: the theme of *Tristan und Isolde.*

In the *Ring of the Nibelungen* the tragic hero is a god whose soul thirsts for power and who, by pursuing every path to gain it, binds himself by pacts, loses his freedom, and is entangled in the curse that lies on power. He comes to know his lack of freedom precisely in the fact that he is no longer capable of possessing the golden ring, embodiment of all earthly power and, at the same time, his supreme danger so long as his enemy possesses it. Fear of the end, of the twilight of all the gods, overcomes him, as well as the despair of being able to foresee, not to avert, this end. He needs the free, fearless man who, without the gods' counsel and support—indeed, in conflict with the divine order—himself accomplishes the deed denied to god. He does not see this man, and precisely when a fresh hope awakens, he must obey the constraint that binds him: with his own hand he must destroy the man he most loves, and punish the man who showed the purest compassion for his affliction. Now at last he is disgusted with power, which carries evil and lack of freedom in its womb; his will falters, and he himself longs for the end that menaces him from afar. And only now what he had previously most longed for happens: the free, fearless man appears. His birth is in violation of all tradition; his parents expiate the blood that has united them against the order of nature and morality: they perish, but Siegfried lives. When Wotan sees Siegfried's magnificent thriving and flourishing, the loathing in his soul mellows; he follows the hero's destiny with the eye of fatherly love and concern. He sees how Seigfried forges the sword for himself, slays the dragon, wins the ring, escapes the extremely cunning ruse, and awakens Brünnhilde. He sees how the curse dormant in the ring spares not even Siegfried, how it comes ever closer to him. He sees him, faithful even in infidelity, out of love wounding what he most loves, enveloped in the shadow and fog of guilt; but finally, pure as the sun, emerging and succumbing, inflaming whole heavens with his fiery splendor, and purifying the world of the curse—all of this is seen by the god whose sovereign spear is shattered in combat with the freest man and who had lost his power to this man, who is full of joy at his own defeat, full of loving joy and compassion for his conqueror. His eye rests on the final events with the splendor of a painful happiness; he has become free in love, free from himself.

And now ask yourselves, you men of the generation of the living: Was this composed *for you?* Have you the courage to lift your hand to the stars of this vast firmament of beauty and goodness and say: this is *our* life which Wagner has transposed among the stars?

Where among you are the men who can read in their own lives the divine image of Wotan, and who, like him, become greater and greater the more they renounce? Who among you, knowing and learning that power is evil, wants to renounce power? Where are those who, like Brünnhilde, sacrifice their knowledge out of love, and yet finally extract the supreme knowledge from their life: "Deepest suffering of grieving love opened my eyes"?[49] And where are the free, fearless men, growing and flourishing in innocent egotism, where are the Siegfrieds among you?

Whoever asks such questions, and asks in vain, must turn his eyes toward the future. And if his gaze should still discover somewhere in the distance precisely that "people" which can read its own history in the signs of Wagner's art, then he will also finally understand *what Wagner will be for this people*: something that he cannot be to us all—that is, not the seer of a future, as he might seem to us, but the interpreter and transfigurer of a past.

---

49. "Trauernder Liebe tiefstes Leid schloss die Augen mir auf." Nietzsche cites here, from act 3 of *Götterdämmerung,* a passage which Wagner discarded in the final score of the opera. See *Gesammelte Schriften,* 6:363.

Introduction
and translation
by William
Arrowsmith

We
Classicists

Introduction

Classicists often prefer to forget that Nietzsche was for ten years a classicist himself. And if they remember, they like to think that he became a philosopher because he was a failure as a philologist, or that Wilamowitz's attack on *The Birth of Tragedy* so crushed Nietzsche that he threw up his professorship in despair and spite. These, of course, are transparent superstitions, designed to cut Nietzsche down to professorial size or render harmless by ridicule the most radical critique of classical scholarship ever made from within the profession. But mostly Nietzsche has been ignored—or, as one classicist puts it, "His attack was met with the reception it deserved, dignified silence." For "dignified silence" read "calculated oblivion." Thus, Sandys' monumental three-volume *History of Classical Scholarship* (1915 edition) never once mentions Nietzsche or any of his writings. And not so long ago the press committee of an American university rejected a translation of Nietzsche's *Wir Philologen* with the argument—doubtless sound—that it would antagonize the profession. Matters have in this respect improved somewhat in the last decade. But until recently, with few exceptions, classicists have ignored or patronized Nietzsche. From this oblivion he deserves to be rescued, as he deserves to be heeded and honored. For one thing, his critique of philology is coherent, consistent, and radical. For another, it is topical. In fact, so little have the situation and character of classical scholarship changed in a century that Nietzsche's critique has both the power of prophecy and the pungency of the present.

Nietzsche's quarrel with his profession began early in his career and developed apace. His early work, done under the supervision of Ritschl at Leipzig, had been firmly and even brilliantly philological: a lengthy article on the sources of Diogenes Laertius (published serially in *Rheinisches Museum*); a paper on Simonides' *Danae* and a study of Theognis (both published in *Rheinisches Museum*); a discussion of the sources of Suidas; an essay in draft form on Democritean *spuria* intended to form part of a festschrift for Ritschl; a paper on the satire of Varro and Menippus; and, horribile dictu, the index (1868) for a twenty-four-year period of *Rheinisches Museum*. But doubts about the value and purpose of traditional philology were already troubling Nietzsche. "We cannot live for ourselves," he writes to his friend Rohde (May 4, 1868), ". . . but for our part let us see to it that the young philologists conduct themselves with the necessary skepticism, free from pedantry and overvaluation of their discipline, as true promoters of humanistic studies. *Soyons de notre siècle*—a standpoint which no one forgets more easily than the classicist-to-be."

For at least a year he toyed with the notion of quitting philology for philosophy, even roughing out a thesis on the concept of the organic since Kant. But these doubts were very briefly eclipsed when, at the age of twenty-four, he found himself appointed professor of classical philology at the University of Basel. Ritschl was responsible for this signal honor, but even "Papa" Ritschl could not keep Nietzsche from being skeptical about philology and philologists. Writing to Rohde on October 20, 1868, Nietzsche affectionately described Ritschl as a "professional pander" whose desire was "to hold us in the toils of Madame Philology. I have a surprising desire in the essay I have just written *in honorem Ritscheli* to tell the philologists a number of bitter truths." To his friend Deussen he wrote (October 20, 1868): "If I were to speak mythologically, I should view Philology as an abortion begotten on the Goddess Philosophy by an idiot or a cretin." Still later that same year (November 20), he wrote prophetically to Rohde: "Now that I see once more the swarming breed of classicists at close range—so that I must daily observe all the mole-like efforts, the full cheek-pouches and the blind eyes, the joy over the captured worm and the utter indifference to the true and highest problems of life—it seems even clearer to me that we two, if we remain uncompromisingly loyal to our genius, will not proceed along life's path without being struck at and thwarted in many ways." Finally, in a letter to Gersdorff (April 13, 1869), he moves toward that positive concept of humanistic education which was to occupy his mind for the duration of his professorship at Basel: "To be a philistine, a man of the crowd—may Zeus and the Muses preserve me from that! . . . To infuse my discipline with fresh blood, to convey to my audience that Schopenhauer-like seriousness which is stamped on the brow of the high-minded man—this is my wish, my dearest hope. I want to be something more than a taskmaster to virtuous little philologists: the production of teachers of the present, the care for the growing brood that is coming, all this is before my mind."

Nietzsche's published views kept close pace with his private opinions of his profession. In 1869 he delivered his inaugural lecture at Basel, *Homer und die klassische Philologie* (Homer and classical philology), in which his distrust of philology was, for the sake of tact and perhaps persuasion, put disarmingly as a professional philologist's skeptical defense of philology. This lecture was immediately followed by a much more drastic critique, a series of public lectures entitled *Über die Zukunft unserer Bildungs-Anstalten* (On the future of our educational institutions), in which the gauntlet is boldly thrown down. He said:

> I should like to take by the hand every talented or untalented man who feels a certain professional inclination pushing him toward classical studies, and lecture him as follows: "Young sir, do you know what

perils threaten you, with your little store of school learning, before you become a man in the full sense of the word? Are you aware that, according to Aristotle, it is not a tragic death to be slain by a statue? Does this puzzle you? Realize, then, that for centuries classicists have been trying, with ever-failing strength, to re-erect the fallen statue of Greek antiquity, but unsuccessfully; for it is a colossus around which modern men crawl like pygmies. The leverage of the collective representatives of modern culture is enlisted for the purpose; but no sooner is the great column raised from the ground than it collapses again, crushing beneath its mass the luckless creatures below. This might be tolerated, for everybody must die in one way or another; but who can insure that the statue itself will not be destroyed during all these attempts? The classicists are being crushed by the Greeks—well, perhaps we can endure this—but antiquity itself is threatened with destruction by these self-same classicists . . . !"

As for Nietzsche himself, he had come to the crux of his career. On February 15, 1870, he wrote to Rohde: "My love for Greek antiquity keeps on growing; there is no better way of approaching it than that of tirelessly shaping one's own small person. The stage I have reached in the most shameful confession of my own ignorance. The philologist's existence in any critical task whatsoever, but a thousand miles away from the Greek experience, is becoming more and more impossible for me. I doubt I will ever be able to become a true philologist. The unfortunate thing is that I have no model and I run the risk of going mad at my own hands." Two months later he was busily constructing his own "model," a radical revaluation of the classics, to be performed without fear of his profession, without (he hoped) modern preconceptions of Christian prejudices. "I have the best hopes for my own philology," he wrote to Rohde (March 30, 1870), "only I must allow myself several years' time. I am approaching a unified perception of Greek antiquity, step by step and with a timid amazement." A month later (April 30, 1870) he wrote to Rohde again: "When I have finished several minor tasks (on old topics), I want to gather my strength for a book for which new ideas keep coming to me. I am afraid that it will not make a scholarly impression, but how can I oppose my own nature? The period of scandal is beginning for me, after a period in which I aroused a certain benevolence because I was wearing the old, familiar slippers. Theme and title of the future book: Socrates and instinct."

The following year (1871) Nietzsche published the book he had been gestating: *The Birth of Tragedy from the Spirit of Music.* The thesis was a bold one, far too bold for his professional colleagues, who maintained, as he had expected, an ominous silence. Then, a year later, the blow fell—a pamphlet entitled *Zukunftphilologie!* by the young philologist Ulrich von Wilamowitz-

Moellendorff, written with all the passion of outraged *Berliner Wissenschaft* ("It smells of Berlin in everything," wrote Nietzsche) and a profound professional resentment of Nietzsche's "treachery." As to the worth of Wilamowitz's polemic, opinions will differ. Classicists, of course, have almost unanimously preferred to believe that Wilamowitz—who caught Nietzsche in several factual errors—had the better of it. But in point of fact none of Wilamowitz's arguments disproves or even seriously damages Nietzsche's thesis; for the notion that a thesis (or interpretation, translation, and so on) is only as good as its author's philological expertise—the *ad scientiam* argument—is a self-serving fallacy. A sorites of rigorous argument may be relevant to strict philological work (such as the dating of a play), but a thesis like Nietzsche's—a large, intuitive, esthetic insight, addressed finally to esthetic *experience*—cannot be defeated by showing errors of fact in the argument. And to suppose that it could be is the kind of crude category-mistake to which philologists, insofar as they are primarily technicians, are professionally susceptible.

But it is a revealing mistake, the typical *error philologicus*, recurrent in classicists' shoptalk or gossip or the review sections of most classical journals. Stripped to the bone, it is nothing more than the barely suppressed premise that philological method and knowledge of the original languages are in every case the decisive criteria. These may be decisive for philological work as such, but the unreflective readiness with which philologists extend them to areas where they do *not* apply illuminates some of the past and present difficulties of the profession. The trouble is not philology itself (who could quarrel with those who think it important to have one's facts straight and to know Greek and Latin?) but that the pretensions of philologists are often grotesquely exaggerated. Thus, literary discussion, translation, and esthetics are, in classical studies at least, constantly troubled by *mis*application or *over*application of philological principles. Translation, for instance, still suffers from the hard-nosed philological belief that the virtue of a good translation, regardless of whether it is "literary" or merely a scholarly "trot," is finally accuracy, fidelity. Philologists differ, of course, in the latitude they allow translators, and it may be that they are more permissive these days. But the eagerness with which scholarly reviewers assume that any departure from the text argues that the translator's Greek or Latin is deficient—the possibility of a motivated departure, for good and even sufficient reason, seems never to suggest itself—indicates that the latitude is rather less than scholars claim. In any case, what needs pointing out is that this philological theory of translation-as-fidelity-to-the-text is in fact very late, a product of the same age and the same "scientific" principles that created Germanic philology. It begins with Bentley, who infected the Germans and intimidated the others. Augustan Rome and Elizabethan England, both great ages of translation, would have found such a theory absurd, and rightly so. There are more important things than accuracy—there is life, for instance. Only philologists could have built their distinctive professional virtue—"objective" accuracy—into a theory of translation. And the philological view of translation has lasted, not because it is commonsensical, but because philologists have largely succeeded in becoming the policemen of their own theory. In an age of specialization, the specialist usually frightens off the non-specialists and "amateurs." And too often this has meant not only the routing of imaginative intelligence but a real diminution in the life of the classical texts.

Finally, it is only confusion or arrogance about the limits of philological method that could induce scholars and laymen alike to believe that the kind of argument that proved the Donation of Constantine was a forgery also proved that *The Birth of Tragedy* was a failure. The same confusion allows philologists to claim that they "welcome" literary criticism in classical studies; but when it comes to graduate studies, promotions, research, and hiring, it is clear that what still counts in most places is philology. *In petto*, most professional scholars believe that literary criticism is only genteel philology anyway. The problem for the profession is not how to make room for criticism, but rather how to liberate philology from its claim to be coextensive with classical studies and from its naive faith that discipline and method can solve any problem worth solving.

But the consequence of this naiveté is, for classical studies, unfortunate. Not only is method pressed to the point where it finally begins to defeat thought and complexity, but the philologist, by dismissing literary insight as methodically unsound, cuts himself off from the completion of his own purpose and skills. For supposedly philology aims at literary understanding. Certainly insights such as those which pile up triumphantly throughout *The Birth of Tragedy* (even if we acknowledge that Socrates is a straw man, that Nietzsche misunderstands Euripides, that Wagner is very doubtfully classical, and so on) are too precious and rare to be ignored by a profession notoriously long on method and sadly short on insight.

A single example may illustrate the point. In his attack Wilamowitz sharply rapped Nietzsche for exaggerating the antiquity of the Greeks and failing to understand the true lateness of Homer—the fashionable scholarly consensus in Germany at the time was that Homer was late. Commenting on Wilamowitz's argument in a letter to Rohde (July 16, 1872), Nietzsche remarked: "The soft thesis of the Homeric world as a youthful world has begun to irritate me. *In the sense* in which it is expounded, it is false. That an enormous struggle—savage, of gloomy roughness and cruelty—precedes it; that Homer is, as it were, a conqueror at the close of this long and desolate period—this is for me one of my firmest convictions. *The Greeks are much more ancient than anyone thinks.* One can talk about springtime, provided one puts the winter before the spring. But this world of purity and beauty certainly didn't fall from the skies." Time and recent scholarship have, of course, vindicated not Wilamowitz, but Nietzsche, the man who "arrogantly" dared to defy the scholarly consensus of his time for the simple reason that it did not make literary or cultural sense to him. And though for factual accuracy Wilamowitz may take the prize, what is instructive about Nietzsche (or Goethe or Matthew Arnold or Leopardi) is that his insight— literary, philosophical, and intuitive in nature—is, in the big things, importantly accurate. Philologists, in short, should cultivate modesty, for their skills are modest skills, and must always be supplemented by a larger vision. Besides, as Nietzsche himself observed, "The errors of great men are venerable because they are more fruitful than the truths of little men."

So far as Nietzsche was concerned, Wilamowitz's pamphlet was merely the declaration of war, and it was in fact shortly followed by practical sanctions imposed by the philologists against the offender. "The Establishment has condemned me to death," Nietzsche wrote to Rohde (July 7, 1872), "but that it is strong enough to kill—of this I have my doubts." The Establishment made an attempt, however—a subtle whispering campaign, at Basel and elsewhere, which had the effect of frightening off Nietzsche's few students and bearing out Nietzsche's contention that timid careerism was the dominant trait of classical scholarship in his time. His ordinary class at Basel the following autumn simply withered away, and not even Rohde's strong counterattack on Wilamowitz (*Afterphilologie*, October 1872) succeeded in removing the ban of ostracism. Undisturbed, Nietzsche threw himself into the completion of his extremely ambitious *Unmodern Observations*, whose thirteen books were intended to inaugurate, under the aegis of Schopenhauer, Wagner, and the classics, a renaissance of German culture. Above all this renaissance was to be based upon a new, reformed classical humanism, which in turn would be based upon a thorough revaluation (often a transvaluation, at least in Nietzsche's practice) of antiquity, and, finally, a concerted effort to supersede or surpass classical culture. If for Nietzsche the classical world, and the Greek world in particular, was par excellence man's supreme cultural achievement to date—it had been an age of both *genius* and *liberation*, for Nietzsche the essentials of any great human culture—then the only conceivable curriculum of modern education must be a vigorous and lively study of classical culture. But by "vigorous" and "lively" Nietzsche meant something very different from *Philologie* as practiced in the German universities of his time. Indeed, traditional philology— with its worship of the "objective" fact, its naive faith in the "accumulation of data," its subservience to official Christian culture, and its obvious lack of any great ideal or love—not only hindered, but directly blocked any lively reform of education or any new insight into the Greeks. As such, it was an enemy of education and, since for Nietzsche education meant care for the future of man, it was the enemy of man. What education required was both the example and the challenge of a great past, and anything that veiled or obscured that past also obscured man's model and challenge. What was needed was, first, an *imitation* of the classics—to be imitated as a young artist imitates his great predecessor—and then an attempt to *surpass*, to *overcome* the past. Cultures, like men, could realize and fulfill themselves only by transcending their past taken at its highest peak. Education bared the past, and thereby laid bare the height of the future.

Culture was, or should be, liberation. For Nietzsche, active culture is closely linked to struggle, and intellectual freedom lies precisely in the struggle to achieve what one does *not* possess but which one *needs*, to create future institutions for what does not yet exist. This struggle requires but also releases the heroic virtues: courage, pugnacity, resourcefulness, good cheer. Once institutions were created, they necessarily became illiberal, making men *unfree*, thwarting and smothering the instincts that had originally created them. Classical education—the developed German system of professorships, universities, curriculum, and scholarship which Nietzsche calls Philologie—was precisely such an illiberal institution. Still, however decadent philology had become, it had begun as an instrument of freedom, liberating Renaissance man from medieval theology and everything which that implied. Textual criticism, for instance, once had a vital purpose: to know *for freedom's sake* precisely what a text did and did not say, which text was corrupt and which was not. But institutionalized, and its original lively motive replaced by technical virtuosity flourishing ostensibly in the service of truth but actually for its own sake, it had withered into an illiberal and largely functionless "discipline." As for classical philology as a whole, the situation was just the same, and nothing more vividly dramatized the death that had overtaken it than the great disparity visible at every level—between the classics and the classicists, between the Greeks with their genius and their freedom as men, and the staid, subservient respectability of professional philology. What mattered to Nietzsche was the classics, not philology, and the classics mattered only because they represented human life at its highest peak. In order that life should be served, it was therefore crucial that the classics should survive in a manner worthy of them, that is, both as a model and a challenge to the present. What was needed therefore was a worthy *new* philology (or *Zukunftphilologie*, as Wilamowitz contemptuously called it) which would revalue the ancient world as the first, critical step toward surpassing it. In the struggle to surpass a great past, to create fresh cultural institutions, lay freedom. The crucial thing was the drive to release the instincts of men committed to found fresh institutions worthy of their love, and an incarnation of their hunger for freedom as men.

To the passionate presentation of these views Nietzsche devoted the last few years of his professorship at Basel: in *Schopenhauer as Educator* (1874); in *We Classicists* (1874–75); in *Wagner in Bayreuth* (1875–76); in his letters to his friends, and, doubtless, to his few remaining students. But for Nietzsche these were depressing and unhappy years. He was increasingly tormented by acute physical illness, which forced him to take long convalescent leaves; then came the critical break with Wagner, a break which left Nietzsche emotionally scarred and which also deprived the still unfinished *Unmodern Observations* of much of its vital urgency. And, gradually, he seems to have become convinced either that the German university and German philology could not be reformed from within, or that his severe illness disqualified him for the task. In 1879 he resigned his professorship for good and shortly afterward retired to that solitary meditation that eventually made him the German Zarathustra. To his old bitter quarrel with his profession Nietzsche seldom alluded later, but there is one revealing account in *Thus Spoke Zarathustra* (part 2, "The Scholars") in which he tells how a sheep (Wilamowitz) consumed Zarathustra's wreath of scholarly ivy:

> As I lay asleep, a sheep ate of the ivy wreath of my brow—ate and said, "Zarathustra is no longer a scholar." Said it and strutted away proudly. A child told it to me.
>
> I like to lie here where the children play, beside the broken wall, among thistles and red poppies. I am still a scholar to the children, and also to the thistles and red poppies. They are innocent even in their malice. But to the sheep I am no longer a scholar; thus my lot decrees it—bless it!
>
> For this is the truth: I have moved from the house of the scholars and I even slammed the door behind me. My soul sat hungry at their table too long; I am not, like them, trained to pursue knowledge, as if it were nut-cracking. I love freedom and the air over the fresh earth; I would rather sleep on oxhides than on their decorums and respectabilities. . . .
>
> If you seize them with your hands they raise a cloud of dust like flour bags, involuntarily; but who could guess that their dust comes from grain and from the yellow delight of the summer fields? When they pose as wise, their little epigrams and truths chill me: their wisdom often has an odor as though it came from the swamps. . . . They are skillful and have clever fingers: why would my simplicity want to be near their multiplicity? All threading and knotting and weaving their fingers understand: thus they knit the socks of the spirit.
>
> They are good clocks, but take care to wind them correctly! Then they indicate the hour without fail and make a modest noise. They work like mills and like stamps: throw down your seed-corn to them and they will know how to grind it small and reduce it to white dust.
>
> They watch each other closely and mistrustfully. Inventive in petty cleverness, they wait for those whose knowledge walks on lame feet: like spiders they wait. . . .

We are alien to each other and their virtues are even more distasteful to me than their falseness and their loaded dice. And when I lived with them, I lived above them. That is why they developed a grudge against me. They did not want to hear how someone was living over their heads; and so they put wood and earth and filth between me and their heads. Thus they muffled the sounds of my steps: and so far I have been heard least well by the most scholarly. Between themselves and me they laid all human faults and weaknesses: "false ceilings" they call them in their houses. And yet I live over their heads with my thoughts; and even if I wanted to walk upon my own mistakes, I would still be over their heads.

An extremely perceptive and valuable book could, and should, be made from Nietzsche's occasional writings on the classics and his own profession. This would include, not the early philological work of his student days, which is of minor interest and can be left to the decent obscurity of *Rheinisches Museum,* but the mature work of his professorial years (1869–79): the still untranslated lectures on Greek drama and other classical subjects; the very interesting sketch, *Einleitung in das Studium der klassischen Philologie* (1871); the inaugural lecture at Basel; *Homers Wettkampf;* the pertinent sections of *Über die Zukunft unserer Bildungs-Anstalten;* Nietzsche's working notes for a book on the classical profession, *Wir Philologen; Die Geburt der Tragödie* (which should be printed together with Wilamowitz's attack on Nietzsche and Rohde's counterattack on Wilamowitz); and *Die Philosophie im tragischen Zeitalter der Griechen.* These works in turn should be backed by a generous selection of the letters (especially those to Rohde, Gersdorff, and Burckhardt). But the heart of the collection would surely be the brilliant aphorisms and notes on classical subjects scattered everywhere throughout the Nietzschean corpus, but particularly concentrated in *Menschliches, Allzumenschliches, Morgenröte, Die fröhliche Wissenschaft,* and *Götzendämmerung.*

Nietzsche's preferred and characteristic mode of viewing the classics was a form of personal intuition which he called "backward inference" and for which he claimed a special talent. "If there is anything," he wrote, "in which I am ahead of all psychologists, it is that my eye is sharper for that most difficult and captious kind of *backward inference* in which the most mistakes are made: the backward inference from the work to the maker, from the deed to the doer, from the ideal to him who *needs* it, from every way of thinking and valuing to the *want* that prompts it" (*NAW,* "We Antipodes"). Thus, in Greek culture of the classical period, with its overwhelming emphasis upon moral order and control, upon coherence and simplicity and unity, Nietzsche saw the unmistakable creation of a people who wanted those virtues precisely because they did *not* have them. *Sophrosyne* was the desiderated virtue of a culture prone to every kind of excess, to *hybris* in behavior and art alike, just as modern culture, with its characteristic romantic disorder and its *simulated* Dionysiac vitalism, was for Nietzsche the obvious work of a society in which the instincts had been sacrificed to the needs of religious, moral, and political order. How could the stupendous world of glittering Apollonian order manifest in Greek art be anything but the willful triumph over itself of a turbulent and passionate people?

But it was not merely a matter of "backward inference." There was also a tangible difference in cultural courage and talent. Thus, Nietzsche tended to see in classical Greek culture, especially that of the sixth century BC, both a real hunger for freedom and a genius for enlarging it which made that culture the measure of modern decadence and the greatest challenge to modern man. As heirs of a Christian tradition which had made freedom of body and spirit impossible by creating *bad conscience*, and which prevented genius (always selfish and aggressive in origin, whatever gentle transformations it later underwent) by perverting egotism, modern men needed all they could get of their classical heritage. But they needed to get it neat, not adulterated by a moralizing, Christian education and a timorous philology that served not the truly subversive cause of the classics, but the oppressive, official forces of church and state. And for this reason Nietzsche almost everywhere tended to report, and then to emphasize for good measure, what in classical culture was undeniably *there* and what philologists persistently refused to see: vulgarity, energy, good cheer and good conscience, turbulence and suffering, courage, health of instinct, aggressiveness of spirit. It is this double vision—this classicist's perception, exacerbated and sharpened by the modern man's passionate habit of contrasting classical culture with his own in order to confer the genius and freedom of the past upon the future—that makes Nietzsche's perceptions valuable and unique. He sees as much as he does because he everywhere insists, surely rightly, that the only criterion of knowledge, of value, is its usefulness for life, *our* life.

Thus, it is not Thucydides' *accuracy* that takes Nietzsche's eye, but his saving *realism*, that hard-headed shrewdness about political behavior and human nature that make him important for life and not merely for Greek history. In Epicurus he sees not the customary doctrine of escapism, but an idyllic and philosophical heroism which is typically Greek because based upon a sense of necessary, rather than superfluous, pleasure, upon deliberate economy in appetite and a civilized control of the passions. The good Epicurean is, in some respects at least, a Nietzschean artist, controlling, in firm human tension, Dionysiac experience with Apollonian form. In Pompeii and the ancient feeling for festival Nietzsche observes the vulgarity that links it with Italian opera, a vulgarity with nothing unwholesome about it because it derives from man's nature and in its joyful exuberance totally lacks a tainting sense of shame. Everywhere the good competitive spirit (not war, nor class conflict, nor the Nazi perversions of Nietzschean *eris*) seizes his heart, not because he regards strife as intrinsically valuable, but because it is ineradicably rooted in human nature and because rivalry and emulation (*aemulatio*) are the sources of cultural striving and individual self-mastery. Once competition is destroyed (as Christian ethics destroyed the classical sense of competition in order to found a new altruistic rivalry), the agonistic values are also destroyed, with appalling results for man.

In art Nietzsche sees convention as the crucial limitation against which the artist competes, the bond or chain that makes his dance a spectacle of bravery and cunning. As for the Christians, if they perverted the classical world, they had pagan precedents, especially Plato, in so doing; but even in the case of the Christians, Nietzsche characteristically sees that Christian control over the passions is preferable to the decadence of Juvenal's world, sunk in torpor and self-loathing. To generations of artists and tourists who report the melancholy of Roman ruins, Nietzsche counters with the melancholy of "eternal buildings" which Christians must have felt in the face of Rome's dreary secular eternity, and which set them to transfiguring and surpassing the old in their new way. Point for point, it seems, Nietzsche turns the old clichés inside out, purposely challenging the scholarly views to yield at last something like a sense of the greatness of the classical past. If the scholars are right, Nietzsche seems to be asking, how in the world can all that ancient brilliance be explained? Against the scholar who, no less than the ordinary man, tends to live uncritically, tacitly accepting the prejudices and assumptions of his own time and culture as though they were self-evident and timelessly human, Nietzsche counterposes a classical world which is both his inference from known facts and an implicit criticism of his own culture. Doubtless it was this criticism of his own culture that at bottom motivated him, but his vision of the classical world cannot be written off simply because it derives from his quarrel with his own age. Most classicists study the ancient world without ever really recognizing their own cultural conditioning. They are historians of a world which they know only from their books, and this bookishness prevents them from sharpening their sense of their own culture, with which they seldom have any real quarrel except as classicists—*laudatores temporis acti* to such a degree that they have often written off present and future altogether. With Nietzsche it was different, and this difference gave him a special access to the past.

To scholars, however, Nietzsche's revaluation of the classics has often seemed a merely peevish inversion of that modern culture he despised. There is some small truth in this. Certainly "backward inference" is susceptible of abuse and, consistently applied, produces insights that are ingenious but bizarre; at other times Nietzsche seems to be mythologizing Greek experience simply in order to provide ideal standards from which to measure modern lapses. But these are the failures characteristic of his judgment and insight, just as his excesses are to some degree the consequence of his polemic against professional philology. But Nietzsche's passion, it needs to be said, was not that of wounded vanity or pique, but of frustrated mission. More than anything he wanted to refresh classical experience in living men, above all in the classicist, and thereby to invigorate contemporary culture. The chief obstacle was the philology of his time, which, despite its claim to scientific dispassion, was in fact disfigured by most of the received ideas of the age. It was Nietzsche's conviction that, by removing the crippling and crudifying accretions of bourgeois idealism, Christian values, and romanticism on the classics, the classics could once again be seen for what they were: revolutionary documents of unmistakable genius which, honestly confronted, must have a truly regenerative effect upon the individual and his culture.

But mere removal of the patina was not enough. Whatever Greek culture was, it was not merely *non*bourgeois and *non*-Christian, but generically distinct. What this meant for Nietzsche was that the job of classical scholarship was to construct something like a general field theory that would unify the complex features of Hellenic experience by taking account of its typical achievements, but above all of its genius and freedom. And what Greek culture as a whole suggested to Nietzsche was precisely what was so manifestly lacking in the fragmented, multiform, confused texture of modern life—a *single style*, an unmistakable animating coherence whose very existence among the Greeks implied that a general field theory was possible. The description and appraisal of this cultural style of Greek antiquity was, to Nietzsche's mind, the exhilarating task of classical scholarship—the only task that could redeem a profession which had disgraced itself and betrayed the classics by turning its back on the present and refusing to speak to living men. In the reappraisal of the past, in the work of redefining past greatness, classical scholarship, he hoped, might take the contagion of greatness, emulating instead of merely emending its authors, and recovering its lost relation to life. Once the classical world had been revalued, the failure and the successes (above all, the astonishing success in the physical sciences) of the contemporary world could be assessed, and a general renewal of modern culture carried out by that society of collaborating (and competing) men of genius which Nietzsche, in his professorial period, hoped to create. "I dream," he wrote (*WC*, 194), "of a fellowship of men who are uncompromising, unindulgent, and want to be called 'Destroyers.' They apply the standard of their criticism to everything and sacrifice themselves to Truth. . . . We don't want to build prematurely. We don't know whether we can ever build, or whether the best thing might be not to build at all." Nietzsche's "destroyers" are not, of course, a foreshadowing of Nazi bookburners (as the Nietzsche myth has it), but those conspirators of genius, those unmodern men, who, by surpassing the classics, become destroyers of the intolerable culture of the present, and creators of the future.

Doubtless all very visionary: who but a visionary would have dreamed of asking classicists to live classically or proposing that the present should compete with the past? Predictably Nietzsche's appeal fell on deaf ears; even his best friend Rohde was unconvinced, and elsewhere in the profession his program aroused nothing but scorn ("Zukunftphilologie!" sneered Wilamowitz). With the drastic deterioration in his health and his resignation from his Basel professorship in 1879, Nietzsche's plans for professional and institutional reform collapsed completely, leaving him to work out his fate on his own. This new loneliness, however, was as much a matter of deliberate choice on Nietzsche's part as the consequence of events, and behind the choice lies his recognition that loneliness freed him and liberated his personal genius by imposing upon him, in isolation and physical suffering, the essential conditions of classical heroism. He chose, that is, as a convalescent duty, to enact in person his own counsels to his profession: to live classically, to pay for his convictions with his life, and, like a Sophoclean hero, to become his own fate. The lonely convalescent exile in Sils Maria and elsewhere which his body exacted of him accorded with his own will to realize himself, and it is on the experience of these years that Nietzsche drew for his profound commitment to *amor fati,* the loyalty to an inward daimon which is synonymous with a sense of a personal fate. A vocation for Sophoclean heroism is, of course, not now easily sustained without false heroics or self-congratulation, but Nietzsche chose to suffer alone, nailed to his mountainside at Sils Maria, and this voluntary, meditative exile was both climax and coda, in action, to his unfinished *Unzeitgemässe Betrachtungen,* his most unmodern meditation. Where persuasion, polemic, and diatribe had failed, example might succeed; there was nothing else left. And from 1879 on Nietzsche's whole life was a heroic attempt to put his vision into personal practice, to realize his daimon by becoming his own Overman and surpassing the classics by the power of his example and the originality and beauty of his thought.

In our time no nobler homage has been paid by genius to the classics than this, and a fully moral and philosophical appraisal of their molding influence in Nietzsche and, through him, on the life of the twentieth century, is woefully overdue. The *saturation,* for instance, of the early Nietzsche's mind in the poetry and thought of archaic Greece is crucial to the understanding of the late Nietzsche's tragic metaphysics. Thus, his philosophy is above all, like that of the pre-Socratics, a *teaching,* the unfolding thought of a self-mastering nature enacting its daimonic text: "Become the thing you are!" Whatever the truth of the Nietzsche now affirmed by the literary theorists, the older Nietzsche, the persisting humanist and educator, cannot, I believe, be expunged or even displaced. Early and late, Nietzsche extols human greatness and the chrysalis or entelechy from which, not without struggle, it emerges; his canonical texts are passionately privileged; his *trans-valuations* are anything but value-free. Archaic and classical are, in Nietzsche's thought, not to be superseded but rather fulfilled. And of all modern philosophers, *pace* Heidegger, it is Nietzsche in whom the ancients are most fully realized. Scratch Zarathustra, and one comes up against his avatar—Prometheus or Oedipus, even Philoctetes. Pre-Socratic doctrines of flux, of love and strife, are renewed, recreated, in the "teaching" of the Eternal Recurrence. What the Greeks meant by sophrosyne in the largest sense is transformed by Nietzsche into an esthetic that is also, like the Greek esthetic, a morality: Dionysus and Apollo fused. But the supreme example of classical influence, of true emulation, is Nietzsche's own life, spent in conscious competition with the classical, sealed by suffering, and lived in the determination to make of himself "an exemplary destiny."

We Classicists

I[1]

[1]
Romundt, January 9: Must complete the draft of it by March 9 or 10; by April 10 at the latest.[2]

[2][3]
Passage on Faust
Hölderlin
Finish Empedocles

[3][4]

1874	4	5	Philologist. Wagner.
1876	6		Press.
1877	7	8	Religion. School.

1. The only full German text of Nietzsche's notes and jottings for this uncompleted work is in *NWKG*. Nietzsche's notes for his projected *Wir Philologen* are contained in eight notebooks dating from 1875, winter to the end of the summer.

2. H. Romundt, friend of Nietzsche and Privatdozent in philosophy at the University of Basel. He shared living quarters with Nietzsche and Overbeck in what they called their *Baumannshöhle* house in Basel. Presumably, Romundt had promised Nietzsche to deliver a certain draft—the subject is not known—by early spring. In this same period, it should be added, Romundt underwent a religious crisis involving his conversion to Roman Catholicism, which both Nietzsche and Overbeck viewed with dismay as a philosophical defection.

3. Memo presumably relating to various projects—for reading or writing—of which nothing else is known. Empedocles is conspicuously absent from the philosophers discussed in *Philosophy in the Tragic Age of the Greeks*; but the pointedly unanswered question that closes the third section of *SE* shows that Empedocles was much on Nietzsche's mind during this period when he was trying to clarify his relationship to Schopenhauer in terms of the pre-Socratics, above all Heraclitus, Empedocles, Parmenides, Anaxagoras, and Democritus.

4. Like the following entry, this contains one of a number of Nietzsche's outlines for the complete series of *Unmodern Observations*. The first three titles consisted of the essays already published at this time (*DS, HSDL, SE*). The fact that the series, at least in this outline, was to consist of thirteen essays is, one might infer, indicative of Nietzsche's interest in challenging and confronting Christianity and the Christian values, unconscious or unexamined, underlying contemporary behavior. In European culture the ominousness of the number thirteen, for instance, is, for Nietzsche, a superstition obviously deriving from the Last Supper (Christ and his twelve disciples)—and therefore a religious survival which Nietzsche's essentially pagan renaissance must, if possible, deny and destroy.

1878   9   10   Socialism. State.
1879   11–12   My plan. Nature.
1880   13   Road of liberation.

[4]
Prelude. The Culture-philistine.
  1. History.
  2. Philosophy.
  3. Antiquity.
  4. Art.
  5. Religion.   1876 Easter.   April, May, June
  6. School.   July, August, September
  7. Press.   October, November, December
  8. State.   1877   January, February, March
  9. Society.   April, May, June
  10. Man as I.   July, August, September
  11. Nature.   October, November, December
  12. Road of Liberation.   1878   January, February, March

Easter 1869–Easter 1878. Seven years of university.
Easter 1876–Easter 1878. 800 pages in 24 months,
24:800 | 33, that is, a page a day, one "Unmodern" every three
   72 | months.
At age 33 I will have finished the "Unmoderns."[5]

[5]
Age 13–19 at Schulpforta
Age 19–24 at Bonn and Leipzig
Age 24–31 at Basel
Age 31–33   ?[6]

II[7]

[1]
The conch is rounded inside, rough on the outside. Blow it, and it booms.

5. Already, even here in the notebooks of Nietzsche's professorial period, a hint of the emerging Antichrist, tangible in that "at age thirty-three" as well as the "Easter" dating of Nietzsche's autobiographical projection.
6. Still another hint of Nietzsche's gestating decision to abandon his academic career as professor of philology at Basel and devote himself to philosophy. In point of fact, largely because of his mother's anxiety about his stipend, Nietzsche delayed his resignation for another three years, until May 1879.
7. Archive notebook: U II 8a. To March 1875. See *NWKG*, 1:87–89.

Then, for the first time, it gets the respect it deserves.

(*Ind. Spräche*, ed. Böthlingk, I, 335)[8]

An ugly-looking wind instrument: first you have to blow it.

[2]
Themata.
Theory of the ridiculous. Collected examples.
Theory of the horrible. With collected examples.
Description of my musical experience with regard to Wagner.
The question in music.

A large notebook to be set up for daily ideas, experience, projects, etc.—
in which scholarly insights can be briefly entered. All literary projects to be
put aside. *Mihi scribere.*[9]

[3]
We Classicists
Tentative Outline
1. Origin of the contemporary philologist.
2. The contemporary philologist and the Greeks.
3. Consequences for nonphilologists.
4. Hints about the Greeks.
5. The future education of the philologist.

8. Quotation in Gersdorff's handwriting at the beginning of the notebook. The source
is a collection of Indian texts by Otto Böthlingk, *Indische Spräche: Sanskrit und Deutsch*
(Petersburg, 1870–73).
9. "To write for myself." For Nietzsche a central and enduring maxim, in fact, a life-
text. Cf. *Mixed Maxims* (1879), 167: "*Sibi scribere.* The sensible author writes for no other
posterity than his own, that is for his age, in order then to be able to have more joy. . . ."
The maxim was adapted from V. Roses, ed., *Aristotle Pseudepigraphus* (Leipzig, 1863),
717: *sibi quisque scribit.* Nietzsche frequently cited this passage; cf. H. J. Mette, *Die un-
vollendet gebliebene historisch-kritische Gesamtausgabe der Werke Nietzsches* (Munich, 1938–
42), 4:599.
Compare, for instance, Emerson's "Spiritual Laws" in *Essays: First Series*: "The effect
of any writing on the public mind is mathematically measurable by the depth of
thought. . . . The way to speak and write what shall not go out of fashion is to speak and
write sincerely. . . . He that writes to himself writes to an eternal public. . . . 'No book,'
said Bentley, 'was ever written down by any but itself.'" Nietzsche read this essay—along
with "Circles"—in the translation by G. Fabricius (Hanover, 1858) and made jottings in
his student years. In July 1882 he wrote to his friend Rohde: "And if today I'm above
everything, with the joyful mind of a conqueror and full of new and difficult projects . . .
nobody can blame me for thinking well of my own medical specific. *Mihi ipsi scripsi*: this
is always what counts; and in this way everyone should do his best for himself and in his
own way; this is my morality, the only morality I still possess."

6. Greeks and Romans—and Christianity. Wolf's[10] dissociation.

Better:

a. The preference for the Greeks.
b. Origin of the contemporary philologue.
c. Their effect on nonphilologists.
d. Their stand on the Greeks as they actually were.
e. Future matters.

[4]

Perhaps cite against the enemies of antiquity Cicero's remark (*In Pison.* 30): *Quid, te, asine, litteras doceam? Non opus est verbis, sed fustibus.*[11]

10. Friedrich August Wolf (1759–1824), one of the very greatest of German classical scholars and, in effect, the founder of classical philology as a "scientific" (*wissenschaftlich*) discipline. Educated at Göttingen, he successfully elected philology as his field—though until then philology had not been academically recognized as a discipline. In 1782 he published an edition of Plato's *Symposium*, and consequently won the chair of philosophy and pedagogic at the University of Halle. There Wolf carried out his educational reforms, establishing philology as a rigorous discipline—for classical studies and education generally a momentous event, according to Nietzsche (see *WC*, 3.2). Following the French victory at Jena and the closing of Halle, Wolf moved to Berlin, where he spent the remainder of his life in productive, though hardly contented, forced retirement. His best-known work is his celebrated *Prolegomena to Homer* (1795), a work whose main tenets— the crucial importance of oral tradition, the reduction of the poems to written form, multiple authorship—pose the essential questions even now. His most far-reaching work, however, was *Darstellung der Altertumswissenschaft* (Representation of antiquity), published in 1807.

As the numerous citations of Wolf's *Kleine Schriften* (Minor writings) in *WC* attest, Nietzsche regarded Wolf with enormous respect and admiration. "Where," he asks in the final section of *SE*, "has the spirit of Friedrich August Wolf vanished? Wolf, of whom Franz Passow could say that he seemed a genuine patriot, a truly human spirit, with the sort of power that could set a continent in ferment and in flames?" Impressive praise, given Nietzsche's normally dismissive or downright contemptuous attitude toward his own profession and most of its luminaries. But for good reason. Wolf, after all, was a pioneer; he had established a great discipline in the teeth of opposition from vested academic interests, thereby revolutionizing both education and classical studies (as Nietzsche in these years yearned to do); above all he was a teacher, and plainly (according to Goethe) a great one; and finally he was, like Nietzsche, committed, in the most intense and self-demanding way, to the ideal of a culture—"a purely human education"— founded on a vigorous, a *living*, Hellenism. In Mark Pattison's words, Wolf was devoted to "an elevation of all the powers of the mind and soul to a beautiful harmony of inner and outer man."

By Wolf's "dissociation," Nietzsche appears to be referring to Wolf's insistence that philology must be separated from theology, and that Hellenism cannot be an object of rigorous and perceptive scrutiny if that scrutiny is based upon essentially Christian purposes and preconceptions.

11. "How shall I teach you literature, ass? It isn't words that are needed, but blows." The passage is cited by Friedrich August Wolf, *Kleine Schriften* (Halle, 1869), 1046.

[5]

A considerable *doubt* remains whether inferences can be made from *language* to nationality and the *relationship* with other *nations*. A victorious language is often (not always) merely a sign of a successful conquest. Where have autochthonous peoples ever existed? To talk about Greeks who have not yet settled in Greece is a wholly foggy idea. What's peculiarly Greek isn't so much the result of native disposition as of adapted institutions, and also an adopted language.

[6]

I want to make short catechisms for my students, e.g.
—on reading and writing.
—on Greek literature.
—the chief characteristics of the Greeks.
—Greeks and Romans.
—what can be learned from the Greeks.

[7]

a. Preference for the ancient world, its motives and their refutation.
b. Formation of the philologist to date; also his audience.

[8]

Klinger[12] says: "Culture is a product of free and courageous feelings."

III[13]

[1]

> Go and conceal your good works,
> and confess before the people the sins
> you have committed.
>
> —Buddha

[2]

April 8, 1777, when F. A. Wolf devised the name of *stud. phil.* for himself, is the birthday of philology.[14]

---

12. Friedrich Maximilian Klinger (1752–1831), friend and close associate of Goethe's youth in the inner circle of the Sturm und Drang movement (the term itself derived from Klinger's 1776 drama of the same name). The passage cited here by Nietzsche comes from Klinger's later (1809) collection *Betrachtungen und Gedanken über verschieden Gegenstände der Welt und der Literatur*, 581.

13. Archive notebook: Mp XIII 6b (U II 8, 239–300). March 1875. See *NWKG*, 1:90–114.

14. See J. F. J. Arnoldt, *Friedrich August Wolf in seinem Verhältnisse zum Schulwesen und zur Paedagogik* (Braunschweig, 1861–62), 1:26. Nietzsche borrowed this book from the University of Basel library in 1871.

1

[3]
There would be no objection to the discipline of philology, if the philologists weren't the educators too. That's the problem; this is why even philology is subject to a higher court. —And would we still have philology if philologists weren't professional teachers?

[4]
It's hard to justify the *preference* accorded the classics, since it's founded on prejudices:

  1. Ignorance of nonclassical antiquity.
  2. A false idealization of humanitarian mankind[15] in general—whereas Indians and Chinese are more humane in any case.
  3. Schoolmaster snobbery.
  4. Traditional admiration—which began with the Romans.
  5. Opposition to, or support of, the Christian church.
  6. Impression made by long centuries of work by philologists, and the nature of their work. The classics must really be a gold mine, the onlooker thinks.
  7. Skills and knowledge acquired from antiquity. Preparatory school for scholarship.

  In sum: partly on *ignorance, mistaken judgments,* and *sophistic conclusions,* partly through *the self-interest of a class,* the philologists.

  Preference later accorded the classics by the artists, who instinctively assumed that the sense of proportion and *sophrosyne* were the property of the entire classical period. Pure form. Similarity with the writers too.

  Preference for the classics as a small-scale history of mankind—as though they were some autochthonous creation in which all Becoming could be studied.

  In fact, the basis for this preference is now gradually disappearing, and if the fact hasn't been noticed by classicists, it has been noted with great clarity outside their circle. History has had an effect; then the language sciences caused enormous defection, even desertion, among the philologists. Now all that's left is the schools; but for how long? In the form in which it has *hitherto* existed, classical philology is *dying out*: the ground has vanished from under it. Whether philologists will survive *as a profession* is extremely doubtful; in any case, they're a dying breed.

15. In German, *Humanitäts-Menschheit,* Nietzsche's effort to distinguish the *human* quality of the Greeks, which he intensely admired, from the *humane* or even *humanitarian* emphasis, essentially Christian in origin and much in vogue among contemporary classicists of liberal Christian persuasion.

[5]

Our *terminology* already indicates our tendency to misrepresent the ancients. E.g., the exaggerated taste for *literature*, or Wolf who, speaking of the "inner history of classical erudition," calls it "the history of *learned enlightenment.*"[16]

[6]

What a mockery of the *humanities* that they are also called "belles lettres" (*bellas litteras*)![17]

[7]

Wolf's reasons why Egyptians, Hebrews, Persians, and other Oriental people can't be put on a level with the Greeks and Romans: "The former peoples have either not raised themselves at all, or only a few rungs, above that level of culture which ought to be called *civil polity* or *civil government*, as opposed to the *true higher spiritual culture.*" He presently explains that this culture is intellectual and *literary*: "In a successfully organized people, this can commence before peace and order in external life ('civilization')." He then contrasts the easternmost inhabitants of Asia ("resembling such individuals as want for nothing in the cleanliness, decorum, and comfort of their dwellings, clothing, and entire environment, but who never feel the lack of a higher enlightenment") with the *Greeks* ("among the Greeks, even among the most educated people of Attica, the opposite often occurs to a remarkable degree, and they neglected as unimportant what we, thanks to our love of order, have come to regard as the basis of spiritual refinement").[18]

[8]

"At the end of his life Markland,[19] like so many of his peers before him, felt such revulsion for all scholarly fame that he destroyed several projects on which he had long been engaged, tearing some up and burning others."

---

16. Wolf, *Kleine Schriften*, 844.

17. Ibid., 814 and footnote. Speaking of the name given to classical studies by the French, Wolf remarks that "if some scholar used this term [*belles lettres*] in Latin and proceeded to write *litteras bellas*, he would clearly have intended it as a joke."

18. Ibid., 817.

19. Jeremiah Markland (1693–1776), English philologist and friend of Richard Bentley, editor of Statius's *Silvae* and several plays of Euripides. He twice declined the Regius Professorship of Greek at Cambridge. The quotation comes again from Wolf, *Kleine Schriften*, 1,110. The fact that Nietzsche noted this particular passage in Wolf tells us something of Nietzsche's own increasing disgust with his profession—and, it seems likely, with his own earlier philological work.

[9]

"In the period of Winckelmann's youth, philological studies as such did not exist, apart from the common service of professorial disciplines—in those days men read and explained the ancients in order to prepare themselves better for interpreting the Bible and the Corpus Iuris."[20]

[10]

F. A. Wolf recalls how feeble and cautious were the first steps taken by our predecessors in developing a scholarly discipline, how even the Latin classics had to be smuggled into the university market, as though contraband. In a Göttingen book catalogue of 1737, J. M. Gesner advertises a copy of Horace's Odes: "ut imprimis, quid prodesse in *severioribus studiis* possint, ostendat."[21]

[11]

Newton was astonished that men like Bentley and Hare (since they were both theological dignitaries) should come to blows over a volume of ancient comedies.[22]

[12]

It's so difficult to achieve close rapport with anything classical; you have to know how to wait until you manage to hear something. The *human element* that the classics show us is not to be confused with the *humane*.[23] The antithesis to be strongly emphasized; what ails philology is its effort to smuggle in the humane. This is the only reason why the young are introduced to the classics, to be made humane. I believe that a good deal of history is enough to achieve that end. Brutality and overconfidence are cut down by seeing how things and values change. —The humanity of the Greeks lies in a certain naiveté in which, among them, man is revealed—his art, government, society, military and civil law, sexual relations, education, politics. It's precisely the human element that appears among all peoples at any time, but among the Greeks in a state of nakedness and inhumanity that makes it indispensable for education. The Greeks, moreover, have created the greatest number of individuals—this is why they're so instructive about *man*: a Greek cook is more of a cook than any other.

20. A running paraphrase of Wolf, *Kleine Schriften*, 735ff.
21. Ibid., 1,175. "In order above all to demonstrate the advantage of *more disciplined* studies." Johann Mathias Gesner (1691–1761), German philologist and professor of philosophy at Göttingen. His chief works were editions of Quintilian, Horace, the younger Pliny, and the Orphic poems, as well as the *Scriptores rei rusticae*.
22. Wolf, *Kleine Schriften*, 1,005. For Bentley, see n. 29 below. Bentley and Francis Hare were involved in a fierce polemical dispute over the comedies of Terence.
23. Once again Nietzsche pointedly contrasts human (*menschliche*) with humane (*human*).

[13]
Christianity has overcome the classical world—very easily said. In the first
place, Christianity itself is a part of antiquity; second, it has preserved the
classical world; third, it has never been at war with the pure classical period.
On the contrary: in order to survive, Christianity had to let itself be conquered by the spirit of antiquity, e.g., the idea of *imperium*, the community,
etc. We suffer from the extreme impurity and obscurity of *human affairs*,
from the clever *mendacity* that Christianity has introduced among men.

[14]
Greek antiquity has not yet been assessed as a whole. I'm convinced that if
it weren't wrapped in the radiance of tradition, modern men would kick it
aside with loathing. The radiance, I mean, is spurious, a gilding.

[15]
It's a great advantage for a classicist that so much of the initial spadework
in his discipline has been done. Hence, if he has the *talent*, he can claim
possession of his heritage—that is, undertake the *assessment* of the whole
Hellenic mind. So long as scholarship puttered at details, *misunderstanding*
of the Greeks prevailed. *Stages in misunderstanding* to be noted: second-
century sophists, the scholar-poets of the Renaissance,[24] the classicist as
teacher of the upper classes (Goethe, Schiller).

[16]
Imitation of antiquity: hasn't this principle finally been refuted?
    Escape from reality to the classics: hasn't the understanding of antiquity
already been falsified in this manner?

[17]
One sort of consideration is left: to *understand* how the greatest creations of
the spirit have evil and terror as their background. The *skeptical* consideration: examination of Hellenism as the most beautiful example of life.
    Accurate judgment is hard.

[18]
It's not true that culture can be acquired *only* from the classics. But some
culture *can* be got from them. Not, needless to say, what's called "culture"
nowadays. Our culture can only build on an utterly castrated and mendacious study of the classical world.

24. A glancing allusion to Burckhardt's well-known observations on the classicizing poets
of the Renaissance in *Die Kultur der Renaissance in Italien* (1860), 194ff.

To see how ineffective this curriculum is, we need only glance at our classicists. Yet they *most of all* should be *educated by the classics.*

2

[19]
How much men are ruled by chance, and how little by reason, is shown by the almost regular disparity between the so-called vocation and the aptitude for it. Successful cases, like successful marriages, are exceptions, and even these aren't the result of reason. A man *chooses* his career at an age when he's not fit to choose. He doesn't know the various professions; he doesn't know himself; and then he wastes his most active years in this career, giving his whole mind to it, acquiring experience. His judgment reaches its peak, and by then it's usually too late to start something new. And earthly wisdom almost always smacks of the weakness of old age and lack of physical strength.

The task is largely that of repairing, of correcting as far as possible, what was bungled at the beginning. Many will recognize that their later life shows a sense of purpose that sprang from an original disharmony. It makes living hard. But by the end of his life a man has gotten used to it—then he can deceive himself and praise his own stupidity: *bene navigavi cum naufragium feci.*[25] And he may even sing a hymn of praise to "Providence."

[20]
I ask about the development of the classicist, and I maintain:
  1. A young man can't possibly know who the Greeks and Romans are.
  2. He doesn't know whether he's fit to study the classics.
  3. And, above all, he has no idea to what extent this knowledge fits him

---

25. In this paragraph Nietzsche plays ironically on Schopenhauer's words at the beginning of "Transcendent Speculation on the Apparent Deliberateness in the Fate of the Individual," in *Parerga and Paralipomena,* 1:201 ff.: "Belief in a special providence . . . has at all times been universally popular. . . . Opposed to it . . . is the fact that, like all belief in a God, it has sprung not really from *knowledge* but from the *will*; thus, it is primarily the offspring of our miserable state. The data for this, which might have been furnished merely by *knowledge,* could perhaps be traced to the fact that chance, which plays us a hundred cruel and malicious tricks, does sometimes turn out particularly favorable to us. . . . In all such cases, we recognize therein the hand of providence, and this most clearly when it has led us to a fortunate destiny against our own insight and even in ways that we abominate. We say then *tunc bene navigavi, cum naufragium feci,* and the contrast between chance and guidance becomes unmistakably clear." The Latin phrase means: "I made a good voyage, although I shipwrecked."

to be *a teacher*. The decisive factor, then, isn't knowledge of himself and his discipline, but:

    a) imitation;

    b) laziness, since he goes right on doing the sort of work he used to do in school;

    c) sooner or later, his goal of earning a living.

I mean: ninety-nine classicists out of a hundred *shouldn't be* in the profession.

[21]

Stricter religions require that man view his activity solely as a means in a metaphysical scheme; so a mistaken choice of profession can be regarded as a test of the individual. Religions are only concerned with the individual's salvation; whether he is slave or free, merchant or scholar, his goal in life doesn't lie in his profession, hence a wrong choice is no great misfortune. This may serve to console classicists. But for real classicists the conclusion is obvious: what can come of a discipline professed by ninety-nine such men? This genuinely unqualified majority legislates for the profession and makes its demands according to the abilities and inclinations of the majority. By so doing it *tyrannizes* the hundredth, the only competent man in the lot. If it controls education, it *educates* consciously or unconsciously in *its own* image. What happens in that case to the *classical quality* of the Greeks and Romans?

    To be pointed out:

a) the incongruity between classicists and classics;

b) the unfitness of the classicist to *educate* even with the aid of the classics;

c) *the perversion of the discipline through the unfitness of the majorities; false requirements; disavowal of the actual goal of this discipline.*

[22]

In what way is a man *best fitted* for this *evaluation?* —In any case, not when he is trained in philology as he is now. Discuss: to what degree methods make this last aim impossible. —That is, the philologist himself is *not* the aim of philology. —

[23]

Leopardi is the modern ideal of a classicist. The German classicists can't *create* anything. (Take a good look at Voss!)[26]

26. For Nietzsche's regard for Leopardi, see n. 7 of *HSDL*. Johann Heinrich Voss (1751–1826) was a German poet and philologist, best known for his incredibly prolific career as a translator. His immense translator's oeuvre includes the *Iliad* and *Odyssey*, the corpus of Vergil, Ovid's *Metamorphoses*, Aratus, Horace, and the plays of Shakespeare.

[24]

Vanity is the involuntary tendency to pose as an individual when one isn't; to pose, that is, as independent when one is dependent. Wisdom is the opposite: appearing to be dependent when one is independent.

[25]

One great value of the ancient world is that its *writings* are the only ones which modern men still *read carefully*.[27]

[26]

Overstraining of *memory*—very common among classicists; underdeveloped judgment.

[27]

In the education of the modern philologist the influence of linguistics to be noted and assessed. Preferably to be avoided by a philologist. Questions of the prehistoric origins of Greeks and Romans shouldn't concern him. How can people spoil their subject like this?

[28]

I notice in the classicist:
  1. lack of respect for the ancient world,

Nietzsche's contrast of Leopardi and Voss is pointed and deserves more than casual scrutiny. At least I take Nietzsche's point to be the strikingly different ways in which Voss and Leopardi—both poets, both equipped with professional knowledge of Greek and Latin—engaged the classical writers. Voss's approach was essentially *imitative*—not interpretive—a very close, sometimes slavishly close, rendering of his original in a mechanical jogtrot meter, whereas Leopardi is essentially *emulative*, writing a poetry which, while saturated in ancient models, effectively renews and thereby continues the tradition from which it derives. Leopardi, in short, is *creative*; he engages and revives the texts which in Voss's hands are newly embalmed in accessibly literal German.

For Nietzsche's view of the proper nature of the translator's task, there is no better statement than that in *GS*, 83.

27. A central theme in Nietzsche's thought. Compare Zarathustra's cry: "I hate lazy readers!" See also "On Reading and Writing" in *Z*, part 1, and Archive notebook 7 = Mp VIII 6a. 1875, 7:5. Whatever contempt Nietzsche may have felt for philologists in general, he valued the habit of close reading acquired from his Leipzig and Basel years: "It is not for nothing that one has been a philologist; perhaps one is a philologist still, that is, a teacher of slow reading: —in the end one also writes slowly. . . . For philology is that venerable art which demands of its votaries one thing above all: to go aside, to take time, to become still, to become slow. . . . This art does not so easily get anything done, it teaches to read *well*, that is to say, to read slowly, deeply, looking cautiously before and aft, with reservations, with doors left open, with delicate eyes and fingers. . . . My patient friends, this book desires for itself only perfect readers and philologists: *learn to read me well!*" (Preface to *Dawn*, 1886).

2. effeminate and flowery style; perhaps a note of apology,
3. simple historicizing,
4. self-importance,
5. underrating of gifted classicists.

[29]

Bergk's *Literaturgeschichte*,[28] not a spark of Greek fire and Greek *sense*!

[30]

I like reading Bentley's remark: *non tam grande pretium emendatiunculis meis statuere soleo, ut singularem aliquam gratiam inde sperem aut exigam.*[29]

[31]

Bentley summoned Horace before a tribunal which Horace would certainly have repudiated. The admiration which a discerning man acquires as a philologist is in proportion to the scarcity of intellectual acuteness among philologists.[30] —Bentley's brief against Horace has something schoolmasterish about it, except that the target isn't Horace but Horace's transmitters. But actually and in general, Horace is the accused. I am firmly convinced that to have written a single line worthy of comment by scholars of a later age outweighs the merit of the greatest textual critic. The philologist's role is profoundly modest. The improvement of texts is an amusing task for scholars, like solving riddles; but it shouldn't be regarded as an important matter. A pity that the classics should speak to us less clearly because a million words stood in the way!

---

28. Theodor Bergk (1812–81), German philologist, whose *Griechische Literaturgeschichte*, vol. 1 (Berlin, 1872) Nietzsche borrowed from the University of Basel library in April 1873. A student of Hermann (cf. n. 63) at Leipzig, he was professor of philology at Bonn from 1869 to 1881. Writing to Rohde (Nov. 1867), Nietzsche remarks that Bergk "bored us with an incomprehensible lecture that lasted three hours." Elsewhere he speaks of Bergk with ill-concealed contempt.

29. "I am not accustomed to assigning such value to my little emendations as to expect or demand any special praise thereby." Cf. Wolf, *Kleine Schriften*, 1,043n.

Richard Bentley (1662–1742), greatest of English textual critics and classical scholars. Educated for the church, he wrote a *Confutation of Atheism* (1692). Perhaps his greatest achievement was his triumphant demonstration that the so-called *Letters of Phalaris* was a second-century forgery; it was this that earned him the mastership of Trinity College, Cambridge. In that post he found time—while feuding endlessly with his colleagues— to edit the works of Horace (1711), to write his *Proposals for a New Edition of the Greek Testament* (1720), and his justly celebrated *Terence* (1726). He was greatly admired by German Hellenists, above all by Wolf in his *Literarische Analekten*, vol. 1 (1816).

30. Wolf, *Kleine Schriften*, 1,051.

[32]
A schoolmaster said to Bentley, "Sir, I'll make your grandson as great a scholar as you." "How so," Bentley replied, "when I've forgotten more than you ever knew?"[31]

[33]
Wolf says that Bentley, both as a man and as a man of letters, was misunderstood and persecuted, or even maliciously praised, most of his life.[32]

[34]
Wolf calls it the summit of historical research to rise to a large, comprehensive view of the whole and a profound grasp of the differences in artistic advances and the various styles. But Wolf admits that Winckelmann lacked, or failed to apply, that commoner talent, which is textual criticism: "a rare blend of cool intelligence and a petty, nervous concern for a hundred irrelevant matters, combined with a fire that inspirits everything and devours particulars, and an intuitive talent that offends the uninitiate."[33]

[35]
"Textual criticism often makes its best show of strength in just those places where it offers reasons as to the degree of persuasion attainable on both sides, and why an expression, a passage, cannot be emended. It seems to us that doctors, to whom textual critics sometimes compare themselves, are familiar with wholly similar triumphs in their art."[34]

[36]
So profoundly and frequently oppressive is the *uncertainty* in *prediction*[35] that it now and then becomes a morbid passion for believing at any price and a desire to be *certain*: e.g., as concerns Aristotle, or in discovering numerical necessities—almost a disease in Lachmann.[36]

31. Ibid., 1,071 note.
32. Ibid., 1,087.
33. Ibid., 739.
34. Ibid., 833.
35. Ibid., 832.
36. Karl Lachmann (1793–1851), professor of classical philology at Berlin, chiefly known for his magisterial edition of Lucretius (1850), but also for his work on Horace, Catullus, and Tibullus. Severely methodological, he tended to schematize ancient literature according to reductive numerical patterns; he held, for instance, that the total number of lines assigned to chorus and actors in a Greek tragedy was invariably divisive by seven; that the Nibelungen epics could be reduced to twenty distinct lays; that the *Iliad* contained eighteen such primitive lays; and so forth.

3

[37]
By this time we will no longer be surprised if, given such teachers, the
culture of our age is worthless. I cannot stop describing their lack of culture.
And precisely with regard to those matters where, if a man can learn at all,
he *must* learn from antiquity (e.g., writing, speaking, etc.).

[38]
Besides the great number of incompetent classicists, there is the converse—
a number of men who are born classicists but who are prevented for several
reasons from realizing themselves. But the most serious obstacle in the way
of these born classicists is the misrepresentation of classical studies by classicists without vocation.

[39]
The *false enthusiasm* for antiquity, in which many classicists live. When we're
young, antiquity actually overwhelms us with a mass of trivia; above all we
think we have outgrown ancient ethics. And between Homer and Sir Walter
Scott—who takes the prize? Be honest. If this enthusiasm were great, men
would hardly expect to make a living out of it. I mean: what we can get
from the Greeks only begins to dawn on us *later*; after we've lived a good
deal, experienced much.

[40]
Where is the influence of antiquity visible? Surely not in language, not in
the imitation of this or that, surely not in the perversity exhibited by the
French. Our museums are crammed; I always feel nauseated when I see
pure, naked figures in Greek style—confronted with this mindless philistinism that will soon devour everything.

[41]
In school graduation programs speakers actually compare our age with the
age of Pericles, they congratulate themselves on the reawakening of patriotism. And I recall a parody of Pericles' Funeral Oration by G. Freytag,[37]

37. Gustav Freytag (1816–95), German playwright and novelist, regarded in Nietzsche's
time as one of the greatest writers of the age. His novel *Soll und Haben* (1835), a paean
in praise of the new German middle class as the bulwark of German morality and national
spirit, was enormously popular in Germany and elsewhere. As editor and owner of the
liberal periodical *Der Grenzbote*, he ardently supported the hegemony of Prussia. His
popular history of Germany, *Bilder aus der deutschen Vergangenheit* (5 vols., 1859–67), was
similarly nationalistic and influential. An observer of the battles of Wörth and Sedan, he
hailed the German victory over the French in 1870 as "the poetry of the historical
process." Hence, at least in part, Nietzsche's consistent contempt for Freytag's (Straussian) mindless "contemporaneity." See also *WC*, 5.46.

in which that pompous prig of a poet described the happiness now felt by men in their sixties—all pure *caricature*! This is the effect of the classics! Deep sorrow and scorn and seclusion is all that's left to those who have *seen* more than this.

[42]
They have forgotten how to speak to other men, and because they can't speak to the older generation, they can't speak to the young either.

[43]
They lack a real pleasure in the rugged and powerful elements of the ancient world. They become eulogists and make themselves ludicrous in the process.

[44]
Wolf says: "The intellectual sap and nourishment to be gotten from well-digested scholarship is always extremely little."[38]

[45]
"Only the ability to write as the ancients wrote, only personal creative talent, fit us for fully grasping unfamiliar creations of a similar sort and thereby understanding more than certain secondary virtues."[39]

[46]
Wolf thereupon points out that the ancient world was acquainted only with theories of rhetoric and poetry that aided creation, τέχναι and *artes* that actually developed orators and poets—"whereas we at the present time will soon have theories by whose help a man could no more write a speech than he could create a thunderstorm from a thesis on brontology."[40]

[47]
"In the final analysis really consummate scholarship should be restricted to those few born with artistic talent and equipped with erudition, who take advantage of the best opportunities for acquiring the requisite technical knowledge, both practical and theoretical."—Wolf.[41] True!

38. Wolf, *Kleine Schriften*, 1,117.
39. Ibid., 833.
40. Ibid., 834 and note. τέχναι = "skills, crafts."
41. Ibid., 849.

[48]
According to *Goethe*[42] the classics are "the despair of the imitator."

Voltaire remarked: "If Homer's admirers were honest, they would admit the boredom which their favorite so often causes them."[43]

4

[49]
When I say the Greeks were generally *more moral* than modern man, what does this mean? The utter visibility of the soul in behavior shows that they were without shame; that they lacked bad conscience. They were more open, more passionate, like artists. There's a sort of childlike naiveté about them, which gives a touch of purity, something close to holiness, to everything they do. Their individuality, very marked; isn't there a higher morality in that? Bear in mind that character develops slowly: what is it then? What produces such individuality? *Vanity* in conflict perhaps? Emulation? Maybe. Little taste for the conventional.

[50]
Consider how differently a discipline and a special family talent are transmitted. Physical transmission of a particular discipline is something extremely rare. Are the sons of classicists likely to become classicists? *Dubito.* So there's no accumulating of philological talent as there was, say, of musical talent in Beethoven's family. Most scholars start from scratch, and they're helped of course by *books*, not by traveling, etc. But certainly education.

[51]
The *shades* in Homer's *Hades*—what sort of existence are they actually modeled on? I think it's a portrait of the *classicist*. Surely it's better to be the lowest serf on earth[44] than such a bloodless memory of the past—of things great and small. (Sacrifice of many sheep.)[45]

42. See *Winckelmann und sein Jahrhundert in Briefen und Aufsätzen* (Tübingen, 1805), 12–14.
43. This tag of Voltaire was borrowed by Nietzsche from Klinger's *Betrachtungen und Gedanken*, 94.
44. The words of Achilles in Hades, *Odyssey* 11.489–91.
45. An ironic glance at *Odyssey* 11.35–36, where Odysseus sacrifices sheep in order to summon up the shades in Hades. The sheep are the *living* blood by which the *bloodless* shades in Hades are lured to appear. In Nietzsche's passage the sacrificial animals are the great texts on which the anemic scholars feed. Later on, in *Zarathustra* (part 2, "The Scholars"), the scholar who goes along with the herd—Wilamowitz?—will become the sheep. "As I lay asleep," says Zarathustra-Nietzsche, "a sheep ate of the ivy wreath on my brow—ate and said, 'Zarathustra is no longer a scholar'."

[52]
The classicist's attitude toward the ancient world is *apologetic* or inspired by his purpose of proving that what is valued highly in our times was valued by the ancients. The right starting point is the reverse: that is, to proceed from the recognition of modern perversity and then to look backward—many very shocking things in the ancient world then appear as profoundly necessary.

We have to see clearly that we make ourselves look utterly *absurd* when we justify and apologize for antiquity: who are *we*?

[53]
For the highest images in every religion there is an analogue in the state of the soul. *Mohammed's* god—the loneliness of the desert, distant roar of the lion, vision of a terrible warrior. The god of the *Christians*—everything men and women mean by the word *love*. The god of the *Greeks*: a beautiful dream-figure.

[54]
The man with no feeling for the *symbolic* has no feeling for the ancient world. Apply this principle to pedestrian classicists.

[55]
It's the *free man's* task to live for himself, without regard to others. That's why the Greeks considered manual labor inappropriate.

[56]
Not much can be achieved by sheer industry if the mind is dull. The classicists who hurl themselves on Homer think that violence succeeds. Antiquity speaks to us when it wants to, not when we want it to.

[57]
Bentley's remarkable daughter Joanna expressed regret to him that he spent so much time and talent criticizing the texts of others rather than on his own writing. "Bentley was silent for a long time, as though pondering. Finally he said that her remark was justified. He himself felt that he might perhaps have used his natural talents for other purposes. In his younger days, however, he had done something for the glory of God and the benefit of his fellow men (a reference to his *Confutation of Atheism*). But afterwards the genius of the pagan writers had lured him away and, *despairing of achiev-*

ing their level in any other way, he had climbed onto their shoulders so as to look out over their heads."[46]

[58]
"The moderns are indebted to the Greeks because they always sought the Useful rather than the Beautiful, and because knowledge with them was not exclusively a class privilege; because high culture was not wholly employed in the service of civil government; because various studies, which as a kind of luxury were unremunerated, were never denied anyone who renounced help from the state."[47]

[59]
Wolf's opinion of amateurs in classical studies is worth noting: "If they were by nature endowed with talents akin to the genius of the ancients or capable of nimbly adapting to alien intellectual modes and conditions of life, they surely acquired from their middling knowledge of the best authors more of the wealth of those powerful natures and great patterns of thought and action than most of those who devoted their entire lives to the interpretation of the classics."[48]

[60]
As a man stands towards his own profession—skeptically and pessimistically—so we ought to stand towards a nation's highest profession: the *understanding* of what *life* is.

[61]
My consolation applies particularly to the tyrannized individuals. Let them simply treat all those majorities as their helpers. Similarly, let them make use of that prejudice which still prevails in favor of classical studies. They need *many* helpers. But they must have total *understanding of their goals.*

[62]
Classical studies as knowledge of the ancient world can't, of course, last forever; their material is exhaustible. What can't be exhausted is the always-new adjustment every age makes to the classical world, measuring itself against it. If we set the classicist the task of understanding *his own* age better by means of antiquity, then his task has no end. —This is the antinomy of

46. Wolf, *Kleine Schriften,* 1,077 note. For Bentley, see n. 29. Bentley's *mot*—*pigmei gigantum humeris impositi plusquam ipsi gigantes vident*—has a long and interesting history, stretching (at least) from Didacus Stella to Burton, Herbert, Newton, and later authors.
47. Wolf, *Kleine Schriften,* 820ff.
48. Ibid., 836.

philology. *The ancient world* has in fact always been understood only *in terms of the present*—and will *the present* now be understood *in terms of the ancient world*? More accurately: men have explained the ancient world from their own experience; and from what, by so doing, they have acquired of the classical world, they have *appraised* and evaluated their own experience. Hence, *experience* is clearly the absolute prerequisite for the classicist. Which means: the classicist must first be a man; only then will he be creative as a classicist. It follows that older men are suited to be classicists, so long as they *weren't* already classicists in that period of life that was richest in experience.

But, generally speaking, only through knowledge of the present can *the passion for classical* antiquity be acquired. Without this knowledge, where could the passion come from? If we note how few classicists there are, apart from those who earn a living at it, we can judge how matters really stand with this passion for antiquity. It *barely* exists, since there are no disinterested classicists.

So this is the *task* set us: to overcome the educational effect of philology everywhere. *Means*: reduction of the philological profession; doubtful whether the young should be acquainted with it. Critique of the philologist. The value of the ancient world: it sinks with you. How terribly you must have sunk, since it has so little value now!

[63]

Most men obviously don't regard themselves as *really being individuals*; their lives show this. The Christian demand that *each* man look *solely* to his own salvation is opposed to the general life of mankind, in which each man lives merely as a point between other points, at once wholly the product of preceding generations, yet also living exclusively with a view to posterity. Only in three forms of existence does man remain an individual: as philosopher, saint, and artist. Merely note how the scholar kills off his own existence: what does the teaching of Greek particles have to do with the meaning of life? —Here too we see how countless men actually live only as forerunners of a real man; the scholar, for instance, as forerunner of the philosopher, who knows how to make use of the scholar's antlike labor in order to make his own statement on the *value of life*. Obviously, when it's done without *guidance*, the *greatest part* of the ant-work is simply *nonsense*, superfluous.

[64]

Most men are obviously in the world *by accident*: no higher necessity is visible in them. They putter at this or that, their talent is mediocre. Strange! Their way of living shows that they have no self-respect, they reveal their low estimate of themselves in the way they degrade themselves (whether in petty passions or professional minutiae). In the so-called vocations of life where everybody must make a choice, men reveal a pathetic *modesty.* They say in effect, "We are 'called' to serve our fellow men and be useful to them, and the same is true of our neighbor and his neighbor too." And so each man serves another, nobody has a "calling" to exist for himself, but always for others. So we have a tortoise resting on another tortoise, etc., etc. When each man finds his own goal in someone else, then *nobody has any purpose of his own in existing.* And this *"existing for others"* is the most comical of comedies.

[65]
The organizing of social and political conditions to produce the greatest comfort and happiness is found least of all among the Greeks. This is the goal that hovers before our visionaries of the future. Horrible! So we have to judge according to this principle: the greater the intelligence, the greater the suffering (as the Greeks demonstrate). By the same token: the greater the stupidity, the greater the comfort. The culture-philistine is the most comfortable creature the sun ever shone on; and he'll have the corresponding stupidity.

[66]
It's a misconception to say, "There has always been a class that managed a nation's culture; that's why *scholars* are necessary." For all that scholars possess is knowledge about culture (and this only in the best of cases). There may well be cultured men even among us, hardly a whole class. But there could only be a *very few.*

[67]
Preoccupation with past cultural epochs is gratitude? We look to the past in order to explain the state of contemporary culture, surely not to eulogize our own condition. But perhaps we have to do this so as not to be too *hard* on ourselves.

[68]
My aim is: to create complete hostility between our modern "culture" and the ancient world. Whoever wants to serve the former must *hate* the latter.

[69]
Very strict reflection leads to the view that we are a multiplication of many pasts: how can we also be a final end? —But why not? But this is what most of us don't want to be; we want to join the ranks again, work in a corner, and hope that our work won't be utterly lost to posterity. But this is actually

the Danaids' jar.[49] It's no use, we have to do everything all over again, for ourselves and only for ourselves. Measure scholarship, for instance, in relation to ourselves by asking: What's scholarship to *us*? But not: What are we to scholarship? We make living too easy for ourselves when we take such simple historical views and make ourselves servants. "Your own salvation is more important than anything else," we should tell ourselves: "and there's no institution you should rate more highly than your own soul." —But as things now stand, a man comes to know himself: he discovers he's miserable, he despises himself, and he's delighted to find something outside himself worthy of his respect. And so he throws himself away by filling a niche somewhere, sternly doing his duty, atoning for his existence. He knows he doesn't work for himself; he'd like to help those who dare to live for themselves; like Socrates. Most men drift in mid-air like a bunch of balloons, swaying with every breath of wind. —*Result: The scholar must be a scholar from self-knowledge, that is, out of contempt for himself. In short, he must know himself as the servant of a higher man who will come after him. Otherwise he's a sheep.*[50]

[70]
It's thought that philology is finished—and I think it hasn't yet begun.

The greatest events in philology are the appearance of Goethe, Schopenhauer, and Wagner. Thanks to them, we can really look into the distance. The fifth and sixth centuries can be discovered now.

[71]
In place of Latin, I recommend cultivation of the Greek style, especially Demosthenes. Simplicity. Refer to Leopardi,[51] probably the greatest stylist of the century.

[72]
Graiis—praeter laudem nullius avaris,[52] says Horace. He calls their chief activities *nugari* (*Epistles* 2.93),[53] which is typical of a Roman.

49. The daughters of Danaus murdered their husbands on their wedding night and were condemned to the never-ending task—the punishment of futility—of filling a great perforated jar in Hades.
50. See n. 45 above.
51. See n. 26 above and *HSDL*, n. 7. On Jan. 2, 1875, Nietzsche wrote to Hans von Bülow: "I know his [Leopardi's] prose pieces only very slightly; one of my friends who lives with me in Basel has translated and read several passages, always to my great surprise and admiration." The Leopardi prose pieces would presumably be the *Pensieri* and the *Zibaldone*, in which Leopardi's philological expertise is vividly evident. At this time Nietzsche also possessed a copy of Hamerling's translation of Leopardi's poetry.
52. "To the Greeks—covetous of nothing but praise" (Horace *Ars poetica*; also cited by

[73]
Wolf: "In any case it is a prejudice to suppose that the history of political conflict becomes more credible as it approaches our own times."[54]

[74]
Chief viewpoints with regard to the future value of antiquity:
1. It is not for the young, since it reveals man in freedom from shame.
2. It is not to be imitated directly, but learned, in what way art achieved its highest perfection to date.
3. It is accessible to only a few, and there should be a cultural police in charge of it, as there should be for bad pianists who play Beethoven.
4. These few, as critics of the present, measure our own times against antiquity, and they also measure antiquity in terms of their own ideals, and in this respect are critics of antiquity.
5. The contrast between Hellenic and Roman, and again between early and late Hellenic, to be studied. —Clarification of the differences in culture.

[75]
I want to say once and for all everything that I no longer believe—also what I do believe.

Man stands in a great maelstrom of forces and imagines that this maelstrom is rational and has a rational purpose. A mistake!

The only rational thing known to us is the little bit of reason man possesses. He must strain it to the utmost, and if ever he wants to abandon himself to "Providence," it always ends in his ruin.

The only happiness lies in reason, everything else in the world is miserable. But I see the highest reason in the work of the artist, and can experience it as such. There may be something which, if it could be consciously produced, would give a still greater sense of reason and happiness; for instance, the movement of the solar system, the creation and development of a man.

Happiness lies in swiftness of feeling and thinking; everything else is slow, gradual, stupid. Since light is very swift, the man who could experience the movement of light would be a very happy man.

Thinking about ourselves brings little happiness. But if we feel very happy when doing so, the reason is that we're not really thinking of ourselves, but of our ideal. This is distant, and only the swift man reaches it and rejoices.

Wolf, *Kleine Schriften*, 820n.). The Latin words have been—probably deliberately—transposed by Nietzsche and displaced from their context.
53. *Epistles* 2.1.93 (also cited by Wolf). *Nugari* = "to trifle."
54. Wolf, *Kleine Schriften*, 827n.

Organizing a great center for producing better men is the task of the future. The individual must accustom himself to such demands that, when he affirms himself, he also affirms the will of that center, e.g., in choosing a wife, or the way in which he educates his child. Until the present no individual was free, apart from very rare exceptions; and these individuals were conditioned by similar ideas, although the goals of the individual were poorly and incoherently organized.

[76]
If we look from the character and culture of the *Catholic Middle Ages* backwards to the *Greeks*, the Greeks shine in the radiance of a higher *humanity*. For every reproach brought against the Greeks must be brought a fortiori against the Middle Ages. Thus, the veneration of the ancients in the Renaissance is entirely honorable and just. We for our part have made progress in one area, directly on the basis of that dawning ray of light. In natural and human history, we've surpassed the Greeks in *illuminating* the world; and our information is much greater, our judgment more moderate and accurate. Thanks moreover to the Enlightenment, a gentler humanity now prevails, which has *weakened* mankind—but that weakness, transformed into morality, looks very good and does us proud. Man now enjoys great freedom, and if he makes little use of it, that's his affair. Fanaticism of opinion has become much milder. Finally, the fact that we'd rather live in the present age than in any other is essentially due to scientific knowledge. And surely no other generation has had so many noble enjoyments as our own, even though our generation has neither the stomach nor the palate for feeling much joy. — But life amid all this freedom is only good provided we all want it to understand it, not participate in it—that's the modern dilemma. The participants appear less charming than ever; how stupid they must be!
So the danger arises that knowledge may revenge itself on us just as ignorance took its revenge on men during the Middle Ages. Religions that believe in gods, providences, rational world-orders, miracles, and sacraments are done for; certain types of the holy life, of asceticism, are also obsolete, since it's easily inferred that they originate in a damaged brain and sickness. There's no doubt that the antithesis between a pure, incorporeal soul and a body has almost been discarded. Who believes nowadays in the immortality of the soul? Everything related to salvation and damnation—founded on certain mistaken physiological assumptions—became untenable as soon as these assumptions were seen to be false. Modern scientific hypotheses, however, can just as well be interpreted and used for a stultifying philistinism—bestiality even—as for the domain of grace and the spirit. In comparison with all earlier ages, our foundations are new; this is why something can still be expected from the human race. —*As regards culture*, this means: until now we've known only *one* perfect form of it, the city-state of

the Greeks, whose basis is mythical and social; and *one* imperfect form, the Roman, as enhancement of life, derived from the Greek. At present, all bases, the mythical and sociopolitical, have changed; our pretended culture has no stability because it's been built on shaky, indeed already crumbling, conditions and beliefs. —So if we fully understand Greek culture, we see that it's gone for good. Hence the classicist is *the great skeptic* in our cultural and educational circumstances: that's his mission. —Lucky the classicist who, like Wagner and Schopenhauer, has a presentiment of those auspicious strengths in which a new culture is stirring.

IV[55]

[1]
Agenda:
   Books to be bought and exchanged
   Historians, e.g., all of Ranke.
   Geographers, e.g., Peschel's Atlas.
   Biographers, e.g., Cardanus.
   Patristic writers in translation.
      Bible in modern translation.
   Graeco-Roman classics, e.g., Aristotle.
   Schopenhauer.
   Library of *natural sciences*.

[2]
To be excerpted: "The Population of the Alps" by Rütimeyer, in *Jahrbuch des Schweizer[ischen] Alpenclubs*. First year, 1864.
   Later: *From the Sea to the Alps*, by L. Rütimeyer, Bern, 1854. Dalpsche Bookstore.

[3]
To autumn, 1876.
   Summer, 1875. "Philology."
   Autumn until Christmas. Preparatory studies for "Wagner."
   Summer, 1875. History of Literature.
   Winter, 1875–76. *Choephoroe*, with critical text and interpretation.

55. Archive notebook: N I 3b. Spring 1875.

Summer, 1876— — —
Work on Burckhardt notebook.[56]

[4]
Difficulty in Producing the Artist[57]

1. Lack of naiveté in education—limited concept of Nature.
2. Where will the artist find a place for himself? Music a language that can be understood only in resistance to the rest of the culture. The artist's restlessness in official posts.
3. How can he defend himself from being misunderstood? If he writes, who is his audience?
4. He takes play seriously (Cervantes, romances of chivalry; Wagner, the theater); the pathos appears wasted unless it serves as summons and symbol for strengths of the same sort.
5. He cleaves to life with greater pleasure than other men.
6. A modern artist must have *intentions*.

[5]
School of Educators
Where is:
   the doctor
   the scientist
   the economist
   the cultural historian
   the scholar of ecclesiastical history
   the Hellenist
   the political scientist

V[58]

[1]
Beginning anew is always an illusion; even the impulse driving us toward this supposed "beginning" is the effective result of something earlier. But

56. Since May 1875 Nietzsche had possessed a complete transcript of his Basel colleague Burckhardt's *Griechische Kulturgeschichte,* prepared for him by his student Louis Kelterborn. He also had a transcript prepared by a second student, Adolf Baumgartner. On May 30, 1875, Nietzsche wrote to Overbeck: "Little Kelterborn has presented me with an impressively bound book, of 448 dense quarto pages; it is Burckhardt's Greek Culture; and to be sure it has merits greater than Baumgartner's preparation; it is richer in material and better ordered and more fully supplemented, whereas Baumgartner has a finer eye for Burckhardt himself and greater imitative skill."
57. An early effort at outlining what was to become *Richard Wagner in Bayreuth.*
58. Archive notebook: U II 8b. Spring–summer 1875.

a break of such violence and decisiveness is indicative of the violence and extremity of our former momentum. The radical nature of our opinions and our truth stems from the radical nature of our mistakes and failures. The great law of *transformation*—all so-called progress lies in this. Basically, moral judgment must always remain the same. But whereas intellect and experience grow, the moral quality is always transformed. In the last analysis, we value a theory according to its *effects*, e.g., whether it kills or cripples many men. This isn't right.—

[2]
To reconstruct the ancient world in writings—still a wholly unresolved problem.

[3]
The belief in individuality—could it conceivably not exist? In any case, we are moving toward times in which human opinions could become extremely uniform; but at the same time that individuals become more and more alike, they will be more and more divided. Hostility then appears in small but ever sharper differences.

[4]
An exact cross-comparison of Greeks and classicists is needed, why mutual understanding *must* be difficult. This would mean characterizing the Greeks.

[5]
Finally, all religions rest on certain philosophical assumptions which *already* exist, and which adapt the religions to themselves. E.g., in Christianity, contrast of body and soul, absolute importance of the earth as the "world," miraculous events in nature. As soon as opposed views come to prevail— e.g., strict natural law, impotence and irrelevance of all gods, extremely narrow view of the soul as bodily process—*then everything's over. At present the whole of Greek culture rests on such views.*

[6]
In Thucydides the agreeable feeling, as of turning a lock with a key: a gradual, reluctant giving way, but always functional, always achieving its end.

In Aristotle we see whitening bones.

[7]
The tyrants of the mind have almost always been assassinated too, and have only scant posterity.

[8]
Transmission of emotion is hereditary: as we might say of the effect of the Greeks on classicists.

[9]
How can we exalt and glorify merely a whole nation? It is individuals that count, even among the Greeks.

[10]
There is a great deal of *caricature* even among the Greeks; e.g., the Cynics' concern with their own happiness.

[11]
It is only the relation between a people and the education of the individual that interests me. And in this respect there are certainly some things among the Greeks very favorable to the individual's development, coming, however, not from the nation's good quality, but from the conflict of evil instincts.
   Thanks to happy discoveries, we can educate the great individual in a wholly different and better way than by leaving his education to chance, which has been the case until now. My hopes lie here: training of significant men.

[12]
Until now the history of Greece has always been written optimistically.

[13]
The desire to have some sort of certainty in esthetics led to Aristotle-worship. It will gradually be shown, I think, that he understands nothing about art, and that what we admire in him is merely the echo of clever Athenian conversation.

[14]
The Greeks are interesting and desperately important because they have so many great individuals. How was that possible? A problem for study.

[15]
With the disappearance of Christianity a good part of antiquity has also become incomprehensible. That's why an imitation of antiquity is a false direction; the classicists who still consider it are either betrayers or betrayed. We live in an age when different views of life exist side by side: this is why the age is so instructive—as few are—and why it is so sick, since it suffers the evils of every direction simultaneously. Man of the future: the European man.

[16]
Historical knowledge at present means: recognizing that all those who believe in a Providence have made things simple for themselves. There is no Providence. If human affairs move violently and chaotically, don't suppose that a god intended something by it or permitted it. We can generally observe that the history of Christianity on earth is one of the most frightful chapters in history, and that it *must* be brought to an end for good. Clearly, through Christianity the ancient world directly overlaps with our own period; and if Christianity dwindles away, our understanding of antiquity dwindles still more. Now is the best time to recognize it: we are no longer guided by a prejudice in favor of Christianity, but we still understand it and the antiquity still contained in it, insofar as it agrees with Christianity.

[17]
The decline of the *scholar-poets* is due in large part to their own personal perversity. The breed thrives again later. Goethe and Leopardi, for instance, are manifestations of it. Behind them plod the pure philologists. The whole species emerges in the sophistic movement of the second century.

[18]
At the end of antiquity, there are still completely unchristian figures, who are more beautiful, purer, and more harmonious than any Christian, e.g., Proclus.[59] His mysticism, his syncretism are things for which Christianity can least of all reproach him. In any case, it's with *men like this* that I would like to live. In contrast to *them*, Christianity seems merely the coarsest vulgarization, designed for rabble and criminals.

[19]
Every historical school has tried its hand with the ancient world. *Critical* consideration is all that's left. By which I don't of course mean textual and literary-historical criticism.

[20]
To bring to light the irrational in human affairs, without any *shame*—that is the aim of *our brothers and colleagues*. Hence, a distinction will have to be made between what is fundamental here and cannot be improved upon, and

59. Proclus (AD 410–85), perhaps the most important of the later Neo-Platonists, and a passionate champion of the older pagan religion in its struggle against Christianity. The bulk of his surviving work is devoted to exegesis of Plato and includes commentaries on the *Parmenides, Republic, Timaeus, Cratylus,* etc. But the writings that most impressed Nietzsche were Proclus's seven extant hymns (to Helios, the gods, Aphrodite, the Muses, Hecate, Janus, and Athena).

what can still be improved. But "Providence" is to be kept out of it: that's a concept by which things are simplified. I want to breathe the breath of *this* purpose into scholarship. To advance *the knowledge of man*! The good and the rational in man is fortuitous, fictitious, or the opposite of something very irrational. Someday there will be no thought of anything but education.

[21]

I do not teach submission to *Necessity*—since we would first have to *know* it to be necessary. Maybe there are many necessities, but generally speaking it is still a lazy evasion.

[22]

Signs and *wonders* are not believed; only a "Providence" needs that sort of thing. There's no help, either in prayer, or asceticism, or visions. If this is all religion is, then there's no longer any religion for me.

My religion, if I must use a word of that sort, lies in the task of producing the genius. Education is everything we hope for; all consolation is called art. *Education* is *love for the procreated,* an excess of love beyond love of self. Religion is *"love beyond ourselves."* *The work of art is the image of such self-transcending love, and a perfect image.*

[23]

The stupidity of the will is Schopenhauer's greatest thought, if we judge thoughts by their power. We can see how Hartmann[60] immediately juggled this thought away. Something stupid will never be called God.

[24]

This, then, is the novelty in all future human activity: men must never again be *ruled* by religious concepts. Will they in that case become worse? I don't find their behavior is moral and good under the yoke of religion. I'm not on Demopheles' side.[61] The fear of the next world and above all the religious fear of divine punishment have hardly made men better.

60. See *HSDL,* n. 39 and passim.
61. Demopheles ("people-deceiver") and Philalethus ("truth-lover") are the interlocutors in Schopenhauer's dialogue "On Religion" (*Parerga and Paralipomena,* 2:324ff.). Demopheles takes the line that religion is really a necessary "pious fraud," i.e., metaphysics for the masses, a set of contrived illusions which should be supported and inculcated because they are socially expedient as well as morally useful: "The fabric of society, the state, stands perfectly firm only when a universally acknowledged system of metaphysics serves as its foundation. Naturally, such a system can be only popular metaphysics, i.e., religion. . . . The great mass of the human race must somehow be guided and controlled, even if only by actually superstitious motives, until they become susceptible to those that are better and more correct. . . . Religious conceptions are a means of rousing and drawing out his [the average man's] moral nature."

[25]

When something great appears and lasts for a fair length of time, we can infer that it was preceded by a very painstaking training, e.g., among the Greeks. How did so many men among them achieve their freedom?

Educators, educate! But first educators must educate themselves. It's for them I write.

[26]

The *denial of life* is no longer so easily achieved: you can become a hermit or a monk—what's denied by that? This notion will be deeper these days: it's above all *a discriminating denial, a denial founded on the desire to be fair, no longer the blanket denial it once was.*

The man who wants to be good and holy nowadays would have a harder time of it. In order to be good, he can't be so *unfair* to knowledge as the earlier saints were. He has to be a knowledge-saint, blending love and wisdom; and he mustn't have anything more to do with a belief in gods or demigods or Providence (just as the Indian saints had nothing to do with them). He must also be healthy and stay healthy; otherwise he'll begin to doubt himself. And perhaps he'll be quite unlike an ascetic saint, he could even be a man-about-town.

[27]

Every type of history has already been applied to the ancient world. Above all we've learned enough to make use of the history of antiquity—without foundering on antiquity itself.

[28]

The German Reformation cut us off from the ancient world: was this necessary? It revealed anew the old contradiction of paganism vs. Christianity. At the same time it was a protest against the *decorative culture* of the Renaissance; it was a victory over the same culture that was defeated in Christianity's beginnings.

[29]

With respect to "worldly things," Christianity has preserved precisely the coarser views of the ancients. Everything noble in marriage, slavery, the state, is unchristian. Christianity *required* the distorting aspects of worldliness in order to prove *itself.*

[30]

I dream of a fellowship of men who are uncompromising, unindulgent, and want to be called "Destroyers." They apply the standard of their criticism to everything and sacrifice themselves to Truth. What is bad and false has to be exposed! We don't want to build prematurely. We don't know whether we can ever build, or whether the best thing might be not to build at all. There are lazy pessimists, fatalists who won't fight—to whom we refuse to belong!

[31]
Peculiarly significant position of the classicist: a whole profession to which the young are entrusted and which has to study a special antiquity. Obviously the highest value is assigned to this antiquity. But if antiquity has been misvalued, then the basis for the classicist's lofty position suddenly vanishes. In any case antiquity has been very *differently* evaluated, and the value assigned the classicist has always been adjusted accordingly. This profession has acquired its power from the strong prejudices in favor of antiquity. — This point to be elaborated. —At present the classicist feels that, if these prejudices were at last closely compared and antiquity were accurately described, the bias in favor of the classicist would promptly vanish. *It is therefore a matter of professional self-interest to prevent a more accurate view of antiquity from appearing; above all, the view that antiquity makes a man uncontemporary in the deepest sense.*

Secondly, it is in the professional interest of classicists to prevent the appearance of any view of the teacher's mission higher than what they are capable of satisfying.

[32]
There are, I hope, a few people who find it a problem just why the classicists should be the educators of the nobler youth. Perhaps it won't always be this way. —It would be much more natural in itself if the young were taught the essentials of geography, natural science, political economy, sociology; if they were gradually introduced to the study of life and finally, later on, to the most remarkable periods of the past. In this way *knowledge of antiquity* would be the last knowledge to be acquired; is *this educational position of the classics more honorable* than the usual one? —At present antiquity is used as a propaedeutic for thinking, speaking, writing. *There was a time when it was the sum total of human knowledge, and students wanted mastery of it in order to acquire what they now want to acquire through the curriculum described (which has changed in accordance with the advanced knowledge of the age).* So the inner *purpose* of classical education has completely changed; what was once *material* education is *now merely formal.*—

[33]
The blending of *humanism* and *religious rationalism* is rightly emphasized as a Saxon trait by Köchly:[62] the type of these classicists is *G. Hermann.*[63]

62. Hermann Köchly (1815–76), professor of philology at Zurich and Heidelberg, a disciple of Gottfried Hermann (see n. 63), who fled Saxon Dresden in the wake of the

[34]

Is it true that the classicist, insofar as he employs antiquity in *formal education*, is himself *formally educated*?

But what an antithesis! Formal and material indeed! *Material* here means information, facts. *Formal* means the way people think, speak, write, quite *as though* one acquired information and then diffused it!

[35]

If it were the classicist's joy to provide *formal education*, he would have to teach walking, dancing, speaking, singing, deportment, conversation. And this was pretty much what was taught by the formal teachers of the second and third century. But nowadays all we think about is the education of the *professional scholar*, and here *formal* means: thinking and writing, hardly any speaking.

[36]

Selected aspects of antiquity, e.g., the power, the fire, the verve of the ancient sense of music (shown by the first Pythian ode); the purity of his-

---

political upheavals of May 1849. He is best known for his studies of Greek tragedy (*Prometheus, Alcestis, Hecuba,* and *Iphigenia in Tauris*) and the structure of the Homeric poems.

63. Gottfried Hermann (1772–1848), one of Germany's three greatest classical scholars, whose students and disciples (including Nietzsche's teacher, Ritschl) constituted something like a distinct philological school. Sternly, often narrowly, insisting on the crucial importance of language (grammar, style, meter), Hermann's approach was vigorously opposed by that of August Boeckh (1785–1876) and Müller (see n. 105), who argued for a broader, more spacious investigation of the ancient world based upon the study of history, social institutions, and archaeology. A student of Wolf, Boeckh held the chair of philology at Heidelberg, where he lectured on topics ranging from Plato's *Timaeus* to the Greek tragedians, Pindar's metrics, and ancient chronology; he is perhaps best known for his *Staatshaushaltung der Athener* (English version published under the title *The Public Economy of Athens*). On classical studies, both in Europe and in America, his influence was immense; and gradually his broad cultural approach, wholly compatible with scholarly rigor, prevailed over the older philology as represented by Hermann, with its narrowing emphasis upon minute textual analysis. Jacob Burckhardt, for instance, clearly reveals the influence of Boeckh, above all in the Basel lectures on Greek cultural history (posthumously published under the title of *Griechische Kulturgeschichte*—but see n. 56 above), the studies of the age of Constantine, and of the Italian Renaissance.

Nietzsche's comment here upon Hermann is unmistakably pejorative in the implied aspersion on Hermann's proudly professed "scholarly objectivity":—a (spurious) objectivity rooted, in Nietzsche's judgment, in the scholar's *uncritical* relation to his own time and his unawareness of his own Christian and humanistic preconceptions. The scholar's "objectivity" was in fact only too often an impediment to the *accurate* and *overall* valuation at which Nietzsche believed classical philology should ideally aim. For Nietzsche's general opinion of "scholarly objectivity," see *BGE*, 206 and 207.

torical sense, and gratitude for the blessings of civilization, fire-festivals, corn-festivals. The ennobling of jealousy; the Greeks the most jealous people. Suicide, hatred of old age, e.g., of poverty. Empedocles on sexual love.

[37]

I *deplore* an *education* in which an understanding of Wagner is not achieved, which makes Schopenhauer sound crude and dissonant. That education is a failure.

[38]

The German has waged a long war against antiquity, that is, against the archaic culture. Certainly it's precisely what's best and most profound in the German that resists it. But the main point is this: this resistance is only justified in the case of Romanized culture. But this culture is already a decline from a much more profound and nobler culture. It's this culture that the German is wrong to resist.

[39]

I see in classicists *a conspiratorial society that wants to educate the young in classical culture.* I could understand it if this group and its aims were criticized on all sides. A great deal would then depend on what these classicists *mean* by "classical culture." —If I see, for instance, that their education is opposed to German philosophy and music, I would fight either *them* or *classical culture*—in the former case perhaps by showing that these classicists have not understood classical culture. At present I see: 1) great changes in the value assigned antiquity by the classicists; 2) something deeply unclassical in classicists, something unfree; 3) confusion over *which* ancient culture they mean; 4) considerable perversity in their methods, e.g., scholarship; 5) adulteration by Christianity.

[40]

Healthier, more active bodies; purer and deeper feeling in the observation of things close at hand; free manliness; belief in good race and good education; military ability; jealousy in ἀριστεύειν;[64] delight in the arts; respect for free leisure; feeling for free individuals, for the symbolic.

[41]

A Course on "Principles of Culture"
  1. The aim of culture, at last clearly recognized.

---

64. The cardinal tenet of Greek heroic morality, as embodied in the life and person of Achilles. See *Iliad* 6.208, where Glaukos asserts that his father sent him to Troy with this advice: "Always to be best [*aien aristeuein*] and to surpass others."

2. History of previous aims and their errors.

3. Means of culture.

[42]
Life Plans
　Unmodern Observations. For my thirties.
　The Greeks. For the years before forty and fifty.
　Discourse on Humanity. For my fifties.

[43]
Supposedly the gymnasium educates students for a discipline. But it's now said that it can no longer prepare students for any discipline, so extensive have all branches of learning become. So students must be trained generally, that is, for all fields of knowledge, which is to say for *professional scholarship* itself—and classical studies are useful for this! A marvelous leap! A very desperate argument. What exists must be viewed as right, even after it's clearly seen that the right on which it was hitherto based has become wrong.

[44]
It's the same with the simplicity of antiquity as it is with simplicity of style. It's the highest trait, something to be recognized and imitated, but also the last. Bear in mind that the classical prose of the Greeks is also a late development.

[45]
The basis for the general esteem for antiquity is prejudices. Do away with these, and the esteem would necessarily turn into a deep hatred. Do the classicists at present foster these prejudices? Then they're ignorant of the ancient world. If they don't foster them—then what about their honesty? But where is it apparent that they deliberately destroy antiquity?

[46]
Do the classicists know the present? Their view of it as "Periclean"; their errors of judgment, when they talk of Freytag's[65] "Homeric genius," etc.; their tagging behind while the literary men lead the van. Their disavowal of the pagan sense, that same ancient quality that Goethe detected in Winckelmann.[66]

65. See n. 37 above.
66. Johann Joachim Winckelmann (1717–68), archaeologist and historian of art. His great *Geschichte der Kunst des Altertums* (History of ancient art), published in 1764, revolutionized European knowledge of antiquity and the modern perception of the ancient world. In German literature, his writings were enormously influential, profoundly affecting Lessing (whose *Laokoön* takes Winckelmann's work as its starting point) and stimulating and informing Goethe's classicism.

[47]
Our attitude toward classical antiquity is basically the deep cause of modern culture's sterility: in point of fact, we've borrowed this whole idea of culture from the Hellenized Romans. We have to *distinguish* within antiquity itself: at the same time we learn to recognize its only creative period, we also *condemn* the whole Alexandrian-Roman culture. *But at the same time we condemn our entire attitude toward antiquity and our classical scholarship along with it!*

[48]
An example, and a common one, of the way classical studies are carried on. A man throws himself unthinkingly—or is thrown—into some field of study or other. From this vantage he looks to right and left, he sees much that's good and new. But in an unguarded moment, he says to himself: "What the devil does all this have to do with me?" In the meantime he's grown old, he's used to it, and keeps on going, just as in marriage.

[49]
Generally speaking, modern philology has lost its leading-strings; those who led it earlier have now been repudiated. But all of its value and influence rest on the fame of that earlier leadership, e.g., the leadership of humanity.

[50]
There are matters about which antiquity is instructive, on which I would hardly like to express myself in public.

[51]
It's almost laughable to see how almost all the sciences and arts in the modern period sprout from seeds sown by the ancient world, and how in this respect Christianity seems nothing more than a hard frost on a long night in which men must have thought that everything rational and honest among men had vanished for good. The war against the natural man has created the unnatural man.

[52]
There's something disrespectful in the way we acquaint the young with the classics. Even worse, it's poor pedagogy. What, after all, can come of acquaintance with things that it's impossible for a young man to honor consciously? Perhaps he'll learn to *take it on faith*; and that's why I want none of it.

[53]
Those who say, "But certainly classical culture survives as an object of pure scholarship, even if all its educational aims are disavowed," deserve this

reply: Where is pure scholarship here? Achievements and qualities have to be *assessed*, and the assessor has to stand above what he assesses. So your first concern must be to *surpass antiquity*. Until you do that, your scholarship isn't pure, but impure and limited: as it palpably is.

[54]
How it stands with the classicists is clear from their indifference to the appearance of Wagner. They could have learned even more from him than from Goethe—and they didn't even glance in his direction. Which shows: they have no strong needs, or they would have had a feeling where to find their food.

[55]

Plan of Chapter 1

Of all disciplines of learning *philology* until nowadays the most favored; the greatest numbers; promoted in every country for hundreds of years; charged with training the nobler youth, hence the handsomest inducement for propagating themselves, for inspiring *respect*. How did it acquire this power?

Reckoning of the various prejudices against it.

But suppose these were recognized as prejudices? —Would philology survive if professional interest and livelihood were no longer involved? What if the truth were told about the classics and their capacity to educate for the present?

Chapter 2

In answer to the above, review the philologist's education, his origin: when self-interest is removed, he fails to put in an appearance.

Chapter 3

If the general public ever discovered how utterly unmodern antiquity really is, the classicists would lose their posts as teachers.

Chapter 4

Philology owes its present power only to the coalition between philologists—who *will not*, or *cannot*, understand the ancient world—and public opinion, which is guided by prejudices favoring antiquity.

Chapter 5

The classicist of the future as skeptic of our entire culture, and thereby destroyer of professional philology.

[56]
Would philology still exist as a discipline if its servants weren't salaried teachers? In Italy such men existed. What German could we set beside Leopardi, for instance?

[57]

Effect on nonclassicists exactly nil. If the classicists were demanding and said No, how they would be persecuted! But they grovel.

The Greeks as they actually are, and their enfeeblement by classicists.

[58]

Up to the present all history has been written from the viewpoint of success, in fact with the assumption of intelligence behind success. The same with Greek history; we still don't have one. But it's the same everywhere: where are the historians who can view events without succumbing to the universal humbug? I see only one—Burckhardt. Everywhere in the discipline expansive optimism. The question "What would have happened if this or that event hadn't happened?" is almost unanimously rejected, yet it's precisely the key question, whereby everything turns ironic. We merely have to look at our own lives. If we seek for a design in history, we should look for it in the purpose of a powerful man, or a generation perhaps, or a political party. Everything else is chaos. —Even in natural science the same deification of the *necessary*.

Germany has become the hothouse of historical optimism; Hegel may be responsible for this. But in no other respect has the influence of German culture been more disastrous. Everything suppressed by success gradually rebels; history as the victor's scorn; slavish feelings and prostration before the fact—a "sense of the state," they call it now! As though that needed to be implanted! The man who doesn't grasp the brutality and senselessness of history won't understand the impulse to make history meaningful. Note how rarely a man understands the meaning of his own life, as Goethe did. So what sort of rationality will emerge from all these veiled and blind existences working chaotically together and at cross purposes?

It's particularly naive when Hellwald,[67] the author of a cultural history, rejects all "ideals" because history has persistently disposed of them, one after another.

[59]

                              Greeks and Classicists

        The Greeks: *The Classicists:*
pay homage to beauty   are windbags and triflers
develop the body   are repulsive
speak well   stutter

67. Friedrich Anton Heller von Hellwald (1842–92), a cultural historian in the tradition of David Strauss and E. Häckel. Nietzsche is referring here to Hellwald's *Kulturgeschichte in ihrer natürlichen Entwicklung von den ältesten Zeiten bis zur Gegenwart* (History of culture in its development from the most ancient times to the present) [Augsburg, 1874].

are religious transfigurers of ordinary things	are filthy pedants
are listeners and observers	are hairsplitters and screech-owls
are prone to symbolism	are incapable of symbolism
possess freedom as men	are passionate slaves of the state
have a pure outlook on the world	are twisted Christians
are intellectual pessimists	are philistines

[60]

It's true, humanism and the Enlightenment have made an alliance with antiquity. And so it's natural that the enemies of humanism should be hostile to antiquity. Except for the fact that antiquity was badly understood and wholly falsified by humanism. Clearly understood, it's evidence *against* humanism, against the notion that human nature is essentially good, etc. The enemies of humanism are wrong when they fight against antiquity, in which they have a powerful ally.

[61]

I regard religions as *narcotics*. But when they're given to such peoples as the Germans, they're pure *poison*.

[62]

On what one condition do the Greeks model their life in Hades? Bloodless, dreamlike, weak: it's *old age* all over again, intensified, in which the memory grows constantly weaker and the body still more so. The old age of old age—in the eyes of the Greeks, that's our life.

[63]

How *real* the Greeks were, even in free invention! How they made poetry out of reality, instead of yearning to escape it!

[64]

Education is, first, instruction in the *necessary*, then in the *changing* and the *variable*. The student is introduced to Nature and everywhere shown the power of her laws; then the laws of civil society. Here the question will soon arise: *Must* things be as they are? Gradually he feels a need for history to learn how things become what they are. But at the same time he learns that they could also be different. How much power over things does man have? That is the question in all education. To show how completely different things can be, look at the example of the Greeks. The Romans are needed to show how things *became* what they are.

[65]

The Greeks as the only people of *genius* in world history. Even as learners they have genius. This is what they understand best, and they don't know how to primp and dress up in borrowed clothes, like the Romans.

The constitution of the *polis* is a Phoenician invention; even this was copied by the Greeks. For a long time, like happy dilettantes, they studied everything around them; even Aphrodite is Phoenician. And they refuse to disown their importations, the nonindigenous.

[66]

The Egyptians are a *much more literary* people than the Greeks. Here I disagree with Wolf.[68]

[67]

The first grain at Eleusis, the first vine at Thebes, the first olive, the first fig.

[68]

Egyptians had essentially lost their myth.[69]

[69]

The *living epiphanies* of gods, as in Sappho's hymn to Aphrodite,[70] should *not* be taken as poetic license, they are frequently hallucinations. Many things, like the *wish for death*, we view too baldly as rhetoric.

[70]

Greeks the *genius* among the peoples.[71]

    Childlike nature. Credulous.

    Passionate. They live unconscious of the genius they produce. Enemies

---

68. Wolf, *Kleine Schriften*, 817–19. Cf. *TI*, "What I Owe to the Ancients," 2. Nietzsche, like his soi-disant follower, Prof. H. J. Lloyd-Jones, connects Plato's apostasy from archaic Hellenism with the supposed influence of Egypt and the Orient in the minds of Athenians: "My mistrust of Plato goes deep: he represents such an aberration from all the basic instincts of the Hellene, is so moralistic, so pre-existently Christian . . . that for the whole phenomenon Plato I would sooner use the phrase 'higher swindle,' or, if it sounds better, 'idealism.' . . We have paid dearly for the fact that the Athenian got his schooling from the Egyptians (or from the Jews in Egypt?). In that great calamity, Christianity, Plato represents that ambiguity and fascination called an 'ideal,' which made it possible for the nobler spirits of antiquity to misunderstand themselves and set foot on the bridge leading to the cross."
69. Burckhardt, *Griechische Kulturgeschichte*, 1:28.
70. Ibid., 1:28.
71. Ibid., 1:12.

of constraint and stupidity. Pain. Imprudent behavior. Their way of intui-
tively understanding misery, combined with a sunny temperament,[72] genial
and cheerful. Profundity in understanding and glorifying everyday things
(fire, agriculture). Deceitful. Unhistorical. The cultural importance of the
polis instinctively comprehended; its center and periphery are favorable to
great men (affording a prospect over an entire community, also the possibility of addressing it as a whole).[73] The individual raised to his highest
powers through the polis.[74] Envy, competition, as among talented people.

[71]
The recreations of the Spartans consist of festivals, hunting, and war; their
daily life was too harsh. In general, their state is really a caricature of the
polis and a perversion of Hellas.[75] The training of the ideal Spartan—what
greatness did he have that his production required such a brutal state?

[72]
Greek culture rests on the domination by a very small class over a slave
population four or five times greater.[76] *Statistically*, Greece was a country
inhabited by barbarians. How can the ancients be viewed as *humane*? Contrast between the genius and the worker, half ox, half beast-of-burden. The
Greeks believed in racial difference. Schopenhauer wonders that Nature
didn't think to invent two distinct species.[77]

[73]
The Greek is related to the barbarian as "freely moving or winged animals
stand to the mussel fastened to its rock, compelled to wait whatever chance
brings it." Schopenhauer's image.[78]

[74]
"Always to see the universal in the particular is precisely the basic trait of
genius"—Schopenhauer.[79] Think of Pindar, of the $\Pi\varrho o\mu\eta\theta\varepsilon\tilde{\iota}\alpha$,[80] etc.
Greek "composure," according to Schopenhauer, is largely rooted in the

72. Ibid., 2:363.
73. Ibid., 1:73.
74. Ibid., 1:80.
75. Ibid., 1:91ff.
76. Ibid., 1:147.
77. Schopenhauer, *Parerga and Paralipomena*, 2:245.
78. *WWR*, 2:379.
79. Ibid., 2:379.
80. Aeschylus's Prometheus trilogy, of which only the *Prometheus Bound* survives, but
whose general outlines can, in the main, be reasonably reconstructed.

clarity with which they looked at the world and themselves, and by which they arrived at consciousness.

[75]
The "wide separation between the will and the intellect"[81] is a trait of the genius, and also of the Greeks.

[76]
"The *melancholy* associated with genius rests on the fact that *the more brilliantly the will-to-live is illuminated by the intellect, the more clearly it perceives the misery of its condition.*" Schopenhauer.[82] Cf. the Greeks!

[77]
What a contrast between the Romans, with their boring seriousness, and the cheerful Greeks! Schopenhauer: "The firm, practical seriousness about life, which the Romans designated *gravitas*, presupposes that the intellect does *not forsake* the service of the will in order to wander away in quest of other concerns."[83]

[78]
The *moderation* of the Greeks in sensual consumption, in drinking, and the pleasure they took in those things; the Olympian games and their worship—this shows what they were.

[79]
In the case of genius, "the intellect will show the faults that are usually bound to appear in the case of every tool used for a purpose for which it is not made." "It often leaves the will very inopportunely in the lurch; and, accordingly, the individual genius becomes more or less useless for life; in fact, by his conduct we are sometimes reminded of madness."[84]

[80]
"When that abnormally enhanced power of knowledge occasionally directs itself suddenly with all its energies to the affairs and miseries of the will—where everything is enlarged to monstrous proportions, too vividly, in too glaring colors, in too bright a light—then the individual falls into mere extremes."[85]

81. *WWR*, 2:382.
82. Ibid., 2:383.
83. Ibid., 2:386–87.
84. Ibid., 2:389.
85. Ibid., 2:389.

[81]

The Greeks lacked sobriety. Excessive sensibility; abnormal excitement of nerves and brain; vehemence and ardor of the will.[86]

[82]

The happiest fate that can befall genius is release from practical activity and free leisure;[87] and for this reason the Greeks were aware of the value of leisure. The blessing of work! *Nugari*[88] was the Roman word for all the straining and striving of the Greeks.

Genius has no happy course of life—it is opposed to, and at war with, its age.[89] Similarly with the Greeks: they instinctively took enormous pains to make (out of the polis) a safe refuge for themselves. Finally, everything collapsed into politics. They were forced to resist the outside world. This became more and more difficult, finally impossible.

[83]

By changing a single word of Lord Bacon of Verulam, we can say: *infirmarum Graecorum virtutum apud philologos laus est, mediarum admiratio, supremarum sensus nullus.*[90]

[84]

The *childlike character* of the Greeks[91] perceived by the Egyptians.

[85]

The *heightening* of the present into the *vast* and *eternal*, e.g., in Pindar.

[86]

The unmathematical curvature of the columns at Paestum is analogous to variation of tempo: vitality instead of mechanical movement.

[87]

The work of all education is to transform conscious actions into more or less unconscious action; and the history of mankind is in this sense its education. The classicist now performs a great many such unconscious

86. Ibid., 2:389.
87. Ibid., 2:390.
88. See n. 53 above.
89. Schopenhauer, *The World as Will and Representation*, 2:390.
90. "Among classicists there is praise of the lowest virtues of the Greeks, admiration of the average virtue, no understanding of the highest." The sentence has been adapted from Schopenhauer's citation of Bacon in *WWR*, 2:391.
91. Schopenhauer, *WWR*, 2:393.

actions: what I propose to study is how his behavior, that is, his instinctive behavior, is the result of activities that used to be conscious, which he has gradually ceased to experience as such. But *that consciousness consists of prejudices. His present* power rests on *those prejudices*, e.g., the high regard for *ratio,* as in Bentley and Hermann. Prejudices, as *Lichtenberg* says,[92] are the *artistic instincts of man.*

[88]

We expect *skills* from the study of the classics. In past times, writing and speaking. But what is expected nowadays? —Thinking and drawing inferences. But this can't be learned *from* the ancients, but at best *through* the ancients, by means of scholarship. Besides, all historical inference is conditional and very uncertain; the inferences of the natural sciences are preferable.

[89]

Proclus,[93] who gravely worships the rising moon.

[90]

The hereditary training of the contemporary classicist. A certain sterility in basic perceptions is the result, since the discipline is advanced, but not the classicist.

[91]

The political subjection of Greece is culture's greatest defeat, since it is the origin of the monstrous theory that culture can only be promoted by arming yourself to the teeth and putting on boxing gloves. Christianity's rise was the second greatest defeat. Brute strength on one side, and stupidity on the other, overcame the aristocratic genius among the nations. To be a Philhellene means being an enemy of brute strength and stupidity. Sparta was the ruin of Athens insofar as she forced Athens to form a confederation and throw herself wholly into politics.

[92]

Generally speaking, the *increase* in the *military strength of mankind* is quite certain. Victory of the stronger nation: "little by little" is the rule not only for *greater power of being* of a *bodily* sort, but even more for that of *mind and spirit.*

92. *Vermischte Schriften,* 1:186.
93. See n. 59.

[93]
In *Socrates* we confront an *example of the consciousness* out of which the *instincts of theoretical man* later developed. One would rather die than grow old and weak in spirit.[94]

[94]
In Christianity, a religion corresponding to a pre-Greek condition of mankind achieved ascendancy: belief in magical causes for everything, bloody sacrifices, superstitious terror of punishment by demons, failure of nerve, ecstatic brooding and hallucinations, man converted to a battlefield for good and evil spirits.

[95]
It would have been much *more fortunate* if the *Persians*, rather than the *Romans*, had conquered the Greeks.

[96]
Its splendid feeling for *order* and organization has made the city of the Athenians immortal. —The board of ten generals in Athens! Madness! Much too big a sacrifice on the altar of jealousy.

[97]
> ### Statute of the Society of the Unmoderns
Each member required to submit a written report of his activities every three months.
O.R.G.B.N.[95]

[98]
For a preface to the complete publication of "Unmodern Observations":
Description of its origins: my desperation with regard to Bayreuth; I no longer see a thing that I know isn't packed with flaws. In my more searching second thoughts, I find I've been thrust into the most fundamental problem of all culture. At times I lack the desire to go on living. But then I tell myself: If you have to live, it's best to live today. —In point of fact, I thought Strauss too small for me; I didn't have to take him on. Several words spoken by Wagner at Strassburg.[96]

---

94. Burckhardt, *Griechische Kulturgeschichte*, 2:374.
95. The initials of Nietzsche's circle of intimate friends at Basel in this period: Overbeck, Rohde, Gersdorff, Baumgartner, Nietzsche.
96. Nietzsche and Wagner met at Strassburg on Nov. 22–25, 1872. It was evidently at one of these meetings that Wagner suggested to Nietzsche that he devote a polemical pamphlet to the work of David Strauss.

[99]
Suppose the Romans had rejected Greek culture: it might have been totally destroyed. Where could such a culture have rearisen? Christianity and Romans and barbarians—that would have been an onslaught. Utterly destructive. We perceive the dangers in which genius lives. That's why Cicero is surely one of mankind's greatest benefactors. —There's no Providence for the genius; only for the ordinary masses of mankind and their needs does such a thing exist. The masses find their satisfaction, and later their justification.

[100]
The Greek polis and the αἰὲν ἀριστεύειν[97] grow out of mutual and deadly enmity. "Hellenic" and "humane" are contradictory, though the ancients flattered themselves a good deal.

[101]
In the world of Hellenic strife, Homer is the Panhellenic Greek.
    Greek competition is also visible in the symposium, in the form of clever conversation.

[102]
Genius makes tributaries of all half-talented people. Hence, even the Persians dispatched embassies to the Greek oracles.

[103]
A Greek polytheism requires great intelligence; it's possible, of course, to economize on intelligence if you have only *one* [god].[98]

[104]
Greek morality rests not on religion, but on the polis.
    There were only priests of individual gods, not representatives of the religion as a whole. That is, no clergy. Likewise no sacred scriptures.

[105]
The "laughter-loving gods"[99] is the highest epithet ever conferred on the world. Meaning, how hard it is to live!

[106]
Have there been *many gifted philologists?* I doubt it. Reason has been too slow in making inroads on them (numbering manuscripts, etc.). —Philology

97. See n. 64. See also Burckhardt, *Griechische Kulturgeschichte*, 2:330, 360.
98. Ibid., 2:29ff.
99. Presumably an allusion to the "unquenchable laughter" of Homer's gods.

of words-and-things—stupid struggle!—and then the exaggerated esteem for any clever man in their ranks.

[107]
Humanism was strongly cultivated by Charlemagne, whereas the harshest measures were taken against heathenism. Classical mythology was encouraged; German mythology was treated as a crime. I believe the reason for this was the feeling that Christianity had already done away with ancient religion. People no longer feared it, but made use of the ancient culture which it supported. They were afraid of the old German gods. —A gross *superficiality* in the idea of the ancient world—little more than regard for its formal skills and knowledge—*must* have been implanted in this way. The forces that hindered a deepening of our insight into the ancient world deserve mention. First (1), ancient culture was used as an *inducement* to the *acceptance of Christianity*—the reward, so to speak, for conversion, the sugar in this poisonous concoction. Second (2), the help of ancient culture was needed as a *weapon* in the intellectual defense of Christianity. Even the Reformation couldn't dispense with classical studies in this sense. In reaction, the Renaissance, in a *purer* but quite anti-Christian way, inaugurates classical studies; the Southern Renaissance shows, like the Northern Renaissance, an awakening of *honesty*. Generally speaking, it's the church that *succeeded* in turning classical studies in a *harmless* direction. *The philologist was discovered*, a scholar who is in other respects a priest or something of the sort. And even in the sphere of the Reformation they managed to castrate the scholar. Friedrich August Wolf is remarkable in this respect because he *liberated* his profession from philology. But his achievement wasn't wholly understood, since no aggressive, active element of the sort we associate with the poet-scholars of the Renaissance developed. Scholarship, not men, profited from the liberation.

[108]
The *unpopularity* of the new Renaissance culture! A frightful fact!

[109]
What is antiquity *now*, with respect to modern art, science, and philosophy? No longer the repository of all knowledge; in knowledge of nature and history, it has been surpassed. Oppression by the church has been stopped. A *purer* knowledge of antiquity is now possible, but also a *less effective*, a weaker knowledge? —That's right, if by "effect" we mean *effect on the masses*; but for the molding of the greatest men the classics are now *more* potent than *ever*. Goethe as *German poet-classicist*. *Wagner* at a still higher level: clear recognition of the only position worthy of art. Never has an ancient work had so powerful an effect as that of the *Oresteia* on Wagner. The

classicist castrated by objectivity, who in other respects is a philistine and a jingoist, and who also dabbles in pure scholarship, is obviously a sorry spectacle.

[110]
Bentley was at the same time *defensor fidei*;[100] and Scaliger[101] was certainly an enemy of the Jesuits, and a very aggressive one.

[111]
Between our highest art and philosophy and the *truly* understood <u>archaic</u> period of antiquity, there is no contradiction: they are mutually supporting and sustaining. My hopes are founded on this.

[112]
There are areas where *ratio* will produce nothing but mischief, and the classicist who has nothing else is thereby lost and can never see the truth, e.g., in the study of Greek mythology. Not even a visionary, of course, has a claim: you have to have Greek imagination and something of Greek religious feeling. Even the poet needn't be consistent, and, in general, consistency is the last thing the Greeks would have understood.

[113]
Almost all the Greek gods are accumulations, layer on layer, some firmly fused, others barely touching. Scholarly sorting out of these strata looks to me hardly possible, since there's no good method for doing it. The wretched conclusion of the analogy is here a very good conclusion.

[114]
How far removed from the Greeks you have to be to attribute to them the stupid autochthony of O. Müller![102] How Christian, to maintain with

100. "Defender of the faith," an allusion to Bentley's *Confutation of Atheism*. See Wolf, *Kleine Schriften*, 1,033ff.
101. Joseph Justus Scaliger (1540–1609); not to be confused with his father, Julius Caesar Scaliger. Founder and practitioner of a rigorously methodical textual criticism, and one of the half-dozen truly great classical scholars of post-classical times. So impressive were his erudition and authority that he incurred the hostility of the Jesuits who perceived, in the great erudition and passionate candor of this Protestant scholar, an obstacle to their efforts at conversion and their order's intellectual supremacy both inside and outside the Church.
102. Carl Ottfried Müller (1797–1840), student and disciple of Boeckh at Berlin, later professor of classical antiquity at Göttingen. His *Geschichte der griechischen Literatur* was borrowed from the Basel library by Nietzsche in April 1875.

Welcker[103] that the Greeks were originally monotheists! The way classicists torture themselves asking whether Homer could write, without grasping the much more important principle that Greek art exhibited a long inner hostility to writing and didn't want to be read.

[115]
The Greeks were monstrously given to the passion for fabulizing.[104] Even in daily life it was hard for them to hold back from the "mythical," from dizziness, in the same way that every poetic people has a passion for lying, along with the innocence that passion requires. The neighboring peoples found this quite infuriating.

[116]
Living on mountains, traveling a lot, moving about quickly—in this we can now compare ourselves with the Greek gods. We know the past, we almost know the future. What would a Greek say if he could see us!—

[117]
The gods make men even *worse*; it's the same with human nature. When we don't like someone, we want him to be worse and in that way make us happy. This belongs to the darker philosophy of hate, which hasn't yet been written because wherever one goes it's the *pudendum* that everyone feels.[105]

[118]
The Panhellenic Homer delights in the frivolousness of the gods. But it's astonishing how he can give them back their dignity. But this immense power of heightening—this is Greek!

[119]
Thucydides on the *state*.
    The *tyrannical* element strongly nourished in every aristocrat; this is revealed in prayers (Xenophon, Socrates). They mutually kept each other within limits; the people held them all together within limits, as best they could.

---

103. Friedrich Gottlieb Welcker (1784–1868), archaeologist and philologist, professor of classical antiquity at Göttingen, later librarian and museum director at Bonn. He is best known for his study of Greek mythology, *Griechische Götterlehre* (1857–62), and his edition of Hesiod's *Theogony*. His other essays and studies were published in five volumes in his *Kleine Schriften* (1844–67), which Nietzsche borrowed from the Basel library in Feb. 1875.
104. Burckhardt, *Griechische Kulturgeschichte*, 2:326.
105. Ibid., 2:97.

[120]

What is the origin of *divine envy*? The Greeks don't believe in calm, tranquil happiness, but in a happiness that's arrogant. That must have made them feel bad, their feelings are all too easily wounded. It irritated them to see a man happy. That's *Greek.* When an exceptional talent appeared, the crowd of jealous people must have been enormous. If a misfortune struck him, people said, "Aha. He was too arrogant." And every one of them would have behaved the same, had he been similarly talented; and every one of them would have gladly played the part of the god who sent the misfortune.

[121]

The Greek gods demanded no conversions and were generally not so tiresome and importunate. It was even possible to take them seriously and believe in them. The Greek character, after all, was ripe in the Homeric period: frivolity in images and imagination is necessary to calm and liberate that excessively passionate spirit.

　　If the Greeks let their intellect speak, how bitter and cruel their life seems! They don't deceive themselves. But they veil life with lies; Simonides advises them to take life as a game; seriousness they knew well in the guise of pain. Man's suffering is a delight to the gods, when they hear songs on that theme. The Greeks knew this, that only by means of art can suffering become delight; *vide tragoediam.*[106]

[122]

The really *scholarly people,* the people of literature, are the Egyptians, not the Greeks. What looks like learning among the Greeks derived from the Egyptians and later returned home to blend its waters with the old current. Alexandrian culture is a blend of Hellenic and Egyptian. And if the modern world links itself to Alexandrian culture, then . . .

[123]

The *seer* must be kind, otherwise he'll have no credit among men:[107] Cassandra.

[124]

Classical philology is the focus of the shallowest enlightenment. Always dishonestly employed, it has gradually become utterly ineffective. Its effect is one more of modern man's illusions. Actually, it's simply a matter of a

---

106. Ibid., 2:359. "See tragedy." Nietzsche's point is implicit, if not explicit, in Euripides' *Trojan Women* 1,424ff., *Hercules Furens* 673ff., and *Andromache,* passim.
107. Burckhardt, *Griechische Kulturgeschichte,* 2:277.

class of teachers, which is not composed of priests. This is why the state is interested in it.

It has completely exhausted its usefulness, whereas, for instance, the history of Christianity still shows its power.

[125]

Nothing can be learned from talk about philology when it comes from philologists. It's the purest rubbish; for example, Jahn's *Bedeutung und Stellung der Altertumsstudien in Deutschland*.[108] Absolutely no feeling for what should be justified, what defended. This is how people talk who have never even imagined they could be attacked.

[126]

It's just not true that the Greeks only paid attention to this life.[109] They also suffered the terror of death and hell. But no repentance and contrition.

[127]

"Wanton, mutual destruction inevitable so long as a single polis wanted to live; its envy of all superiority; its greed; its moral confusion; enslavement of women; unscrupulousness in oaths, in murder and manslaughter." B[urckhardt].[110]

[128]

Tremendous power of self-conquest, e.g., in the citizen, in Socrates, who was capable of any evil.[111]

[129]

In the average Greek we encounter the traits of the genius who lacks genius, in essence all the most dangerous peculiarities of spirit and character.

---

108. Otto Jahn (1813–69), German archaeologist, philologist, and historian of music. Author of numerous works on Greek art, he also wrote a biography of Mozart and was one of Wagner's most outspoken opponents.
109. Cf. Kelterborn's transcript (p. 76a) of Burckhardt's lectures on Greek culture: "It is quite false to believe that the Greeks were completely this-worldly and cared little about the world beyond."
110. Burckhardt, *Griechische Kulturgeschichte*, 1:80.
111. Ibid., 1:80, 2:373. See also Kelterborn's transcript (p. 84): "We will never learn how often the highly talented, passionate selfishness overcame itself in the service of a collective enterprise."

[130]
The "sufferer" is Hellenic. Prometheus, Heracles.

The *myth of the hero* became *Panhellenic;*[112] obviously this was the work of a poet.

[131]
Wagner develops man's inward imagination; later generations will be spectators of the visual arts. Poetry must precede the visual arts.

[132]
"Classical education"! What do people see in it? Something quite useless— except for getting exemption from military service and taking a doctorate!

[133]
The philological profession—to see this as a problem.

[134]
Wagner rates his art much too highly to go hide in a corner like Schumann. Either he surrenders to the audience (*Rienzi*) or it surrenders to him. He raises it to his level. Minor artists want an audience too, but they seek it by nonartistic means, such as the press, Hanslick,[113] etc.

[135]
When *philologists* discuss their discipline, they never get to the *root of the matter;* they never propose philology itself as a problem. Bad conscience? Or mindlessness?

[136]
It's "enlightenment" and Alexandrian culture—in the best of cases!—that classicists want. Not Hellenism.

[137]
The consistency we praise in a scholar is pedantry when applied to the Greeks.

---

112. Burckhardt, *Griechische Kulturgeschichte,* 2:353ff., and the chapter titled "Greek Hero Cult."
113. Eduard Hanslick (1825–1904), music critic and influential music editor of *Weiner Zeitung* (1848–49), *Presse* (1855–64), and later, *Neue freie Presse.* A stern formalist of markedly conservative taste, he attacked the work of Wagner and Liszt while promoting that of Schumann and Brahms. Wagner revenged himself by caricaturing Hanslick as Beckmesser in *Die Meistersinger* (1867).

[138]
Classical education! Yes, if there were only at least as much paganism as Goethe found and praised in Winckelmann—that would be none too much. But as it is now, mixed with, or concealed beneath, the whole false Christianity of our age—this is too much for me, and I have to relieve myself while I express my disgust once and for all. —With regard to this "classical education," people really believe in magic. But of course those who most possess antiquity ought to have most of this education—i.e., the classicists. But *what's* classical about them?

[139]
In earlier days men attributed their desires and temptations to the devil or evil spirits; nowadays that's a fairy tale. By the same token it's a fairy tale to thank a god for one's better impulses and successes. They're both tranquillizers, we use them to comfort ourselves. To point out how, in the case of *religion*, every conceivable effort has been made to provide *comfort*; evasions and excuses readily available.

[140]
Five years of silence. Student, tutor, educator.

[141]
What is talent? Willing a lofty purpose along with the means for accomplishing it.

[142]
Classical scholars are men who exploit the hollow feeling of personal inadequacy in modern man in order to earn a living.
I know them, I'm one of them myself.

[143]
German scholars and so-called thinkers, though remote from real history, have taken history as their theme and tried, like good theologians, to prove its rationality. I fear that a later age will recognize in this German contribution to European culture the most miserable of dowries: their history is false!

[144]
We treat our young people as though they were mature, educated men when we introduce them to the Greeks. *What*, after all, in the Greek character is particularly suited to the young? In the end they're left with *formal matters, details*. Are considerations of this sort suited to the young?—
And of course we offer young men the best, the loftiest, comprehensive

view of the ancients? Or don't we? That's the way *reading* of the classics will be emphasized.

I believe that preoccupation with antiquity has been assigned to the *wrong* stage in life. By the end of our twenties the light begins to dawn on us.

[145]

All difficulties of historical study *to be made clear* by the most striking examples.

To what extent young people are unsuited to the Greeks.

Consequences of philology:

> Arrogant expectations
>
> Philistinism
>
> Overrating of reading and writing
>
> Shallowness
>
> Alienation from the people and the people's needs

The philologists themselves (and historians and philosophers and jurists, all steeped in this nonsense).

Young people should be taught *real* disciplines.

Similarly, *real* art.

Then, at a riper age, they'll crave *real* history too.

> *Philologist*: his origin generally and his origin now.
>
> *The young and the philologist.*
>
> *The consequences of philology.*
>
> *Task for philology*: Disappearance.

Cruelty: even from Antigone, even from Goethe's Iphigenie.

Absence of *Enlightenment*.

Politics incomprehensible to the young.

The poetic—a bad expectation.

[146]
Critique of Development

False assumption of a *natural* development.

Degeneration lies behind *every* great manifestation here; at any moment the beginning of the end is visible. Degeneration lies in the facile imitation and outward grasp of great models. That is, the model provokes vainer natures to imitation and reproduction and surpassing.

The link between a genius and others is rarely a straight line. Thus, between Aeschylus and Sophocles there is none at all. After Aeschylus numerous paths of development lay open; Sophocles took *one* of them.

The fatal element in all great talents: they sweep everything else away with them and make a desert around themselves—like Rome in the midst of her own wilderness.[114] In this way great energies, still in an embryonic state, are suffocated.

To be noted: how *prevalent* degeneration is, even in Hellas; how rare and transient greatness is, how inadequately (on the false side) evaluated.

How awkward the beginnings of tragedy in Thespis must have been! That is, the artistic imitation of primitive orgies. So too prose was at first extremely awkward in relation to real speech.

The dangers are: pleasure in content, or indifference to content and a craving for the sensual charms of sound, etc.

The agonistic element is also the danger in every development; it overstimulates the creative drive. —The luckiest thing in development: when several men of genius mutually impose limits on each other.

Weren't a great many glorious possibilities nipped in the bud? Who could have thought a Theocritus, say, was possible at the time, unless he already existed?

The greatest event is still the precociously *Panhellenic Homer*. Everything good comes from him; yet at the same time he remained the most potent obstacle of all. He made others *superficial*, which is why the really serious spirits struggled against him. But to no avail. Homer always won.

The *destructive* element in great spiritual forces is also visible here. But what a difference: Homer or the Bible as such a force!

The delight in *drunkenness*, delight in *cunning, revenge*, envy, *slander, obscenity*—in everything which the Greeks *recognized* as human and therefore built into the structure of society and custom. The wisdom of their institutions lies in there being no gulf between good and evil, black and white. Nature, as she appears, isn't denied but merely *ordered*, restricted to specific days and religious cults. This is the root of all spiritual freedom in the ancient world; they sought to release natural forces moderately, not to destroy them or suppress them. —The whole systematizing of a new order becomes the *state*. It was built not on limited individuals but on the recurrent human traits; manifest in its founding are that *keenness of observation* and that *feeling for facts*, especially the typical fact, which fitted the Greeks for science, history, geography, etc. It was no narrow priestly *customary law* that prevailed in the founding of the state. Where did the Greeks acquire this freedom? Clearly from *Homer*. But where did Homer get it? —Poets aren't the wisest and most logical of creatures, but they delight in particular reality of every kind; and they don't want to destroy this reality, but moderate it so it doesn't destroy everything else.

---

114. The Romans of the empire, according to Tacitus (*Agricola* 30), habitually "make a wilderness and call it peace."

[147]

The necessity of release, of κάθαρσις,[115] a fundamental principle of the Greek nature.

Alternate building-up and release, in powerful, periodic explosions. Is there a clarification of *tragedy* here?

[148]

Philosophical minds must get busy and provide a final overall reckoning of antiquity. Once that's done, antiquity will be overcome. With all the weaknesses afflicting us, we're much too dependent on the ancient world to go on treating it leniently. Mankind's most atrocious crime—making Christianity possible, in the way it became possible—is the *fault* of the ancient world. Antiquity too will be swept away along with Christianity. —It's very close to us now, clearly too close to do it justice. It's been used for oppression in the most monstrous way and, in the guise of "culture," has supported religious oppression. The crowning joke was the statement that "antiquity has been overcome by Christianity!" That was a *historical* fact, and that's why the study of antiquity became harmless. It's so plausible to find Christian ethics "more profound" than Socrates! We're a match for Plato any day! It's all a chewing-over of the same battle that was fought out in the first centuries AD. Except that the ancient world, once so clearly visible, has now been replaced by the palest specter, and Christianity itself has become a spectral affair also. It's a skirmish *after* the decisive battle, an aftershock. Finally, in Christianity all those forces which composed the ancient world have now surfaced in their crudest form. It's nothing new, extraordinary only in its scale.

[149]

Agh, it's a miserable history, the history of classical philology! The most nauseating erudition; lazy, passive indifference, nervous submission. — Who's ever shown the slightest freedom?

[150]

Religious cult is to be traced back to the act of *bribing* or *begging* the gods' favor. What really matters is when men fear their displeasure. —As a result, when a man is unable or unwilling to achieve success *through his own powers*, he looks for supernatural forces—to *alleviate the pain of living.* When a man

---

115. Catharsis. Cf. Kelterborn's transcript (p. 78) of Burckhardt's lectures: "We find atonement, κάθαρσεις, in part already in Homer, later at every possible occasion. One need merely consider how, in that violent age, almost everyone might encounter a murder (as today in Italy), whereupon revenge must be taken!" Cf. Nietzsche's *Mixed Maxims*, 220.

is unable or unwilling to make amends for something *through his own action*, he asks the gods for grace and pardon in order to *lighten his heavy conscience*. The gods were invented for man's *convenience*. Lastly, their cults as the sum total of all *recreation* and *diversion*.

Do away with the gods, and all burdens become heavier, there's much less cheerfulness. —Whenever the Olympians receded, Greek life became darker. —Where we study and do research, the Greeks celebrate festivals. They are the *celebrators of festivals*.

They don't, like the Jews, view the gods as lords and masters, and themselves as slaves. Their conception is that of a luckier and more powerful social class, a mirror image of the most successful specimens of their own class, that is, an idealization, not an antithesis, of their own nature. They feel completely akin to it. There is also a mutual self-interest, a kind of military alliance. Men think *nobly* of themselves when they invent gods like this. And that is why there is something *noble* even in *the bringing and begging of divine favor*. The relation is like that between a greater and lesser nobility. The Romans, in contrast, have a genuine peasant religion, terror of goblins and ghosts.

[151]
I want to master literature so that I can, for instance:
    compare the ἀναγνωρίσεις[116]
    the prologues in the plays, etc.

[152]
Outline for 18 Lectures
  9. *Honors* in cities, among rulers, at festivals, sacrifices, etc. Tyrannies.
18. *Types of death.*
10. *Sets of associates,* of the same aspiration.
11. *Diffusion by discipleship.*
12. *Rebellious disciples.*
  6. Greeks and *non-Greeks,* geographical participation.
  7. *Slaves* and people *at the very bottom.*
  8. *People of high nobility.*
13. *Personal enemies,* contests.
17. *Influence on the state* and remaining neutral.
14. *Keeping silence.*
15. *Disparagement* and *incomprehension* of the past.
16. *Diffusion by means of lectures, travels,* books, libraries.
  2. *What we've lost,* extent of our loss, reasons for it.
  5. *Art for everybody* and art for a limited circle.

116. "Recognitions," i.e., recognition scenes in Greek drama.

3. *A few principles* for the study of literature.
1. *Critique of development*, absolute value.
4. *Falsifications*. Literary-historical mythology.

[153]
A prince is always a caricature, something excessive; and if a people still
needs a prince, that's proof that the political instinct of individuals is still
too weak. The man who has known better days thinks with disgust of always
looking up, and with sorrow on those who need to pose as though they
looked at things "from above."

[154]
When I note how all states are now promoting classical education, I think,
"How innocuous it must be!" And then, "How serviceable it must be!" It
wins these countries the glory of promoting "the liberal arts." But we have
only to look at the classicists to assess the real value of these "liberal arts."

[155]
An *earlier* state of culture—i.e., vestigial survivals—is preserved in *religious
cult*. The ages that celebrate the rite are not those that invent it. The contrast
is often very vivid. Greek ritual takes us back to a pre-Homeric outlook and
culture; it is almost the oldest thing we know of the Greeks, older than the
mythology which, in the form in which we know it, has been substantially
shaped by the poets. —*Can* we call this cult *Greek?* I doubt it. The Greeks
are refiners, not inventors. They *preserve* through the beauty of their refinement.

[156]
What always *cuts us off* from *ancient culture* is that is *foundations* have become
for us completely *invalid*. A critique of the Greeks is at one and the same
time a critique of Christianity, since they are both based on the identical
belief in spirits, religious ritual, and the magical order of Nature. —There
are still numerous *vestigial* stages surviving today, but these are already on
the point of *collapsing*.
  *This would be a thesis: to describe Greek culture as irrecoverable, along with
Christianity and the foundations on which our society and politics have hitherto
been built.*

[157]
Thesis: the *death of ancient culture* inevitable. To characterize Greek culture
as the prototype, and to show how all cultures rest on concepts which are
invalid.
  Dangerous position of *art*: as custodian and energizer of dead and dying

concepts. Of *history* too, insofar as it wants to lead us back to feelings we've outgrown. To feel "historically," to be "just to the past," is only possible if we are at the same time above and *beyond* it. But the danger in the empathy required is great: Let the dead bury their dead, so we don't take the taint of decay ourselves.

[158]
The Death of Ancient Culture
1. Meaning of classical studies to the present: obscure, dishonest.
2. As soon as their goal is recognized, they sentence themselves to death. For their goal is to describe ancient culture as a culture to be destroyed.
3. Compilation of all the ideas out of which Hellenic culture arose. Critique of religion, art, society, state, morality.
4. Christianity is thereby rejected.
5. Art and history—dangerous.
6. Replacing classical studies, which have become invalid for educating the young.

Thus, the problem of the discipline of *history* is resolved, and history itself becomes superfluous, once the whole internally coherent cycle of past aspirations has been *condemned*. Its place must be taken by the scholarship of the *future*.

[159]
The *teacher of reading and writing*, and the *proofreader*, are the prototypes of the philologist.

[160]
Our classicists are to real educators as primitive medicine men are to real doctors. Imagine the astonishment of posterity!

[161]
Everything, with Critique
2. Literature.
2. Religious conceptions.
2. Moral conceptions.
1. Education.
1. Relationships of sex, country, etc., of class.
2. State.
1. Art of speech, concept of civilized and uncivilized.
2. Philosophy and science.
1. On classical philology and antiquity in the modern world.
1. On Greeks and Romans.

After 5½ years, i.e., from autumn 1875–Easter 1881.
Easter '82 + 7½ = 89½, e.g., at age 45–46.

[162]
Poets are naturally out of date and a bridge to very distant ages, always epigones in fact. Are they therefore necessary? They, like religion, can be reproached because they provide *temporary relief,* they're palliatives of a sort. By reducing and distracting the feeling of discontent, they keep men from struggling for real improvement.

[163]
The *devices* men employ *against pain* are often *narcotics.* Art and religion belong to the narcotics of representation. They harmonize and soothe; it's a stage of *lower medicine* for spiritual suffering. *Elimination* of the *cause of suffering* by means of a fiction; e.g., when a child dies, pretending that he's still alive, more beautiful than before, and that someday we'll be reunited. This, with its consolation, must be the poor man's religion.

Is tragedy still possible for the man who doesn't believe in a metaphysical world? We have to show how the *highest peak* achieved by mankind to date rises on the basis of this lower medicine.

[164]
We look back over a considerable span of mankind: what sort of humanity will it be which someday looks back on us from a like distance? Which finds us still wholly submerged in the wreckage of the ancient culture? Which finds its only consolation in "being good and doing good"[117] and spurns all other comforts? —Does beauty also come from the ancient culture? I believe that our *ugliness* depends on our own metaphysical wreckage; the cause is our moral confusion, the misery of our marriages, etc. The beautiful man, the healthy, temperate, enterprising man, makes the surrounding world beautiful, in his own image.

[165]
In the nature and cult of the Greek gods all the signs of a coarse, gloomy, very primitive state are visible. Had the Greeks remained in that state, they would have become something very different. *Homer* freed them with the characteristic frivolity of his gods. The transformation of a *dark, savage religion* into a *Homeric religion* is surely the *greatest of events.* But note the

117. An allusion to Goethe's poem "Das Göttliche." The poem clearly stuck in Nietzsche's memory, especially the last stanza: "Be the man that is noble / Both *helpful and good,* / Unweariedly forming / The right and the useful, / A type of those beings / Our mind has foreshadowed."

cross-currents, the appearance of archaic forms, the adoption of kindred notions of alien origin.

1. Coarse, darker prehistory. Fetishism. Human sacrifice, etc. Dread of death and worship of death.
2. The dramatic spectacles of cult.
3. Later stirrings and revivals of the gloomiest primitive religion.
4. Religious frivolity and lightening. The Ionian poets.
5. Religion as a narcotic against pain and the hardships of life.
6. Poetic invention and interpretation of myth; blending and reconciling.
7. Disbelief.
8. Art as a retrogressive force generally, opposed to enlightenment.
9. The state seeks a basis, in religiosity. Society too.
10. Religion, to amuse the people, to shelter them from misery and boredom.

Cult

1. Prayer. (Curse, oath.)
2. Sacrifice.
3. Ecstasy and its means. Prophecy. Oracles. Exorcism. Magic. The priest.
4. Orientation. Form of the temple.
5. Purification. (Mysteries.)
6. Complex forms: festivals with spectacles.
    a. state cults
    b. family cults
    c. domestic cults
    d. cults of the dead

On Religion

1. Love is the *artistic device* employed by Christian ambiguity. (Sexual love in the ancient world purely conceived in Empedocles.)
2. Christian love, based on denial.
3. Christian activity contrasted with Buddhist calm.
4. No religion of vengeance and righteousness. The Jews the *most evil* people.
5. Imported ideas: dying in place of another.
6. The priestly state. Hypocrite. Aversion to coping seriously with all problems.
7. The greatest sin against the human mind is historical Christianity.
8. God entirely superfluous.
9. Decline of humanity: nothing eternal.
10. Contemptibility of all motives; impurity of thought; delusions of all sorts, classes, aspirations.
11. Either to live wholly subject to illusions, or to live the hard way, without

hope, without deception, without providences, without redemption and immortalities; but with a compassionately loving look towards oneself. Gulf between two worldviews, the everyday view and that of the rarest moments of thought and feeling. (Contempt and love, understanding and feeling, equally intense.) This conception of religion requires knowledge (as an instrument for the scornful understanding of the weaknesses and purposelessness of men). The greater the knowledge of the world, the greater that understanding. —The struggle with necessity—that's a principle of life. Understanding of the delusive nature of all goals and compassion towards oneself—that's another.

[167]
To *surpass* Greek culture by action—that is the task. But to do that, we must first know it. —There is a learned thoroughness which is only an excuse for not acting. Think how much Goethe understood of the ancient world; certainly less than a classicist, yet enough to grapple with it creatively. We *should not* know more of a thing than we could also create. Besides, the only means of really *knowing* something is by trying to *do* it. Try living classically—by so doing you immediately get a hundred miles closer to the classics than with all the learning in the world. —Our classicists never show that they *emulate* antiquity in any such way—hence, *their* antipathy has no effect on their students.

　　Curriculum of *competition* (Renaissance, Goethe) and *curriculum* of *desperation*!

[168]
A correctly emended author is *no great matter*.

[169]
The false idea of preoccupation with the classics is an impediment even to the best.

[170]
Someday scholarly research will be done by women; men should become intellectually *creative*: states, laws, works of art, etc.

[171]
We should study an *exemplary* antiquity only in the same way we study an *exemplary* man: that is, imitating as much of it as he understands and, when the model is very remote, considering his steps and preparations, *devising* proximate approaches.

　　The *criterion* of the curriculum is this: we should study *only what incites us to imitation*, what we understand with love, and what demands to be passed on. The *most appropriate* would be: a *progressive* syllabus of *exemplary models*, suited to *boys*, to *young men*, and to *older men*.

[172]

That's how Goethe grasped the ancient world: always with a competitive soul. But who else? There is no sign of a carefully considered pedagogy of this sort. Who knows whether there is a knowledge of the ancient world that can't be imparted to the young?

[173]

The *puerile* character of philology: invented by teachers for their students.

[174]

Ever *more general* form of the *exemplary model*: first men, then institutions, and finally trends, goals or lack of goals.

Highest form: *surpassing of the model* by a reverse process from trends to institutions, from institutions to men.

[175]

The advancement of learning at the expense of man is the most destructive thing in the world. The stunted man is a backward step for humanity; he casts his *shadow* over every age. It debases conviction, the natural aim of the particular field of knowledge; in this way knowledge itself is destroyed in the end. It is advanced, but its effect on life is nil or immoral.

[176]

Men not to be used like *things!*

[177]

Out of the very imperfect philology and classical scholarship [of the Renaissance] there issued a stream of freedom. Our own highly developed philology enslaves men and serves the idols of the state.

[178]

The better the state is organized, the duller mankind will be.

To make the individual *uncomfortable*: my mission!

Appeal of liberating the individual by struggling!

Intellectual *peak* has its historical *age*; for this, hereditary energy is required. In the ideal state such energy vanishes.

[179]

The intellectual culture of Greece a perversion of the boundless political instinct for ἀριστεύειν.[118] The πόλις adamantly opposed to new culture. *Despite this,* culture existed.

[180]

Supreme judgment on life only to be passed by the supreme energy of life. The mind must be as far from *apathy* as possible.

In *transitional* world history the judgment will be most accurate, since it's in such periods that the greatest *geniuses* exist.

Production of the genius as the only one who can really *value* and *deny* life.

[181]

Walter Scott loved company because he liked telling stories; he practiced at it the way a virtuoso practices his piano for seven hours straight.

[182]

Save your genius! should be proclaimed to the people. Free him! Do everything to unshackle him!

[183]

The dull, the poor in spirit, *must not* pass judgment on life.

[184]

When good friends, etc., praise me, I am often apparently pleased and grateful, out of politeness and good feelings; but actually I am quite indifferent. My true being is in this respect utterly lazy and can't be budged an inch from the shade or sun where it lies. —But men want to give pleasure with their praise, and they would be offended unless we enjoyed it.

[185]

We mustn't expect from man's future what certain epochs of the past have achieved, e.g., the effects of religious feeling. The type of the saint may only be possible in a certain intellectual orientation, which is now gone for good. The highest *peak* of intellect may perhaps have been reserved for another age of mankind. Enormous energy of the will, transferred to intellectual aspiration (aberration)—only possible so long as that savagery and energy were generally cultivated. Mankind probably comes closer to its goal at the midpoint of its journey than at the end. —Certain strengths, by which art is conditioned, could perish, e.g., pleasure in lying, in ambiguity, sym-

118. See n. 64 above.

bolism, etc., drunkenness might even become disreputable. And in fact: once life is organized in an ideal state, there can no longer be a poetry of the *present*. At best, poetry will look back nostalgically to the time when the state was not ideal.

[186]
Infancy and childhood have their ends in themselves, they are not *stages*.

[187]
I would like a book on the *scholar's way of life*.

[188]

Aims

The value of life can only be measured by the *highest intellect* and the warmest heart.

How is the highest intelligence to be produced?

The aims of producing *human welfare* are generally wholly different from those of producing the highest intelligence. Good living is rated too high and understood in a completely superficial way. Likewise the school and education.

The ideal state of which the socialists dream destroys the basis for great intelligence—violent energy.

We have to want life to maintain its *violent* character in order that *savage* powers and energies should be summoned into existence. The judgment on the value of life is the highest result of the most violent *tension* in chaos.

But now the warmest heart wants to eliminate that savage, violent quality, even though it arose from that same quality! It wants to eliminate its own basis. That is, it is not intelligent.

The highest intelligence and the warmest heart cannot coexist in the same person. The highest intelligence is *superior* to any other good, and even *this* is only an item in the overall reckoning of the life *to-be-evaluated*; the wise man stands higher than it.

The *wise man* must *struggle against* the ideas of the unintelligent good man, since his purpose is the reproduction of his type. At least he *cannot further* the ideal state. —Christ furthered man's stupidity; he arrested the production of great intellect. Consistently! His opposite might perhaps be an impediment to the production of more Christs. —*Fatum tristissimum generis humani!*[119]

[189]

Proemium

If I were *free* now, all my struggling would be unnecessary. I could turn to

119. "Mankind's saddest fate."

a work or an action and test all my strength against it. —As things stand now, I can only hope to free myself gradually, and up to the present I feel I am becoming more and more so. So the day of my real *labor* is also coming, and the *preparation* for the Olympic games is *over.*—

[190]
The time is at hand when I will have to reveal opinions which are regarded as *shameful* to the person holding them. Then even friends and acquaintances will become skittish and apprehensive. I will have to pass through this fire too. Then I will belong to myself more than ever.—

[191]
The man who had the knowledge to produce genius and who wanted to practice the method employed by Nature, would have to be as cruel and unfeeling as Nature herself.

[192]
I find Xenophon's *Memorabilia* very interesting. One must still acknowledge Socrates' example: it can still be imitated. The ἀνδραποδισταὶ ἑαυτῶν[120] pierce me.

[193]
Plato's Socrates in a very real sense is a caricature, an excessive Socrates.

[194]
Mistreat men, drive them to extremes, keep it up for thousands of years— and suddenly, because of an *aberration* of nature, because of a spark set flying from the terrible energy ignited in this way, the genius appears! — That's what history tells me. Horrible vision! Ah, I can't endure you!—

[195]
The *Greeks* of the *Roman Empire* are *tired* and give us a splendid idea of future humanity. They seem kindly, especially towards Rome, they loathe gladiatorial games, etc. —It's completely wrong to draw conclusions from this as to what they were in an earlier age.

120. "Those that sell themselves into slavery," i.e., the sophists. Cf. Xenophon, *Memorabilia* 1.2.6: "And those who provided instruction for payment, he [Socrates] called 'sellers of themselves,' since they were compelled to converse with those from whom they received profit." Nietzsche is clearly glancing at his own professorship at Basel as a form of sophistic prostitution and duress. See also *SE,* 2 and 10, and Nietzsche's sympathetically envious remarks on Schopenhauer's happy exemption from the need to earn a living, as well as his comments on the effective prostitution of university philosophers.

[196]
Homer is so much at home in the humanized world of his gods and, as a poet, takes such delight in it, that he must have been profoundly irreligious. His relation [to his gods] is like that of a sculptor to his clay and marble.

[197]
The Greek polis tends to exclude culture, its political instinct was on this side extremely paralyzing and conservative. There could be no *history,* no *development* in culture; everything had to be fixed for all time. Later Plato too felt the same way. *Despite* the polis, higher culture appeared, indirectly through the polis, since through the polis the individual's ambition was raised to the highest pitch. If a Greek set out to distinguish himself intellectually, he went to the farthest limits.

[198]
Earliest inhabiting of Greek soil: people of Mongolian origin, worshippers of trees and snakes. A fringe of Semites along the coast. Thracians here and there. The Greeks took all these elements into their own bloodstream, along with gods and myths (several of the Odysseus stories are Mongolian). The Dorian invasion is a *later push*; all Greece had gradually been overwhelmed before the arrival of the Dorians. What are "racially pure" Greeks? Can't we simply suppose that Italic peoples, mixed with Thracian and Semitic elements, became *Greek?*

[199]
Considering the vast horde of slaves on the mainland, the *Greeks* must always have been numerically very few. A *higher* class of leisured politicians, etc. The *enmities* kept them in physical and intellectual tension. They had to maintain their *qualitative superiority*—that was their spell over the masses.[121]

[200]
Pericles' [funeral] speech is a great optimistic illusion,[122] the sunset in which the disagreeable day is forgotten—and after it the night!

---

121. Burckhardt, *Griechische Kulturgeschichte,* 1:147.
122. Ibid., 4:175ff.

About the Contributors

WILLIAM ARROWSMITH is University Professor and professor of classics at Boston University. He has translated numerous Greek plays, both tragedies and comedies; the *Satyricon* of Petronius; and the poetry of Cesare Pavese and Eugenio Montale. With Herbert Golder, he is general editor of the Oxford University Press series *The Greek Tragedies in New Translation.*

GARY BROWN is a graduate of the University of Texas and a postgraduate autodidact. Novelist, computer specialist, and translator, he is also, in both practice and theory, a professing Nietzschean who turned to philosophy in an effort to unify "the chaos within."

WERNER DANNHAUSER is professor of government at Cornell University. In addition to numerous articles on Nietzsche, he is the author of *Nietzsche's View of Socrates*. His own translations from the German include essays by Gershon Sholem, Walter Benjamin, and Karl Reinhardt.

HERBERT GOLDER teaches classics at Boston University. He is general editor (with William Arrowsmith) of *The Greek Tragedies in New Translation* and editor of *Arion, A Journal of Humanities and the Classics*. He has done translations from Greek writers, including a version of Euripides' *Bacchae* now being produced as a film in England. He is at work on a study of visual meaning in Greek drama and a book on the films of Werner Herzog.

RICHARD SCHACHT is professor and chairman of the Department of Philosophy at the University of Illinois at Champaign-Urbana. His publications include *Alienation*; *Hegel and After*; *Classical Modern Philosophers*; and a study of Nietzsche's political thought, *Nietzsche*. The author of numerous articles and essays on Nietzsche, he is also executive director of the North American Nietzsche Society and editor of *Nietzsche Studies*, published by Routledge.

Index